Oxford AQA History

A LEVEL AND AS

Component 1

Tsarist and Communist Russia 1855–1964

Sally Waller

OXFORD
UNIVERSITY PRESS

Great Clarendon Street, Oxford, OX2 6DP, United Kingdom

Oxford University Press is a department of the University of Oxford. It furthers
the University's objective of excellence in research, scholarship, and education by
publishing worldwide. Oxford is a registered trade mark of Oxford University Press
in the UK and in certain other countries

© Oxford University Press 2015

The moral rights of the authors have been asserted

First published in 2015

British Library Cataloguing in Publication Data
Data available

978-019-835467-3

10 9 8 7 6 5 4

Paper used in the production of this book is a natural, recyclable product made
from wood grown in sustainable forests.
The manufacturing process conforms to the environmental regulations of the
country of origin.

Printed in India by Multivista Global Pvt. Ltd

Acknowledgements

The publisher would like to thank the following for permissions to use their
photographs:

Cover: Popova Valeriya/Shutterstock; **p1**: akg-images/Alamy; **p3**: (r) Everett Collection
Historical/Alamy; (l) dpa picture alliance/Alamy; **p7**: INTERFOTO/Alamy; **p12**: GL
Archive/Alamy; **p14**: Three Lions/Stringer/Getty Images; **p16**: SZ Photo/Scherl/
Mary Evans Picture Library; **p19**: World History Archive/Alamy; **p22**: World History
Archive/Alamy; **p24**: Hulton Archive/Stringer/Getty Images; **p28**: World History
Archive/Alamy; **p32**: INTERFOTO/Alamy; **p33**: (r) Heritage Image Partnership Ltd /
Alamy; (l) World History Archive/Alamy; **p36**: Pictorial Press Ltd/Alamy; **p38**: E. O.
Hoppe/Contributor/Getty Images; **p41**: INTERFOTO/Alamy; **p43**: AKG-images;
p45: ITAR-TASS Photo Agency/Alamy; **p47**: (t) ullstein bild/AKG-images; (b) Keystone
Pictures USA/Alamy; **p49**: Peter Horree/Alamy; **p54**: INTERFOTO/Alamy;
p56: INTERFOTO/Alamy; **p57**: RIA Novosti/Alamy; **p61**: AFP/Stringer/Getty Images;
p62: Central Press/Stringer/Getty Images; **p64**: Popperfoto/Contributor/Getty
Images; **p67**: INTERFOTO/Alamy; **p68**: Bettmann/Corbis UK Ltd.; **p71**: (t) John Frost
Newspapers/Alamy; (b) picture-alliance/dpa/Mary Evans Picture Library;
p73: AKG-images; **p75**: (t) dpa picture alliance/Alamy; (b) Archivart/Alamy;
p76: CBW/Alamy; **p79**: (t) Photo 12/Contributor/Getty Images; (b) AF archive/Alamy;
p80: PHAS/Contributor/Getty Images; **p82**: Pictorial Press Ltd/Alamy; **p86**: AKG-
images; **p87**: Hulton Archive/Stringer/Getty Images; **p90**: (t) dpa picture alliance/
Alamy; (b) Imagno/Getty Images; **p92**: (l) Everett Collection Historical/Alamy;
(r) The Print Collector /Alamy; **p93**: Hulton-Deutsch Collection/Corbis UK Ltd.;
p94: INTERFOTO/Alamy; **p96**: dpa picture alliance/Alamy; **p100**: John Frost
Newspapers/Alamy; **p103**: Hulton Archive/Staff/Getty Images; **p105**: John Frost
Newspapers/Mary Evans Picture Library; **p108**: Popperfoto/Contributor/Getty Images;
p109: (t) dpa picture alliance/Alamy; (b) AKG-images; **p114**: Larry Burrows/The LIFE
Picture Collection/Getty Images; **p119**: Pictorial Press Ltd/Alamy; **p121**: dpa picture
alliance/Alamy; **p125**: war posters/Alamy; **p126**: Topical Press Agency/Stringer/Getty
Images; **p129**: World History Archive/Alamy; **p131**: Mary Evans Picture Library/
Alamy; **p133**: Sueddeutsche Zeitung Photo/Mary Evans Picture Library; **p139**: AKG-
images; **p140**: Mary Evans Picture Library/Alamy; **p144**: Sueddeutsche Zeitung Photo/
Mary Evans Picture Library; **p149**: INTERFOTO/Alamy; **p152**: Mary Evans Picture
Library/Alamy; **p153**: INTERFOTO/Alamy; **p156**: Everett Collection Historical/Alamy;
p157: Heritage Image Partnership Ltd /Alamy; **p167**: akg-images/Alamy; **p169**: World
History Archive/Alamy; **p176**: Adrian Muttitt/Alamy; **p183**: (t) dpa picture alliance/
Alamy; (b) akg-images/Alamy; **p185**: AKG-images; **p188**: Bettmann/Corbis UK Ltd.;
p189: dpa picture alliance archive/Alamy; **p191**: Alessandro0770/Alamy;
p192: Sovfoto/Contributor/Getty Images; **p195**: unbekannt/Stadt Koeln NS-
Dokumentationszentrum; **p197**: George (Jürgen) Wittenstein/AKG-images;
p198: Everett Collection Historical/Alamy; **p201**: World History Archive/Alamy

We are grateful for permission to reprint from the following copyright texts:

Archie Brown, *The Rise and Fall of Communism* (Bodley Head, 2009), copyright ©
Archie Brown 2009, reproduced by permission of The Random House Group Ltd;
Norman Davies, *Europe: A History* (OUP, 1996), reproduced by permission of Oxford
University Press; **David Christian**, *Imperial & Soviet Russia: Power and privilege and
the challenge of modernity* (Palgrave Macmillan, 1986), copyright © David Christian
1986, reproduced by permission of the author; **Edward Crankshaw**, *Kruschev's
Russia* (Penguin, 1959, 1964), reproduced by permission of Peters Fraser & Dunlop
(www.petersfraserdunlop.com) on behalf of the Estate of Edward Crankshaw;
Terence Emmons, *The Russian Landed Gentry and the Peasant Emancipation* of
1861 (CUP, 1968), reproduced by permission of Cambridge University Press;
M. E. Falkus: *The Industrialisation of Russia 1700-1914* (Macmillan, 1972), reproduced
by permission of Palgrave, an imprint of Macmillan Publishers Ltd; **Orlando Figes**,
Revolutionary Russia 1891-1991 (Pelican Books, 2014), copyright © Orlando Figes
2014, reproduced by permission of Penguin Books Ltd; *A People's Tragedy* (Cape,
1996), copyright © Orlando Figes 1996, reproduced by permission of The Random
House Group Ltd and the author c/o Rogers, Coleridge & White Ltd, 20 Powis
Mews, London W11 1JN; **G. Freeze**, *Russia: A History* (OUP, 2009), reproduced
by permission of Oxford University Press; **Neil Harding**, 'Lenin, socialism
and the state in 1917' in Edith Rogovin Frankel, Jonathan Frankel and Baruch
Knei-Paz (Eds): *Revolution in Russia - reassessments of 1917* (CUP, 1992), reproduced
by permission of Cambridge University Press; **Geoffrey Hosking**, *Russia & the
Russians: From the Earliest Time to the Present* (Penguin, 2002), copyright © Geoffrey
Hosking 2002, reproduced by permission of Penguin Books Ltd; **Lionel Kochan**,
The Making of Modern Russia: From Kiev Rus' to the Collapse of the Soviet Union (Penguin
1962, 1997), copyright © Lionel Kochan 1962, reproduced by permission of
Penguin Books Ltd; **Walter Moss**, *A History of Russia since 1855*, Volume 1 (Anthem
Press, 2003), reproduced by permission of the Wimbledon Publishing Company
Ltd; **David Offord**, *Nineteenth Century Russia: Opposition to Autocracy* (Routledge,
1999), copyright © Taylor & Francis 1999, reproduced by permission of Taylor &
Francis Books UK; **Christopher Read**, *Tsar to Soviets* (UCL Press, 1996), copyright
© UCL Press 1996, reproduced by permission of Taylor & Francis Books UK;
Robert Service, *The Penguin History of Modern Russia from Tsarism to 21st Century* (Allen
Lane 1997, Penguin, 1998, 2003,2009), copyright © Robert Service 1997, 2003,
2009, reproduced by permission of Penguin Books Ltd; **Martin Sixsmith**, *Russia*
(BBC Books, 2011), Copyright © Martin Sixsmith 2011, reproduced by permission
of The Random House Group Ltd; **Adam B. Ulam**: *A History of Soviet Russia* (Praeger/
Harcourt College Publishers, 1976), reproduced by permission of the publishers
via the Copyright Clearance Center; **Dimitri Volkogonov**, *The Rise and Fall of the
Soviet Empire: Political Leaders from Lenin to Gorbachev* edited and translated by Harold
Shukman (HarperCollins, 1999), English translation copyright © Harold Shukman
1998, reproduced by permission of HarperCollins Publishers Ltd; **Peter Waldron**,
The End of Imperial Russia 1855-1917 (Palgrave Macmillan, 1997), reproduced by
permission of the author and Palgrave, an imprint of Macmillan Publishers Ltd;
J. N. Westwood, *Russia since 1917* (B T Batsford, 1980), reproduced by permission
of Pavilion Books Company Ltd; **Alan Wood**, *The Romanov Empire 1613-1917*
(Bloomsbury Academic/Hodder Arnold, 2007), copyright © Alan Wood 2007,
reproduced by permission of Bloomsbury Academic, an imprint of Bloomsbury
Publishing Plc.

We have made every effort to trace and contact all copyright holders before
publication, but if notified of any errors or omissions, the publisher will be happy
to rectify these at the earliest opportunity.

The author would like to thank the following people: Margaret Haynes, for her
invaluable support and encouragement, and colleagues and pupils at Cheltenham
Ladies' College, past present and future, who provide daily inspiration.

The publisher would like to thank the following people for offering their
contribution in the development of this book: Jonathan Bromley, Roy Whittle

---

Approval message from AQA

This textbook has been approved by AQA for use with our qualification. This
means that we have checked that it broadly covers the specification and we
are satisfied with the overall quality. Full details of our approval process can be
found on our website.

We approve textbooks because we know how important it is for teachers and
students to have the right resources to support their teaching and learning.
However, the publisher is ultimately responsible for the editorial control and
quality of this book.

Please note that when teaching the AQA A Level History course, you must refer
to AQA's specification as your definitive source of information. While this
book has been written to match the specification, it does not provide complete
coverage of every aspect of the course.

A wide range of other useful resources can be found on the relevant subject
pages of our website: www.aqa.org.uk.

The Practice Questions in this book allow students a genuine
attempt at practising exam skills, but they are not intended to replicate exam
questions in every respect.

Contents (continued)

Introduction to features

The *Oxford AQA History* series has been developed by a team of expert history teachers and authors with examining experience. Written to match the new AQA specification, these new editions cover AS and A Level content together in each book.

How to use this book

The features in this book include:

TIMELINE

Key events are outlined at the beginning of the book to give you an overview of the chronology of this topic. Events are colour-coded so you can clearly see the categories of change.

LEARNING OBJECTIVES

At the beginning of each chapter, you will find a list of learning objectives linked to the requirements of the specification.

SOURCE **EXTRACT**

Sources introduce you to material that is primary or contemporary to the period, and **Extracts** provides you with historical interpretations and the debate among historians on particular issues and developments. The accompanying activity questions support you in evaluating sources and extracts, analysing and assessing their value, and making judgements.

KEY QUESTION

The six key thematic questions in the specification for this topic are highlighted to help you understand and make connections between the themes.

 PRACTICE QUESTION

Focused questions to help you practise your history skills for both AS and A Level, including evaluating sources and extracts, and essay writing.

STUDY TIP

Hints to highlight key parts of **Practice Questions** or **Activities**.

ACTIVITY

Various activity types to provide you with opportunities to demonstrate both the content and skills you are learning. Some activities are designed to aid revision or to prompt further discussion; others are to stretch and challenge both your AS and A Level studies.

CROSS-REFERENCE

Links to related content within the book to offer you more detail on the subject in question.

A CLOSER LOOK

An in-depth look at a theme, event or development to deepen your understanding, or information to put further context around the subject under discussion.

KEY CHRONOLOGY

A short list of dates identifying key events to help you understand underlying developments.

KEY PROFILE

Details of a key person to extend your understanding and awareness of the individuals that have helped shape the period in question.

KEY TERM

A term that you will need to understand. The terms appear in bold, and they are also defined in the glossary.

Part One content

Autocracy, Reform and Revolution: Russia, 1855–1917

1 Trying to preserve autocracy, 1855–1894
2 The collapse of autocracy, 1894–1917

Part Two content

The Soviet Union, 1917–1964

3 The emergence of Communist dictatorship, 1917–1941
4 The Stalinist dictatorship and reaction, 1941–1964

AS examination papers will cover content from Part One only (you will only need to know the content in the blue box). A Level examination papers will cover content from both Part One and Part Two.

The examination papers

The grade you receive at the end of your AQA AS History course is based entirely on your performance in two examination papers, covering Breadth (Paper 1) and Depth (Paper 2). For your AQA A Level History course, you will also have to complete an Historical Investigation (Non-examined assessment).

Paper 1 Breadth Study

This book covers the content of a Breadth Study (Paper 1). You are assessed on the study of significant historical developments over a period of around 100 years, and associated interpretations or extracts.

Exam paper	Questions and marks	Assessment Objective (AO)*	Timing	Marks
AS Paper 1: Breadth Study	**Section A: Evaluating historical extracts** One compulsory question linked to two historical interpretations (25 marks) • The compulsory question will ask you: *'with reference to these extracts and your understanding of the historical context, which of these extracts provides the more convincing interpretation of…'*	AO3	Written exam: 1 hour 30 minutes	50 marks (50% of AS)
	Section B: Essay writing One from a choice of two essay questions (25 marks) • The essay questions will contain a quotation advancing a judgement, and <u>could</u> be followed by: *'explain why you agree or disagree with this view'.*	AO1		
A Level Paper 1: Breadth Study	**Section A: Evaluating historical extracts** One compulsory question linked to three historical interpretations with different views (30 marks) • The compulsory question will ask you: *'using your understanding of the historical context, assess how convincing the arguments in these three extracts are, in relation to…'*	AO3	Written exam: 2 hours 30 minutes	80 marks (40% of A Level)
	Section B: Essay writing Two from a choice of three essay questions (2 x 25 marks) • The essay questions require analysis and judgement, and <u>could</u> include: *'How successful…'* or *'To what extent…'* or *'How far…'* or a quotation offering a judgement followed by *'Assess the validity of this view'.*	AO1		

*AQA History examinations will test your ability to:

AO1: Demonstrate, organise and communicate **knowledge and understanding** to analyse and evaluate the key features related to the periods studied, **making substantiated judgements and exploring concepts**, as relevant, of cause, consequence, change, continuity, similarity, difference and significance.

AO2: **Analyse and evaluate** appropriate source material, primary and/or contemporary to the period, within the historical context.

AO3: **Analyse and evaluate**, in relation to the historical context, different ways in which aspects of the past have been interpreted.

Visit **www.aqa.org.uk** to help you prepare for your examinations. The website includes specimen examination papers and mark schemes.

Breadth Studies

The study of history concerns the study of change and continuity over time. Sometimes it is easy for you to over-concentrate on the former and forget that, for long periods throughout history, much remained the same. In undertaking a historical breadth study covering approximately 100 years of history, you will have the opportunity to reflect on the processes of change and continuity and, in so doing, come to appreciate what drives and hinders change and how historical development is a multi-faceted process.

The course of history brings together many different strands or themes, so, in order to understand any broad period as a whole, it is helpful to divide it into its various aspects or perspectives. This book reflects the AQA **Key Questions** which address a range of perspectives. These Key Questions are given at the beginning of the book and regularly through the text of the chapters. The most common themes in all the questions relate to the differing political, economic and social developments, but sometimes they highlight the place of religion, ideology or cultural movements across time.

Sometimes specific individuals colour history, changing the course of events or affecting others for good or ill, and the **Key Profile** features in this book will help you to identify the major influences on the period you are studying.

> **Practice Questions** help familiarise you with the new exam-style questions, while **Study Tips** highlight key parts of Practice Questions and words to look out for

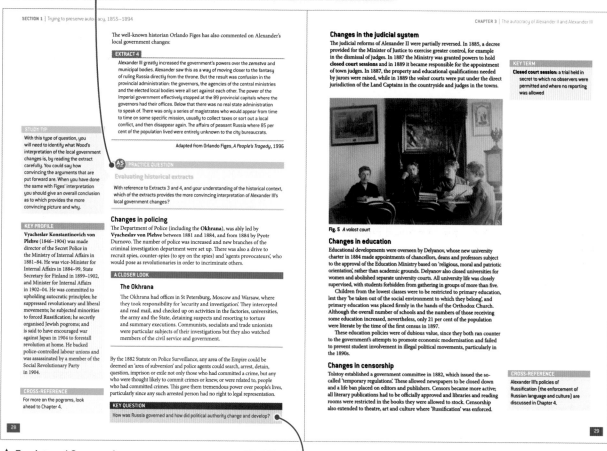

▲ Tsarist and Communist Russia 1855–1964

> **Key Questions** in each Breadth Study help you to understand and make connections between the key themes

While this book is designed to impart a full and lively awareness of a significant period in the history of one or more countries, far more is on offer from the pages that follow. With the help of the text and activities in this book, you will be encouraged to analyse past events, rather than merely learn to describe them. You will thus build up key historical skills that will increase your curiosity and prepare you, not only for A Level History examinations, but for any future study.

This book also incorporates passages of historical interpretation. These **Extract** features will encourage you to reflect on the way in which the past may be seen in different ways by academic historians and how the same factual evidence may support a variety of conclusions. The accompanying **Activity** features pose questions that are designed to stimulate debate on these interpretations. Suggestions for research also encourage you to read further and understand for yourself how history is a 'living' discipline and subject to constant revision.

The chapters which follow are laid out according to the content of the AQA specification, in four sections. Obviously, a secure chronological awareness and understanding of each section of content will be the first step in appreciating the historical period covered in this book. However, on reaching the end of each section, you should pause to reflect on the key questions posed and consider the 'big picture' which has emerged by that point, and the interpretations that have accompanied this. In this way, a broad and satisfying appreciation of history and historical processes will emerge.

Developing your study skills

You will need to be equipped with a paper file or electronic means of storing notes. Organised notes help to produce organised essays and sensible filing provides for efficient use of time. This book uses **Cross-References** to indicate where material in one chapter has relevance to that in another. By employing the same technique, you should find it easier to make the final leap towards piecing together your material to produce a broad historical picture. The exercises and research activities in this book are intended to guide you towards making selective and relevant notes with a specific purpose. Copying out sections of the book is to be discouraged, but selecting material with a particular theme or question in mind will considerably aid your understanding.

For students preparing for the AQA A Level examination, the essay questions posed in the examination will cover around 20–25 years of history or more. AS questions will also be broad, although there is no specific minimum timeframe for these. There are plenty of

examples of such 'breadth' **Practice Questions** in these books, both at AS in Part One and A Level in Parts One and Two of this book, as well as **Study Tips** and activities to encourage you to think about change, continuity, historical perspectives and interpretations. You should also develop timelines, make charts and diagrams, for example, to illustrate causation and consequence, analyse interpretations of key events, dissect broader developments thematically and identify the significance of major issues.

It is particularly important for you to have opinions on and be able to make informed judgements about the material you have studied. Some of the activities in this book encourage pair discussion or class debate, and you should make the most of such opportunities to voice and refine your own ideas. The beauty of history is that there is rarely a right or wrong answer, so this supplementary oral work should enable you to share your own opinions.

Writing and planning your essays

At both AS and A Level, you will be required to write essays and, although A Level questions are likely to be more complex, the basic qualities of good essay writing remain the same:

- **read the question carefully** to identify the key words and dates
- **plan out a logical and organised answer** with a clear judgement or view (several views if there are a number of issues to consider). Your essay should advance this judgement in the introduction, while also acknowledging alternative views and clarifying terms of reference, including the time span
- use the opening sentences of your paragraphs as stepping stones to take an argument forward, which allows you to **develop an evolving and balanced argument** throughout the essay and also makes for good style
- **support your comment or analysis** with precise detail; using dates, where appropriate, helps logical organisation
- **write a conclusion** which matches the view of the introduction and flows naturally from what has gone before.

While these suggestions will help you develop a good style, essays should never be too rigid or mechanical. This book will have fulfilled its purposes if it produces, as intended, students who think for themselves!

Sally Waller

Series Editor

The colours represent different types of event as follows:

● Blue: economic events   ● Red: political events   ● Green: religious events

● Yellow: social events   ● Black: international events
(including foreign policy)

Note that at this period these factors were very much interlinked.

1855	1856	1861	1860
● Alexander becomes Tsar	● Treaty of Paris ends Crimean War	● Abolition of serfdom	● Creation of state bank. Reform of tax collection

1866	1867–69	1870	1872
● Assassination attempt on Alexander II	● Church reforms	● City/town government reform and the introduction of *dumas*	● Russian publication of Karl Marx's *Das Kapital*

1881	1881–82	1883	1884
● Assassination of Alexander II	● Pogroms; May Laws ● Counter-reform in censorship	● Creation of Peasant Land Bank ● 'Emancipation of Labour' founded by Plekhanov	● Counter-reform in education ● Counter-reform in the Church

1889	1890	1891–1902	1892–1903
● Land Captains established	● Zemstvo counter-reform (restricting franchise)	● Widespread famine	● Sergei Witte becomes Minister of Finance

1899	1901–05	1901	1903
● Social Revolutionary Party established	● Economic slump follows world-wide depression and failed harvests ● Agrarian and industrial unrest	● Lenin publishes *What is to be Done?* ● Peasant disorder ● Commission on Agriculture set up	● Main section of Trans-Siberian Railway completed ● Union of Liberation (moderate) established ● Social Democrats split into Bolsheviks and Mensheviks

1905	1905	1906	1907
August ● Portsmouth (USA) Peace Treaty with Japan	**October** ● October Manifesto promises political reform and civil rights	● First State Duma ● Stolypin begins programme of agrarian reform	● Second Duma meets and is dissolved after four months ● Stolypin alters electoral laws

1915	1916	1917	1917
6 September ● The Tsar assumes command of the armed forces ● Progressive bloc formed ● Political crisis	**June–October** ● Brusilov offensive **30 December** ● Murder of Rasputin	**January–February** ● Strikes and civil unrest in Petrograd **23 February** ● International Women's Day march in Petrograd ● Women's Day march turns into a workers' demonstration	**27 February** ● Troops refuse to fire on demonstrators and join the revolutionary movement instead

1862–74
- Military reforms

1863
- Polish revolt
- University statute
- Publication of Chernyshevsky's *What is to be done?*

1864
- Local self-government *zemstva* established
- Judiciary reform
- Elementary school reform

1865
- Censorship reform

1874
- Military service reforms
- Populists begin 'Go to the People'

1876–79
- Revolutionary populist organisation: Land and Liberty

1877–78
- Russo-Turkish War

1879
- Terrorist organisation, The People's Will, established

1885
- Nobles' Land Bank; abolition of poll tax

1885–1900
- Russification in borderlands

1886
- Revival of The People's Will by St Petersburg students

1887–92
- Ivan Vyshnegradsky becomes Minister of Finance

1892
- Town/city government counter-reform (restricting franchise)

1894
- Death of Alexander III; accession of Nicholas II

1897
- Russia adopts the Gold Standard

1898
- Foundation of Russian Social Democratic Workers' Party

1903
- Labour strikes
- Anti-Semitic pogroms

1904
- Struve initiates liberal campaign of political banquets
- Minister of the Interior, Plehve, assassinated by the Socialist Revolutionaries

1904
- War breaks out between Russia and Japan over Korea and Northern Manchuria

1905
- 'Bloody Sunday' massacre

1907–12
- Third State Duma

1911
November
- Stolypin is assassinated

1912
- Lena goldfields massacre
- Industrial unrest
- Fourth State Duma

1914
1 August
- Germany declares war on Russia

26 August
- Russia defeated at the Battle of Tannenberg

1917
1 March
- Formation of the Petrograd Soviet and first Provisional Government

1917
2 March
- The Tsar abdicates

3 April
- Lenin returns and formulates his April Theses

1917
3–4 July
- Anti-government demonstrations in Petrograd – the 'July Days'

27–30 July
- Kornilov's coup fails and Red Guards are given arms

1917
September
- Trotsky becomes Chairman of the Petrograd Soviet; Bolshevik majorities in Petrograd and Moscow Soviets

1917

25–27 October
- Provisional Government members arrested
- Bolshevik coup announced at the second Congress of Soviets
- Congress adopts decree on peace;
- and decree on land;
- and appoints the first Soviet government

1917

December
- Establishment of the Cheka

1918

January
- The Constituent Assembly is forcibly dissolved

1918

- Civil war commences; first Soviet constitution
- "Treaty of Brest-Litovsk"

1922

- Stalin elected General Secretary
- Lenin dictates his testament

1924

- Lenin's death

1926

- United Opposition formed; Zinoviev, Kamenev and Trotsky removed from Politburo

1927

- Defeat of left opposition

1934

- Assassination of Kirov

1935

- Beginning of Stakhanovite movement

1936

- Family law restricts abortion and divorce
- Show trial of Zinoviev, Kamenev and others; Yezhov appointed head of NKVD
- New constitution

1937

- Show trial of Radek and others
- Execution of Marshal Tukhachevsky and Red Army officers

1941

- Nazi invasion of USSR
- Emergency legislation
- Siege of Leningrad begins

1941

- US Lend-Lease agreed
October
- Battle for Moscow
December
- Soviet counter-offensive

1942

- Battle of Stalingrad

1943

- Nazis driven back from Stalingrad
- Battle of Kursk
- Deportations from North Caucasus

1948

- Czech coup
- Berlin blockade

1949

- Leningrad affair
- Soviet atomic bomb

1952

- Doctors' plot

1953

- Stalin's death
- Malenkov becomes Head of State
- Khrushchev becomes First Secretary of Party
- Beria executed

1958

- Pasternak awarded Nobel Peace Prize for *Dr Zhivago*

1959

- Khrushchev launches 'maize' campaign

1961

- First manned space flight

1962

- Publication of Solzhenitsyn's *One Day in the Life of Ivan Denisovich*
- Cuban missile crisis

1919
- Establishment of Politburo and Orgburo; Communist Party is reorganised

1920
- Polish-Soviet War

1921
- Kronstadt revolt
- Tenth Party conference
- New Economic Policy
- Ban on factions

1921–22
- Great Famine

1928
- Shakhty Trial
- First Five Year Plan

1929
- Defeat of right opposition
- Celebration of Stalin's 50th birthday
- Call for mass collectivisation and liquidation of *kulaks*

1932–33
- Famine in Ukraine and elsewhere

1933
- Second Five Year Plan

1937–38
- Height of Great Terror

1938
- Third Five Year Plan
- Trial of Bukharin, Rykov and others
- Labour book for workers introduced
- Beria replaces Yezhov

1939
- Nazi-Soviet Pact; Soviet invasion of Eastern Poland and Finland

1940
- Soviet annexation of Baltic states

1944
- Siege of Leningrad broken
- Soviet armies advance into Eastern Europe

1945
- Soviet invasion of Germany
- Yalta Conference
- German surrender
- Potsdam conference

1946
- Beginning of Zhdanovshchina

1947
- Famine in Ukraine
- Cominform established

1954
- Publication of Ehrenburg's *The Thaw*
- Khrushchev's Virgin Lands Scheme adopted

1955
- Malenkov replaced by Bulganin as Head of State

1956
- 20th Party Conference; Khrushchev's 'secret' speech begins de-Stalinisation

1957
- Economic decentralisation adopted
- Anti-Party group defeated; demotion of Marshal Zhukov
- Sputnik launched

1963
- Exceptionally poor harvest

1964
- Removal of Khrushchev

The period between 1855 and 1964 encompasses the reigns of the last three **Tsars** of Russia and the first three communist rulers of what became known as the USSR or the Soviet Union. These 100 years were a time of great change for the nation. The Tsars Alexander II, Alexander III and Nicholas II, whose family had ruled Russia for 300 years, were replaced by a new communist line-up, following some months of instability in 1917. Russia's chequered and sometimes turbulent history will be the subject of the following chapters in this book.

Politically, Russia was transformed between 1855 and 1964. While there remained one man 'at the top', the circumstances of his coming to power and the way in which he ruled the country was entirely different. However, the problems faced by the communist rulers were not entirely dissimilar from those which beset the Tsars. Maintaining control and preventing political opposition preoccupied the rulers of both regimes and both relied heavily on methods of repression in order to stay in power.

Another major change which occurred across the 100 years covered by this book was the transformation of the Russian economy. When Alexander II came to the throne, Russia was still undeveloped and reliant on agriculture, but by 1964 it was an industrially advanced country which had even sent the first man into space. However, in economic matters, as in political ones, there was some continuity. Nikita Khrushchev, who was leader of the Soviet Union from 1955 until 1964, was just as concerned to develop Russian agriculture, make the best use of Russia's resources and run an efficient economy as was Alexander II and the finance ministers of the late nineteenth century.

The years 1855 to 1964 were also years of profound social and cultural change, as the predominantly rural peasant society of the mid-nineteenth century gave way to a modern urbanised society by the mid-twentieth century. A previously superstitious and strongly religious Christian society was replaced by one in which the political doctrine of communism (which promised a better future for the ordinary working people), offered a new form of belief. Despite these changes, working and living conditions, while much improved since 1855, still posed significant problems and social discontent did not go away.

This book is concerned both with understanding and explaining the sweeping changes which took place across this 100 year period of Russian history. It also identifies and accounts for those issues that remained the same. The following chapters will explore the developments and narrative of Russian history and, importantly, will consider the many varied influences which shaped this country's development. You will be taken on a journey through Russian history, considering both the rulers and the ruled and in so doing you will come to understand for yourself how individuals, groups and ideas all played their part in the emergence of the Russian/Soviet nation.

As you study this period of Russian history, you are invited to consider the following key questions:

- How was **Russia** governed and how did political authority change and develop?
- Why did opposition develop and how effective was it?
- How and with what results did the economy develop and change?
- What was the extent of social and cultural change?
- How important were ideas and ideology?
- How important was the role of individuals and groups and how were they affected by developments?

Try to keep these questions in mind as you work your way through this book; you will find them highlighted in the text too. These are the 'big' questions which have occupied historians studying the 1855 to 1964 period and by reflecting on them you will come to appreciate the development of the Russian/Soviet state over this period more fully. Remember too that political, economic, social and cultural developments go hand-in-hand and to build up a full picture you will need to explore the links between them.

There is plenty to learn and much to think about in the following pages. If you approach your studies in a spirit of enquiry, anxious to piece together past events to enrich your understanding of the whole, you will not only find much to enjoy in your study of Tsarist and Communist Russia, you will also emerge the wiser from it.

A CLOSER LOOK

The calendar in Russia

The Russians used the Julian calendar until 31 January 1918, rather than the Gregorian calendar adopted by the rest of Europe in the seventeenth and eighteenth centuries. Although they had added an 'extra day' (in addition to leap years) in some centuries, by 1918 Russia was 13 days behind Western Europe. This book uses the old-style Julian calendar for dates to 1 February 1918 and the new-style Gregorian calendar thereafter.

Trying to preserve autocracy, 1855–1894

The Russian autocracy in 1855

The Russian Empire was deeply divided between the government and the Tsar's subjects; between the capital and the provinces; between the educated and the uneducated; between Western and Russian ideas; between the rich and the poor; between privilege and oppression; between contemporary fashion and centuries-old custom. Most people (and over 90 per cent of the Emperor's subjects were born and bred in the countryside) felt that a chasm divided them from the world inhabited by the ruling elites. Russia was an empire, but national consciousness was only patchily developed and local traditions and loyalties retained the greatest influence. National consciousness was not a dominant sentiment among Russians. Except in times of war, most of them were motivated by Christian belief, peasant customs, village loyalties and reverence for the Tsar rather than by feelings of Russian nationhood. Christianity itself was a divisive phenomenon; Russian Orthodox teachings were not accepted universally. But the Tsar and the Church hierarchy wanted obedience and they had the authority to secure just that.

Adapted from Robert Service, *History of Modern Russia*, 1997

The well-respected modern historian Robert Service has painted a picture of tsarist Russia as it was in the mid-nineteenth century and was to remain, scarcely changed, until the end of tsarist rule in 1917. His account of the state of the Russian Empire stresses its geographic, social, intellectual, economic and even religious divisions. Above all, he emphasises the **localism** of Russian society and the lack of national consciousness. The empire he describes seems to be held together by a 'reverence for the Tsar', and by the power of that Tsar and the Russian Orthodox Church to demand obedience.

The political context

In 1855, Russia was an **autocratic empire**. At its head was a Tsar, who took the title 'Emperor and Autocrat of all Russia'. According to the 'Collected Laws of the Russian Empire' compiled by Tsar Nicholas I in 1832, 'The Emperor of all the Russias is an autocratic and unlimited monarch; God himself ordains that all must bow to his supreme power, not only out of fear but also out of conscience.'

A CLOSER LOOK

Empire

An empire is made up of a number of lesser states ruled over by one monarch. Nineteenth-century Russia was a vast empire of around 21 million square kilometres, twice the size of Europe and a sixth of the globe's surface. It had been acquired through military conquest and colonisation, and was still growing.

LEARNING OBJECTIVES

In this chapter you will learn about:

- the powers of the Tsar of Russia in the mid-nineteenth century
- the way in which Russia was governed and the problems the rulers faced
- the economic state of Russia in c1855
- the social make-up of Russia in c1855.

KEY QUESTION

As you read this chapter, consider the following Key Question:
How was Russia governed and how did political authority change and develop?

KEY TERM

Localism: loyalty to the local community or local area

ACTIVITY

As you read this chapter, see if you can find evidence that agrees with Service's interpretation in Extract 1. Later in the chapter, you will be asked to assess how convincing his argument is.

KEY TERM

Autocratic: autocracy means having no limits on a ruler's power; such a ruler was called an autocrat

Fig. 1 *The Russian Empire in 1855. What can be learned from this map about the likely problems of governing Russia in the mid-nineteenth century?*

Nicholas' statement is a reminder that the Tsar was, in name only, also the Head of the Russian **Orthodox Church** and was regarded by Orthodox believers as the embodiment of God on Earth. The vast lands of the Russian Empire were his private property and the Russian people were his children. Russians were taught to show devotion to their Tsar and to accept their conditions on Earth as the will of God. The Patriarch of Moscow, who worked in close harmony with the Tsar, provided spiritual guidance, while the **Over-Procurator** of the **Holy Synod**, a post created in 1721, was a government minister appointed by the Tsar to run Church affairs. This meant that the structures of Church and State were entwined, as archbishops and bishops at the head of the Church hierarchy were subject to tsarist control over appointments, religious education, most of the Church's finances and issues of administration.

The Tsar's imperial **edicts** (*ukazy* in Russian) were the law of the land. The Tsar did, of course, have advisers and ministers, but these were all chosen by the Tsar himself and no-one could do anything without the Tsar's approval. His main advisory bodies were the Imperial Council or Chancellery, a body of 35 to 60 nobles specially picked by the Tsar to advise him personally and provide their 'expert' opinion; the Council of Ministers, a body of 8 to 14 ministers in charge of different government departments; and the Senate, which was supposed to oversee all the workings of government but in practice was largely redundant by 1855.

The Tsar and the central government were based in the Imperial capital of St Petersburg but the regime also depended on the **provincial** nobility for support. Nobles had not been obliged to serve the State since 1785, although many continued to do so, for example as a provincial governor of one of the Empire's fifty provinces. However, their sense of obligation remained strong and all landowners were expected to keep order on their estates. Furthermore, when circumstances demanded, Tsars might choose to appoint a special committee to carry out an investigation or prepare a report. Such committees were usually headed by trusted nobles but, even so, there was no need for the Tsar to take any notice of their findings.

The **civil servants** who made up the **bureaucracy** were paid noble officials, selected from a 'table of ranks' that laid down the requirements for office.

There were 14 levels, from rank 1, held by members of the Council of Ministers, to rank 14, which covered the minor state positions, for example, collecting taxes or running a provincial post office. Each rank had its own uniform, form of address and status. This bureaucracy was riddled by internal corruption and incompetence, but through it orders were passed downwards from the central government to the provincial governors and, in turn, to district governors and town commandants. It was a one-way operation though; there was no provision for suggestions to travel upwards from the lower ranks.

Fig. 2 *The Tsar's palace in St Petersburg*

As well as his civilian officials, the Tsar also had at his disposal the world's largest army of around 1.5 million **conscripted serfs**, each forced into service for 25 years and made to live in a '**military colony**'. This huge army and the much smaller navy absorbed around 45 per cent of the government's annual spending. The higher ranks of the military were prestigious posts, reserved for the nobles who bought and sold their commissions, but for the lower ranks discipline was harsh and army life was tough. This army could be called upon to fight in wars or to put down risings and disturbances inside Russia. The Tsar also had the service of elite regiments of mounted **Cossacks**, with special social privileges. The Cossacks acted both as a personal bodyguard to the Tsar and as police reinforcements.

A CLOSER LOOK

Cossacks

The Cossacks came from the Ukraine and Southern Russia. They were known for their skills in horsemanship and their strong military tradition. By the nineteenth century, the Cossacks formed a special and prestigious military class serving the Tsar. They were provided with arms and supplies by the tsarist government, but each soldier rode his own highly trained horse.

To maintain the autocracy, the country had developed into a **police state**. The police state prevented freedom of speech, freedom of the press and travel abroad. Political meetings and strikes were forbidden. Censorship existed at every level of government and the police made sure that the censorship exercised by the State and Church was enforced. The secret state security network was run by the 'Third Section' of the Emperor's Imperial Council. Its agents kept a strict surveillance over the population and had unlimited powers to carry out raids, and to arrest and imprison or send into exile anyone suspected of anti-tsarist behaviour. They sometimes acted on the word of informers, and were greatly feared.

Following the **French Revolution**, Alexander I, Tsar between 1801 and 1825, considered setting up an advisory representative assembly and possibly giving it law-making powers, but he never put this into practice. His brother Nicholas I, who ruled between 1825 and 1855, totally rejected such a thought. A military uprising against his rule in December 1825 encouraged him to follow a path of repression, and he deliberately sought to distance Russia from

KEY TERM

Civil servant: someone working for the government

Bureaucracy: a system of government in which most of the important decisions are taken by state officials rather than by elected representatives

Conscription: compulsory enlistment of a person into military service

Serf: a person who was the property of the lord for whom he or she worked; serfs and serfdom are further discussed later in this chapter (on page 4, in A closer look: What was serfdom?) and will be covered in detail in Chapter 2

Military colony: where the conscripts lived (with their families) and trained, all under strict military discipline

Police state: a state in which the activities of the people are closely monitored and controlled for political reasons

ACTIVITY

Draw a diagram to show the political structure of Russia in c1855.

S-REFERENCE

han half the total population
of around 69 million people in 1855
was Russian. Read more in A Closer
Look: Problems of governing the
Empire on page 2.

A CLOSER LOOK

The French Revolution

The French had risen up against their
absolutist King in 1789 and a republic
had been set up in 1792. The French
example of representative government
(as already practised in Great Britain)
was spread across Europe by Napoleon
before 1812. French 'liberal' ideas
ignited a demand for greater political
freedom in the European states.

KEY TERM

Entrepreneur: someone who invests
money to set up a business
despite the financial risks

Cottage industry: work done in the
worker's own home or a small
workshop, typically spinning,
weaving and small-scale wood
and metal work; occasionally
whole villages specialised in a
particular trade, such as making
samovars for boiling water for tea

the West where the liberal ideas he most feared were spreading. He believed
in strict autocracy and severe restrictions were imposed on Russia's other
nationalities. While leading intellectuals argued for a civil society based on
the rule of law, Nicholas tightened censorship and set up the secret police, or
Third Section. His reign ended in military defeat in the Crimea, which finally
brought the long-ignored need for change to the new Tsar's attention.

The economic and social context

KEY QUESTION

How and with what results did the economy develop and change?
What was the extent of social change?

The economic situation

When Alexander II came to the throne in 1855, Britain, Belgium, France and
the states comprising Germany were already well advanced industrially. Mills,
factories, coal pits, quarries and railways were transforming the landscape and
trade was flourishing. However, the Russian economy remained mostly rural
with a ratio of 11:1 village to town dwellers, compared with 2:1 in Britain.

There were good reasons for Russia's economic backwardness. Although
the Russian Empire was vast, much of its territory was inhospitable (over
two thirds lay north of the 50th parallel north), comprising tundra, forests
and stretches of barren countryside, especially to the north and east. As a
result, both size and climate placed severe strains on economic development.
Although mid-nineteenth century Russia was Europe's main exporter of
agricultural produce and possessed vast reserves of timber, coal, oil, gold
and other precious metals, much of its potential remained untapped and
communications between the different parts of the Empire were poor.

However the lack of progress was primarily due to Russia's commitment to
a serf-based economy. The landowning aristocracy, the tsarist government and
the army were all reliant on the **serfs**. This inhibited economic development
by limiting the forces that drive change, such as wage-earners, markets and
entrepreneurs. The serfs were poor. Most just about managed to survive on the
produce they grew for themselves on the land made available by their landlords,
and '**cottage industries**' provided the little extra cash they needed for special
purchases and taxes. However, they often suffered with starvation in the winter,
particularly in years of bad harvest, and systems of land management within
the serf communes (*mirs*) meant that individual serf families worked scattered
strips and were obliged to follow a communal pattern of farming. There was
little incentive or opportunity, therefore, for them to develop into 'wage-earners'.

A CLOSER LOOK

What was serfdom?

Russian peasants (serfs) were men, women and children who were
classified as the 'property' of their owners, rather than as 'citizens' of
the State. Serfs could be bought and sold, were subject to beatings, and
were not allowed to marry without permission. Serfs were also liable for
conscription into the army. There were two main types: a little over half
were privately owned, with around 30 per cent of these paying rent (*obrok*)
and around 70 per cent providing labour (*barshchina*). The remainder
were 'state serfs' who paid taxes and rent. Most serfs worked on the land in
village communes (*mirs*) run by strict rules imposed by the village elders.
Some performed domestic service.

Markets existed (and indeed were growing) although 'business' was mostly small-scale. The most common peasant purchases were vodka (for celebrations), metal tools and salt (to preserve food), which they bought in the nearest town, or at a fair. However, self-sufficiency meant that comparatively few goods were actually 'purchased' and in peasant markets, money was not the usual form of payment. Exchanges took place 'in kind'; for example some eggs might be given in return for a length of wool. In some areas, particularly near large cities, market forces were beginning to develop as peasants sought wage-work in nearby towns at slack times in the farming year, but for the vast majority, money was simply irrelevant and there was no **internal market demand**.

At the other end of the scale was the small **landowning elite**, who obtained most of what they needed from their serfs in the form of service and feudal dues. They were generally uninterested in how efficiently their estates operated. For many, serf-owning merely provoked idleness. So long as their bailiffs squeezed sufficient amounts out of the peasants for their own benefit, the aristocratic landowners saw little need to do more. There was no opportunity for **capital accumulation**, since income was generally falling. This was thanks to the rural population growth and the **agricultural changes** in Western Europe that had increased the competitiveness and productivity of the European markets. Many landowners had been forced into debt and had to take out **mortgages** on estates which had previously been owned outright by their families. Sometimes they even mortgaged their serfs, but despite their despair, they did not seek alternative ways of 'making money', because money as such was of little use in Russia's under-developed economy.

A CLOSER LOOK

Agricultural changes

Crop rotation, new fertilisers and developments in agricultural machinery had all helped to transform Western agriculture.

Fig. 3 *A peasant woman tilling the soil*

KEY TERM

Internal market demand: the desire and ability to buy the products of manufacturing within the country; if a country's inhabitants are poor, there will be little internal demand

Landowning elite: those who owned land and who were a privileged minority in Russian society

Capital accumulation: building up money reserves in order to invest

Mortgage: this involves borrowing money by providing a guarantee; in this case a landowner's serfs provided the guarantee for a state loan, and if the borrowed money and additional interest was not repaid, the State could seize the serfs

A CLOSER LOOK

Serf poverty

The serfs' working and living conditions were, by Western standards, primitive. It was normal for corn to be cut by hand with sickles and for peasants to share their huts with their animals. In such circumstances, it is perhaps unsurprising that most peasants were illiterate but deeply religious, inclined to superstition and deeply hostile to change.

KEY QUESTION

What was the extent of social and cultural change?

KEY TERM

Urban artisan: a manual worker in a town who possessed some skills, e.g. a cobbler or a leather-maker

Intelligentsia: the more educated members of Russian society, including writers and philosophers with both humanitarian and nationalist concerns; many opposed the State for various cultural, moral, religious, philosophical and political reasons

ACTIVITY

According to Extract 2, what were the consequences of the absence of a middle class in Russia?

The social context

Socially, Russia was, as Service suggested in Extract 1, starkly divided between the privileged land-owning elite and the serf majority; the non-productive and the productive classes. The former consisted of the clergy, nobility, civil and military officials, army and naval officers and, at the very top, the royal court. In addition to the serfs, there were some **urban artisans**, manufacturers and merchants within the ranks of the 'productive classes', but the striking feature of mid-nineteenth century Russian society was the absence of any coherent 'middle class', as was becoming increasingly dominant elsewhere in Europe. There were a small number of professionals (doctors, teachers and lawyers, for example) some of whom comprised an educated '**intelligentsia**', but these were often the sons of nobles.

EXTRACT 2

It is impossible to overstate the importance of the late survival in Russia of serfdom, an institution that in Western Europe is associated with medieval times and had begun to decline from the end of the thirteenth century. By tying the bulk of the population to the land and preventing the movement of a free labour force, it acted as an impediment to the development of a middle class. This social gap had a profound effect on political as well as economic development. It accounts for the relative weakness in nineteenth-century Russia of moderate liberal political opinion. It may also explain the lack of sympathy shown by thinkers at both ends of the political spectrum for entrepreneurial activity, the lack of practicality in much of their thought – which tended towards the visionary rather than the concrete – and their disdain, even contempt, for prosperity and material gain.

Adapted from Derek Offord, *Nineteenth Century Russia: Opposition to Autocracy,* 1998

The word 'class', with its connotation of 'economic status' is actually a rather modern term to use of nineteenth-century Russian society, which was still based on birth, land and service. As in the past, in 1855 legal barriers still limited social mobility. Serfs were liable for dues, as demanded by past custom, to their masters (from whose bond it was almost impossible to escape). They also paid direct and indirect **taxes** to the government. The nobility and clergy, however, were exempt from the payment of any direct monetary taxes.

A CLOSER LOOK

Taxes

The government was financed from taxes and dues. The main direct tax, paid by all except the merchants, was the poll tax, literally a 'tax on heads', which had been introduced in 1719 in order to cover the costs of maintaining Russia's large army. It was levied, at the same rate, on every male peasant in the Empire, no matter what his circumstances. This, together with the *obrok* paid by state serfs in lieu of land and service dues, made up 25 per cent of 'ordinary' government income. Indirect taxes (on services and goods) included a tax on salt, and, even more importantly, on vodka. This had grown during the nineteenth century to represent 30 per cent of ordinary government income by 1855, suggesting that a change was already underway towards a more 'commercial' source for government revenue. Overall, the taxes hit hard at the peasantry who, together with the urban workers and tradesmen, provided around 90 per cent of Imperial finance.

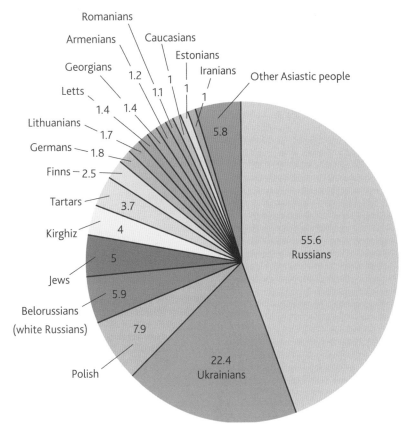

Fig. 4 *Ethnic groups within the Russian Empire, as given in the first national census of 1897 (population in millions)*

Most of the structures present in mid-nineteenth century Russia were still typical of the pre-modern world. A small ruling group, unified by the structures of autocracy, lived off resources mobilised directly from a large agrarian population through the system of serfdom. Most of the peasant population lived lives little different from those of the Middle Ages. The family, the household and the village were the crucial institutions of rural life. Largely self-sufficient peasants used traditional ways of working the soil, and levels of productivity were little higher than those of the Middle Ages. However, new forces were already beginning to undermine the traditional patterns. In some areas, market forces were beginning to transform village life, while the government's revenues came increasingly from commercial sources. At the upper level of society, the increasingly westernised outlook of Russian elites undermined the autocratic political culture of Russia's ruling group. The government became aware of how threatening these various changes might be to its own power only in the middle of the nineteenth century.

Adapted from David Christian, *Imperial and Soviet Russia*, 1986

So, while Russia was still considered a 'great' power in Europe because of its size and huge army, politically, economically and socially it remained undeveloped and 'backward' in comparison with the West. Small changes were taking places but, as yet, these had been insufficient to promote extensive modernisation.

STUDY TIP

When faced this with type of question, look carefully at each extract and make a note of the arguments it puts forward in your answer. Comment on the overall argument and the specific, lesser arguments, using what you have learned so far to assess how convincing these arguments are.

 **PRACTICE QUESTION**

Evaluating historical extracts

Re-read Extracts 1, 2 and 3. Using your understanding of the historical context, assess how convincing the arguments in these three extracts are in relation to the condition of Russia in 1855.

The impact of the Crimean War 1853–56

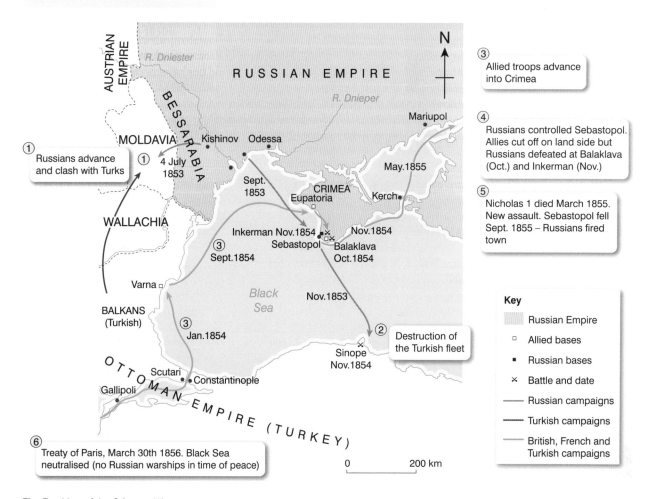

Fig. 5 *Map of the Crimean War*

In the mid-nineteenth century, the empire of the Ottoman Turks stretched from the Middle East across the Black Sea Straits and into the Balkans. However, ever since the 1820s, the Sultan had struggled to control the Christians in his European dominions and consequently Tsar Nicholas I had seized the opportunity to increase Russian influence in the area by posing as the Protector of Slavs and Christians.

In June 1853, Nicholas sent a Russian army to Moldavia and Wallachia (now part of present-day Moldova). This provoked the Turks into declaring war in October. The Russians were the stronger, and triumphantly sank a squadron from the Turkish Black Sea Fleet, which had been at anchor in Sinope Bay on the Black Sea. This brought the British and French, who were anxious to protect their own trading interests in the area, into the war in defence of Turkey. They sent a joint expeditionary force of more than 60,000 men to the Russian Crimea, where they mounted a land and sea attack on the major Russian naval base of Sebastopol.

The war was marred by incompetence on both sides, and the death toll was made worse by an outbreak of cholera. Russia suffered badly from outdated technology, poor **transport** and inadequate leadership and while the Russian conscript army was larger in number, it lacked the flexibility and determination of the smaller French and British units. The Russians were defeated at Balaclava in October 1854 and at Inkerman in November 1854.

Shortly before his death in March 1855, Nicholas I addressed his son, the future Alexander II, with the words, 'I hand over to you my command, unfortunately not in as good order as I would have wished'. By September, the fortress of Sebastopol had fallen to its enemies, leaving the tsarist government shocked and humiliated.

Although they had gone to war in a spirit of utmost confidence, the course of the fighting had revealed Russia's military and administrative inadequacies. In every respect, the war was little short of disastrous. Trade had been disrupted, peasant uprisings escalated and the intelligentsia renewed their cries for something to be done to close the gap between Russia and the West. The concluding Treaty of Paris (1856) added the final humiliation by preventing Russian warships from using the Black Sea in times of peace.

A CLOSER LOOK

Transport was a major problem for the Russians. It took them longer to get equipment to the front line than it took France and Britain to send soldiers and materials from the channel ports. Russian equipment was also outdated. Their muskets were inferior and there was only one to every two soldiers. The Russian navy still used sails and wooden-bottomed ships, while Western ships had metal cladding and were powered by steam. Furthermore, the inshore fleet contained galley boats, rowed by conscripted serfs.

Fig. 6 *The siege of Sebastopol*

Failure in the Crimean War provided the 'wake-up call' that Russia needed. With the death of Nicholas I, decades of stagnation came to an end. In 1855 there came to power not only a new Tsar, Alexander II, but also a new generation of liberal-minded nobles and officials who were to have a major influence on his reign. The dilemma was how to match the other European powers in economic development without weakening the autocratic structure that held the Empire together.

Fig. 7 *Alexander II receiving congratulations from his family after his coronation*

SUMMARY

Activity

1. Draw a chart, as illustrated below, and complete it with bullet point notes, based on what you have learned in this chapter.

	Strengths	Weaknesses
Political		
Economic		
Social		

2. Using this chart, assess the validity of the statement, 'The Russian Empire had more strengths than weaknesses in 1855.'

2 Alexander II, the 'Tsar Reformer'

The emancipation of the serfs

ACTIVITY

As you read this chapter, reflect on how convincing Emmons' interpretation in Extract 1 is. At the end of the chapter, you will be asked to provide your own critique of Emmons' view.

Tsar Alexander II's decision to **emancipate** [i.e. free] Russia's 51 million serfs in 1861 has often been hailed as the product of the Tsar's own liberal, humanitarian ideas. Alexander has been praised for making this bold move, challenging accepted convention and setting Russia on a new path of reform, so transforming Russian society. The measure was followed by a series of reforms in other areas (the army, local government, the judiciary, education, publishing and elsewhere), which have collectively led to his being given the nickname 'Tsar Liberator'.

However, it is worth looking closely at the historian Terence Emmons' interpretation of this major edict. He refers to the serfs' Emancipation as a piece of 'state-directed' manipulation of society that aimed to 'strengthen social and political stability', rather than as the product of 'liberal' thinking from an enlightened Tsar who is only concerned for the welfare of his subjects. The edict and the reforms that followed were government-driven, and Emmons claims that the outcome was little short of disastrous, producing serious long- and short-term 'stresses and strains'. Emmons' interpretation suggests that, far from being a solely selfless reform, Alexander's reforms were intended to maintain tsarist authority. However, he also suggests that the calculation seriously backfired, creating division between the Tsarist government and the landed gentry (on whom that government relied). In short, Alexander's reforms actually weakened faith in the Tsar as being capable of leading effective change, and ultimately created a desire for 'popular participation in government'.

LEARNING OBJECTIVES

In this chapter you will learn about:

- the reasons why Alexander II embarked on a programme of reform
- the emancipation of the serfs
- other domestic reforms
- interpretations of Alexander II's reforms.

KEY TERM

Emancipation: freeing from bondage

Enlightened despotism: a system of government in which an all-powerful ruler granted domestic reforms in order to benefit his people

CROSS-REFERENCE

For more context on the role of serfs in Russian society, and to understand why their emancipation is considered a major event in European history, read Chapter 1, pages 4–5.

Fig. 1   *Alexander II liberating the serfs, 1861*

Motives for reform

KEY QUESTION

How important were ideas and ideology?

KEY TERM

Party of St Petersburg Progress:
a loose title given to the more
liberal nobles and officials who
frequented the salons of the Tsar's
aunt, or gathered around his
brother

Whether Alexander II's views on serfdom were shaped by his Romantic poet tutor, Vasily Zhukovsky, and Alexander's own travels around the Empire during his father Nicholas I's reign, or by the political circle of progressive nobles known as the '**Party of St Petersburg Progress**' who came into prominence at his court, we cannot be sure. However, his brother the Grand Duke Konstantin, his aunt the Grand Duchess Elena Pavlovna, and other 'enlightened bureaucrats' (such as the **Milyutin brothers**) who had all been committed to the abolition of serfdom for some time, no doubt helped fuel his determination to act.

CROSS-REFERENCE

The economic and social
implications of serfdom, and the
views of the Russian intelligentsia,
are discussed in Chapter 1,
pages 4–6.

You can read about Slavophiles on
page 42.

Zemstva, the new elected local
councils with power to improve
public services, will be discussed
later on page 16.

KEY PROFILE

The Milyutin brothers

Nikolai Alexander Milyutin (1818–72) was an influential voice in the Ministry of Internal Affairs, favouring reform within the Slavophile tradition. In 1859–61 he was largely responsible for drafting the terms of the Emancipation Edict, and he also supported the establishment of the *zemstva*.

  Dmitry Alekseyevich Milyutin (1816–1912) had trained in a military academy and earned a reputation as a military scholar. He analysed the reasons behind Russia's defeat in the Crimean War and was an obvious choice for Alexander II's Minister of War from 1861 to 1881. He was made a count in recognition of his services for military reform.

  Their views were shared by other members of the Russian intelligentsia who believed that, as well as holding Russia back economically and weakening her 'Great Power status', serfdom was morally wrong.

Alexander, whose natural tendencies were conservative rather than liberal, may not have been fully convinced by such arguments, but the increase in peasant uprisings since the 1840s would certainly have been likely to alarm him. While serf disorder posed no real threat to the autocracy, it certainly added weight to the arguments for emancipation.

Fig. 2 *The economic motives behind emancipation*

KEY QUESTION

How effective was opposition?

A CLOSER LOOK

Between 1840 and 1844, there had been fewer than 30 outbreaks of disorder per year on privately owned estates, but the figure more than doubled over the next 15 years. This increase was partly the result of:

- landowners pushing peasants to produce more or pay higher rents in order to maintain their own incomes
- protests against military conscription during the Crimean War. Nor did the disturbances subside once the war ended in 1856. Since it was traditional for the Tsar to announce the freedom of serfs conscripted to fight at the end of a war, Alexander II's delay (while he considered the future) increased tensions.

The humiliations and inefficiencies of the Crimean War were the main catalyst for action. Dmitry Milyutin, Minister of War 1861–81, pleaded for reform in order to 'strengthen the State and restore dignity'. He believed that the army had to be modernised, and that only a 'free' population would provide the labour needed for much needed military improvement.

 PRACTICE QUESTION

'The decision to emancipate the serfs was the result of peasant unrest.' Explain why you agree or disagree with this view.

Alexander was as determined as his ancestors to maintain the tsarist autocracy and uphold his 'God-given' duties, but he felt the pressure for reform. He began his reign by releasing political prisoners and pardoning the Decembrists, a group who had been involved in a plot to assassinate his father. He relaxed controls on censorship, lessened restrictions on foreign travel and university entrance, cancelled tax debts, and restored some of the rights [liberties] of Poland and the Catholic Church. In March 1856, Alexander followed up this 'enlightened' start by asking a small group of nobles to produce suggestions for an emancipation measure.

SOURCE 1

The contradictions behind Alexander's views and intentions can be seen in his address to the Moscow nobility in 1856:

There are rumours abroad that I wish to grant the peasants their freedom; this is unjust, and you may say so to everyone to right and left; but a feeling of hostility between the peasants and landlords does, unfortunately, exist, and this has already resulted in several instances of insubordination to the landlords. I am convinced that sooner or later we must come to it. I believe that you too, are of the same opinion as I; consequently, it is far better that this should come about from above, rather than from below.

CROSS-REFERENCE

The impact of the Crimean War is outlined in Chapter 1, pages 8–9.

STUDY TIP

When faced with this type of question, you should firstly consider the importance of peasant unrest and then balance this against other factors promoting emancipation. Look back to Chapter 1, for further ideas.

CROSS-REFERENCE

Catholic Poland, at this time, was part of the Russian Empire, as illustrated by the map on page 1. Chapter 3 covers the treatment of non-Russian nationalities within the Empire under Tsars Alexander II and III.

The Emancipation Edict, 1861

In 1858–59, Alexander II set off on a tour of the countryside making pro-emancipation speeches to try to win noble support for emancipation. His decree was not ready until February 1861 and finally came into force that Lent.

The 1861 Emancipation Edict initially applied only to the privately owned serfs, although the state serfs received their freedom in 1866. It granted them freedom and an allotment of land, while landowners received government compensation. Freed serfs were required to pay '**redemption payments**' to the government over 49 years, for their land, and were to remain within their peasant commune (*mir*) until these redemption payments had been made. The *mir* was made responsible for distributing the allotments, controlling the farming, and collecting and paying the peasants' taxes, while **volosts** were established to supervise the *mirs*. From 1863, the *volosts* ran their own courts, replacing the landlords' jurisdiction over serfs.

There was a two-year period of 'temporary obligation' before freedom was granted, during which allocations were worked out. Landowners kept the meadows, pasture, woodland, and a personal holding, although open fields were given to the *mirs*.

The abolition of serfdom was a huge undertaking which took far longer to carry out than anticipated. Around 15 per cent of peasants still remained 'temporarily obligated' to their landlords until 1881, when redemption was made compulsory.

The results of emancipation

Fig. 3 *A holiday crowd in Moscow celebrates the Emancipation*

Some peasants, the **kulaks**, did well out of the land allocations. They bought up extra land so they could produce surplus grain for export. Others who sold up their allocation, or obtained a passport to leave the *mir*, raised their living standard by finding work in the industrialising cities. Similarly, some landowners used the compensation offered to get out of debt, and enterprising individuals made profits through investment in industry.

However, many peasants felt cheated, not least because the land allocations were rarely fair. The small allotments (which provided little opportunity to adopt new farming methods) were increasingly divided as several sons inherited and the land was shared between them. The *mir* system also proved to be a highly traditional institution, and subsistence farming and technical backwardness persisted, so that in 1878 only 50 per cent of the peasantry was capable of producing a surplus.

The loss of former benefits, restrictions on travel (which required an internal passport) and the burden of the redemption payments made rural life difficult. Resentment of *kulaks* easily led to further violent outbreaks in the countryside.

Landowners, too, resented their loss of influence. The newspapers ran articles about their disappointments and a wave of student protests and riots occurred in St Petersburg, Moscow and Kazan.

A CLOSER LOOK

Unrest in the countryside continued after the Edict as disputes erupted over land-holding and redemption payments. There were 647 incidents of riot in the four months that followed the decree, and a peasant riot in Bezdna (in the area of Kazan) was brutally crushed with 70 peasant deaths. Noble bankruptcies also continued, as landowners had to sell or mortgage their own allocated land. Some nobles found an opportunity to air their resentments in another of Alexander II's reforms, the new local elected governments called *zemstva*.

KEY QUESTION

How and with what results did the economy develop and change?

 PRACTICE QUESTION

'The emancipation of the serfs caused more problems than it solved.' Explain why you agree or disagree with this view.

Other domestic reforms

The changes to the rights and position of peasants and landowners had wide implications for both society and government, and further reforms soon followed.

Military reforms (1874–75)

Dmitry Milyutin reorganised the armed forces to create a smaller, more professional, more efficient, and less expensive army:

- Conscription was made compulsory for all classes (including nobles) from the age of 21, but the length of service was reduced from 25 to 15 years of active service, and 10 years in the reserves.
- Punishments were made less severe and the system of military colonies (where conscripts had been forced to live) was abandoned. Better provisioning and medical care were established.
- Modern weaponry was introduced and a new command structure was established.

ACTIVITY

Divide into three groups to consider the impact of the Emancipation Edict for:
- the Tsar and his government
- the nobility
- the peasantry.

You should write a speech and deliver your verdict to the other groups. In each case, try to make some positive and some negative comments.

STUDY TIP

With this type of question, you need to decide whether you are going to support or challenge the view before writing your answer. In your essay you need to weigh up the arguments carefully. For example you could put forward the ways in which the Emancipation Edict caused problems and the ways in which it solved them. Try to write in a way that leads naturally to your conclusion.

ACTIVITY

As you read about these 'other reforms' create a chart to show what changed and what remained the same. Rate the significance of each reform for the tsarist autocracy on a scale of one to ten, where 'one' would be a reform that strengthened the autocracy and 'ten' would be a reform that weakened it.

CROSS-REFERENCE

The problems of supply and leadership facing the army are discussed in Chapter 1, page 9.

- Military colleges were set up to provide better training for the non-noble officer corps.
- Literacy within the army was improved, with mass army-education campaigns in the 1870s–90s.

These were improvements but the better-off found substitutes to serve in their place, while the officer class remained largely aristocratic. More importantly, problems of supply and leadership continued. The army struggled to win in the **war against Turkey** (1877–78), and, in the longer term, was defeated at the hands of the Japanese in 1904–05 and again by Germany in 1914–17.

A CLOSER LOOK

War against Turkey (1877–78)

In an attempt to recover the losses of the Crimean War, the Russians went to war in 1877 in support of the Balkan states fighting against Turkish rule. In March 1878, after some hard fighting, Russia concluded the Treaty of San Stefano with Turkey. This created a large Bulgaria under Russian protection. Alarmed by such Russian gains, Britain and Austria-Hungary forced Russia to accept the Treaty of Berlin in July 1878, which split up the new Bulgaria.

KEY QUESTION

How was Russia governed and how did political authority change and develop?

A CLOSER LOOK

Electoral colleges

In a system of electoral colleges, individuals vote for others who then cast votes on their behalf. In this case, the peasants would elect members of an 'electoral college'. The electoral college would then vote for nominee(s) to sit on the *zemstvo*. The nobles, townspeople and Church did the same. Obviously this meant that, proportionately, the nobles, who dominated the *zemstva*, had more weight than the peasants.

Local government reforms (1864–70)

To replace the rights and obligations of the former serf-owning gentry, a system of elected local councils was established, both at district and provincial levels. They were known as *zemstva* (singular *zemstvo*). These were chosen through a system of '**electoral colleges**', with separate colleges for nobles, townspeople, Church and peasants. However, the voting procedure was arranged in a way that allowed the nobility to dominate.

The *zemstva* were given power to improve public services (roads, schools, public health, prisons), develop industrial projects and administer poor relief in times of hardship. In 1870 this reform was extended to towns, when elected town councils called dumas were set up.

The establishment of a degree of representative government at a local level raised the hopes of those members of the intelligentsia who wanted a representative National Assembly. However, the power of the *zemstva* was strictly limited. They had no control over state and local taxes. Provincial governors continued to appoint officials, took responsibility for law and order, and could even overturn *zemstvo* decisions if they chose.

Nevertheless, the *zemstva* provided a valuable addition to local government, not least because they were composed of men who understood the locality and its needs. However, despite some peasant representation, they were never truly 'people's assemblies'. They attracted doctors, lawyers, teachers and scientists who, to the dismay of the regime, used meetings as an opportunity to debate political issues and criticise central government.

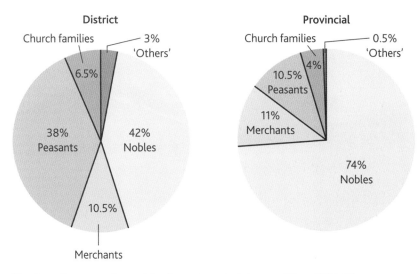

Fig. 4 *The proportions of district and provincial assemblies, 1865–67*

Judiciary reforms (1864)

Emancipation also demanded an overhaul of the law, particularly concerning property rights, and a change in the administration of local justice. This had formerly been in the hands of a judge examining written evidence, usually prepared by the landowner and police. There had been no jury system, no lawyers and no examination of witnesses. The accused was considered guilty until proven innocent and the judge's decision was final.

The new system was modelled on the West:

- Equality before the law was established with a single system of local, provincial and national courts (although *volost* courts dealt with exclusively peasant cases). The accused was presumed innocent until proven guilty and could employ a lawyer to defend himself.
- Criminal cases were heard before barristers and a jury, selected from lists of property owners. Judges were appointed by the Tsar and given improved training and pay.
- Local Justices of the Peace were elected every three years by the *zemstva*, and were to be independent from political control.
- Courts were opened to the public and proceedings could be freely reported. National trials were recorded in a government newspaper, the *Russian Courier*.

While the new system was fairer and less corrupt, and the public flocked to the open courts, a new opportunity arose for the articulate lawyers of the intelligentsia to criticise the regime, becoming 'celebrities' in their own right. Furthermore, the new juries sometimes acquitted the guilty because they sympathised with their plight. To counter such behaviour, a new decree had to be issued to permit political crimes to be tried by special procedures.

There were other limitations too. Trial by jury was never established in Poland, the western provinces and the Caucasus, while **ecclesiastical and military courts** were excluded from the reforms, and the peasantry in the *volost* courts were still treated differently from those of higher status.

KEY TERM

Ecclesiastical and military courts: an ecclesiastical court was a Church court where punishments were in the hands of priests; in military courts, army officers awarded the sentences

Education reforms (1863–64)

Fig. 5 *St Petersburg University*

The abolition of serfdom increased the need for basic literacy and numeracy among peasants trying to run their private smallholdings, while the establishment of the *zemstva* provided an opportunity for a change in the control and funding of education.

Under Alexander Golovnin (Minister for Education 1862–67):

- universities were given the opportunity to govern themselves and appoint their own staff
- responsibility for schooling was transferred from the Russian Orthodox Church to the *zemstva*
- primary and secondary education was extended, with 'modern schools' established at secondary level for those who did not want the traditional classical education offered in a *gimnaziya* (plural: *gimnazii*). Students from both could progress to university.
- schools were declared 'open to all' regardless of class and sex (allowing women to attend secondary school for non-vocational education from 1870).

Educational provision grew markedly, but the new independence given to the universities had the effect of increasing the number of radical and militant thinkers. Indeed, the education reforms were so 'successful' that after 1866, it was deemed necessary to reassert government control.

A CLOSER LOOK

The number of primary schools rose from 8000 in 1856 to 23,000 in 1880, and the number of children in primary education from 400,000 to over a million. However, the primary curriculum, with the aim of 'strengthening religious and moral notions and spreading basic knowledge' was still restricted. At secondary level, students had a choice of study in classics or modern subjects, although these still largely remained the preserve of the professional and upper classes. The number of students in the universities grew from 3600 to 10,000 by the 1870s.

Censorship reform (1858–70)

In accordance with the greater 'liberalisation' of the new reign, there was an initial relaxation of press censorship, which under Nicholas I had extended to all books and newspapers. Restrictions on publishers were reduced, foreign publications were permitted with government approval, and the press was allowed to print editorials with comment on government policy.

This led to a short-lived growth in the numbers of books, journals and newspapers on sale in Russia. The numbers of books published grew from 1020 in 1855 to 1836 in 1864, and 10,691 by 1894. However, a growth in critical writing brought a re-tightening of government control in the 1870s.

Other reforms

There was a half-hearted attempt to eliminate corruption in the lower reaches of the Russian Orthodox Church and there was some reform of the condition of the Jews and ethnic minorities undertaken in the earlier years of Alexander's reign. At the Ministry of Finance, Mikhail Reutern also brought about some economic liberalisation. However, the period of reaction in the 1870s ended hopes of Church reform, while the 1863 Polish rebellion led to a reversal of the lenient treatment of both Poles and Jews. Only the financial liberalisation survived, and this was largely at the expense of the peasants.

CROSS-REFERENCE

The influence of the Church is discussed in Chapter 6.

Treatment of Jews and ethnic minorities under Alexander II is covered in Chapter 4.

ACTIVITY

Summary – evaluative thinking

While there were clearly limitations to Alexander's reforms, there was an extraordinary amount of positive change. Whether these changes were perceived as hugely beneficial or deeply unsettling depended on the perspective of those affected.

In this activity, weigh up these different perspectives, and then step outside modern perceptions of reform to look at the changes from, for example, the point of view of the contemporary peasants, landowners, priests, military commanders, radical university students, the Tsar and government officials. You will need to think carefully about how the reforms affected these people's lives: their concerns, their suspicions and their perspectives on new government initiatives.

1. Divide into pairs or groups. Each should consider the effects of Alexander II's reforms for one of the groups listed above, and complete the table below.
2. In a whole group session, discuss and justify your various suggestions.
3. Create a summary chart based on the material in this chapter, which considers the overall impact of the reforms, both positive and negative.

The impact of reforms on ... (indicate the group you will consider)		
	Positive	Negative
Military reform		
Local government reform		
Judicial reform		
Educational reform		
Economic reform		
Church reform		

Summary

In the 15 years that followed his accession, Alexander II had brought immense change to Russia. His reforms had altered the social, economic, political, and military structure of the Russian Empire.

There was some continuity with earlier years:

- Agriculture still retained its dominant place in the Russian economy and its problems (both geographical and technological) remained.
- The noble class retained much of its former dominance.
- Peasant society changed little as illiteracy, religious teachings and superstition, combined with heavy taxation and the control of the *mirs*, worked against progress.

However, Russia had changed:

- The Emancipation Edict marked a turning point in the government's willingness to take a direct interest in economic matters.
- It changed patterns of land ownership, produced a more mobile labour force, and permitted a substantial increase in grain exports in the second half of the nineteenth century, which helped to finance industrial development.
- Social change was perpetuated by the military, educational, and even local government and judiciary reforms, which empowered a growing group of professionals.

Although the tsarist government approached reform in a piecemeal fashion, it unwittingly created new social alignments, which had important repercussions for the future. Alexander II's reforms taught that change was possible. Expectations were raised, and when they were not fulfilled, the autocracy was in danger.

ACTIVITY

Evaluating historical extracts

Look back at Emmons' interpretation given at the beginning of this chapter, on page 11. In small groups, consider whether you find his interpretation convincing. You will need to find specific evidence to support or refute his views.

STUDY TIP

There are two parts to this quotation and you will need to consider them both when faced with this type of question. Were the concessions half-hearted? Were the protagonists of reform intent on preserving the old ways (and what do you understand by that)? In assessing whether they tried to maintain as much of the past as possible, you will need to look at the reforms individually, as well as the whole group.

 PRACTICE QUESTION

The reforms were 'half-hearted concessions from men intent on preserving the old ways as much as possible'.
Assess the validity of this view of Alexander II's reforms between 1855 and 1870.

The autocracy of Alexander II and Alexander III

Alexander II and reaction

In the later years of the nineteenth century, Russia's internal policies hovered uneasily between two incompatible systems. Alexander II's reforms had severely shaken the traditional personalised power structure but had not managed consistently to replace it with institutions of **civil society** or **rule of law**. To plug the resulting authority gap, the regime had nothing else at hand but the police, backed up by emergency powers. Having set out to demolish an old building and erect a new one, the regime then changed its mind and started repairing the ruins; the resultant hybrid architecture threatened the balance of the entire construction. The regime was in an insoluble dilemma, caught between perception of the need for civic institutions and inability to introduce them without undermining its own stability.

Adapted from Geoffrey Hosking, *Russia and the Russians,* 2001

For a decade after Alexander II's accession, the more enlightened members of Russian society must have felt a certain optimism, as various reforms were begun which promised to transform the Russian State. However, that optimism was not to last. In 1866, an **attempted assassination** attempt shook the Emperor's confidence. After this, a more repressive policy was adopted, interrupted only by a brief flirtation with further constitutional reform in Alexander II's final years. From 1881, the reign of Alexander II's son, Alexander III, was similarly characterised by **reaction**, as made clear in his address to the nation:

'The voice of God orders us to take up the task of ruling, with total faith in the strength and righteousness of our autocratic power. We are summoned to reaffirm that power and to preserve it for the benefit of the people from any encroachment upon it.'

The modern historian Hosking alleges that the problems of the later years of the nineteenth century were primarily the result of Alexander II's failure to set up '**institutions of civil society**' or '**rule of law**', which left the tsarist regime with nothing to fall back on except repression. He accuses the Tsar of a 'change of mind' and suggests that the attempt to 'repair' the tsarist autocracy was a threat to the whole system, producing an 'insoluble dilemma'. To have introduced 'civic institutions', Hosking believes, would have undermined stability.

ACTIVITY

As you study this chapter, not only look for evidence to support Hosking's interpretation of the autocracy of Alexander II and Alexander III, but also try to find evidence that challenges it. Is it appropriate, for example, to speak of a 'change of mind' and was there really an 'insoluble' dilemma? Is Hosking correct in assuming the introduction of civic institutions would bring instability? You might like to reflect on whether statements like this are the result of 'reading history backwards'. This means being aware of later events and mistakenly assuming that everything beforehand automatically led to this outcome.

LEARNING OBJECTIVES

In this chapter you will learn about:

- the reasons why Alexander II's reign became more reactionary after 1866

- the extent of tsarist reaction before 1881

- the personality and influence of Alexander III

- the tsarist autocracy under Alexander III.

KEY CHRONOLOGY

1865	Death of Alexander II's son and heir
1866	Attempted assassination of Alexander II
1871	Educational reaction
1877–78	War with Turkey
1877	Trial of the 50
1878	Vera Zasulich shoots military governor of St Petersburg but is not convicted; political crimes transferred to special courts
1879	New governor-generals established
1879–80	Famine and industrial recession
1880	Loris-Melikov proposals
1881	Assassination of Alexander II

KEY TERM

Civil society and **rule of law:** key concepts of a democratic society; all members of society enjoy the protection of laws, which are applied equally and fairly, while organisations exist in which the people of the country can express their views and influence decisions

Reaction: implies actions and policies that are backward looking in an attempt to restore the past; those who support reaction are known as reactionaries

Attempted assassinations of Alexander II

In April 1866, a former student of noble status, Dmitry Karakozov, shot at Alexander, but missed. The following year, a Polish immigrant Antoni Berezowski fired on a carriage carrying Alexander and his two sons, but hit a horse and a cavalryman instead. In April 1879, Aleksandr Soloviev, another former student, fired at Alexander five times, without success, and in December 1879, the bomb intended to blow up the Tsar on a railway journey was planted under the wrong train. In February 1880, a mine positioned below the dining room in the Winter Palace, by a revolutionary posing as a carpenter, came nearer to success. It killed 12 people and wounded a further 50, but the Tsar was late in getting to dinner that evening and survived.

KEY QUESTION

How was Russia governed and how did political authority change and develop?

Alexander II's later years

Fig. 1 *Mounted Secret Police in St Petersburg waving down a horse*

KEY PROFILE

Yekaterina (Catherine) Mikhailovna Dolgorukova (1847–1922) had been sent to the Smolny Institute for Noble Maidens in St Petersburg, following the death of her father and, at 16, was spotted by Alexander on an official visit in 1864. He found her a position as lady-in-waiting to his ill wife and by 1866 they were writing to each other at least once a day, despite court disapproval. She bore him four children and he eventually married her 40 days after the death of his first wife. However, their children were debarred from the succession.

In 1865, Alexander II's eldest son and heir had died and his wife, suffering from tuberculosis, had withdrawn from public appearances. The Tsar had sought consolation at the hands of his mistress, **Yekaterina (Catherine) Mikhailovna Dolgorukova**. This distanced him from the reforming elements within his own family: his brother the Grand Duke Konstantin, and the Grand Duchess Elena. These developments, along with the many assassination attempts, all helped to make him more aloof. He became less inclined to resist the reactionary conservatives who believed the Tsar's reforming instincts had gone too far, weakening the props on which the Imperial monarchy relied, the Church and the nobility.

EXTRACT 2

The Emperor faced the solid opposition of the rank and file of the bureaucracy as well as that of his son and heir-apparent, the future Alexander III. The radicals unwittingly assisted this conservative party. Every time they made an attempt on the life of the Tsar or assassinated some high official, opponents of political reform could press for more stringent police measures and further postponement of basic reforms. The terrorists could not have been more effective in scuttling political reform had they been on the police payroll.

Adapted from Richard Pipes, *Russia under the Old Regime*, 1974

The reactionaries feared the spread of 'Western' ideas through the liberal universities and freer press, and argued that the ethnic minorities with their different religions were diluting Russian strength.

Alexander was therefore persuaded to make a series of new appointments in 1866, replacing more liberal ministers with conservatives. These included:

- **Dmitry Tolstoy** as Minister for Education, replacing the liberal Golovnin
- Aleksandr Timashev as Minister of Internal Affairs, to replace Pyotr Valuev
- Pyotr Shuvalov as head of the Third Section (the Secret Police)
- Konstantin Pahlen as Minister of Justice.

Education

KEY QUESTION

- How was Russia governed?
- How effective was opposition?
- How important was the role of individuals and groups?

Dmitry Tolstoy was a staunch Orthodox believer and felt a tight control over education was essential to eradicate Western liberal ideas and growing criticism of the autocracy. As a result, the *zemstva's* powers over education were reduced, the Church regained its authority over rural schools and the higher *gimnazii* schools were ordered to follow a traditional classical curriculum and abandon teaching natural sciences. From 1871, only students from a *gimnaziya* could progress to universities. Students at the modern technical schools were limited to higher technical institutions.

In the universities, more liberal courses were replaced by a traditional curriculum. Subjects that encouraged critical thought such as Literature, Science, Modern Languages and History were forced out, while Maths, Latin, Greek and Divinity were encouraged. Censorship was tightened and there was strict control over student activities and organisations.

More state teacher-training colleges were set up, but this was to increase tsarist control, rather than to improve education. Tolstoy reluctantly accepted Moscow University's decision to organise lectures for women, but he used the government's right to veto university appointments wherever he felt it necessary and many students chose to attend universities abroad rather than in the stifling atmosphere at home.

Police, law and control

Pyotr Shuvalov strengthened the police, encouraged the Third Section, and stepped up the persecution of other ethnic and religious minorities, while Konstantin Pahlen ensured that the judicial system made an example of those accused of political agitation. Searches and arrests increased and new governor-generals were established in 1879 with emergency powers to prosecute in military courts and exile political offenders. Even radicals who fled the country and settled in Switzerland or Germany were liable to be tracked down and recalled to face justice.

Pahlen held open '**show' trials**, with the intention of deterring others from revolutionary activity, but the whole experiment backfired and in 1878, political crimes were transferred from the civil courts to special secret courts.

KEY PROFILE

Count Dmitry Andreyevich Tolstoy (1823–89) was a noble who became Over-Procurator of the Holy Synod in 1865, until 1880. In 1866, he joined the State Council where he was Minister of Education from 1866 to 1880. From 1882 to 1889, Tolstoy was Minister of Internal Affairs and Chief of the Gendarmerie. He was elected President of the St Petersburg Academy of Sciences in 1882 and wrote a number of books on Russian history.

CROSS-REFERENCE

The spread of Western liberal ideas is discussed in Chapter 5.

KEY TERM

Show trial: a trial that took place in front of the general public, usually for 'propaganda' purposes

Fig. 2 *Prisoners on the road to exile in Siberia*

CROSS-REFERENCE

For more on the revolutionary activity and opposition in general, look ahead to Chapter 5.

A CLOSER LOOK

Show trials: the 'Trial of 50' (1877), the 'Trial of 193' (1877–78) and the case of Vera Zasulich, 1878

These were show trials of people accused of revolutionary activities. At the 'Trial of 193', a sympathetic jury acquitted 153 of the 193 defendants and gave only light sentences to the rest, while the defence lawyers' passionate speeches were reported in the press, giving publicity to the revolutionaries' ideas. Vera Zasulich, who sympathised with some of the accused, then shot and seriously wounded the governor of St Petersburg, Dmitri Trepov. She too was found 'not guilty' at her trial in 1878.

CROSS-REFERENCE

The war against Turkey is outlined in Chapter 2, page 16.

The 1880 attempt on the Tsar's life is described on page 22.

The Okhrana is discussed in more detail later in the chapter, on page 28.

The Loris-Melikov Constitution

The late 1870s were a time of political crisis in Russia. The Russian army was bogged down in the Russo-Turkish War (1877–78), famine swept the countryside in 1879–80, and an industrial recession began. However the further attempts on the Tsar's life in 1879 and 1880 led Alexander to accept, at least implicitly, that the violence and unrest might be better curbed by widening democratic consultation.

Count Mikhail Loris-Melikov was appointed Minister for Internal Affairs. He released political prisoners, relaxed censorship, removed the salt-tax, and lifted restrictions on the activities of the *zemstva*. The Third Section was abolished and its powers transferred to the regular police, although a special section which became known as the Okhrana was created, and soon became just as oppressive.

ACTIVITY

Research

Find out as much information as you can about the work of the security services in Russia at this time. You should focus on the Third Section, the methods they used, the trials and detention of suspects, and their treatment in the Tsar's prisons. Compare this to the treatment of political prisoners in other societies either in the past or the present day. How effective are such methods of control? Are such methods justifiable in any circumstances?

In 1880, Loris-Melikov produced a report, in response to *zemstva* demands. It recommended the inclusion of elected representatives of the nobility, of the *zemstva*, and of the town governments in debating the drafts of some state decrees. These proposals became known as 'Loris-Melikov's Constitution', although they did not really create a **constitution** at all.

Alexander II accepted and signed the report on the morning of 13 March 1881, calling for a meeting of the Council of Ministers to discuss the document. The same day, the Tsar was killed by a bomb.

A CLOSER LOOK

The assassination of Tsar Alexander II

On 13 March 1881, Alexander II was travelling to the Winter Palace in St Petersburg in a closed carriage. Members of the revolutionary group, The People's Will, had positioned themselves along the route with concealed bombs. Although the first two bombs thrown missed and landed among the accompanying Cossacks, when the Tsar got out of his carriage to check on the injured men, another terrorist threw a bomb which killed him instantly.

Fig. 3 *Alexander II's assassination, 1881*

Alexander III as Tsar

A change of direction

Tutored by **Konstantin Pobedonostsev**, **Alexander III** had been brought up with a very strong sense of commitment and sincerely believed that, with God's direction, he alone could decide what was right for his country; the duty of his subjects was not to question, but to love and obey.

His reign began with the public hanging of the conspirators involved in his father's assassination and the 1881 'Manifesto of Unshakable Autocracy'. He also issued a Law on Exceptional Measures, which declared that, if necessary, a Commander-in-Chief could be appointed to take control of a locality, using military police courts and arbitrary powers of imprisonment.

KEY TERM

Constitution: set of rules by which a country is governed, for example regarding where power lies and which bodies should make laws and how

CROSS-REFERENCE

For more on opposition to the tsarist regime, look ahead to Chapter 5.

ACTIVITY

Here are three assessments of the reforming activity of Alexander II's reign:
- bold and adventurous
- half-hearted and over-cautious
- inadequate and misdirected.

Choose one of these as your theme and write an obituary for Alexander II in which you assess the reforms of his reign.

Konstantin Pobedonostsev (1827–1907) was chosen as tutor to Alexander from 1865. He became very close to him and earned the nickname 'the Black Tsar'. He probably wrote Alexander's accession manifesto 'on unshakable autocracy'. As Over-Procurator of the Holy Synod from 1880, he spoke out for absolutism, nationalism and anti-Semitism. He also tutored Nicholas II.

Alexander III (1845–1894) had watched his father die and was so fearful of revolutionary activity that he refused to live in the Winter Palace in St Petersburg and moved to a fortified fortress in Gatchina instead. He was a large but ungainly man, 1.9 metres (six feet and four inches) tall and immensely strong. He could tear a pack of cards in half, bend an iron pole over his knees, and crush a silver rouble with his bare hands. He married a Danish princess, Dagmar (Maria Feodorovna), and had six children. He died of a kidney ailment, possibly brought on by heavy drinking, in 1894.

The Empress Maria Feodorovna (1847–1928) was born Princess Dagmar of Denmark, but she adopted the Orthodox religion and a new name in 1865 when she married the future Alexander III. She became an imposing and elegant empress, and a domineering mother. She tried to oppose her eldest son Nicholas' marriage to Alix (Alexandra), a minor German princess, for fear this would diminish her own influence over him.

CROSS-REFERENCE

You will find information about the role of the Over-Procurator of the Holy Synod in Chapter 1, page 5.

KEY QUESTION

- How important was the role of individuals?
- How was Russia governed and how did political authority change and develop?

KEY CHRONOLOGY

1881	Accession of Alexander III; Alexander III's Manifesto of Unshakable Autocracy; beginning of Law on Exceptional Measures; Russification programme
1882	Statute on police surveillance; new regulations of the press
1884	New university charter
1889	Land captains introduced
1890	Change in election arrangements for *zemstva*
1891–92	Great Famine
1894	Death of Alexander III

Fig. 4 *Revolutionaries were hanged*

The Loris-Melikov proposals were abandoned and reforming ministers, including Dmitry Milyutin, resigned. Alexander III relied heavily on conservatives, such as the nationalist Nikolai Ignatiev, his first Internal Minister, who was replaced by Dmitry Tolstoy in 1882; Ivan Delyanov, who became Minister for Education; Konstantin Pobedonostsev, the Over-Procurator of the Holy Synod; and **Mikhail Katkov**, a journalist who helped justify Alexander's conservative views to the literate public.

KEY QUESTION

How important was the role of individuals and groups?

Changes in local government

A new state-appointed office of 'Land Captain' was created in July 1889, with power to override elections to the *zemstvo* and village assemblies and to disregard *zemstvo* decisions. Land Captains were made responsible for law enforcement and government in the countryside and could ignore the normal judicial process, overturning court judgements.

A further act in 1890 changed election arrangements for the *zemstva*, so as to reduce the peasants' vote, and placed the *zemstva* under central government control. This had the effect of channelling their efforts away from political discussion towards the social services, including education, health, local transport and engineering projects.

In June 1892 a similar arrangement was made for the towns. The electorate was reduced to the owners of property above a certain value, and the mayor and members of the town councils became state employees, subject to central government direction.

While it could be argued that these changes helped to ensure a more efficient collection of taxes, the modern historian Alan Wood writes:

EXTRACT 3

Attempts were made to re-impose the leaden hand of central government in all those areas of the Empire's affairs where a degree of local or institutional **particularism** had been allowed to creep in. Of course, the re-enserfment of the peasantry was virtually inconceivable, but in the governance of rural areas, the power of the local nobility, never entirely lost, was reasserted through a number of measures which adjusted their regulations concerning membership and organisation of the *zemstva*. At the same time, the central administration increased its control over the provincial nobility itself, most notably by the creation of a new category of official, the Land Captains. It would be wrong to say that the power of local authorities had been taken away, as they did not have much of that in the first place, but by these counter-reforms the government had re-established the class principle in the countryside.

Adapted from Alan Wood, *The Romanov Empire*, 2007

KEY PROFILE

Mikhail Katkov (1818–87) was an influential right-wing journalist who edited the *Moscow News* from 1863 until his death in 1887. This gave him considerable power over the literate public and he was much favoured by Alexander III for his conservative political views, support of Russian interests and opposition to Polish nationalism.

KEY TERM

Particularism: concern for the immediate locality and an area of personal interest

The well-known historian Orlando Figes has also commented on Alexander's local government changes:

EXTRACT 4

Alexander III greatly increased the government's powers over the *zemstva* and municipal bodies. Alexander saw this as a way of moving closer to the fantasy of ruling Russia directly from the throne. But the result was confusion in the provincial administration: the governors, the agencies of the central ministries and the elected local bodies were all set against each other. The power of the Imperial government effectively stopped at the 89 provincial capitals where the governors had their offices. Below that there was no real state administration to speak of. There was only a series of magistrates who would appear from time to time on some specific mission, usually to collect taxes or sort out a local conflict, and then disappear again. The affairs of peasant Russia where 85 per cent of the population lived were entirely unknown to the city bureaucrats.

Adapted from Orlando Figes, *A People's Tragedy*, 1996

AS LEVEL PRACTICE QUESTION

Evaluating historical extracts

With reference to Extracts 3 and 4, and your understanding of the historical context, which of the extracts provides the more convincing interpretation of Alexander III's local government changes?

Changes in policing

The Department of Police (including the **Okhrana**), was ably led by **Vyacheslav von Plehve** between 1881 and 1884, and from 1884 by Pyotr Durnovo. The number of police was increased and new branches of the criminal investigation department were set up. There was also a drive to recruit spies, counter-spies (to spy on the spies) and 'agents provocateurs', who would pose as revolutionaries in order to incriminate others.

A CLOSER LOOK

The Okhrana

The Okhrana had offices in St Petersburg, Moscow and Warsaw, where they took responsibility for 'security and investigation'. They intercepted and read mail, and checked up on activities in the factories, universities, the army and the State, detaining suspects and resorting to torture and summary executions. Communists, socialists and trade unionists were particular subjects of their investigations but they also watched members of the civil service and government.

By the 1882 Statute on Police Surveillance, any area of the Empire could be deemed an 'area of subversion' and police agents could search, arrest, detain, question, imprison or exile not only those who had committed a crime, but any who were thought likely to commit crimes or knew, or were related to, people who had committed crimes. This gave them tremendous power over people's lives, particularly since any such arrested person had no right to legal representation.

KEY QUESTION

How was Russia governed and how did political authority change and develop?

STUDY TIP

With this type of question, you will need to identify what Wood's interpretation of the local government changes is, by reading the extract carefully. You could say how convincing the arguments that are put forward are. When you have done the same with Figes' interpretation you should give an overall conclusion as to which provides the more convincing picture and why.

KEY PROFILE

Vyacheslav Konstantinovich von Plehve (1846–1904) was made director of the Secret Police in the Ministry of Internal Affairs in 1881–84. He was vice-Minister for Internal Affairs in 1884–99, State Secretary for Finland in 1899–1902, and Minister for Internal Affairs in 1902–04. He was committed to upholding autocratic principles; he suppressed revolutionary and liberal movements; he subjected minorities to forced Russification; he secretly organised Jewish pogroms; and is said to have encouraged war against Japan in 1904 to forestall revolution at home. He backed police-controlled labour unions and was assassinated by a member of the Social Revolutionary Party in 1904.

CROSS-REFERENCE

For more on the pogroms, look ahead to Chapter 4.

Changes in the judicial system

The judicial reforms of Alexander II were partially reversed. In 1885, a decree provided for the Minister of Justice to exercise greater control, for example in the dismissal of judges. In 1887 the Ministry was granted powers to hold **closed court sessions** and in 1889 it became responsible for the appointment of town judges. In 1887, the property and educational qualifications needed by jurors were raised, while in 1889 the *volost* courts were put under the direct jurisdiction of the Land Captains in the countryside and judges in the towns.

KEY TERM

Closed court session: a trial held in secret to which no observers were permitted and where no reporting was allowed

Fig. 5 *A volost court*

Changes in education

Educational developments were overseen by Delyanov, whose new university charter in 1884 made appointments of chancellors, deans and professors subject to the approval of the Education Ministry based on 'religious, moral and patriotic orientation', rather than academic grounds. Delyanov also closed universities for women and abolished separate university courts. All university life was closely supervised, with students forbidden from gathering in groups of more than five.

Children from the lowest classes were to be restricted to primary education, lest they 'be taken out of the social environment to which they belong', and primary education was placed firmly in the hands of the Orthodox Church. Although the overall number of schools and the numbers of those receiving some education increased, nevertheless, only 21 per cent of the population were literate by the time of the first census in 1897.

These education policies were of dubious value, since they both ran counter to the government's attempts to promote economic modernisation and failed to prevent student involvement in illegal political movements, particularly in the 1890s.

Changes in censorship

Tolstoy established a government committee in 1882, which issued the so-called 'temporary regulations'. These allowed newspapers to be closed down and a life ban placed on editors and publishers. Censors became more active; all literary publications had to be officially approved and libraries and reading rooms were restricted in the books they were allowed to stock. Censorship also extended to theatre, art and culture where 'Russification' was enforced.

CROSS-REFERENCE

Alexander III's policies of Russification (the enforcement of Russian language and culture) are discussed in Chapter 4.

CROSS-REFERENCE

To recap on the emancipation of the serfs in 1861, revisit Chapter 2.

Reformist factory legislation is discussed in Chapter 6.

ACTIVITY

Class debate

Divide into two groups. One group should consider the ways in which the actions of Alexander III's government increased the likelihood of opposition to the tsarist autocracy, while the other should consider the ways in which they strengthened the tsardom. Each group should present its views to the rest of the class and you should then try to decide which is the more convincing view.

STUDY TIP

This question invites you to think about the conventional ideas of Alexander II as a 'great reformer' and Alexander III as a 'great reactionary'. Rather than writing chronologically, one approach would be to consider the ways in which the two Tsars lived up to these titles, balanced against the ways in which the titles are false or poor descriptions of them.

Extent and impact of counter-reform

Although Alexander III's policies helped to reverse the trends set in motion by his father, not all of Alexander II's reforms disappeared and there was some positive change. In May 1881, a law reduced the redemption fees payable and cancelled the arrears of ex-serfs in the 37 central provinces of the Empire. In May 1885, the poll tax was abolished and the introduction of inheritance tax helped to shift the burden of taxation a little, away from the lowest classes. Other reforms included the introduction of the right of appeal to higher courts (after trial before the Land Captain), the establishment of the Peasants' Land Bank in 1883 and some reformist factory legislation. These may merely have been introduced in an effort to forestall rebellion, but the same accusation could be levied against Alexander II's reforms.

ACTIVITY

Summary

Make a chart with three columns. Look back at Chapter 2, and in the first column list the reforms introduced by Alexander II. In the second column, note whether this reform continued, was changed or abandoned under Alexander III. In the third column, give brief details.

 PRACTICE QUESTION

'While Alexander II was the "great reformer", Alexander III was the "great reactionary"'.
Assess the validity of this view.

4 Political authority in action

Russification

LEARNING OBJECTIVES

In this chapter you will learn about:

- the reasons why the tsarist regime pursued a policy of **Russification** in the later nineteenth century

- the effects of Russification for the tsarist autocracy and the people of Russia

- the reasons why **anti-Semitic** policies were enforced in Russia

- the impact of anti-Semitism in Russia.

EXTRACT 1

From the time of Alexander III, it was decided that political loyalty would be best preserved by engaging in a policy of Russification, based on making the Russian language and religion the dominant focus of the cultural life of the whole patchwork Empire. This official **chauvinism** brought protests from nationalities as far apart as Latvians and Georgians and gave a great boost to local nationalist and separatist movements. What compensatory benefit Russification brought to the government is unclear. It also entangled the Church in politics, associating it closely with the regime as its spiritual policeman. The situation was made worse by a drift into semi-official anti-Semitism. In the aftermath of the assassination crisis in 1881, when the autocracy was suffering from irrational paranoid fears of insecurity, **pogroms** were encouraged to divert opposition away from the real source of the trouble. Although these never became official government policy, the fateful example was followed with increasing frequency in moments of local and national crisis.

Adapted from Christopher Read, *From Tsar to Soviets,* 1996

ACTIVITY

Evaluating historical extracts

1. a. What is Read's view in Extract 1 of the policy of Russification?
   b. What does he believe to have been the consequences of this policy?
2. As you study this chapter, try to find examples to support Read's analysis.

KEY QUESTION

As you read through this chapter, consider the following Key Question:
How important were ideas and ideology?

The problem posed by ethnic minorities

Tsarist Russia was a multi-national Empire inhabited by over 100 different ethnic groups. Although the Slavs in Russia, Ukraine and Belorussia comprised two thirds of the population, the remaining peoples were a mixture of many different nationalities, languages, religions and cultural traditions.

A CLOSER LOOK

In addition to a host of smaller national groups, Finns, Estonians, Latvians and Lithuanians lived in the north of European Russia, with distinctive national cultures. However, much of the land in the Baltic area was owned by Lutheran Germans, and this added an ethnic twist to the peasant/landowner divide. To the west was the home of the Catholic Poles and many of the Empire's Jews, while to the south and south-west were the Ukrainians, who considered themselves a distinctive nation, as did a million Romanians living in Bessarabia, and Georgians and Azerbaijanis in the Caucasus. Added to this, continual Imperial expansion in Asia in the second half of the nineteenth century helped increase the Muslim population to ten million by 1900.

KEY TERM

Russification: forcing everyone within the Russian Empire to think of themselves as 'Russian', by enforcing the Russian language and culture

Anti-Semitic: being prejudiced against and persecuting Jews, who were known as 'Semitic' as they descended from people who spoke the 'Semitic' language

Chauvinism: exaggerated belief in national superiority and glory

Pogrom: an old Russian word which means 'round up' or lynching; it originally denoted an assault by one ethnic group on another but after 1881 it gained the special connotation of an attack on Jews

CROSS-REFERENCE

The ethnic distribution of Russia in 1897 is described in Chapter 1, page 7.

ACTIVITY

Research

Extract 1 in Chapter 1 says, 'National consciousness was not a dominant sentiment.' Undertake some personal research into the various peoples and religions that made up the Russian Empire in the nineteenth century.

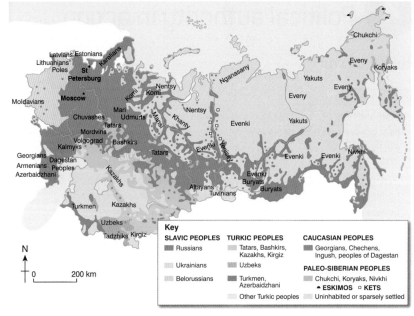

Fig. 1 *Ethnic groups in Russia in 1800s*

This diverse Empire posed a continual challenge for the tsarist autocracy, particularly as the development of **national ideology** in the nineteenth century provoked ethnic groups (including the Russian Slavs) to assert their distinctive identities.

Polish nationalism had surfaced and brought rebellion in 1830. In the 1840s, a Finnish language pressure group was set up and local language newspapers were founded in the Baltic regions. In the Ukraine, the secret 'Brotherhood of Saints Cyril and Methodius' provoked a national consciousness that sought to separate Ukrainian Slavs from their Russian counterparts. Such aspirations were met by a Russian determination to assert their national superiority.

KEY TERM

National ideology: a belief in the strength of one's own country, language and traditions; this became a powerful force in Europe after the defeat of Napoleon (1815) who had tried to extend French influence across the continent

SOURCE 1

The Russian journalist Mikhail Katkov wrote in 1865:

We do not want coercion or persecution or constraints against ethnic peculiarities, dialects and languages, or still less against the religious conscience of non-Russians; but we do indeed propose that the Russian government should be solely Russian, throughout the whole expanse of the possessions of the Russian power, which have been gained by Russian blood.

Alexander II and the ethnic minorities

Alexander II, like his predecessors, was more concerned with control than with matters of racial superiority. He reacted swiftly and strongly when a further Polish rebellion broke out in 1863, sending his own brother, Viceroy Duke Konstantin Nikolaevich, to deal with the rebels. More than 200,000 Poles had joined in creating an underground National Government for Poland, and they waged a form of **guerrilla warfare** against their Imperial masters, although they were soundly crushed after fierce fighting in 1864.

Nevertheless, Alexander II did not engage in systematic persecution of racial minorities and he also used **concessions** as a means of keeping control. For example, through decrees in 1864 and 1875 the Latvians and Estonians were allowed to revert to **Lutheranism**, where previously Orthodoxy had been demanded. Furthermore, he allowed the Finns to have their own *diet* [parliament] and tried to maintain good relations with the Finnish people.

KEY TERM

Guerrilla warfare: a form of fighting conducted by groups of soldiers and armed civilians using methods such as ambushes, sabotage and raids rather than fighting conventionally

Concession: granting a request in response to demand

Lutheranism: a form of Christianity based on the teachings of the sixteenth-century German, Martin Luther

Fig. 2 *Poland rose against Russia and fought the Cossacks in 1863*

However, the period of increased reaction towards the end of his reign saw growing intolerance of national differences on the part of the Tsar's ministers and administrators, who were keen to reinforce the tsarist regime. This led, for example, to a prohibition on the use of the Ukrainian language in publications or performances in 1876. This more hostile attitude was to turn into a far more aggressive campaign in the reign of Alexander's son.

Russification under Alexander III

KEY QUESTION

- How did political authority change and develop?
- How important was the role of individuals and groups?

Alexander III and his ministers, particularly Pobedonostsev, engaged in a policy of 'cultural Russification'. This sought to merge all the Tsar's subjects into a single nation with a feeling of shared identity.

EXTRACT 2

The official creed of Pobedonostsev, 'Autocracy, Orthodoxy, Nationality', became a theory of Russia's apartness from the rest of the world. Everything was done in this period to enforce official Orthodoxy and this unifying policy weighed heavily on nationality.

Adapted from Bernard Pares, *A History of Russia,* 1926

CROSS-REFERENCE

The Church and Orthodoxy were introduced in Chapter 1, and will be covered in more detail at the end of Chapter 6.

ACTIVITY

In groups, taking the role of government ministers, debate the advantages and disadvantages of enforcing nationalism and Orthodoxy on the minority races within the Empire. Make a case to present to the Tsar.

The destruction of non-Russian national cultures was particularly marked in Poland and Finland. In Finland, the *diet* [parliament] was reorganised in 1892 in order to weaken its political influence, the use of the Russian language was increasingly demanded, the independent postal service was abolished, and Russian coinage replaced the local currency. In Poland, the Polish National Bank was closed in 1885, and in schools and universities the teaching of all subjects except the Polish language and religion had to be in Russian. Even Polish literature had to be studied in a Russian translation. The administration of Poland was also changed to curb any independence.

The loyal Baltic Germans, who had enjoyed the special protection of Alexander III's predecessors, also found themselves the subjects of particularly aggressive Russification. Between 1885 and 1889, measures were introduced to enforce the use of Russian in all state offices, elementary and secondary schools, the police force, and judicial system. Even the German University of Dorpar was 'Russified' and became Iurev University (1889–93).

Russification was extended to other provinces, such as Belorussia, Georgia and the Ukraine. In the Ukraine, further laws limited the use of the Ukrainian language in 1883, and in 1884 all the theatres in the five Ukrainian provinces were closed. Military service arrangements were extended into areas previously exempt, and conscripts from national areas were dispersed to prevent national groupings developing in the army, where business was entirely conducted in Russian.

Even the peoples of Siberia and further east were subject to attempts at Russification. Uprisings of ethnic peoples were mercilessly supressed in Guriya in Georgia in 1892, at Bashkira in 1884, in the Uzbek district of Fergana (in modern-day Uzbekistan) and Armenia in 1886, and at Tashkent (also now part of Uzbekistan) in 1892.

Fig. 3 *The Church was an important instrument of government*

Adherence to the Orthdox Church was encouraged everywhere, with laws benefiting those of Orthodox faith. In the Baltic region, 37,000 Lutherans converted to Orthodoxy in order to take advantage of the special measures of support. In Poland, Catholic monasteries were closed down, the influence of Catholic priests was curbed, and incentives were provided for non-Catholics to settle in this area. In Asia, the All-Russian Orthodox Missionary society worked to convert '**heathens** and Muslims' and this included forced mass baptisms. From 1883, members of non-Orthodox Churches were not allowed to build new places of worship, wear religious dress except within their meeting place, or spread any religious propaganda. Any attempt to convert a member of the Orthodox Church to another faith was made punishable by exile to Siberia.

Results of Russification

KEY QUESTION

- What was the extent of social and cultural change?
- How effective was opposition?

ACTIVITY

Write a newspaper article for a local ethnic newspaper of the 1890s, describing some of the developments in your area and giving your views on the Tsar, his ministers and his policies.

The process of Russification was not accepted without resistance. In June 1888, the Department of Police estimated 332 cases of mass disturbance in 61 of Russia's 92 provinces and districts. This included 43 disturbances in 9 of the 12 central provinces. Nevertheless, troubles were swiftly curbed. In 51 of these cases, the military was employed.

As well as popular disturbances, Russification caused particular resentment among the more educated and wealthy Finns, Poles and Baltic Germans in the west of the Empire. Here, national groups constantly petitioned the Tsars for more liberties, and the secret publication of local language books continued. Some ethnic schools also survived (particularly in Poland) and fanned the flames of resentment against the tsarist impositions.

Supporters of Russification genuinely believed they were acting for the greater good of Russia. They believed it was necessary to 'unite' the country in order to improve its administration, to allow for modernisation, and to reassert Russian strength. Moreover, this was a time of strong nationalistic feeling throughout Europe. The historian Walter Moss has provided an explanation for Russification in Extract 3.

EXTRACT 3

Although in retrospect Russification may seem foolish and counterproductive, there were many factors nudging the government in the direction it took, primarily the desire to maintain a stong unified Russia. Among the foreign powers, Germany's growing strength after 1870 most impressed its neighbours. In minority areas, such as its Polish lands, it imposed Germanisation by such measures as demanding the use of German in administration and schools. Austria-Hungary was weaker than Germany, and some Russian nationalists believed this was partly due to the Dual Monarchy's inability to impose a unifying nationality policy on its peoples. Besides the German example, there was a growing fear of Germany, especially by the 1890s, and Russification measures were especially prevalent in border areas that could be threatened by Germany. Other causes also stimulated Russification. Economic modernisation sped up centralising tendencies that were often accompanied by Russifying measures. Russification was part of the counter-reform mentality, a reaction to the growing forces threatening autocracy and the Empire's political stability.

Adapted from Walter Moss, *A History of Russia since 1855,* 2003

However, it is more generally believed that Russification was a misguided policy that had the opposite effect from that intended. The historian Peter Waldron writes that Russification 'failed to achieve its ends' and 'intensified national feeling among the non-Russians of the Empire'. Furthermore, it drove some of the wealthier citizens to emigrate and persuaded others, who might otherwise have proved loyal, to join political opposition groups.

STUDY TIP

This type of question requires an examination of policy, for example from the time of the Polish rebellion to the end of Alexander III's reign. You could make it clear that policy changed during this period and you may wish to distinguish between the results of policies pre- and post-1881 in responding to the question.

AS LEVEL PRACTICE QUESTION

'Tsarist policy towards the national minority groups in the years 1863 to 1894 weakened the tsarist regime.'
Explain why you agree or disagree with this view.

Anti-Semitism

Fig. 4 *Bodies of Jews killed in a pogrom*

ACTIVITY

What impression is conveyed by this picture in Fig. 4? When you have read the section on anti-Semitism, judge for yourself whether this image is fair or exaggerated.

The racial group that suffered the most from this intense nationalism was the Jews. This group possessed both a distinctive ethnic background and religion. There were around five million Jews within the Russian Empire, and since 1736 most had been confined to an area of western Russia known as the **Pale of Settlement.**

A CLOSER LOOK

Pale of Settlement

This refers to a region in the south and west part of European Russia, created in 1791, which included much of present-day Lithuania, Belarus, Poland, Ukraine, Moldova and parts of western Russia. It comprised around 20 per cent of European Russia. A number of cities within the Pale were excluded, however, while a limited number of categories of Jews were allowed to live outside the Pale.

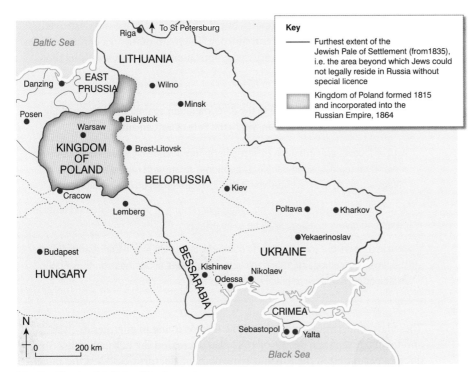

Fig. 5 *The Jewish Pale of Settlement*

During Alexander II's reign, anti-Semitism had existed among the poorer elements in society, who not only hated Jews because of the teachings of the Orthodox Church, but also resented their money-lending and personal riches. Nevertheless, Alexander II had allowed the wealthier Jews to settle elsewhere until the Polish revolt frightened him into withdrawing his concessions and reducing participation of Jews in town government. This action encouraged the growth of anti-Semitism. It was further encouraged in the reign of Alexander III by ministers such as Pobedonostsev, who used inflammatory slogans such as, 'Beat the Yids – Save Russia' and suggested that 'one third should emigrate, one third die, and one third assimilate [i.e. be converted]'.

Alexander III was himself anti-Semitic, largely on religious grounds. He wrote in the margin of a document urging him to reduce Jewish persecution, 'but we must never forget that the Jews have crucified our Master and have shed his precious blood'. However, he also had political concerns. The right-wing Russian press had helped encourage the belief that Jews had orchestrated Alexander II's assassination, and there was a real fear of Jewish involvement in the growing opposition movements.

CROSS-REFERENCE

Opposition movements will be discussed in Chapter 5.

The Jewish pogroms of 1881–84

The Jewish concentration in the areas of the Pale made them ready targets for the anti-Jewish pogroms that broke out in April 1881, in Yelizavetgrad in the Ukraine. The immediate cause of these pogroms is unknown. They may have started because of some business competition, involving Jews, for lucrative railway contracts, but it is regarded as highly probable that they were encouraged by the Okhrana using the link to Tsar Alexander II's assassination as an excuse to stir up trouble. The governing authorities certainly did little to curb the violence. They were slow to act and the 'Holy League' organisation, which was supported by Pobedonostsev, helped to coordinate the early attacks, although this was banned in 1882.

From Yelizavetgrad, the riots spread to other Ukrainian towns such as Kiev and Odessa, and beyond to Warsaw and Nizhny Novgorod, causing many Jews to flee across the border into western Europe. Around 16 major cities

CROSS-REFERENCE

The Okhrana, or Secret Police, was introduced in Chapter 3, page 28.

were affected, with Jewish property burnt, shops and businesses destroyed, and many incidences of rape and murder. The main outbreaks continued into 1884, but there were still sporadic pogroms after this, as in Odessa in 1886.

SOURCE 2

The May Laws of 1882 added to the discrimination against the Jews, making life even harder for them, even within the Pale of Settlement:

Article 1. Jews are forbidden to settle hereafter outside cities and towns of fewer than ten thousand people. Exception is made with regard to Jewish villages already in existence where the Jews are engaged in agriculture.

Article 2. All contracts for the mortgaging or renting of property situated outside cities and towns to a Jew, shall be of no effect.

Article 3. Jews are forbidden to do business on Sundays and Christian holidays; the laws compelling Christians to close their places of business on those days will be applied to Jewish places of business.

These laws effectively condemned the Jews to living in ghettoes in cities and towns. A separate decree of 1882 also decreased the number of Jewish doctors permitted in the Russian army because doctors possessed the rights of army officers, a privilege otherwise unattainable for Jews. These laws were supposedly temporary but were, in practice, constantly revised and tightened.

KEY CHRONOLOGY

Anti-Semitic legislation 1882–94

1882	May Laws and Army Law. The Governor-General of St Petersburg orders 14 Jewish apothecaries to shut down their businesses
1886	No Jew can be elected to a vacancy on the board of an orphan asylum
1886	Jews engaged in the sale of alcohol can only do so from their own homes or personal property
1887	Jews who have graduated from a university outside Russia no longer possess the right to reside outside the Pale by virtue of their qualifications
1887	The number of Jews admitted to schools and universities is regulated by quotas: ten per cent within the Pale; five per cent outside the Pale; and three per cent in the capitals (Moscow, St Petersburg and Kiev). Jews are prohibited from settling in Finland. Rostov-on-Don and Taganrog are removed from the Pale
1889	Jews need a special permit from the Minister of Justice to be elected to the Bar (the legal professional body). Any Jewish lawyer who wishes to become a barrister needs the express consent of the Minister of Justice
1891	Non-Christians are forbidden from buying property in the provinces of Akmolinsk, Semirietchensk, Uralsk and Turgai
1892	Jews are banned from participation in local elections and prohibited from the right to be elected to town dumas. The mining industry in Turkestan is closed to Jews
1893	It is illegal for Jews to adopt a 'Christian' name
1894	Jews who graduate from veterinary college can no longer be admitted to the service of the State. Jews are no longer eligible for any licences to sell alcohol

ACTIVITY

In pairs, consider how far the Jews' lives would have been affected by these measures. Which do you think would have had most effect? Compare your ideas with the rest of the class.

The impact of anti-Semitism

KEY QUESTION

- What was the extent of social and cultural change?
- How effective was opposition?

Fig. 6   *Torah scrolls desecrated during the pogroms in 1881*

Following the pogroms, many Jews left the country. Some went of their own free will but others were forcibly expelled, for example from Kiev in 1886.

From 1890, foreign Jews began to be deported from Russia along with Russian Jews who had settled outside the Pale. In the winter of 1891–92, around 10,000 Jewish artisans were expelled from Moscow where they had legally settled during the reign of Alexander II. More expulsions followed when the Grand Duke Sergei Alexandrovich, Alexander III's brother, was made Governor-General in 1892. He forced around 20,000 Jews from the city during the Passover and closed down a newly built synagogue.

The effect of such policies among the Jews that remained in Russia was to drive a disproportionate number of them towards revolutionary groups, and in particular Marxist socialist organisations. It is perhaps not surprising that the revolutionary movement in Russia in the early twentieth century would contain a disproportionate number of Jews, including Trotsky, Martov, Zinoviev and Litvinov.

CROSS-REFERENCE

The growth of opposition is the subject of Chapter 5.

You can read more about these significant figures (Leon Trotsky, Julius Martov, Grigorii Zinoviev and Maxim Litvinov) in Section Three of this book.

ACTIVITY

Summary

Copy and complete the chart below, with examples of tsarist policies, to provide a revision checklist.

Area	Language	Culture	Religion
European Russia			
Poland			
Finland			
Baltic provinces			
Ukraine, Belorussia and Georgia			
Asian Russia			
Jews and the Pale			

STUDY TIP

With this type of question, read each extract carefully and note down the key points made by each author. Your answer should identify these key points (or arguments) and consider whether they seem convincing in the light of what you have learned about Russification in this chapter. After dealing with each extract, write a short summary conclusion, giving your overall view of the arguments put forward by both authors. Concentrate on what each says, rather than on what is 'missed out'!

 PRACTICE QUESTION

Evaluating historical extracts

Look back at Extracts 1, 2 and 3. Using your understanding of the historical context, assess how convincing the arguments in these extracts are in relation to the policy of Russification.

The growth of opposition to tsarist rule

EXTRACT 1

There was a symmetry between the concentrated autocracy of government and the violence of political action. These extremes often go hand-in-hand; the rigorous demand for unquestioning obedience, the extreme claim of sovereign authority and its challenge with bomb or gun. Russia was a mass of **polarised** contradictions. This polarisation was self-reinforcing; the tendency was repression and greater extremism, not compromise or reduction of conflict. There might be a startling **plethora** of views as to what was wrong, or what should be done to put it right, but on one thing almost all critics were agreed – a sense of impending catastrophe. Resistance to the government moved on the same conflicting dimensions as official policy; national resentment on the part of suppressed and disorganised minorities, revolutionary leaders speaking for an, as yet, disorganised and mute peasantry, a small group of westernising intellectuals determined to fashion Russia in a more democratic and liberal image, socialists voicing the demands of the new industrial **proletariat** and, finally a tradition of violence which complemented the often repressive system of government.

Adapted from John P. Nettl, *The Soviet Achievement*, 1973

LEARNING OBJECTIVES

In this chapter you will learn about:

- ideas and ideologies
- individuals who opposed tsarist rule
- liberal and radical opposition
- the tsarist reaction to opposition.

KEY TERM

Polarised: opposite 'extremes', such as the North Pole and the South Pole

Plethora: a lot, probably too many

proletariat: urban working class

ACTIVITY

Evaluating historical extracts

Nettl's picture of Russia by the 1880s provides a picture of the opposition to the tsarist autocracy that emerged during the reigns of Alexander II and Alexander III. Make a note of Nettl's key ideas and reflect on these as you read this chapter.

CROSS-REFERENCE

The resentment and opposition of minorities was introduced in Chapter 4.

KEY QUESTION

As you read this chapter, consider the following Key Questions:
- How effective was opposition?
- How important were ideas and ideology?
- How important was the role of individuals and groups?

The emergence of new ideas and opposition

Both the hope and disappointment brought by Alexander II's reforms stimulated opposition to the tsarist regime. The initial relaxation in censorship encouraged the spread of radical literature, while the relaxation of controls in higher education increased the number of independently minded students. The creation of the *zemstva* and dumas also provided a platform for the educated intellectuals to challenge tsarist policies, while reform to the judicial system produced professionally trained lawyers skilled in the art of persuasion and ready to question and challenge autocratic practices. The more repressive atmosphere which existed in Alexander II's later years, and continued through the reign of Alexander III, only served to reinforce the demands for change. These came from many quarters, ranging from the mostly mildly behaved, liberally minded intelligentsia to the more vociferous student radicals and **socialist** groups.

KEY TERM

Socialist: person who believes that society should be egalitarian; in the nineteenth century this meant taking from the rich to give to the poor, to create a more equal and fair society

CROSS-REFERENCE

The liberal intelligentisa are introduced in Chapter 1, page 6.

The economic changes of the nineteenth century are discussed in Chapter 6, pages 50–55.

KEY TERM

Nihilism: the belief that all values are baseless and that nothing can be known or communicated

Anarchism: the belief in self-governed institutions; the State is considered unnecessary or even harmful

KEY PROFILE

Ivan Sergeyevich Turgenev (1818–83) was a Russian novelist and playwright who developed 'Westernising' ideas while travelling in Europe. His publication *A Sportsman's Sketches* (1852) helped to influence educated Russian opinion in favour of the abolition of serfdom. His novels, including *Fathers and Sons*, published in 1862, also addressed the problems of contemporary Russian society.

Count Leo Tolstoy (1828–1910) began his career in the army and wrote as he travelled through Europe, including *Sevastopol Sketches* (1855–56) and *The Cossacks* (1863). After returning to his family estates, he set up a school for peasant children and wrote *War and Peace* (1865–69), which established his reputation. This was followed by *Anna Karenina* (1875–77). Both novels were concerned with the meaning of life. In his later years, Tolstoy devoted himself to social reform, advocating simplicity and non-violence.

Moderate liberal opposition

Although a relatively small group, since there were comparatively few literate and educated Russians, the size and influence of the liberal intelligentsia grew with the reforms and economic changes of the later nineteenth century. Liberal intellectuals not only had the benefit of education, but possessed the wealth, time and interest to reflect on political matters. Many had travelled abroad and despaired at the political and social stagnation in their country.

Some of the intelligentsia sought 'the truth' via philosophical ideas such as **nihilism** or **anarchism**. However most fell into one of two broad categories: the **Westernisers** who wanted

Fig. 1   *Liberal intellectuals were of the noble class*

to 'catch up with the West' by copying Western ways, and the **Slavophiles** who favoured a superior 'Russian' path to a better future. The writer **Ivan Turgenev** was a Westerniser, while **Leo Tolstoy** was a Slavophile.

A CLOSER LOOK

Slavophiles and Westernisers

Slavophiles believed Russia had a unique culture and heritage centred on the prevailing peasant society and the principles of the Orthodox Church, which should be preserved as the country modernised. The Westernisers thought that Russia should abandon Slavic traditions and adopt modern Western values. This included not only economic and military reform but also reforms to 'civilise' society by providing representative assemblies, reducing the authority of the Orthodox Church, and establishing civil liberties.

ACTIVITY

Extension

You may be interested to discover more about the life and works of Turgenev, Tolstoy and their contemporaries such as Fyodor Dostoevsky. All these thinkers and novelists were concerned with the problems of Russian society and a dip into their writings would greatly enhance your appreciation of nineteenth-century Russia.

The *zemstva* provided a natural home for Westernising liberal opposition voices, as local decision-making encouraged members to think more nationally. Their members' hope was to reform the autocracy, so that the Tsar would listen to and rule in conjunction with his subjects. However, although Alexander II had created the representative *zemstva*, he was not prepared to give them national influence. When the St Petersburg *zemstvo* demanded a central body to coordinate the regional councils, the Tsar stood firm against the proposal. He did, at least partly, change his mind at the end of the 1870s and, had the Loris-Melikov proposals taken effect, they would have increased representation. However, the restriction of the *zemstva* powers by Alexander III in 1889–90 bitterly disappointed the *zemstva* liberals.

After peaking in 1881, the attractions of the Slavophiles diminished in the 1890s, as the country moved forward in its march towards industrialisation, creating conditions in which Western-style **socialism** began to take root. This split the intelligentsia. Some were attracted by Marxist theory and were drawn to socialism, others maintained a more moderate liberal stance and continued to pin their hopes on a reform of tsardom.

The experience of the 1891–92 famine, when the inaction of the over-bureaucratic tsarist government left the *zemstva* largely responsible for relief work, both increased convictions that the tsarist system had to change and provided the confidence needed to demand this. Orlando Figes emphasises the importance of the famine as a turning point in the development of opposition in Extract 2. By the mid-1890s there were renewed *zemstva*-led calls for a national body to advise the government.

CROSS-REFERENCE

For the Loris-Melikov proposals, look back to Chapter 3, 24–25.

The restriction of the powers of the *zemstva*, when they became subject to the Land Captains in 1889, is described in Chapter 3, pages 27–28.

KEY TERM

Socialism: the political and economic theory that the means of production, distribution, and exchange should be owned by the community as a whole and that people would work cooperatively together; the Bolsheviks were committed to socialism through Marxist ideology

CROSS-REFERENCE

Find out about the Great Famine of 1891–92 in Chapter 6, page 52.

Marx's ideas of capitalist development are described later in this chapter, on page 44.

EXTRACT 2

Russian society was polarised by the Great Famine, and from 1891 it became more organised in opposition to the government. The *zemstva* expanded their activities to revive the rural economy. Doctors, teachers and engineers began to demand more influence over public policy. In the press and periodicals, in universities and learned societies, there were heated debates on the causes of the crisis in which Marx's ideas of capitalist development were generally accepted as the most convincing explanation of the peasantry's impoverishment. The socialist movement sprang back into life making the famine a vital landmark in the history of the Russian revolution by heightening the expectations of the upper classes.

Adapted from Orlando Figes, *Revolutionary Russia 1891–1991*, 2014

Radical opposition

Fig. 2 *St Petersburg ablaze in June, 1862*

Another, far more radical strand of opposition developed among the younger generation who, although often the children of liberals, wanted to go further than their parents.

In the 1860s, there was a vogue for nihilism, and in 1862, a group of students calling themselves 'Young Russia' published a manifesto, in which they argued that revolution was the only way forward:

Society is at present divided into two groups that are hostile to one another because their interests are diametrically opposed. The party that is oppressed by all and humiliated by all is the party of the common people. Over it stands the landowners, the merchants, the government officials – in short all those who possess property, either inherited or acquired. At their heart stands the Tsar. They cannot exist without him, nor he without them. There is only one way out of this oppressive and terrible situation which is destroying contemporary man and that is revolution – bloody and merciless revolution.

In June 1862, a series of fires in St Petersburg destroyed over 2000 shops. Young Russia was immediately held responsible and a commission was appointed to investigate, but little came of this. In 1863, 'The Organisation' was set up by students at Moscow University and more calls for reform were made. Student idealism and determination were heightened by the increased repression of the later 1860s and the influence of radical socialist writers.

Radical thinkers

Nikolai Chernyshevsky was the author of a radical journal, *The Contemporary*, and the book, *What is to be done?*, which he wrote in 1862 while confined to the Peter and Paul Fortress in St Petersburg. His writings suggested that the peasants had to be made leaders of revolutionary change.

Aleksandr Herzen was the editor of the radical journal *The Bell* which was produced abroad and smuggled into Russia illegally. In this, he advocated a new peasant-based social structure. In 1869, he called on followers to 'go to the people'.

Mikhail Bakunin was both an anarchist and a socialist. He put forward the view that private ownership of land should be replaced by collective ownership and that income should be based on the number of hours worked. Bakunin had been forced to live in exile, but he helped to introduce Marxism into Russia by translating **Karl Marx**'s *The Communist Manifesto* into Russian in 1869. The first volume of Marx's *Das Kapital* was subsequently published in Russia in 1872.

Fig. 3 *Karl Marx*

Karl Marx (1818–83) was a German Jew who studied law and worked as a journalist. He moved from Germany to France in the early 1840s, but his writings on the social and economic conditions of Paris led to his expulsion from the city and he settled in Belgium. He wrote *The Communist Manifesto* with his friend Friedrich Engels in 1848, immediately prior to the European revolutions of 1848–49. After moving to London, he wrote his major work *Das Kapital*. The first volume was published in 1867 and subsequent ones (after Marx's death) in 1885 and 1894.

Marxist Theory

The theories of Karl Marx were based on the idea that all history was composed of class struggles. Marx had predicted that a struggle between the working class 'proletariat' and the factory-owning capitalist 'bourgeoisie' would ultimately (after a short dictatorship of the proletariat) herald the perfect 'communist' society in which everyone would be equal. Marxist teaching proved attractive intellectually, but in the 1870s its message seemed largely irrelevant to a predominantly rural country, with hardly any proletariat and still fewer bourgeoisie.

In 1869, Bakunin and Sergei Nechaev, a student radical activist who had fled from Russia illegally after calling on St Petersburg students to assassinate the Tsar, wrote a manifesto, *Catechism of a Revolutionary*. This was published in Switzerland and secretly smuggled into Russia. It exhorted opponents of autocracy to be merciless in their pursuit of revolution, laying aside all other attachments – family, friends, love, gratitude and even honour – in order to find the steely resolve required to pursue a revolutionary path.

CROSS-REFERENCE

Sergei Nechaev was a populist. The activities of the populist movement are described below.

SOURCE 2

Catechism of a Revolutionary included the famous lines:

The Revolutionary is a doomed man. He has no private interests, no affairs, sentiments, ties, property nor even a name of his own. His entire being is devoured by one purpose, one thought, one passion – the revolution. Heart and soul, not merely by word but by deed, he has severed every link with the social order and with the entire civilised world; with the laws, good manners, conventions, and morality of that world. He is its merciless enemy and continues to inhabit it with only one purpose – to destroy it.

In 1871, Nechaev used underground contacts to return to Russia, determined to 'go to the people' and carry out a revolution. However, he was soon forced to flee again, after the murder of a student who disagreed with him.

The Tchaikovsky Circle

The Tchaikovsky Circle, named after its most prominent member, Nikolai Tchaikovsky, was set up in 1868–69 in St Petersburg. It was primarily a literary society that organised the printing, publishing, and distribution of scientific and revolutionary literature, including the first volume of Marx's *Das Kapital*. The circle was never large; probably no more than 100 people spread between St Petersburg and other major cities, but it sought social (although not political) revolution. From 1872, the Tchaikovsky Circle began organising workers with the intention of sending them to work among the peasants in the countryside.

The Narodniks (Populists)

ACTIVITY

Research

Russian intellectuals and students were influenced by a host of writers and thinkers both from abroad and within Russia in the second half of the nineteenth century. As well as Marx, these included foreigners (such as Friedrich Engels, Gieuseppe Mazzini and Louis Auguste Blanqui) and Russians (such as Herzen, Nechaev, Lavrov, Bakunin and Chernyshevsky). Try to find out more about these thinkers and the views that they put forward.

Fig. 4   *Pyotor Lavrov (left), preparing a revolutionary publication*

The idea of 'going to the people' became known as Narodnyism (Populism) and in 1874 Pyotr Lavrov encouraged a group of around 2000 young men and women, mainly from the nobility and intelligentsia, to travel to the countryside in order to persuade the peasantry that the future of Russia depended on the development of the peasant commune. They aimed to exploit the resentment felt since Emancipation about the peasants' lack of land and the heavy tax burden they still carried.

Some Narodniks even tried dressing and talking like peasants but the romantic illusions of the young were soon shattered by peasant hostility. The peasants' ignorance, superstition, prejudice and deep-rooted loyalty to the Tsar ensured that the incomers were reported to the authorities. Around 1600 of them were arrested.

There was a second attempt to 'go to the people' in 1876, but this proved no more successful than the first. More arrests followed and a series of show trials were held in 1877–78.

Despite its immediate failure, Narodnyism had helped to take radical opposition away from the underground meeting rooms and into the countryside and, in so doing, helped to make the government more aware of the depth of feeling of its opponents.

CROSS-REFERENCE

For information on the show trials of 1877–78, look back to Chapter 3, page 24.

EXTRACT 3

The experience was enough to convince the revolutionaries that the people were never going to be a reliable basis on which to stage a revolution. It was a realisation that would have a dramatic impact. From that point onwards, the conviction began to grow that the revolution must be brought about and imposed on society by a clique of dedicated professionals. The 'people's revolution' was going to be based, not on the will of the people, but on the determination of a small group of activists. Lavrov, champion of the 'going to the people' movement, was appalled. He recognised that the revolutionaries were taking on the same character as the regime they were fighting against.

Adapted from Martin Sixsmith, *Russia*, 2011

STUDY TIP

With this type of question, you need to look for the key difference between the two extracts. Figes and Sixsmith have chosen to highlight different turning points in the evolution of revolutionary opposition. Nevertheless, both extracts contain some common points. Make a note of these and when you have read the rest of this chapter, try to write an answer to the question using your own understanding of the context.

 PRACTICE QUESTION

Evaluating historical extracts

Re-read Extract 2 (Figes) and compare it with Extract 3 (Sixsmith). Which provides the more convincing interpretation of the reasons for the growth of a revolutionary challenge to the tsarist autocracy?

A CLOSER LOOK

Populism in practice

Mikhail Romas tried to put his populist ideas into action by setting up a cooperative store selling fruit and vegetables. The peasants were suspicious of the cheap prices offered and some of the richer peasants, who had made their own deals with urban merchants, caused an explosion by filling one of his firewood logs with gunpowder. They intimidated any poorer peasants who bought Romas' goods and his peasant assistant was brutally murdered; his mutilated body scattered along the bank of the river, as a warning to others. Eventually Romas' shop was blown up and he was set upon and forced to flee for his life.

'Land and Liberty'

'Land and Liberty' (*Zemlya i Volya* in Russian), set up in 1877, continued the populist tradition. Its members sought work within the peasant communes – as doctors, teachers or workmen – but in a less obtrusive manner. Some carried out political assassinations, including that of General Mezemtsev, head of the Third Section, in 1878. They elicited considerable public sympathy. There were even some talks between *zemstva* and the Land and Liberty organisation to try to place more pressure on the autocracy for constitutional reform.

The tsarist government, however, failed to respond. Although Dmitry Milyutin, Minister of War, saw all too clearly the state of the country, none within court circles seemed willing to listen to the growing pressure for change.

SOURCE 3

Dmitry Milyutin, 20 April, 1879:

It must be acknowledged that our entire government structure demands basic reform from top to bottom. The structure of rural self-government, of the *zemstva*, of local administration, as well as of institutions on the central and national level have outlived their time. They should all take on new forms in accordance with the spirit of the great reforms carried out in the sixties. The higher strands of government think only of protective police measures. I am convinced that the present leaders in government are powerless, not only to solve the problem, but even to understand it.

In 1879 Land and Liberty split into two different groups:
- Black Repartition (*Cherny Peredel* in Russian), organised from St Petersburg by **Georgi Plekhanov** and other colleagues. It was so called because it wanted to share or partition the black soil provinces of Russia among the peasants. It continued to work peacefully among the peasantry, developing ties with students and workers and publishing radical materials in the hope of stimulating social change without resorting to violence. However, it was severely weakened by arrests in 1880–81, when it ceased to exist as a separate organisation. Plekhanov and some of the early leaders turned instead to Marxism.
- The People's Will (*Narodnaya Volya* in Russian) was ably led by Aleksandr Mikhailov who successfully planted a spy in the Tsar's Third Section, to keep the group informed of the Secret Police's activities and so evade harassment and arrest. This was a bigger group than Black Repartition and it advocated violent methods, undermining government by assassinating officials. In 1879, it declared that the Tsar had to be removed – although it did offer to withdraw the threat if the Tsar agreed to a constitution, which, of course, he did not. After a number of unsuccessful attempts against Tsar Alexander II's life, their aim was finally achieved in March 1881.

ACTIVITY

Creative thinking

Design a poster or write a short pamphlet encouraging fellow students to join the populist cause and 'go to the people'. You should make it clear what you hope to achieve and what this will entail.

CROSS-REFERENCE

Dmitry Milyutin is profiled in Chapter 2, page 12.

KEY PROFILE

Georgi Plekhanov (1856–1918) had been attracted by Populism and became a leader of Land and Liberty and Black Partition. He was exiled in 1880 and settled in Geneva where he studied Marxism. This led him to co-found the Marxist group 'Emancipation of Labour' in 1883 (with Lev Deutsch and Vera Zasulich). This merged with other socialist groups to form the Social Democratic Labour Party in 1898. In 1903, Plekhanov became a Menshevik. He remained an exile until 1917, when he returned briefly, but he never approved of the Bolsheviks.

ACTIVITY

Analysis

Draw a Venn diagram of two overlapping circles. Label one circle 'Black Repartition' and the other 'The People's Will'. In each circle, describe the main features of that movement and where the circles overlap, fill in what the two groups had in common.

CROSS-REFERENCE

The attempts on Alexander II's life are described in Chapter 3, page 22.

ACTIVITY

Revision

Use the following table to compare the ideas and actions of the liberal intelligentsia and the populists.

	Liberal intelligentsia	Populists
Aims		
Supporters		
Methods		
Key influences (books and personalities)		
Achievements by 1881		

STUDY TIP

Before writing your response to this type of question, you need to establish what your argument is. In this particular case, you need to show that you understand that there were many different opposition groups. You could also look at the regime's success and failure in suppressing each type of opposition group as well as providing an overall judgement.

AS LEVEL **PRACTICE QUESTION**

'The tsarist regime was successful in suppressing opposition between 1861 and 1881.' Explain why you agree or disagree with this view.

Tsarist reaction and the radical opposition after 1881

Fig. 5 *An execution of nihilists*

Alexander II's assassination marked a turning point. Security was stepped up and and the new Tsar retired to the fortified castle of Gatchina lest some 'madmen' try to kill him too. This effectively ended the Populist movement, as it had been known, although some of its supporters managed to meet in secret and commit acts of terrorism.

'Self-education' circles, such as the Muscovite Society of Translators and Publishers, which translated and reproduced the writings of foreign socialists, continued underground, and contact with radicals in exile and in the West was maintained. From Switzerland, **Georgi Plekhanov** established the 'Emancipation of Labour' group in 1883, which not only translated and arranged for Marxist tracts to be smuggled into Russia but also sought to demonstrate that Marxism was fully applicable to Russia. Emancipation of Labour had a limited impact at the time, and the group received a setback when its German contact, Deich, responsible for the smuggling of materials into Russia, was arrested by the German police (advised by tsarist agents) in 1884. However, **Plekhanov**'s development of the 'two-stage revolutionary strategy' was vital in advancing Marxism in Russia.

A CLOSER LOOK

Plekhanov, 'the Father of Russian Marxism'

In *Socialism and the Political Struggle* (1883) and *Our Differences* (1885), Plekhanov argued that Russian revolutionaries had to accept the inevitability of Marx's 'stages of development'. He stressed that Russia had to pass through the capitalist phase of development and that this was clearly underway. Revolutionaries, he believed, should concentrate their activities among the Russian workers in the cities, rather than wasting their energy on the peasantry, for it was from the Russian proletariat that the dynamism to drive a socialist revolution would emerge. Since the proletariat of Russia was still small and backward, he wanted revolutionary leaders to organise the workers so as to be ready for Marxism, but, he warned, their first task was to cooperate with the bourgeoisie to fight autocracy, in order to accelerate the capitalist stage.

In 1886, students in St Petersburg tried to reform The People's Will and in March 1887 a group, who made bombs with the intention of assassinating Alexander III, were arrested. Two months later, five of these, including **Aleksandr Ulyanov**, Lenin's elder brother, were hanged.

KEY PROFILE

Aleksandr Ulyanov (1866–87) was the son of a government official from Simbirsk and part of Russia's small bourgeoisie. He and his brother Vladimir (later known as Lenin) attended St Petersburg University, where Aleksandr participated in radical student politics; attending illegal meetings and running propaganda campaigns. Aleksandr helped reform The People's Will (*Narodnaya Volya*) in 1886, with a commitment to terrorism, but following his arrest for attempting to assassinate Alexander III, he was hanged.

Summary

By the 1890s, opposition movements appeared to stand little chance of success in the face of tsarist repression. However, as industrialisation speeded up, a number of workers' organisations, illegal trade unions, Marxist discussion circles and other groups developed, spreading radical Marxist ideas more widely. It was from these small beginnings that changes in thinking that were to have massive long-term importance began to take root.

ACTIVITY

Evaluating historical extracts

Look back at Extract 1. How convincing are Nettl's arguments about the condition of Russia in the 1880s?

STUDY TIP

When analysing extracts, it is a good idea to identify the 'big argument' first and then look for more specific ideas which can be assessed and challenged. You should use your own understanding of the historical context to comment on how convinced you are by what Nettl writes.

(A LEVEL) PRACTICE QUESTION

'Opposition to the tsarist regime achieved nothing in the years 1866 to 1894.' Assess the validity of this view.

STUDY TIP

Remember to consider all the different strands of opposition and to distinguish between their aims. 'Nothing' is a deliberately provocative word; it should be possible to argue that 'something' was achieved, even if the opposition's aims were not fulfilled. Try making a plan in which you list successes (however small) and failures before you begin to write.

6 Economic and social developments

LEARNING OBJECTIVES

In this chapter you will learn about:

- the development of Russian industry

- the problems of Russian agriculture and issues concerning the land

- the social divisions within Russia

- the cultural influence of the Orthodox Church.

KEY QUESTION

As you read this chapter, consider the following Key Question:
How and with what results did the economy develop and change?

EXTRACT 1

The emancipation of the serfs in 1861 removed a considerable barrier to industrial growth. Serfdom was clearly incompatible with the requirements of an industrialising society. The basis of such a society was agriculture, and serfdom ensured a restricted home market, a low level of agricultural technology, and a largely immobile population. The simple pyramid structure of this stratified society, with its huge peasant base and small elite of landed gentry, left little room for the development of a prosperous middle class. Above all, serfdom bred values and attitudes inimical to modernisation. Emancipation can therefore be seen as a decisive turning point. Total industrial production grew by about five per cent a year after 1861, accelerating markedly after the mid-1880s. As the economy developed, peasants marketed crops, which had sometimes previously remained unharvested, and were able to obtain passports to work away from the commune. Furthermore, a large number of Russians were left with no land at all and could therefore supply a factory labour force.

Adapted from Malcolm E. Falkus, *The Industrialisation of Russia 1700–1914*, 1972

ACTIVITY

In Extract 1, Falkus identifies one possible 'turning point' in Russia's economic development. Failure in the Crimean War might well be identified as another. As you read this chapter, see if you can pick out any other crucial turning points or important dates. Compile a key chronology and highlight the most important.

Economic change

Fig. 1 *A train of tankers carrying oil from the oil wells at Baku*

The beginnings of state-promoted industrial growth

In the absence of an entrepreneurial middle class, industrialisation in Russia was largely driven by the State in a deliberate attempt to match the economic development of Western Europe. Following Emancipation, Alexander II's Minister of Finance from 1862–78, **Mikhail von Reutern**, produced a series of reforms designed to boost the economy and provide funds to drive industrial growth.

- The Treasury was reformed and new arrangements for collecting taxes, auditing the accounts of government departments, and publishing budgets was put in place.
- Tax-farming (whereby groups bought the right to collect certain taxes) was abolished and the tax system was reformed to include more indirect taxation.
- Banks and the credit facilities were extended with the establishment of a state bank in 1860, municipal banks in 1862 and a savings bank in 1869.
- Trade was promoted with the reduction of import duties from 1863.
- Government subsidies were offered to enable private entrepreneurs to develop railways.
- Foreign investment in Russia was encouraged with a government-guaranteed annual dividend.
- New legislation regulated **joint-stock companies**, to encourage 'safe' investment.
- Government support was offered for the development of the cotton industry (seizing the opportunity created by the American Civil War in 1861–65 to capture former American markets), and mining in the Donets Coalfield.

Mikhail von Reutern (1820–90) was a German from the Russian Baltic landowning class. He believed that state money and control should direct economic change, and he used his position to carry these beliefs into action. He particularly encouraged the development of railways; selling contracts to many of his own friends and acquaintances. He became Chairman of the Council of Ministers in 1881.

KEY TERM

Joint-stock company: a business owned by shareholders who invested their own capital in the enterprise

ACTIVITY

Consider each of von Reutern's reforms. In what ways would they contribute to economic growth? Can you anticipate any limitations or drawbacks?

Von Reutern's reforms forced former tax farmers to look elsewhere to invest, while the opportunities provided by government subsidies and trade treaties encouraged enterprise. The use of foreign technical expertise and capital also supported industrial expansion and the railway network saw a marked expansion. Overall, there was an annual average growth rate of six per cent during von Reutern's term of office.

Although textiles remained the dominant industry, there were also new developments. Oil extraction began in the Caspian Sea port of Baku in 1871 and an ironworks was set up in Donetsk in 1872, which started mining the rich ironfields of the Krivoi Rog region. In 1879, the Naphtha Extraction Company was established by the Nobel brothers, to exploit the coal and oil extraction further.

However, despite these improvements, Russia's economy remained comparatively weak. A third of all government expenditure went on the repayment of debts and the Russian currency – the rouble – was subject to wild variations in its value. The limitations of the Emancipation Edict, and a taxation system which left 66 per cent of government revenue coming from indirect taxation, kept the peasantry poor and the domestic market small. Furthermore, tariff reductions meant a decline in government revenues and the decision was taken to raise these again from 1878.

KEY QUESTION

How important was the role of individuals?

The industrial 'take-off' under Vyshnegradsky and Witte

Ivan Vyshnegradsky (1832–95) began life as a priest but his entrepreneurial skills enabled him to accumulate wealth through investments. In 1884, he was made a member of the Council of Ministers where he drew up a new programme for technical education. In 1886, he joined the Council of State and from 1887–92 was head of the Ministry of Finance. Here he successfully reduced the budget deficit but only because of harsh measures.

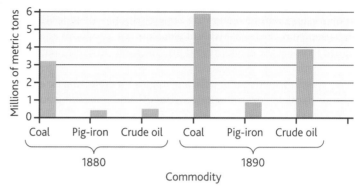

Fig. 2   *Production of raw materials, 1880–90*

Tariffs were raised in the 1880s, and under **Ivan Vyshnegradsky**, who took over in 1887, a prohibitive import tariff of 30 per cent of the value of raw materials was introduced. This was designed to boost home production and considerably helped the iron industry of southern Russia as well as the development of industrial machinery.

Vyshnegradsky needed to balance the budget while financing enterprise. As well as negotiating some valuable loans, for example from the French in 1888, he also increased indirect taxes and mounted a drive to swell grain exports. On the surface, the policy appeared very successful. Between 1881 and 1891, grain exports increased by 18 per cent, as a percentage of total Russian exports, and by 1892 the Russian budget was in surplus.

However, this remarkable export drive was achieved at the expense of the peasants who paid the taxes and saw their grain requisitioned by the State. Many were left with no reserve stores for the winter and it was put about that Vyshnegradsky said, 'We ourselves shall not eat, but we shall export'. A result of this policy was witnessed in 1891–92 when bad harvests brought widespread **famine**, in which many thousands died. Vyshnegradsky was dismissed in 1892, largely because of this disaster, made worse by his own policy.

Sergei Witte (1849–1915) had worked in railway development. In 1892, he was promoted, firstly to Minister of Communications, and then to Minister of Finance, a post he held until 1903. He was an able minister and the author of the 1905 October Manifesto (see page 65). He became Russia's first Prime Minister that year, but resigned after six months. He opposed the entry of Russia into the First World War on economic grounds, and died shortly afterwards, in 1915.

The Great Famine of 1891–92

The 1891–92 famine affected 17 of Russia's 39 provinces. There had been an early winter and a long, hot, dry summer, which ruined crops. A population weakened by hunger became susceptible to disease, so that when food began growing again, cholera and typhoid still continued to kill more. This was a double tragedy as the able-bodied workers who succumbed to disease left families destitute with no breadwinner to provide for them. Over 350,000 died from starvation or disease. The government failed to organise adequate relief and it was left to volunteer groups to help the stricken peasants.

Vyshnegradsky's successor, **Sergei Witte**, was totally committed to economic modernisation as a means to curbing revolutionary activity. Witte believed that the only way forward was to continue with protective tariffs, heavy taxation and forced exports to generate capital.

ACTIVITY

Thinking point

Do you think Witte was correct in his analysis of Russia's needs and the likely outcome of a programme of economic modernisation?

Witte also sought additional loans from abroad and, as can be seen in Table 1 below, foreign investment increased considerably.

Table 1 Foreign investment, 1880–95

Year	Foreign investment (millions of roubles)
1880	98
1890	215
1895	280

Much of this investment went into mining, the metal trades, oil and banking. Witte also encouraged engineers, managers and workers, from France, Belgium, Germany, Britain and Sweden, to oversee industrial developments and advise on planning and techniques. With their help, there was a huge expansion of the **railway network**.

Russia's rate of growth enabled it to move up the league table of industrialised nations to become the world's fourth-largest industrial economy by 1897. This growth helped to increase Russian exports and foreign trade, although the bulk of the export trade was still in grain rather than industrial goods.

A CLOSER LOOK

The railways

Russia's first railway had been completed before this, in 1837, and a line linking St Petersburg and Moscow had opened in 1851. However, thanks to state support, there was a huge expansion of the railway network in the years 1855–94, and by the mid-1890s 60 per cent of the whole Russian railway system was owned by the State.

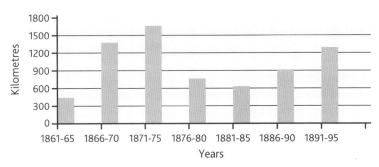

Fig. 3 *Annual average railway construction, 1861–95*

CROSS-REFERENCE

You can find out more in Chapter 2 about *mirs*, on page 14, and about *kulaks*, on page 15.

A CLOSER LOOK

Land Banks

The Peasants' Land Bank held funds and reserves of land. They were set up to assist peasants who wished to acquire land directly or through purchase from nobles. The Nobles' Land Bank was designed to help nobles with the legal costs involved in land transfer and in land improvement schemes. Interest rates on loans from these banks were kept deliberately low. They helped to increase peasant ownership and between 1877 and 1905, over 26 million hectares passed into peasant hands. However, they also helped to prop up some inefficient farms, which continued in their traditional ways.

 PRACTICE QUESTION

'The foundations for Russia's industrial growth were firmly laid in the years 1855 to 1895.'
Explain why you agree or disagree with this view.

Agriculture and the land issue

Fig. 4   *Sheep shearing in a Russian village, 1877*

KEY QUESTION

How and with what results did the economy develop and change?

Emancipation failed to bring any fundamental change in agricultural practice. Aleksandr Engelgardt, a radical writing in the mid 1870s, was to say, 'everything carries on as it was before the Emancipation. The only differences are that the quantity of ploughland has been reduced, that cultivation is carried on even less well, and the meadows are not kept in good condition.'

Although there was considerable variation, the average peasant received only a little less than four hectares. High taxes, grain requisitions, redemption payments and the traditional farming practices perpetuated by the *mir* elders hampered agricultural change. Yields remained low in comparison to Western Europe and although the government established Peasants' (1883) and Nobles' (1885) **Land Banks** to facilitate land purchase, the loans they offered often merely increased debts.

There was an overall increase in agricultural production in the 1870s and 1880s, largely thanks to the efforts of the *kulak* class to respond positively to Vyshnegradsky's export drive. However, the disastrous 1891–92 famine showed that the basic economic problem, which Emancipation had been expected to solve, remained: the average Russian peasant had too little land to become prosperous.

Table 2 Comparison of grain production in the 1880s

	Country	*Puds* per *desiatin*
Grain production	Russia	45
	UK and Germany	146
Rye production	Russia	54
	France and USA	68

A *desiatin* was an old Russian measurement, little more than one hundredth of a square kilometre. A *pud* was a weight of 16.38 kg.

Social divisions: nobles, landowners and the position of the peasantry

As industrialisation spread, Russia's traditional land-based society began to move towards one more focused on money, capital and wages. Of course, this was a slow procedure and until 1895 society was still strongly divided. However, the period saw the beginnings of an emergent new middle class and urban working class, which found themselves placed somewhere between the landowning elites and the mass of peasants. While still in their infancy in the period to 1895, these changes were eventually to have a profound impact on the stability of the State.

KEY QUESTION

What was the extent of social and cultural change?

The landed elite

The landed elite was a small but diverse group, mostly of noble status. After the Emancipation, their personal landholdings had considerably declined, as some sold out to **pay off debts** and others abandoned farming in favour of more rewarding professional activities. In 1880 nearly one fifth of university professors, for example, came from the hereditary nobility. Yet others saw the future in business and, by 1882, more than 700 nobles owned their own businesses in Moscow, while nearly 2500 were employed in commerce, transport or industry. State service was another option, while some found places in the *zemstva* and the provincial governorships.

Consequently, although there were changes to their position, most former serf-owners retained much of their previous wealth and status, and society remained highly stratified (arranged in layers, according to wealth).

The middle class

With urban and industrial expansion and an increase in educational opportunities, Russia's middle class began to grow. Bankers, doctors, teachers and administrators were in greater demand, although their numbers added up to no more than half a million in the 1897 census. Government contracts to build railways, and state loans to set up **factories**, provided tremendous opportunities for those who were enterprising. At the lower end of the scale, there were more opportunities to take up management positions or set up as workshop owners and traders.

A CLOSER LOOK

Paying off debts

One eighth of the money that nobles gained through land sales went to pay off mortgages with the Nobles' Land Bank.

A CLOSER LOOK

Factory ownership

As industry began to develop in Russia in the 1860s–80s, most private industrial enterprises were in the hands of the traditional nobility. However in the 1890s non-nobles found a new niche as factory owners, supervisors and foremen. This is one potential reason why harsh discipline and disregard for workers' wellbeing became more marked. These new figures had none of the old noble 'paternalism' which made them feel morally obliged to look after their workers.

The urban working class

The expansion of industry was accompanied by a growth in the urban population. The number of urban workers was, however, still very small in this period – probably no more than two per cent of the population. Indeed, it was still relatively common for peasants to move to the towns to work temporarily, while returning to their villages to help out at peak times, such as harvest. However, some peasants sold up and left the countryside, either to join a migrant group building railways or to become urban workers. By 1864 one in three of the inhabitants of St Petersburg were peasants by birth, and the proportion continued to rise.

Conditions in the cities could be grim and the early factories paid little heed to their workers' welfare, despite some reforming legislation. In 1882–90 there was a series of reforms: regulation of child labour, a reduction in working hours (and in particular the hours worked by women at night), a reduction in excessive fines and **payment in kind**, and the appointment of inspectors with powers to check up on working and living conditions. However, these contributed very little towards improving the lives of the growing working class.

Although peasants were attracted by the prospect of regular wages, payments were rarely generous. Unsurprisingly, although they were illegal, there were around 33 strikes per year between 1886 and 1894. However, nothing stopped the relentless drive from countryside to city.

The position of the peasantry

CROSS-REFERENCE

The poor conditions of city life are discussed in Chapter 9, pages 84–87.

KEY TERM

Payment in kind: payment in goods or services, such as accommodation, rather than money wages

ACTIVITY

Analysis

Make a list of the social consequences of industrialisation in Russia and rank them in order of importance. Consider which group benefited and which suffered the most. In pairs, discuss your ideas and justify your own order.

Fig. 5 *Russian peasants at a farm house*

Like the landed elites, the peasantry was also divided. At the top were the *kulaks* who bought up land, perhaps with the aid of loans from the Peasants' Land Bank. They employed labour and sometimes acted as 'pawn brokers' to the less fortunate, buying their grain in the autumn to provide them with money to tide them over the winter, but selling it back at inflated prices in the spring. When their clients could not afford the repayments, the *kulaks* sometimes accepted land instead.

In contrast, the poorest peasants found life getting harsher as they turned into landless labourers, dependent on others. According to a *zemstvo* survey in the 1880s, two out of every three of the former serfs in the Tambov region were unable to feed the household without falling into debt.

Living standards varied throughout the country. Areas of former state peasants tended to be better off than those of the emancipated privately owned serfs, because they had been granted more land. Despite improvements in health care, provided through the *zemstva*, a large proportion of the peasantry were turned down as unfit for military service and mortality rates were higher than those in any other European country. Average life expectancy was around 27 years for males and 29 years for women; in England the average age of death was 45 years. It would therefore be fair to say that economic change failed to improve the lot of the peasantry and may even have affected them for the worse.

EXTRACT 2

Russia's problems were deeply rooted in its economy and society, although it must be emphasised that the picture varied from one part of the Empire to another. However, there was one underlying factor of pre-eminent importance. The survival of serfdom to 1861 was, in many important respects, a fundamental source of many other difficulties. Reliance on unlimited cheap labour had inhibited the development of a productive labour force, distorted the distribution of the population, and removed incentives to modernise and mechanise agriculture. It had instilled deep-seated attitudes on the part of peasants that included in-built hostility to the masters and a disastrously inefficient attitude to work. Only work on one's own plot brought the best; work for the master – whether landowner, employer or State was a resented extortion and diversion. Such attitudes survived abolition. It was also the case that state institutions and the reliance on police, army and brute force in order to govern the peasants had been built up under serfdom. The Russian State remained essentially a serfowners' state with corresponding powers and attitudes. The cultural and institutional survivals of serfdom were to be found everywhere and their impact has too often been underrated.

Adapted from Christopher Read, *From Tsar to Soviets*, 1996

 A LEVEL PRACTICE QUESTION

Evaluating historical extracts

Using the contextual knowledge you have acquired in this chapter, how convincing are Extract 1 (Falkus) and Extract 2 (Read) in relation to economic and social development in Russia after 1861?

 AS LEVEL PRACTICE QUESTION

Evaluating historical extracts

Using your understanding of the historical context, which of Extracts 1 and 2 provides the more convincing interpretation of economic and social developments in Russia after 1861?

ACTIVITY

Extract 2 is concerned with the limitations to the economic and social change in Russia after 1861. Read it carefully and compare it with Extract 1. When you have done so, attempt either the A level or AS level question.

STUDY TIP

Firstly, note the main and lesser arguments that each author puts forward. In order to assess their arguments you may need to refer to earlier chapters. You will need to find evidence to both support and reject their ideas, and you should also write a summative conclusion. There is no 'right' or 'wrong' answer here. The idea of this exercise is to make you think!

STUDY TIP

You will need to identify the interpretation given in each extract, noting the differences between them and making a judgement about which is the more convincing, in light of your contextual knowledge.

The cultural influence of the Church

KEY QUESTION

- How important were ideas and ideology?
- What was the extent of social and cultural change?

Fig. 6 *The Church of the Assumption, Moscow*

CROSS-REFERENCE

The Orthodox Church, the Holy Synod, and its highest official, the Over-Procurator, are introduced in Chapter 1, page 2.

KEY TERM

Secular: not connected with religious or spiritual matters

CROSS-REFERENCE

The educational policies of Ivan Delyanov are outlined in Chapter 3, page 29.

Russification is discussed in more detail in Chapter 4, pages 31–36.

The **Orthodox Church**, to which 70 per cent of the population subscribed, had a close bond with the tsarist regime. According to tradition, Russia was a Holy Land that had been chosen by God to save the world. The Tsar possessed not only a 'divine right' to rule, but a holiness which made him a saint on Earth. By the late-nineteenth century, Church administration had been moved to the Holy Synod and the Tsar's position had become more **secular**. Nevertheless, Imperial Russia remained a strongly Orthodox State and the moral domination of the Orthodox Church over the superstitious and ill-educated peasantry was hugely beneficial to the regime as a means of control.

Religious observance was a significant part of life in the Russian countryside. Every peasant hut held its icon and the mix of religion and superstition was an integral part of peasant culture. Priests had close ties with the village, as well as a role assigned by the State. They were expected to read out Imperial manifestos and decrees, keep statistics (for example on births, marriages and deaths), root out opposition, and inform the police of any suspicious activity. Priests were even encouraged to pass on statements given in Holy Confessions to the secular authorities, even though by Church law these should never be divulged.

After a report expressing concern about clerical poverty and behaviour in 1858, Pyotr Valuev, the Minister of Internal Affairs, set up an Ecclesiastical Commission to look into the Church organisation and practice in 1862. In 1868, reforms were introduced to improve the education of priests.

Alexander III and his minsters were certainly conscious of the power of the Church and under Ivan Delyanov (Minister of Education) the Orthodox Church was given increased control over primary education.

The Church also possessed strict censorship controls and the Church courts judged moral and social 'crimes', awarding punishments, such as a spell in a monastery, to those found guilty.

Alexander III's policy of Russification enabled him to promote Orthodoxy throughout the Empire. It became an offence to convert from the Orthodox to another faith, or even to publish criticisms of it. Radical sects, which had broken away from true Orthodoxy – in particular the '**Old Believers**' who had settled in remote parts of Siberia – were all persecuted by the State. The Ukrainian **Uniate Church** and the **Armenian Church** were subject to persecution and in Central Asia and Siberia there was enforced baptism of pagans, accompanied by scenes of ritual humiliation. More than 8500 Muslims and 50,000 pagans were (in theory at least) converted to Orthodoxy during Alexander III's reign as well as around 40,000 Catholics and Lutherans in Poland and the Baltic provinces.

The influence of Orthodoxy

Despite the dominance of the Orthodox Church, there is evidence to suggest that its control over the lives of the people was weakening. One nineteenth-century priest despaired, 'Everywhere, from the most resplendent drawing rooms to smoky peasant huts, people disparage the clergy with the most vicious mockery, with words of the most profound scorn and infinite disgust.'

The provision of Churches and priests had not kept pace with the growth of urbanisation and, in any case, the Orthodox religion often seemed to have little relevance for the workers in the factories and tenement blocks, who were often more attracted by the teachings of the socialists. Even in the countryside, where faith and religious practices seemed stronger, superstition often held a stronger sway than the Orthodox priests who were often regarded a money-grasping and less than perfect role-models.

Some liberal clergy expressed the wish to regenerate the Church and reform its relations with the tsarist state but their calls were silenced by the senior conservatives and in particular by Pobedonostsev, the Over-Procurator between 1880 and 1905.

Old Believers: this group had rejected reforms to the Orthodox liturgy in the seventeenth century and had fled to Siberia to escape persecution; some remain there to this day, despite various bouts of state persecution

Uniate Church: this recognises the Pope as the Head of the Church but observes the rites of the Orthodox Church

Armenian Church: this has its own hierarchy and non-Orthodox practices

Summary

- The backward Russian economy began to develop after defeat in the Crimean War and emancipation
- The State played an active role in promoting industry. Financial policies and the encouragement of overseas investment and expertise were crucial
- The peasantry was forced to support industrialisation by the drive to export grain and an increase in indirect taxation
- Railway development was a crucial first step and, in addition to traditional textiles, heavy industry and oil grew more important
- Emancipation and industrialisation also brought social change affecting landowners, a growing 'middle class', expanding the ranks of urban workers and causing greater social division in the countryside
- Throughout this period the Orthodox Church maintained a strong cultural influence and was used by the State to help keep the population under control.

CROSS-REFERENCE

The teachings of the socialists are discussed in Chapter 5, pages 41–43.

A **LEVEL** **PRACTICE QUESTION**

'There was more continuity than change in Russian society in the years 1855 to 1894.'
Assess the validity of this view.

STUDY TIP

You could plan your answer to this question by making two columns; one headed 'continuity' and the other 'change'. Consider each social group and try to find evidence on both sides. Decide what you will argue and ensure you support your comments with precise examples.

Nicholas II and the challenge to autocracy

ACTIVITY

Evaluating historical extracts

1. Extract 1 is by the modern historian Orlando Figes, who has written several influential books on modern Russia. What impression of Nicholas II is given in this extract? Try to summarise Figes' view of the Tsar in one sentence.

2. As you read this chapter, reflect on this view and look for evidence that both supports and disagrees with what Figes has written.

KEY QUESTION

As you read this chapter, consider the following Key Question:
How was Russia governed and how did political authority change and develop?

CROSS-REFERENCE

Konstantin Pobedonostsev is profiled in Chapter 3, pages 25–26.

EXTRACT 1

Nicholas had been blessed with neither his father's strength of character, nor his intelligence. That was Nicholas' tragedy. With his limitations, he could only play at the part of an autocrat, meddling in (and in the process, disrupting) the work of government, without bringing to it any leadership. He was far too mild-mannered and shy to command any real authority among his subordinates. Being only five feet seven inches tall and feminine in stature, he didn't even look the part of an autocrat. Yet it would be a mistake to assume that Nicholas' failure stemmed from a fundamental 'weakness of will'. Beneath his docile exterior, Nicholas had a strong sense of his duty to uphold the principles of autocracy. He stubbornly defended his autocratic rights against the encroachments of his ambitious ministers and even his own wife. It was not a 'weakness of will' that was the undoing of the last Tsar but, on the contrary, a wilful determination to rule from the throne, despite the fact that he clearly lacked the necessary qualities to do so.

Adapted from Orlando Figes, *A People's Tragedy*, 1996

Political authority and government under Nicholas II, 1894–1904

KEY PROFILE

Tsar Nicholas II (1868–1918) was small, naturally reserved and regarded by his father as a dunce and a weakling. He even referred to Nicholas as 'girlie'. Nicholas had excellent manners, a good memory and could speak several languages, but he was not a practical man. Politics bored him and when his father died in 1894, Nicholas is said to have said to his cousin, 'What is going to happen to me and to all of Russia? I am not prepared to be a Tsar. I never wanted to become one. I know nothing of the business of ruling. I have no idea of even how to talk to the ministers.' However, he accepted his inheritance as God-given and set out to rule in 'the Romanov way', asserting himself against the demands of the growing reform movement. His reign was to be marked by revolutions in 1905 and February 1917, after which he abdicated.

Nicholas II had been brought up to take his duties as a ruler seriously, and to believe that any concessions or signs of weakness would be indications of cowardice and failure on his part. No doubt such attitudes had been instilled in him by Konstantin Pobedonostsev, his tutor. As he declared shortly before his coronation, he was resolved 'to maintain the principle of autocracy just as firmly and unflinchingly as it was preserved by my unforgettable dead father.'

Nicholas's commitment to Orthodoxy also ensured that the Church maintained its powerful influence. Continued Russification and support for the **'Black Hundreds'** organisations, with their right-wing and anti-Semitic ideals, ensured that Nicholas was no more popular with the ethnic minorities than his father had been.

A CLOSER LOOK

An ominous start

Nicholas' reign did not begin well. In May 1896, attracted by the promise of free food, drink and gifts, crowds gathered on Khodynka Field just outside Moscow to celebrate Nicholas II's coronation. However, in the crush to see their new Tsar, and his wife Alexandra, around 1400 men, women and children were trampled to death and others were badly injured. The coronation ceremonies and dancing went ahead as though nothing had happened, although Nicholas later visited the hospital where the injured had been taken and gave money to the families of those who had died.

Demands for change and the government reaction

The years after 1894 were a time of serious unrest in Russia. Although opposition movements were nothing new, Russian society had become more politicised in the years after the Great Famine of 1891–92. The failure of the over-bureaucratic tsarist government to cope with the crisis, which had left the *zemstva* and voluntary organisations to provide the necessary relief work, had bred scorn and despair. As a result, there was not only greater public mistrust of the government's competence, but also a firmer belief in the power of ordinary members of society to play a role in the nation's affairs. Reformist groups had consequently developed a broader support base, by 1900, than ever before.

There were new outbursts of trouble in Russian universities. These were met by the increased use of the Okhrana, whose activities ensured rebellious young people were expelled, exiled or drafted into the army and, when necessary, submitted to military force. In 1901, for example, a squadron of mounted Cossacks charged into a crowd of students in St Petersburg, killing thirteen, and in the aftermath of the incident, 1500 students were imprisoned in the Peter and Paul Fortress.

Fig. 1 *Soldiers executing a group of rioters*

The years 1902 to 1907 were marked by widespread disturbances in both towns and countryside. There were so many instances of arson in the rural communities

KEY TERM

Black Hundreds: nationalist gangs, devoted to 'Tsar, Church and Motherland', emerging from c1900 and supported by clergy, landowners and government officials; they played a major role in crushing the 1905 Revolution

ACTIVITY

Prepare a group presentation on Nicholas II and Alexandra. You should try to find out something about Nicholas' personality and background before becoming Tsar, and the influence of his wife. You might conclude with a summary of the qualities and limitations of the royal couple for their positions.

KEY QUESTION

- Why did opposition develop and how effective was it?
- How important was the role of individuals and groups?

CROSS-REFERENCE

The Great Famine of 1891–92 is covered in Chapter 6, page 53.

CROSS-REFERENCE

The disturbances in the towns and countryside are covered in Chapters 8 and 9.

Stolypin is profiled, on page 70. You will find more detail on his work in the countryside in Chapter 8.

The Cossacks are discussed in Chapter 1, page 3.

KEY PROFILE

Father Georgi Gapon (1870–1906) studied at the St Petersburg Theological Academy and became an Orthodox priest and prison chaplain, working in the working-class districts of St Petersburg. Believing he had a divine mission to help the workers, he began organising workers' unions from 1903, but remained intensely loyal and taught that the Tsar was obliged by God to respond to the workers' demands. He escaped with his life after the Bloody Sunday march of 1905, and briefly spent time in exile, supported by Socialist Revolutionaries (SRs). On returning to Russia in December, he regained contact with the Okhrana, but was found hanged in March 1906, possibly murdered by SR agents angered by his double-dealing, or by the Okhrana.

CROSS-REFERENCE

Plehve is profiled in Chapter 3, page 28.

that the nickname 'the years of the red cockerel', referring to the leaping flames which resembled a rooster's comb, was coined. The unrest was at its worst in the central Russian provinces, where the landord/peasant relationship was still at its most traditional, but it also spread into Georgia, the Ukraine and Poland. Peasants set fire to their landlords' barns, destroying grain, or vented their anger by seizing woodland and pasture or even physically attacking landlords and officials.

The Tsar's minister, Pyotr Stolypin, dealt with the disturbances with a ferocity that aggravated the situation further. Peasants were flogged, arrested and exiled, or shot in their thousands. The gallows was in such constant use that it became referred to as 'Stolypin's necktie'.

Industrial strikes escalated in the towns, numbering around 17,000 in 1894 to around 90,000 in 1904. In 1901, the Obukhov factory in St Petersburg saw violent clashes between armed police and whip-carrying Cossacks and such sights became commonplace over the ensuing years.

In an attempt to control the proliferation of illegal unions, in 1900 the Moscow chief of the Okhrana, Sergei Vasilevich Zubatov, began organising his own police-sponsored trade unions with the approval of the Governor-General of Moscow, the Grand Duke Sergei Alexandrovich. The idea was to provide 'official' channels through which complaints could be heard, in an attempt to prevent workers joining the radical socialists. The experiment only lasted to 1903, when Zubatov was dismissed and exiled after one of his unions became involved in a General Strike in Odessa. However, another union on the Zubatov model, the Assembly of St Petersburg Factory Workers, was formed in 1904 by **Father Georgi Gapon**. The union was approved by Nicholas' Minister for Internal Affairs, Plehve, and had the support of the Orthodox Church. It soon had twelve branches and 8000 members.

The Russo-Japanese War

Fig. 2 *Map of the Russo-Japanese War*

Plehve is accredited with encouraging the Tsar to respond to a Japanese assault on the Russian far eastern naval base at Port Arthur, in January 1904, with a 'short swift victorious war', which would detract from the tide of unrest at home. However, the Russians really had very little idea of their enemy, or the inadequacies of their own forces. Running a war 6000 miles from the capital was never going to be easy and a series of defeats turned the initial surge of anti-Japanese patriotism into one of opposition to the government.

When Plehve was assassinated in July 1904, crowds in Warsaw turned out to celebrate on the streets. There were renewed cries for a representative National Assembly (or **Duma**), and in November 1904, the moderate Pyotr Mirsky, who replaced Plehve, reluctantly agreed to invite *zemstvo* representatives to come to St Petersburg for discussions. However Nicholas declared, 'I will never agree to the representative form of government because I consider it harmful to the people whom God has entrusted to me.' All he would concede was an expansion of the rights of the *zemstva*.

The events and outcome of the 1905 Revolution

Bloody Sunday, 9 January 1905

On 20 December, after a long siege, the Russian forces in Port Arthur surrendered to the Japanese. The humiliation added to the growing discontent and on 3 January 1905 a strike began at the Putilov Iron Works in St Petersburg, which soon involved around 150,000 workers. Economic grievances mixed with political ones and Father Gapon, to whose union many of the strikers belonged, decided to conduct a peaceful march to the Tsar's Winter Palace in the centre of St Petersburg on Sunday 9 January. Gapon wished to present a petition to Nicholas II, demonstrating the workers' loyalty but also requesting reform. Although Gapon was warned of the likelihood for trouble, the march went ahead. While Nicholas chose to spend the weekend at Tsarskoe Selo, his summer palace a little way from the city, 12,000 troops were used to break up the demonstration. The day became known as 'Bloody Sunday' and it sparked an outbreak of rebellion, which spread throughout the Empire.

Fig. 3 *This painting depicts the shootings during the Bloody Sunday March*

The origins of the Russo-Japanese War lay in the Russian 'drive to the East' and the building of the Trans-Siberian Railway to Vladivostock (see Chapter 8). In 1896, the Chinese had allowed an additional line to be constructed south from Vladivostok through northern Manchuria to Harbin. In 1898 a spur line was added to Port Arthur, which was granted to Russia on a 25-year lease. Since the expansionist Japanese had briefly held this peninsula in 1895, they objected and began shelling the Russian naval base of Port Arthur on 2 January 1904.

CROSS-REFERENCE

Plehve's assassination was the work of the Social Revolutionaries. You will read about this group in Chapter 8.

KEY TERM

Duma: an elected governing assembly; a state or national Duma is usually capitalised, while town dumas are lower case

A CLOSER LOOK

Around 150,000 unarmed workers and their families marched on 9 January, singing hymns and carrying icons, patriotic banners, crosses and pictures of former Tsars. They set out from various points around the city, heading for the Winter Palace. At the Narva Gates, Gapon's column was charged and shot at by cavalry, leaving around 40 dead and hundreds wounded. At Troitskaya Square, there was more firing, leaving around 150 dead and wounded. In the Winter Palace Square the marchers met more Cossacks, cavalry and some heavy artillery, but they refused to disperse. When troops with bayonets assumed a shooting position, many fell to their knees and crossed themselves – but the troops still fired.

ACTIVITY

Write a newspaper editorial commenting on the events of Bloody Sunday. Decide first whether this will be for an official 'tsarist' paper or an underground radical publication.

Only after 4 February, following the assassination of Grand Duke Sergei, the Tsar's uncle, did Nicholas finally agree to meet the workers' representatives at Tsarskoe Selo. Even then he inflamed sentiment by suggesting that the marchers had been badly advised and that strikers should return to work. He dismissed the moderate Mirsky and brought in two new officials who were prepared to follow a hard-line policy: Alexander Bulygin as his Minister for Internal Affairs, and Major-General Dmitri Feodorovich Trepov as the new military governor of St Petersburg.

The developments of 1904–05 can be seen in Table 1. The dates in Table 1 are from the Julian calendar, which was used in Russia until 1918 (see the introduction to this book, page xv, for an explanation of this).

Table 1   Events of 1904/05

1904/05 (Julian calendar)	Events in Russo-Japanese War	Events in Russia
December	20th Russia's naval base at Port Arthur surrenders to the Japanese	
January		3rd Strike at the Putilov Iron Works 9th Bloody Sunday
February	9th Battle of Mukden begins (ends 25 March, by which time the Russian army is defeated and 90,000 troops are killed)	4th Assassination of the Grand Duke Sergei Aleksandrovich, the Tsar's uncle, killed by a Socialist Revolutionary bomb 18th Nicholas reaffirms his faith in autocratic rule but also promises an elected consultative assembly; he asks Bulygin to prepare draft proposals
March		*Zemstvo* liberals meet in Moscow
April		All-Russian Union of Railway Workers is established and everywhere workers begin forming illegal trade unions
May	14th and 15th The Russian Baltic fleet is sunk in the Tsushima Strait by the Japanese forces under Admiral Togo	8/9th 'Union of Unions' is set up: a federation of liberal/left professional unions, demanding full civil and political rights, universal suffrage and nationwide elections to an assembly with full legislative powers; Peasants' congress in Moscow calls for All-Russian Union of Peasants.
June		14th Mutiny on the Battleship *Potëmkin* 2nd Congress of Union of Unions prepares for a General Strike
July		Spread of peasant unrest 24th Bulygin publishes details of his plan for constitutional reform
August	23rd Treaty of Portsmouth ends Russo-Japanese War; Russia concedes territory to Japan including the southern half of the island of Sakhalin (although less than Japan had demanded)	
September		12–15th *Zemstvo* conference rejects Bulygin's draft proposal, known as 'Bulygin's Duma' and demands a Duma elected by universal suffrage 29th Printers' strike sets off wave of strikes in Moscow

The mutiny on the Battleship *Potëmkin*

Protest on the *Potëmkin* – one of the Russian Black Sea ships – began over a mouldy meat ration and led to a full-scale mutiny in which seven officers were killed. The sailors hoisted the red revolutionary flag and sailed to Odessa, where they placed a dead sailor's body at the bottom of the 'Potëmkin steps' between the city and the harbour. When the townsfolk arrived to pay respects and show solidarity with the sailors, troops fired on them. Many jumped into the sea and more than 2000 were killed and around 3000 were wounded.

Fig. 4 *Battleship Potëmkin*

The sinking of the Baltic fleet

On 2 October 1904, the government ordered the Baltic fleet, moored off Finland, to sail via Africa and the Indian Ocean to Manchuria. It reached the Tsushima Strait seven months later, in poor shape. The old ships were, in any case, less manoeuvrable than the Japanese vessels and the Japanese had more modern rangefinders and superior gunners and shells. These soon wrecked the Russian superstructures and fatefully ignited the large quantities of coal stored on the Russian decks. The battle lasted a day during which the entire Russian Baltic fleet was lost at the expense of three Japanese torpedo boats.

AS LEVEL PRACTICE QUESTION

'The political unrest of January–September 1905 was brought about by failures in the Russo-Japanese War'.
Explain why you agree or disagree with this view.

October Manifesto

By October 1905, the Russian Empire seemed to be near to total collapse. There were strikes and demonstrations in all the major cities, peasant uprisings throughout the countryside, and demands for independence from the Poles, Finns, Latvians and other minority groups.

A St Petersburg **Soviet**, inspired by the Union of Unions, and dominated by radical revolutionaries, was set up to direct a **General Strike**, which began in Moscow at the beginning of October 1905. Sergei Witte, the Chairman of the Tsar's Council of Ministers, warned that the country was on the verge of a revolution that would 'sweep away a thousand years of history', while Trepov declared the need for some moderate reform and the Grand Duke Nikolay Nikolayevich Romanov, another of the Tsar's uncles, reputedly threatened to shoot himself unless reforms were instituted.

KEY QUESTION

How important were ideas and ideology?

STUDY TIP

Table 1 should help you to see the correlation between the events of 1905 and the failures in the Russo-Japanese War. However, to provide a balanced answer you will also need to address the other reasons for the political unrest. Some of the reasons will be long-term, so you may need to look back at earlier chapters.

KEY TERM

Soviet: a council of workers

General Strike: a strike that involves all workers so that the country is brought to a standstill

CROSS-REFERENCE

More detail on the radical revolutionaries is provided in Chapter 10.

On 17 October the Tsar finally agreed to sign a decree promising constitutional reform. The Tsar's 'October Manifesto' promised:

- To grant civic freedom (personal rights and freedom of conscience, speech, assembly and union).
- To establish a state Duma so allowing a voice to all classes of the population.
- To give the state Duma the power to approve laws.

The manifesto was greeted with celebrations on the streets of St Petersburg. Crowds sang the French revolutionary anthem, '**La Marseillaise**', and waved red flags. The General Strike was called off although the radicals urged workers to fight on. A radical workers' bulletin read: 'We have been granted a constitution, yet autocracy remains. We have been granted everything, and yet we have been granted nothing.' In some ways their view accorded with that of the Tsar himself. Nicholas had no intention of becoming a '**constitutional monarch**' and few of his ministers had a real commitment to the manifesto promises.

Counter-revolution

Despite the October Manifesto's promise of 'full civil rights,' Trepov ordered troops to 'fire no blanks and spare no bullets' in forcing striking workers back to their factories. Furthermore, in the final months of 1905, the Jews, whom the right wing associated with 'socialists and revolutionaries', suffered in terrible pogroms while gangs were sent to round up and flog the peasants in a bid to restore order.

On 3 December, the headquarters of the St Petersburg Soviet was surrounded and its leaders arrested, tried and subsequently exiled to Siberia. This weakened the revolutionary movement in the capital and gradually the authorities regained control. However, there was still a further month of street warfare in Moscow and troops and heavy artillery from St Petersburg had to be dispatched to restore order. There were outbreaks of trouble in the countryside for a further two years.

The major events of October–December 1905 are detailed in Table 2.

KEY TERM

La Marseillaise: a song (that became the National Anthem) sung by the revolutionary movement in France which forced the execution of the French King, Louis XVI

Constitutional monarch: a monarch who rules in conjunction with an elected assembly and whose powers are limited by that assembly

CROSS-REFERENCE

One of the leaders of the St Petersburg Soviet who was arrested was its chairman, Trotsky. More details on Trotsky can be found in Chapter 10.

Table 2 Events of October–December 1905

October	6th Railway strike begins
	10th Moscow railways are brought to a halt; General Strike in the city
	12th General Strike in St Petersburg; Liberal Kadet party is established by the Union of Unions and *zemstva* groups
	13th St Petersburg Soviet is set up to direct strikes
	17th October Manifesto is issued pledging a constitution, extended franchise and civil liberties; Witte becomes Prime Minister and issues an amnesty for political prisoners; the General Strike in St Petersburg is called off
	18th Demonstrations for and against the October Manifesto – Trotsky publicly denounces it – right wing violence is led by the Black Hundreds and strikers begin to return to work; Pobedonostsev is dismissed but the reactionary Durnovo replaces Bulygin as Minister for Internal Affairs
	Military mutinies continue
November	3rd Peasants' redemption payments are halved amidst heightened rural unrest
	4th–7th Second General Strike in St Petersburg ends and demand for an eight-hour day is abandoned
	8th Lenin arrives in St Petersburg
	6th–12th Second Congress of Peasants' Union demands nationalisation of land
	14th Peasant union leaders are arrested
	14th Press censorship ends
	26th Head of St Petersburg Soviet is arrested and Trotsky takes over
December	3rd Government arrests 250 members of the St Petersburg Soviet, including Trotsky
	7th General Strike in Moscow paralyses the city
	11th New electoral law grants wide, but indirect male suffrage; ruthless suppression of rural unrest using the army begins
	16th Durnovo orders mass dismissal of all 'politically unreliable' local government employees; full-scale artillery barrage of working-class district (Presnya) of Moscow by government
	19th Last remnants of Moscow revolt are crushed

The era of the Dumas

The new constitution

Over the following months, a new constitutional arrangement was drawn up, as shown in Figure 5.

Lower Chamber (The State Duma)

- Lower Chamber – The State Duma – members elected under a system of **indirect voting** by estates – heavily weighted in favour of the nobility and peasants (who were assumed to be the crown's natural allies).
- Deputies were to be elected for a five-year term.

Upper Chamber (The State Council)

- Upper Chamber – The State Council – half elected by zemstva, half appointed by the Tsar – noble representatives from the major social, religious, educational and financial institutions.

The two houses had equal legislative power and all legislation also had to receive the approval of the Tsar. Any one of the three bodies could veto legislation.

Government (Council of Ministers under the Prime Minister)

- The government (Council of Ministers under the Prime Minister) was to be appointed exclusively by the Tsar. The government was responsible to the Crown, not the Duma.

Fig. 5 *The new Russian constitution*

The Fundamental Laws

Five days before the first Duma met, Nicholas issued a series of Fundamental Laws (on 23 April 1906) reasserting his autocratic power and stating in Article 4, 'It is ordained by God himself that the Tsar's authority should be submitted to, not only out of fear but out of a genuine sense of duty.'

The Tsar also claimed the right:

- to veto legislation
- to rule by decree in an emergency or when the Duma was not in session
- to appoint and dismiss government ministers
- to dissolve the Duma as he wished

- to command Russia's land and sea forces
- to declare war, conclude peace and negotiate treaties with foreign states and control all foreign relations
- to control military and household expenditure
- to overturn verdicts and sentences given in a court of law
- to control the Orthodox Church.

Political groupings

There were to be four Dumas between 1905 and 1917. The main political parties that contested the elections (in addition to the independent candidates and fringe groupings) are shown in Table 3.

Table 3 The main political parties

Party	Details
Social Democratic Workers' Party (SD) – divided between the Bolsheviks and Mensheviks	Founded 1898. Committed to Marxism. Split in 1903, into: Bolsheviks: Led by Vladimir Lenin. Believed in discipline, centralisation, organisation, and the role of the proletariat under party guidance. From 1905 favoured a peasant/proletariat alliance. Mensheviks: Led by Julius Martov. Believed in cooperation with bourgeoisie/liberals rather than peasantry and the use of legal channels of opposition.
Socialist Revolutionaries (SR)	Founded in 1899; led by Viktor Chernov. Favoured populist ideas of redistribution of land and nationalisation. Left of party favoured terrorism to achieve aims.
Trudoviks (Labour group)	Non-revolutionary breakaway from SR party of moderate liberal views but with no formal programme. Favoured nationalisation of non-peasant land, democratic representation, a minimum wage and an eight-hour working day. Supported by peasants and intelligentsia.
Kadets (Constitutional Democrats)	Led by Pavel Milyukov (1859–1943), a central liberal party which favoured a constitutional monarchy with parliamentary government; full civil rights; compulsory redistribution of large private estates with compensation and legal settlement of workers' disputes.
Octobrists (Union of 17 October)	Leaders included Aleksandr Guchkov (1862–1936). A moderate conservative party that accepted the October Manifesto and opposed further concessions to workers or peasants. Supported by wealthy landowners and industrialists.
Progressives	A loose grouping of businessmen who favoured moderate reform.
Rightists – including the Union of the Russian People	Leaders included Vladimir Purishkevich (1870–1920). The Union of Russian People was extremely right wing, favouring monarchism, chauvanism, Orthodoxy, **Pan-Slavism** and anti-Semitism. Promoted violent attacks on the left wing and pogroms through its street-fighting gangs, the 'Black Hundreds'. Other rightists shared conservative views but were less extreme.
Nationalist and religious groupings	Ukraininans, Polish, Georgians, Muslims – all seeking rights and greater independence.

The results of elections to the four Dumas were as shown in Table 4.

Table 4 Duma election results, 1906–17

Party	1st Duma 1906	2nd Duma 1907	3rd Duma 1907–12	4th Duma 1912–17
SD (Menshevik)	18	47		
SD (Bolshevik)			19	15
SR		37		
Trudoviks	136	104	13	10
Kadets	182	91	54	53

Party	1st Duma 1906	2nd Duma 1907	3rd Duma 1907–12	4th Duma 1912–17
Octobrists	17	42	154	95
Progressives	27	28	28	41
Rightists	8	10	147	154
National and religious groupings	60	93	26	22
Others		50		42

The four Dumas

The First Duma ('Duma of National Hopes') May–July 1906

The First Duma was boycotted by the Bolsheviks, SRs and the extreme right wing Union of the Russian People. It was therefore overwhelmingly radical-liberal in composition with a third of the new deputies coming from the peasantry. It was strongly critical of the Tsar and his ministers and this brought about Witte's resignation. He was replaced by **Ivan Goremykin**, an old-fashioned conservative.

ACTIVITY

Before reading further, study the results in Table 4. What changes can you observe in the make up of these four Dumas?

Fig. 6 *The Duma opened among great expectations in April 1906*

Ivan Goremykin (1839–1917) was a lawyer with strongly conservative political views. He had served as Minister for Internal Affairs between 1895 and 1899, before becoming Prime Minister in 1906. He was soon forced to resign in July 1906, after disagreements with the First Duma, and was replaced by Pyotr Stolypin. Goremykin was a close ally of Grigorii Rasputin and again became Prime Minister in 1914. He retired in February 1916 but was recognised as an ex-tsarist and murdered by mobs in December 1917.

Pyotr Stolypin (1862–1911) was the governor of Saratov province when the Commission of Agriculture was set up in 1902, following an outbreak of rural violence. He quickly established himself as an influential figure and was thus appointed Minister for Internal Affairs in July 1906; a position he held until 1911, when he was assassinated. He muzzled the Dumas, instituted a new court system, brought in health and educational measures, and carried through a major programme of land reform. It has been suggested that he was responsible for staving off the disaster threatening the Russian monarchy.

Stolypin's agrarian reforms are outlined in Chapter 8, pages 80–83.

The Duma passed an 'address to the throne' in which it requested a political amnesty, the abolition of the State Council, the transfer of ministerial responsibility to the Duma, the compulsory seizure of the lands of the gentry without compensation, universal and direct male suffrage, the abandonment of the emergency laws, the abolition of the death penalty, and a reform of the civil service. Nicholas ordered Goremykin to inform the Duma that their demands were 'totally inadmissible', whereupon, the Duma passed a vote of 'no confidence' in the government and demanded the resignation of the Tsar's ministers. Ten weeks later, the Duma was dissolved and Goremykin was replaced as Prime Minister by **Pyotr Stolypin**, who had an even stronger 'hard line' reputation.

Two hundred delegates travelled to the Finnish town of Vyborg and issued an appeal to citizens to refuse to pay taxes or do military service in protest against the heavy-handed action. However, the authorities stepped in, imprisoned the leaders and disenfranchised those who signed the appeal.

The Second Duma ('Duma of National Anger') February–June 1907

Stolypin's government tried to influence the elections to the next Duma but the number of the more extreme left wing increased enormously because the Bolsheviks, Mensheviks and SRs decided to participate. The Second Duma was therefore even more oppositional than its predecessor. Stolypin struggled to find any support for the agrarian reform programme he had drawn up and resorted to passing legislation under the Tsar's emergency powers while the Duma was not in session. When the Duma refused to ratify these, he spread a story about a plot to assassinate the Tsar and dissolved the Duma, arresting and exiling the more radical delegates. He introduced an (illegal) emergency law to alter the franchise. The weight of the peasants, workers and national minorities was drastically reduced and the representation of the gentry increased.

The Third Duma ('Duma of Lords and Lackeys') November 1907–June 1912

This produced a more submissive Duma which agreed 2200 of approximately 2500 government proposals. However, it is a sign of how unpopular the tsarist regime had become that even this Duma proved confrontational. There were disputes over naval staff, Stolypin's proposals to extend primary education, and his local government reform. In 1911, the Duma had to be suspended twice, while the government forced through legislation under emergency provisions. Although the Duma ran its course, by 1912 it was clear that the Duma system was not working.

The Fourth Duma November 1912–17

This was a relatively docile body and the new Prime Minister, Count Vladimir Nikolaevich Kokovtsov, who replaced Stolypin after his assassination in 1911 and remained in this post until 1914, proclaimed, 'Thank God we still have no parliament.' He simply ignored the Duma and its influence declined. It was too divided to fight back, and in any case, the workers again seized the initiative with a revival of direct action and strike activity in the years before the outbreak of war.

Fig. 7 *'Do I smell something burning?': this cartoon from 1906 shows Tsar Nicholas II on his throne, confronted by the fumes of 'discontent' from the Duma (right), and 'hate' from anarchists (left)*

EXTRACT 2

A tragic drama it certainly was; a revolution it was not. After 1905 there was no real devolution of political power, which still rested in the hands of an irresolute Emperor and his appointed ministers. There was no radical redistribution of property and no realignment of the hierarchical class structure of society. The principles of Orthodoxy, autocracy and nationalism still provided the regime with its ideological bedrock. The traditional institutions of the State — bureaucracy, Church, military and police — continued to function unaltered. And the Romanov Empire remained — bruised but unbroken.

Adapted from Alan Wood, *The Russian Revolution*, 1993

ACTIVITY

Evaluating historical extracts

In the light of what Wood has written in Extract 2, would you agree or disagree that the events of 1905 deserve to be called a 'revolution'? Explain your answer.

Political developments by 1914

In the following years it seemed as though the autocracy had largely recovered from the events of 1905. Stolypin had helped restore order in the countryside. In August 1906, he established court martials led by senior military officers to deal with crimes deemed to be political in intent. In these courts, all cases had to be concluded within two days and the accused was not allowed a defence counsel, while death sentences were carried out within 24 hours. Over 3000 people were convicted and executed by this court system between 1906 and 1909.

However, Stolypin combined this intolerance and ruthlessness with a belief in a radical reform of agriculture as the best strategy for resisting revolutionary demands. By 1914, the agrarian situation was improving, and with the Dumas weakened to the point of meaninglessness, the future looked brighter for the traditional governing classes. The revolutionary groups which had led the

CROSS-REFERENCE

The improvements in agriculture are described in Chapter 8, pages 80–83.

CROSS-REFERENCE

Pan-Slavism is explained in chapter 11, page 102.

More detail on the reappearance of labour troubles is provided in Chapter 9, page 86.

KEY PROFILE

Grigorii Rasputin (1869–1916) was a peasant from western Siberia who had spent three months in a monastery but never took vows. He joined a mystical sect (the Khlysty) and had wandered through Russia, living off charity and displaying a talent for faith healing, with his brilliant penetrating eyes, which seemed to exert a hypnotic power. He enjoyed a dissolute private life – accepting bribes, gifts and sexual favours – and drank heavily. His influence at court led to his murder in 1916.

A CLOSER LOOK

Tsarevich Aleksei and haemophilia

Nicholas and Alexandra had borne five children – the grand duchesses Olga, Tatyana, Mariya and Anastasia, and the eldest son and heir, or *tsarevich*, Aleksei. Aleksei, who had been born in 1904, suffered from the disease of haemophilia, whereby the blood fails to clot and even a small knock causes internal bleeding, bringing swellings and crippled joints. It is an incurable, hereditary disease, transmitted by his mother from his great-grandmother, Queen Victoria.

CROSS-REFERENCE

The economic policies of Witte and Stolypin are discussed in Chapters 6 and 7.

opposition were much weakened, partly because of police activity, and partly because of their own internal quarrels. The revival of Pan-Slavism and a new focus for Russia's Imperial ambitions in the Balkans also offered opportunities for a revival of patriotism which might deflect public attention from the troubles at home.

Nevertheless, none of the issues that had sparked the 1905 troubles had been fully resolved and from 1912, labour troubles resurfaced once again. The court simply turned its back and seemed to believe that all could continue as it always had. The only party with which Nicholas showed any sympathy was the Union of the Russian People, which reinforced his mystical belief in the unassailable bond that existed between himself and his people.

The court's distance from reality was, perhaps, epitomised by the rise of the peasant-born **Grigorii Rasputin**, a self-styled clairvoyant and 'faith-healer'. Rasputin's nickname came from the Russian word for dissolute – *rasputnyi*. By the time Rasputin drifted to St Petersburg in 1903, he was claiming special spiritual powers and he found a receptive audience at a time when an interest in spiritualism, astrology and the occult was strong among those of high society who preferred to turn their backs on the political problems.

When Alexandra discovered that Rasputin appeared to be able to lessen the pain endured by her haemophiliac son, **Aleksei**, she was persuaded that he was indeed a 'man of God' sent in answer to her prayers.

Nicholas' failure to take action, despite Rasputin's obvious misdeeds and the damage caused to the royal family, damaged the reputation of the Tsar with those very people whom he relied upon to prop up the monarchy – politicans inside and outside the court, civil servants, Orthodox bishops and army officers. The Rasputin scandal was probably more a symptom than a cause of the position the tsarist autocracy found itself in by 1914, but it certainly showed that whatever the 1905 Revolution had achieved, it had failed to alter the Tsar's outlook.

Summary

As a result of the events of Bloody Sunday, it would be fair to say that the tsarist regime had, in some respects, 'modernised' along Western lines by 1914. The introduction of the Dumas, together with the economic policies of Witte and Stolypin, all marked major advances. However, Nicholas II had never fully appreciated the social and political consequences of economic modernisation. While he wanted Russia to be a twentieth century power that could compete with the West, he himself disliked Western civilisation and preferred to look back to the old Muscovite traditions. His autocracy was reactionary, oppressive and perhaps worse still, inefficient. While the people of Russia became more more urban, more educated and more politicised, he tried to maintain the seventeenth century autocracy of the dynasty's founder, Mikhail Romanov.

EXTRACT 3

Late Imperial Russia was a magnificent beast. Its obvious defects were offset by a seemingly inexhaustible store of power and energy. It had been identified long since as the only power capable, in the future, of challenging the USA. It possessed the largest consolidated state territory on the globe, the largest population in Europe, and the world's largest army. In European eyes, much of Russia's backwardness was masked by the glittering court of the Tsar and the stream of Russian aristocrats, merchants, artists and professors who were thoroughly integrated into every aspect of European life. Politically, Russia was thought to be making serious liberal progress after 1905; the problem of the nationalities was largely submerged. All Russia needed to realise its enormous potential was an indefinite prolongation of the European peace.

Adapted from Norman Davies, *Europe: A History,* 1996

EXTRACT 4

The growth of liberalism and **capitalism** in late Imperial Russia simply added one more major dimension to the problems facing the country. They made the problems more, not less acute. In the first place the Dumas were arenas for conflict; they were not centres of reconciliation. Secondly, they brought a new round of reaction from traditionalists who resented the changes and began to fear the autocracy was going too far. Even some conservatives saw tsarism as an obstacle to progress. No one at the time seriously believed the autocracy was liberalising. The Tsar and his immediate entourage were happier trying to reimpose traditional authority than they were in experimenting with reforms. Rather than converting to liberalism, they showed signs of moving further towards military dictatorship based on authoritarianism, Russian nationalism and anti-Semitism.

Adapted from Christopher Read, *From Tsar to Soviets,* 1996

KEY TERM

Capitalism: private enterprise, which includes making money out of a 'capital' investment (for example, selling surplus agricultural produce for a profit or running a private industry or business)

AS LEVEL PRACTICE QUESTION

With reference to Extracts 3 and 4 and your understanding of the historical context, which of these two extracts provides the more convincing interpretation of the state of Russia by 1914?

ACTIVITY

Evaluating historical extracts

In the light of what you have read in this chapter, prepare your own 'character profile' of Nicholas II. Does your evidence agree with Figes' arguments in Extract 1, or would you challenge his view?

A LEVEL PRACTICE QUESTION

To what extent did Nicholas II uphold his pledge to 'maintain the principle of autocracy' in the years 1894 to 1914?

STUDY TIP

You should consider the ways in which each extract is both convincing and unconvincing by applying your own knowledge to support or challenge the points made by each author. Try to provide an overall conclusion in which you justify your decision as to which is the most convincing.

STUDY TIP

Clearly, autocracy was not as strong in 1914 as in 1894 and it is often a good idea to present a 'before and after' picture in the introduction to an essay of this type. In your answer, you should be able to provide a variety of examples of change – both in theory and in practice. However you will need to balance these with examples of continuity – particularly the continuity of tsarist behaviour and actions. Don't ignore Nicholas' reference to 'the principle'. Even if the autocracy had been weakened, was 'the principle of autocracy' maintained?

The economic development of Russia to 1914

KEY QUESTION

As you read this chapter, consider the following Key Question:
How and with what results did the economy develop and change?

ACTIVITY

Evaluating historical extracts

Identify the arguments put forward by Falkus in Extract 1. As you read this chapter, find evidence that supports or challenges them.

CROSS-REFERENCE

Sergei Witte is introduced, with a key profile, in Chapter 6 page 52.

Ivan Vyshnegradsky and his economic policies in the 1880s are discussed in Chapter 6, page 52.

KEY TERM

Pud: a Russian measure of weight

EXTRACT 1

It must not be thought that tsarist Russia was a country well-endowed with natural resources. The huge raw-material base of Soviet industrial power does not indicate the resources available to the Tsars. Inadequate and expensive communications hampered the exploitation of even known resources. Siberia remained remote and uncolonised until the very end of the century. Indeed, the industrialisation of Russia before 1914 means, for practical purposes, the industrialisation of European Russia, and then certain regions only. The huge variations in the economies, resources and levels of development that existed among different regions make generalisations about the performance of the Russian economy dangerous. Her agriculture, too, was not well-endowed by nature. Even the famed fertile black-soil belt of Great Russia and the steppes of the Ukraine and south-east Volga regions needed the development of communications before they could be fully exploited, while the vagaries of the climate meant frequent harvest failures. However, the striving on the part of the Russian State to emulate the economic strength of its competitors led to significant advance in Russian industrialisation.

Adapted from Malcolm E. Falkus, *The Industrialisation of Russia 1700–1914*, 1972

Industrial transformation

From the mid-1890s, Russia's economy underwent a major transformation, with an annual growth rate of more than eight per cent per annum from 1894 to 1913. This impressive expansion was initially masterminded by Sergei Witte, the Finance Minister between 1892 and 1903, who built on the policies established by Ivan Vyshnegradsky in the 1880s. Russia's economic progress in the eleven years of Witte's tenure was, by every standard, remarkable. Railway trackage virtually doubled, coal output in southern Russia jumped from 183 million **puds** in 1890 to 671 million in 1900, and foreign investment soared, with France supplying a third of all foreign capital, Britain 23 per cent, Germany 20 per cent, Belgium 14 per cent, and the USA 5 per cent.

Table 1 Foreign investment, 1880–1914

Year	Foreign investment (millions of roubles)
1895	280
1900	911
1914	2000

Witte deliberately sought to state-manage industrial growth, seeking capital, technical advisers, managers and skilled workers from overseas. He introduced a new rouble, backed by the value of gold, in January 1897, in order to strengthen the currency and encourage foreign confidence and investment. Although foreign investment declined proportionately in the early twentieth century, as Russian businessmen accumulated sufficient wealth to expand their enterprises and found new ones, state-involvement remained an essential feature of economic growth throughout the period to 1914. The capital was used to fund public works, develop Russia's infrastructure – railways, telegraph lines and electrical plants – as well as develop mines, oilfields and forests for timber.

By the early twentieth century the State controlled 70 per cent of Russia's railways and held extensive holdings in the growing 'heavy industrial plant'. By the turn of the century, the State was buying almost two thirds of all Russia's metallurgical production and a further injection of money was found after 1905, to make good the losses of the Russo-Japanese War and re-equip the army. Indeed, in the years 1903 to 1913, the government received more than 25 per cent of its income from its industrial investments.

The economic historian, Alexander Gerschenkron dubbed the late 1890s 'the great spurt' as the industrial economy progressed more in one decade than it had in the previous century. This growth was to continue until 1914 and was most marked in the railways and heavy industry.

CROSS-REFERENCE

The Russo-Japanese War is outlined in Chapter 7, pages 62–63.

ACTIVITY

Look back at Chapter 6, pages 50–55, and make a chart like the one below that shows developments across the period 1855–1914.

	Key developments	
	1855–1894	1894–1914
Railways		
Heavy industry		
Agriculture		

Railways

Fig. 1   *The first steam train in Russia, on the railway between St Petersburg and Pavlovsk*

The State continued to buy out the smaller private railway companies, extending lines, so that by 1905, Russia had 59,616 kilometres of railways, 66 per cent state-owned. Although this amount was still limited in comparison with the size of the country, nevertheless the growth rate was impressive. The railways helped open up the Russian interior and allowed more extensive exploitation of Russia's raw materials. They also linked grain-growing areas to the Black Sea ports, so reinforcing the export drive.

The building of the railway lines was itself a stimulus to the development of the iron and coal industries and permitted the development of new industries along the length of the expanding rail network. Transport costs fell, bringing down the price of goods, while the government made made money from freight charges and passenger fares.

From 1908–13, the rate of railway building somewhat slowed. By 1913 Russia had the second largest railway network in the world, with 62,200 kilometres, although this fell well short of the USA's 411,000 kilometres.

The most acclaimed development was the impressive construction of the **Trans-Siberian Railway** line, which crossed Russia from west to east. Its building provided a huge industrial stimulus while the psychological boost it provided, both at home and abroad, was perhaps even greater.

A CLOSER LOOK

The Trans-Siberian Railway

Between 1891 and 1902 (with additions to 1914), at Witte's instigation, a railway was constructed, linking central European Russia and Moscow with the Pacific Ocean. It ran to Vladivostok through an arrangement with the Chinese Eastern Railway in Manchuria – a distance of 7000 kilometres. It brought economic benefits – both through its construction and by opening up western Siberia for emigration and farming. It also had strategic benefits, but it promised more than it delivered.

Heavy industry

In the early stages of industrial growth, the lighter industries, particularly textiles, had led the way. However, Witte believed that, by concentrating production in key areas and by developing large factory units of over 1000 or so workers, big increases in heavy goods production could be achieved and this set the pattern for industrial development to 1914.

The main areas of industrial development were around St Petersburg and the Baltic coast (4); Moscow (1); the provinces of Vladimir, Nizhny Novgorod and the Urals to the east (2); the Donbas (Donets Basin) and Krivoi Rog ironfields of southeastern Ukraine (6); the Baku coalfields on the Caspian Sea (5); and in Poland (3). This is illustrated in Figure 2.

The Donbas region, an area of 23,300 square kilometres, for example, was supplying 87 per cent of all Russian coal by 1913, and combined with the rich ironfields of the Krivoi Rog, produced 74 per cent of all Russian pig iron by 1913. By 1914, Russia was the world's fourth largest producer of coal, pig iron and steel.

The Caspian Sea port of Baku also grew tremendously. Russian oil production trebled from 153 million *puds* to almost 570 million between 1885 and 1913, and Russia became not only internally self sufficient, but also able to compete with the USA on the international market. Russia took second place in world oil production (after Texas, USA), while the country ranked fourth in gold mining.

Moscow overtook St Petersburg as an industrial centre, because of its position as the hub of the entire rail network and the main link between Europe and the East. However, St Petersburg grew too, particularly in the engineering sector, with the expansion of the **Putilov Iron Works**.

A CLOSER LOOK

The Putilov Iron Works

Nikolai Putilov, a retired naval ministry official, purchased a former state ironworks in 1867 to develop a railway factory. By 1885, the company provided nearly a quarter of all state orders for locomotives, wagons and rails. Under Putilov's descendants, the company specialised in machinery, artillery and products made of high quality steel and between 1891 and 1894, the workforce grew by two thousand. By 1903 the firm devoted itself to armaments production, supporting Russia through the First World War.

Table 2 Factories and factory workers, 1887–1908

Year	Number of factories	Number of factory workers
1887	30,888	1.3 million
1908	39,856	2.6 million

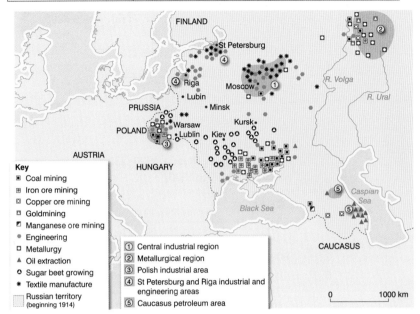

Fig. 2 *Key areas of industrial development*

Table 3 shows the impressive growth in heavy industry.

Table 3 Industrial production (millions of metric tons)

	1890	1900	1910
Coal	5.9	16.1	25.4
Pig iron	0.89	2.66	3.0
Crude oil	3.9	10.2	12.1

Fuelled by a growing internal demand there was also a growth in light industry and textiles, which still accounted for 40 per cent of the total industrial output in 1910. Overall, between 1908 and 1913, Russia experienced an impressive industrial growth rate of 8.5 per cent per year.

The strides made seem impressive and contemporaries certainly thought so (although the relentless drive vastly increased the demands on the State budget). By 1914, Russia was the world's fifth largest industrial power (after the UK, the USA, France and Germany). One of the reasons the German generals urged war against Russia in 1914 was because they feared that delaying war any longer would allow Russian industrialisation to reach a point whereby Russia would outstrip the massive German economy.

How strong was the tsarist industrial economy in 1914?

In order to answer this question, first study the statistics in Figure 3 on pages 78–79.

(i) Industrial development, 1908–14

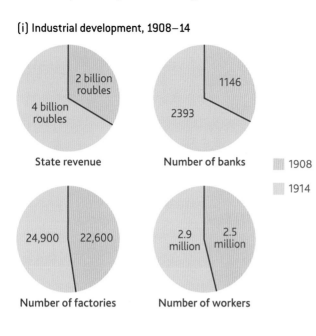

State revenue

Number of banks

Number of factories

Number of workers

1908
1914

(ii) Growth of Russian railways, 1900–13 (in kilometres)

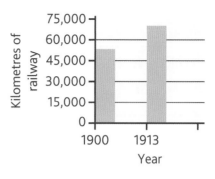

(iii) Russian economy, 1900–13 (annual production in millions of tons)

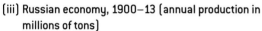

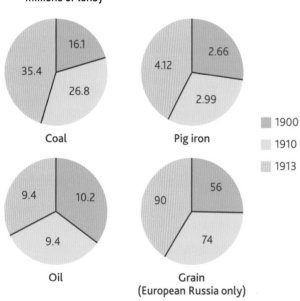

Coal

Pig iron

Oil

Grain (European Russia only)

1900
1910
1913

(iv) Industrial output in Russia, 1900–13 (base unit of 100 in 1900)

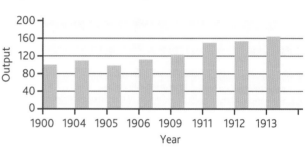

(v) Russian balance of trade, 1891–1920 (in millions of roubles)

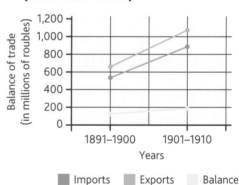

Imports   Exports   Balance

(vi) Population of Russia, 1897–1913

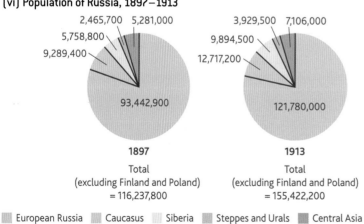

1897
Total
(excluding Finland and Poland)
= 116,237,800

1913
Total
(excluding Finland and Poland)
= 155,422,200

(vii) Growth of population in Russia's two main cities, 1900–14

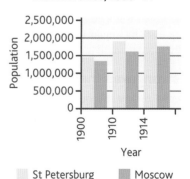

European Russia   Caucasus   Siberia   Steppes and Urals   Central Asia

St Petersburg   Moscow

(viii) Comparative growth in national income, 1894–1913

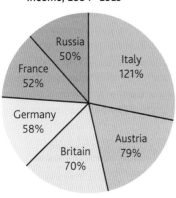

(ix) Foreign trade in 1913 (in £ millions)

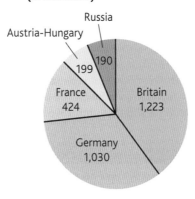

Fig. 3 *The tsarist industrial economy by 1914*

ACTIVITY

Analysis

In groups, copy the chart below. Beneath each heading fill in as much evidence as you can find from Tables 1–3 and the various figures in this chapter that supports of the claim.

Russia had a strong economy in 1914	Russia had a weak economy in 1914

ACTIVITY

Later Marxist Russian historians suggested that Russia had developed a strong industrial economy by 1914, based on the exploitation of the workers. Discuss with a partner, and with reference to what you learned about Marxism in Chapter 5, explain to each other why they made the claim and what truth you feel there may be in this.

EXTRACT 2

In 1914, Russia was the least developed European power, but a European power nonetheless. She was capable of overwhelming militarily and competing economically with a partly-developed European state such as Austria-Hungary. But her development was exceedingly uneven both industrially and geographically. Her modern industry was very modern indeed, with a marked tendency to large well-equipped factories using the most modern up-to-date Western models. These were principally in the areas of St Petersburg and Moscow, in Russian Poland and in the Ukraine. The main metallurgical centre was now in the south using Donets Basin coal. Most of the rest of the country had very little industry other than handicrafts. Apart from the oil of Baku, the southern and eastern territories were particularly primitive. About 67 per cent of those engaged in industry worked in small-scale domestic enterprises and most industrial equipment came from abroad.

Adapted from Alexander Nove, *An Economic History of the USSR*, 1972

 PRACTICE QUESTION

Evaluating historical extracts

Using your understanding of the historical context, assess how convincing the arguments in Extracts 1 and 2 are, in relation to the growth of the Russian economy by 1914.

STUDY TIP

Use your contextual knowledge, as developed in this chapter, to both support and question the arguments conveyed in the extracts. Look at each in turn, then give a brief summary conclusion.

Developments in agriculture

KEY QUESTION

How important was the role of individuals?

CROSS-REFERENCE

Stolypin's political work is discussed in Chapter 7, pages 71–72. His key profile is on page 70.

Although the rural economy provided a livelihood for 80–90 per cent of the Russian population, it was largely ignored or sacrificed in the interests of industrialisation until 1906, when Pyotr Stolypin was appointed Minister of Internal Affairs.

Before 1906, most farming had remained small-scale, in the hands of former serfs and state peasants, tied to their local *mir* by redemption dues, and heavily taxed and exploited by the State. Although the Russian population continued to grow, the amount of land available to farm did not, and the subdivision of estates caused the average holding to fall from 35 acres in 1877 to 28 by 1905. Although there was a government initiative from 1896 to sponsor emigration to new agricultural settlements in Siberia, which had been opened up by the Trans-Siberian Railway, this proved insufficient to alleviate the pressure of a growing population on resources.

Traditional agricultural practices continued, for the most part, and were perpetuated by the *mirs*. The *solcha* or wooden plough was still widely used and medieval rotation systems, which wastefully left fallow land each year, were practised. A lack of husbandry also deprived the soil of manure so that the grain output from American farms was on average one and a half times that of Russian farms, for the same amount of land, while that from the British farmland was four times as great.

Nevertheless, some peasants had managed to improve themselves since the Emancipation Edict by buying up land and farming more efficiently, and Stolypin sought to produce more of these *kulaks*, whom he described as the 'sturdy and strong'. His purpose in this was two-fold: he aimed both to win their loyalty to tsardom and to develop the economy by improving agriculture, and creating an internal market for the products of industry.

Stolypin's land reforms

Stolypin wanted the peasants to become the permanent owners of their land. He intended that each peasant's land should be held in one piece, rather than as a collection of scattered strips around the village, and that each peasant owner should be able to develop it as he wished and without interference by the *mir*. This demanded a complete transformation of the communal pattern of Russian rural life.

His programme of agricultural reform began in 1903, when the *mir's* responsibility to pay taxes on behalf of all the peasants in the village was removed. However, it was not until after the unrest and violence of 1905 and Stolypin's promotion that major changes were undertaken. The most important legislation was introduced in 1906, but this was supplemented by further legislation down to 1910.

CROSS-REFERENCE

To review the unrest and violence of 1905, look back to Chapter 7.

Table 4 Legislation for land reform under Stolypin

Legislation	Measure	Comment
September 1906	More State and Crown land is made available for peasants to buy. Government subsidies to encourage migration and settlement in Siberia are increased.	Land Organisation Committee oversees changes.
October 1906	Peasants are granted equal rights in their local administration.	
November 1906	Peasants are given the right to leave the commune. The collective ownership of land by a family is abolished. A peasant can withdraw land from the commune and consolidate the scattered strips into one compact farm. A new Peasants' Land Bank is established to help peasants fund their land ownership.	This makes the land the personal property of an individual (usually the eldest male). Land organisation commissions are set up, containing representatives elected by the peasants, to supervise this procedure. (These reforms become fully operative in 1910 when approved by the Third Duma.)
1 January 1907	Redemption payments are officially abolished – as promised in 1905.	In reality they have long since ceased to be paid in full.
June 1910	All communes which had not redistributed land since 1861 are dissolved.	

Stolypin is said to have claimed that he needed 20 years of peace for his reforms to have an effect. The coming of the war prevented this, but the legislation encouraged land transfers and the development of larger farms, as poorer peasants were encouraged to sell out to the more prosperous ones. The hereditary ownership of land by peasants increased from 20 per cent in 1905 to nearly 50 per cent by 1915. Grain production rose annually from 56 million tons in 1900 to 90 million by 1914. By 1909, Russia was the world's leading cereal exporter.

A run of good harvests – particularly that of 1913 – also played a significant part in increases in production. In addition, Stolypin's encouragement to emigration took 3.5 million peasants away from the over-populated rural districts of the south and west to Siberia, and helped Siberia to develop into a major agricultural region, specialising in dairy and cereals by 1915.

However, changes in the land tenure arrangements took a long time to process and the measures were not entirely successful.
- By 1913, only 1.3 million out of 5 million applications for the consolidation and hereditary tenure of individual farms had been dealt with.
- By 1914, only around ten per cent of land had been transferred from communal to private ownership.

CROSS-REFERENCE

The social conditions that resulted from this rural migration are described in Chapter 9.

- In 1914, 90 per cent of peasant holdings were still in traditional strips, with conservative peasants (partiularly in central Russia) reluctant to give up traditional practice and the security that the *mir* provided for them.
- Landowners were often reluctant to give up land and difficulties of dividing common land brought protracted legal battles. Fifty per cent of the land remained in the hands of the nobility.
- Probably fewer than one per cent achieved *kulak* status. Many of the rest were forced to leave their farms and join the bands of migrant labourers looking for either seasonal farming work or industrial employment.

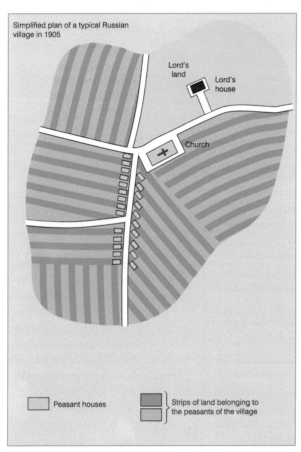

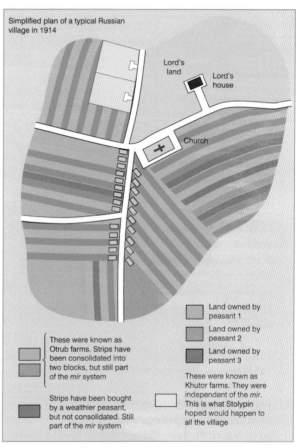

Fig. 4   Changes in farming, 1905–14 (adapted from Richard Radway, *Russia and the USSR*, 1996)

ACTIVITY

Write an obituary for Stolypin following his assassination in 1911. Re-read the section on his political work in Chapter 7 first and try to offer a balanced appraisal of his achievements and failures.

A CLOSER LOOK

Stolypin's reforms – historical debate

Wide variations existed between areas. In some provinces, peasants owned practically all the arable land by 1914, but in others the proportion was much lower. According to Martin McCauley's research into Voronezh province, 37 per cent of the land bought there was purchased by landless peasants, whereas the more prosperous farmers acquired only about four per cent, suggesting that the reforms did benefit poorer peasants in that region. This was not universal, however. The historian Teodor Shanin has argued that there was no clear dividing line between rich and poor peasants, and that a bigger discriminator was family size. Whether Stolypin's policy could have worked if given more time is also subject to differing interpretations. It has been suggested that it not only required fast industrial growth to provide employment for the surplus rural labour, but also a cultural change (desire for self-improvement, more education, and a readiness to think and plan ahead) on the part of the peasantry and that this was lacking before 1914.

 PRACTICE QUESTION

'Russian agriculture changed little in the years 1894 to 1914.'
Explain why you agree or disagree with this view.

ACTIVITY

Summary

Create your own revision chart on the economic development of Russia from 1894 to 1914.

Developments 1894–1914	Industry	Agriculture
Changes which strengthened Russia and its government		
Changes which weakened Russia and its government		
Areas which experienced little or no change		

 PRACTICE QUESTION

'Between 1892 and 1914, the Russian economy was transformed.'
Assess the validity of this view.

STUDY TIP

Since this is a breadth question it is important that you address the years 1894 to 1914 and examine the change and continuity in agriculture in that period, rather than turning this into an essay solely about Stolypin's reforms. You might like to plan the answer by creating two columns: one headed 'change' and the other 'continuity'. This will enable you to offer a balanced appraisal in your essay.

STUDY TIP

You may need to look back at Chapter 6 to answer this question, which is concerned with the degree of change from Witte's appointment in 1892 to the First World War in 1914. 'Transformed' is a forceful word, suggesting a complete change. Rather than simply agreeing or disagreeing with the view, see if you can produce an argument to suggest that the quotation is more valid in some areas than others.

9 Social developments to 1914

LEARNING OBJECTIVES

In this chapter you will learn about:

- developments in working and living conditions in towns
- developments in working and living conditions in the countryside
- social divisions
- cultural changes.

KEY QUESTION

As you read this chapter, consider the following Key Questions:
- How and with what results did the economy develop and change?
- What was the extent of social and cultural change?

EXTRACT 1

The old certainties of Russian society –the dominance of the landed nobility and their explicit control over the peasantry – were destroyed by Emancipation. The rapid growth of factories and the accompanying process of urbanisation which took place down to 1914 also served to unknit rural society. As more people went to live in towns, so they were exposed to new and different influences, shaped by the world of disciplined work. The close ties which migrants maintained with their home villages meant that rural society gradually became exposed to the ideas and values which industrialisation brought. Russian society was fragmenting as traditional relationships broke up. Education meant that the newly literate could absorb information and opinion more easily. Even though change came only slowly to the lives of the 100 million peasants of the Empire, by 1914, the dynamics of Russian society were moving at a pace which the State could no longer regulate. The old social order had irretrievably broken down but a new equilibrium had not yet been reached.

Adapted from Peter Waldron, *The End of Imperial Russia 1855–1917*, 1997

ACTIVITY

Evaluating historical extracts

Read Extract 1 carefully and make a list of (a) the reasons for social change and (b) the consequences of social change, as identified by Waldron. As you read this chapter, try to:

1. Add to your list of reasons for and consequences of social change.
2. Find evidence that supports the views in Extract 1 about social change and its consequences.
3. Find comments and evidence that challenge the views in Extract 1 and suggest that society remained unchanged or was little changed.

Developments in working and living conditions in towns

In Russia's major cities, the arrival of new large factories, in addition to the growing numbers of smaller workshops, swelled the urban population. There were two million factory workers in Russia by 1900, and six million by 1913. Between 1867 and 1917, the Empire's urban population quadrupled from 7 to 28 million, and this was mainly the result of the influx of peasants looking for work in the cities.

Some only settled temporarily, retaining their land and returning to their villages to help out their families for the harvest. Some joined the bands of migrants who might stay in one place for a few years before moving on, while others put down roots and produced children who grew up to think of themselves as urban workers. By 1914, three out of every four people living in St Petersburg were peasants by birth, compared with just one in three, 50 years earlier. What is more, half the city's population had arrived in the previous 20 years. The situation in Moscow was much the same and here an even more 'peasant' atmosphere surrounded the workers' quarters in the city. Livestock roamed the streets and there were numerous outdoor 'peasant' markets, including one on Red Square.

Fig. 1 *Peasants sat on a street in Moscow*

The facilities needed to provide for this growing urban class were grossly inadequate. Workers often found themselves living in barrack–like buildings, owned by the factory owners, and dangerously overcrowded and lacking in adequate sanitation. These workers had to eat in canteens and wash in communal bathhouses. Even those who managed to find 'private' city accommodation fared little better. In St Petersburg at the turn of the century, for example, about 40 per cent of houses had no running water or sewage system. Excrement was simply set in piles in the back yards and collected by wooden carts at night. It is hardly surprising that 30,000 inhabitants died of cholera in 1908–09.

Yet the demand for work and accommodation was such that rents remained high, often taking half a worker's wages. Those who could not afford rents simply lay down in the factory alongside their machines, or lived rough on the streets.

Workers' wages varied tremendously, of course, according to whether they were skilled or unskilled, the occupation followed, and the amount of overtime put in, or, conversely, the amount deducted in fines. Women, who comprised one fifth of the industrial workforce in 1885, but one third by 1914, were among the lowest paid, earning less than half the average industrial wage.

SOURCE 1

According to a female doctor, Kostroma L. Katenina, working for a *zemstvo* in 1913:

One cannot but note the premature decrepitude of the factory woman. A woman of 50 who has worked at the factory 30 or more years, frequently looks ancient. She sees and hears poorly, her head trembles, her shoulders are sharply hunched over. She looks about 70 years old. While in the west, elderly workers have pensions, our women workers, having given decades to the factory so that they are prematurely enfeebled, can expect nothing better than to live out their last days as latrine attendants.

Conditions were, perhaps, at their worst during the industrial depression of 1900–08. However, even when industry began to revive, the wages of industrial workers failed to keep pace with inflation. The average industrial wage increased from just 245 to 264 roubles per month in the years down to 1914, while inflation was running at 40 per cent.

There were some attempts to alleviate the workers' lot, as seen in Table 1.

Table 1   Workers' legislation 1885–1912

Date	Law
1885	Prohibited night-time employment of women and children
1886	Decreed that workers had to be employed according to contracts overseen by factory boards
1892	Employment of children under 12 forbidden and female labour banned in mines
1897	Hours of work reduced to 11 and a half
1903	More efficient system of factory inspection
1912	Sickness and accident insurance for workers

Normal factory working hours were reduced to reach ten hours by 1914, although this did not apply to workshops, which were far more common. Education also spread. There was an 85 per cent rise in primary school provision between 1905 and 1914 and the government promoted the development of technical schools and universities. Investment in education was, however, far less than that in the railways and only 55 per cent of children were in full-time education by 1914. Nevertheless, for some workers, city life offered a new range of opportunities.

EXTRACT 2

The pace of work clearly left little time for leisure, nonetheless, workers did have some time to themselves, much of which was spent in the tavern. The minority who moved away from it attended workers' schools, some of which specialised in Sunday courses to meet their needs; took part in 'social' activities such as dances or out-of-town walks that might involve illicit political discussion; involved themselves in trade union or political activities in the semi-legal conditions of post-1905; attended literary, political or scientific meetings; visited the theatre; or read books borrowed from union or worker-educational libraries. Many workers attended religious services on Sunday, and for some it was a condition of employment.

Adapted from Christopher Read, *From Tsar to Soviets*, 1990

It was easy for towns and cities to become breeding places for political discontent. Political activism was comparatively rare before 1905 – partly because strike activity was illegal and the Secret Police efficient – but also because of the relatively small numbers of workers and their own desperation to get and retain jobs. The strike activity of that year was also followed by a lull, despite the legalisation of trade unions, but from 1912 it escalated again and in 1914 there were 3574 stoppages. The government's only response to such activity was repression. When workers at the **Lena goldfields** in Siberia went on strike for better wages and conditions in 1912, for example, troops were sent in and 270 workers were killed and 250 injured.

CROSS-REFERENCE

You can read more about opposition in Chapter 10.

The Lena goldfields massacre, 1912

The gold miners of the Lena riverbanks in northern Siberia worked long hours for low pay in an inhospitable climate. In 1912, a group of miners went on strike over some inedible horsemeat and the Bolsheviks helped to spread these activities. When their ringleaders were arrested, several thousand miners converged on one mine to present petitions. (They may have been encouraged by the authorities in order to get them together.) As they approached, they were fired on and around 500 were killed. This set off a wave of sympathetic strikes through Siberia and beyond.

Make a two-column table. On one side record the disadvantages of urban life for factory workers, and on the other the benefits. Compare your findings with those of others and, when you have read the next section of this chapter, discuss whether factory workers were better or worse off than their counterparts in the countryside.

Developments in working and living conditions in the countryside

Fig. 2 *Despite Stolypin's reforms there was still widespread rural poverty*

Stolypin's agrarian reforms are discussed in Chapter 8.

Conditions for peasant farmers did not improve substantially. Strip farming persisted on 90 per cent of the land and there was still widespread rural poverty. The gap between richest and poorest sections of the peasantry became wider as the wealthier peasant entrepreneurs or *kulaks* took advantage of the position of the less favoured and, sometimes with the help of loans from the peasant banks, bought out their impoverished neighbours.

In contrast to the upward mobility of the *kulaks*, however, the poorest peasants found life getting harsher. A minority migrated to Siberia, encouraged by government schemes from 1896 to sponsor emigration from the over–populated rural south and west to the new agricultural settlements opened up by the Trans–Siberian Railway. However, only 3.5 million, from a peasant population of nearly 97 million, were able to take advantage of this and the scheme was clearly inadequate to alleviate the pressure of a growing population on resources.

Living standards varied in different parts of the country, with more prosperous commercial farming in the peripheral regions in parts of the Baltic, western Ukraine, the Kuban and northern Caucasus to the south and in western Siberia. The continuation of nobles' landowning and backward farming methods was mainly concentrated in the Russian heartland. Historian Orlando Figes has noted that these were later to become the

Peasant communities

The village commune remained at the heart of peasant life. The proportion of land held by communes fell only from 73 per cent to 60 per cent, even after Stolypin's reforms. Within the commune, peasants supported one another through bad weather and illness, and a peasant could enjoy some community solidarity when faced with an untoward event such as a fire or another personal tragedy. Religion also helped the cohesion of rural society, while festivals and vodka helped punctuate the work cycle.

Evaluating historical extracts

Read Extract 3. According to Figes, why was the commune important to the peasants? Do you agree with Figes that Stolypin made a wrong assessment of the commune? Look back to Chapter 8 and justify your answer.

areas that supported the Bolshevik Revolution from 1917, while the more prosperous areas were centres of counter–revolution. There were other reasons for the differences too. Areas of former state peasants tended to be better off than those of the emancipated privately owned serfs, because they had been granted more land.

The peasants' lot remained a hard one and despite improvements in health care provided through the *zemstva*, a large proportion of the peasantry was turned down as unfit for military service. Mortality rates in Russia were higher than those in any other European country and there were too few doctors for the large rural population. Teachers were also in short supply. Few received much more than the most basic elementary education and in 1914 there was still around 60 per cent illiteracy. With large families, living in their primitive wooden huts, eating a monotonous daily diet, and with few possessions beyond their tools and icons, Russia's land–hungry peasantry remained at the bottom of the social ladder; even though their sense of **community** and their loyalty to Church and Tsar was largely unblemished.

EXTRACT 3

The village commune was an old institution, in many ways quite defunct, but in others still responsive to the basic needs of the peasants, living as they did on the margins of poverty, afraid of taking risks, suspicious of change, and hostile to outsiders. Stolypin assumed the peasants were poor because they had the commune – but the reverse was closer to the truth. The commune existed because the peasants were poor; it served to distribute the burden of their poverty, and as long as they were poor there would be little incentive for them to leave it. For better or worse, the commune's egalitarian customs had come to embody the peasantry's basic notions of social justice and these were the ideals for which they would fight long and hard.

Adapted from Orlando Figes, *A People's Tragedy,* 1996

Social divisions

Fig. 3 *Painting of a ball in Russia by Sapunov, Nikolai Nikolayevich (1880–1912)*

PRACTICE QUESTION

To what extent did standards of living in towns and countryside improve for peasants in the years 1894 to 1917?

Russian society became more complex as economic changes got underway, although the most marked social feature was the continuing division between a small upper stratum [layer] of nobility and the broad mass of peasantry. Huge social and economic inequalities remained.

The nobility

The position of the nobility as a whole had suffered as a result of Emancipation, but some had thrived on the favourable arrangements for land distribution or involvment in industrial enterprises and financial speculation. Others, perhaps serving in government office or with strong military connections, retained much of their former influence and lifestyle.

Around one third of all nobles' land was transferred to townsmen or peasants between 1861 and 1905, and there were certainly nobles who struggled to meet debts, and failed to understand modern money management, investment for the future and the need to adjust living standards accordingly.

However, there was no **redistributive taxation** or attacks on landed wealth to diminish their incomes or substantially harm their traditional ways of life. Indeed Nicholas, like his father, encouraged noble influence and was keen to see their power within the local *zemstva* retained. The nobility were regularly appointed to provincial governorships and vice-governorships and each province and district of the Empire also had its own noble assembly, which met once a year. Indeed, in May 1906, the first meeting of the 'united nobility' took place, which showed nobles determined to retain their property rights and traditional interests in the face of change. The formation of such an organisation reflects the strength and determination of the class. So, while the nobility may have found some adjustments necessary, as a class they retained much of their previous wealth and status.

The middle classes

The traditional legal structure of Russia had been based on four groups – nobles, merchants, clergy and peasantry – but this structure was challenged by the emergence of a small but influential middle stratum that expanded as the pace of economic change quickened. New business and professional men were able to carve out comfortable lives for themselves and their offspring. There was some social mobility as nobles' sons chose to join the business world, or those of peasant stock rose through hard work and enterprise to join the ranks of middle management and, perhaps within a generation, to become factory proprietors.

This group grew as a force as management and professional positions became more in demand in the increasingly complex industrialising society. Within the industrialising regions and in the development of Russia's infrastructure, there were plenty of opportunities for the enterprising. The growth of education and the demand for more administrators also fuelled a growing middle class.

The growing middle classes found their natural home on the councils of the *zemstva*, and in the town and state dumas, where they exerted an influence beyond their size.

STUDY TIP

'Standard of living' is a broad term and it would be advantageous to define it in your introductory paragraph. Remember this refers to both to 'quantity' (i.e. income – in money or food – and what could be bought or obtained) and 'quality' (i.e. living conditions, health, education and pleasures beyond work) of life. It is possible to have a low monetary income but a high quality of life and vice versa. You will need to reflect on the positive as well as the negative side of worker and peasant life in this period.

KEY QUESTION

What was the extent of social and cultural change?

KEY TERM

Redistributive taxation: when richer people are taxed to allow for welfare benefits to be given to the poorer members of society, so 'redistributing' wealth

A CLOSER LOOK

The new industrial society

Russia's industrialising society required specialists and those with professional training, and by 1914 there were growing numbers of 'new positions': managers, statisticians, pharmacists, insurance specialists and civil engineers, as well as over 5000 veterinary surgeons and nearly 4000 agronomists serving the rural community. The number of doctors increased from 17,000 to 28,000 between 1897 and 1914, while the total of graduate teachers doubled between 1906 and 1914, reaching over 20,000. Professional associations, scientific societies and voluntary organisations dominated by professionals, rather than nobility, proliferated and the Association of Industry and Trade was established in 1906 as a political lobbying group.

Workers and peasantry

Population growth and economic development most affected the workers and peasantry. In the countryside, social adjustments were taking place. Although most peasant protest before 1914 was the result of traditional grievances – a failed harvest or unfair land allocation – the slow process of awakening the peasantry from their inertia to political activism was already underway by 1914, although it was to take the exceptional conditions of war to complete the task.

The historian David Moon offers this picture of continuity and change among the peasantry by 1914:

EXTRACT 4

Between 1861 and 1914, the abolition of serfdom and urbanisation forced Russian peasants to adapt to cope with changes. It is inaccurate, however, to speak of processes of change affecting peasants; the peasants themselves shaped the changes. Rather than undermining peasants' ways of life, some changes reinforced peasant customs. Abolition did not fundamentally alter peasant society. It reinforced peasant self-government and reinforced, rather than weakened, peasants' existing legal ties to the land by allowing them to secure control over their land by purchase (redemption). The greater opportunities for wage labour caused industrialisation, which provided experiences that challenged the norms of village life. However, the pace of change was limited, as the numbers that left rural society remained relatively low in comparison with the vast peasant population that remained in the villages.

Adapted from David Moon, *The Russian Peasantry 1600–1930*, 1999

 PRACTICE QUESTION

With reference to Extract 1 and Extract 4, and your understanding of the historical context, which of the two extracts provides the more convincing interpretation of the impact of emancipation and urbanisation on peasant society?

 PRACTICE QUESTION

Using your understanding of the historical context, assess how convincing the arguments in Extracts 1, 2 and 4 are in relation to the extent of social change in the years 1894 to 1914.

In urban areas, former peasants, alienated from their families and their 'roots', gradually lost something of their former identity and began to associate with others who lived and worked in close proximity, sharing grievances. Here they became an easy target for the political agitators and it would not be an exaggeration to say that one of gravest mistakes of the tsarist governments was to fail to respond effectively to the effects of social change in the cities, for it was from the large and discontented urban working class that the impetus to overthrow the regime in 1917 would eventually come.

Cultural changes

Culturally, Russia in 1914 might have appeared little changed. The fundamental **'patriarchal'** structure of Russian society remained untouched with ties of family and household predominating. However, economic and political developments had brought some new opportunities and aspirations for women. Although Alexander III and Nicholas II tried to cut back on women's educational opportunities, these grew from c1900, while increasing numbers of women found greater independence through factory work. In December 1908, the First All-Russian Congress of Women was attended by 1035 delegates in St Petersburg, and it campaigned for a female franchise.

The growth of education also brought change. Government expenditure on primary education grew from 5 million roubles in 1896 to over 82 million by 1914. By 1911, over 6.5 million children between 8 and 11 (44 per cent of that age group) were receiving primary education, although only one third of these were girls, and the spread was uneven with urban areas better provided for than rural ones. There was still 40 per cent illiteracy in 1914, but a basic level of education certainly helped to increase a sense of self-worth among the literate. The number of books and publications proliferated, particularly after 1905 when the popular press boomed. There were 1767 newpapers being published at least weekly by 1914. Reading rooms were also establised and popular literature flourished, in which the portrayal of those who had succeeded in bettering themselves was a common theme.

Secondary and higher education remained elitist, however. Between 1860 and 1914 the number of university students in Russia grew from 5000 to 69,000 (45 per cent of them women). However, although a quarter of students in secondary school in 1911 came from the peasantry, this amounted to only 30,000 individuals.

More serious writers and artists used their art forms to address problems in Russian society during this period. Anton Chekhov, for example, produced a stream of stories and plays from the 1880s until his death in 1904, continuing the realist tradition of Leo Tolstoy and Fyodor Dostoevsky in the 1860s and 1870s. By the early twentieth century the nineteenth-century classics of Russian literature could be obtained in cheap mass-produced editions, and these too were readily sought by the newly literate, as well as the traditional readership of the educated elites.

The relaxation of censorship controls from 1905 produced the 'silver age' of Russian culture, dominated in particular by poets. There were experiments in modernism, for example Igor Stravinsky's music, Serge Diaghilev's ballets, Marc Chagall's pictures and Kazimir Malevich's paintings, which offered new and often 'shocking' challenges to convention and showed that, for all its deficiencies, Russia was culturally as much a part of the 'modern world' as its more advanced economic neighbours.

By 1914, Russian culture had certainly broadened and diversified to encompass a much wider group than the intelligentsia elites, and to some extent it mirrored the many other changes running through Russian society. Nevertheless, some aspects of Russian culture and behaviour seemed to exhibit little change. The year 1913 was the **tercentenary** year of the Romanov dynasty, and Nicholas and Alexandra revelled in the traditional jubilee rituals organised to celebrate the permanency of the Romanovs, encouraging the wearing of traditional Muscovite costumes and Orthodox ceremonies to mark the occasion. Touring his Empire to jubilant and obsequious crowds, Nicholas returned convinced that 'my people love me'. Alexandra added, 'We need merely to show ourselves and at once their hearts are ours.'

CROSS–REFERENCE

For political agitators and their impact, look ahead to the Chapter 10.

KEY TERM

Patriarchal: fatherly, and in this sense, those 'above' looked after the interests of those 'below', as a father would look after his children; in Russia, the male had almost unlimited authority over his family and the head of the household had economic authority for the management of the family's property

CROSS–REFERENCE

Writers, including Tolstoy and Dostoevsky are discussed in Chapter 5, page 42.

ACTIVITY

Choose an art form that interests you and prepare a short class presentation on a Russian writer, poet, artist or musician. Explain how your subject challenged conventional culture and what his/her contribution was to the evolution of Russian culture and society before 1914.

Fig. 4 *The Tsar and his family at the tercentenary celebrations in 1913*

A CLOSER LOOK

The tercentenary celebrations

The Emperor and his family drove through the streets of St Petersburg in open carriages, for the first time since the events of 1905, and attended an elaborate thanksgiving service in Kazan Cathedral. Here, a pair of doves briefly flew from the rafters and hovered over the heads of the Tsar and his son, which was interpreted as a sign of God's blessing on the dynasty. The royal family also undertook a three–month tour of 'old Muscovy' and enjoyed a triumphal entry into Moscow. Nicholas led the way on a white horse, to the adulation of the confetti–throwing crowds who had gathered beneath the Romanov flags that filled the streets. Everywhere the crowds thanked God for their Tsar.

The fundamental bulwarks of autocracy retained their hold on Russian society. The Orthodox Church influenced government and community, and traditions of subservience to authority remained, despite the sporadic outbursts. This traditionalism brought an outpouring of patriotism and support for the Tsar when the decision to go to war was announced in 1914. Soldiers carried icons of Nicholas as they marched to the front and all social groups rallied in defence of the Russian Motherland.

Summary

The years 1894 to 1914 brought social changes in both the towns and the countryside. While it was not always obvious at the time, changes in the position of the middle classes, workers and peasantry in particular were to have political consequences during the war years. Culturally, there was some 'modernist' experimentation, which clashed with an in-built traditionalism. In 1914, Russia was a society of contrasts, but the 'old ways' were soon to be swept aside by the coming of war.

STUDY TIP

Obviously this is a deliberately provocative quotation and it is also deceptively simple. It will need unravelling to answer it well. Dissect what you understand by 'Russian society' and remember that some elements within society may change more than others. While you will want to identify some continuity, you should certainly be able to balance this against changes. You should base your judgement on the degree of both continuity and change across the whole range of 'Russian society'.

 PRACTICE QUESTION

'Russian society changed little in the years 1894 to 1914.'
Assess the validity of this view.

10 Opposition: ideas and ideologies

EXTRACT 1

For at least a decade before the 1905 Revolution, the radicalisation of all sections of Russian society had been taking on more and more extreme forms. The exact number of strikers is unascertainable, but there is no doubt that the general trend was upwards. In the main the government's answer was repression, and the arrest and deportation of strike leaders. In the countryside peasant discontent was aggravated by a series of famines; in 1891–92, 1897, 1898 and 1901. But the difficult character of rural life was evident enough without that. Unmanageable tax arrears, agricultural stagnation, rural over-population, the paralysing effects of communal tenure, all emphasised that the existing order was doomed. A background of rural violence gave birth to more radical Populism. Marxism supported the spread of socialist ideals while, for the first time in Russian history, liberalism began to develop as an independent political force.

Adapted from Lionel Kochan, *The Making of Modern Russia,* 1962

ACTIVITY

Identify the arguments in Extract 1 which help explain why opposition movements increased in the years after 1894. As you read the chapter try to add to your list of factors in the growth of opposition.

LEARNING OBJECTIVES

In this chapter you will learn about:

- the growth of liberal opposition to 1905

- the development of socialism and the emergence of the radical SRs

- the influence of Marxism and the development of the radical SDs

- the extent of opposition between 1905 and 1914.

KEY QUESTION

As you read this chapter, consider the following Key Questions:
- Why did opposition develop and how effective was it?
- How important were ideas and ideology?
- How important was the role of individuals and groups, and how were they affected by developments?

The growth of liberal opposition to 1905

Fig. 1 *Liberal opposition in Russia in 1905*

Liberals had long pressed for changes in the governmental structure of the country. The spread of education, and the emergence of a stronger middle class as a result of industrialisation, added to the numbers favouring more representation and the rule of law. Liberalism was particularly strong in the *zemstva*: their reputation was enhanced by the actions taken in the face of government incompetence during the years of the Great Famine of 1891–92, and their resentments were galvanised by the reduction in *zemstva* powers under Alexander III.

CROSS-REFERENCE

To re-read about the Great Famine of 1891–92, see Chapter 6, page 52.

Prince Georgi Lvov (1861–1925) was a wealthy landowner and liberal Kadet leader who served in the First Duma and became leader of the Russian Union of Zemstva in 1914. He became leader of Zemgor in 1915 and helped to organise the war effort. He favoured decentralised government but was otherwise traditionalist in outlook. He became the first Chairman of the Provincial Government in March 1917 but retired on 4 July, having found it impossible to control the mixture of liberals and socialists that dominated Russia in these months.

CROSS-REFERENCE

The events of 1905 are the subject of Chapter 7.

KEY PROFILE

Pyotr Berngardovich Struve (1870–1944) was a lawyer, economist and philosopher who became interested in Marxism and Populism in the 1890s. By 1900, Struve had become a leader of the moderate wing of Russian Marxists. He was forced into exile in Germany where he produced radical literature, which was smuggled into Russia. In October 1904, he was forced to move operations to Paris, after a raid by the Okhrana. He returned to Russia in October 1905 and became a co-founder of the Kadets, whom he represented in the Second Duma in 1907. He supported the government when the First World War broke out in 1914, and after the Bolshevik Revolution of 1917 joined the Whites.

In 1895, the Tver *Zemstvo* petitioned Nicholas II to set up an advisory body. The Tsar dismissed the request as a 'senseless dream'. This did not, however, deter liberal nobles, like **Prince Lvov**, who continued to demand the creation of an all-class *zemstvo* at district (*volost*) level and a National Assembly. However, when Ivan Shipov tried to set up an 'All-*Zemstvo* Organisation' in 1896, it was immediately banned. This encouraged some of the more radical liberals to establish the Beseda Symposium in 1899 and to meet in secret to discuss matters of liberal interest such as judicial reform and universal education. When, in 1900, the government ordered the dismissal of hundreds of liberals from the elected boards of the *zemstva*, the Beseda Symposium assumed the leadership of the liberal movement, attracting a wide range of support from public figures, town leaders, members of the legal and teaching professions and industrialists.

In 1903, the Union of Liberation (*Soyuz Osvobozhdeniya*) was founded under the inspiration of **Pyotr Struve**. Struve had defected from the Marxist movement, opposing its commitment to violent revolution, and had begun a journal, *Osvobozhdenie* (*Liberation*), published in Germany, to escape censorship. Struve believed that what Russia needed was a period of 'peaceful evolution' in which to adapt to its new industrialising status. He wanted to see a constitutional system put in place through which the urban workers could campaign legally to improve their conditions.

In 1904, the union held a grand meeting to which representatives of the *zemstva* and other professional societies were invited. Members declared their intention to work for the establishment of a constitutional government and arranged a series of about 50 society banquets during the winter of 1904, which were attended by members of the liberal elite.

The liberals, whether moderate campaigners within the *zemstva* or more radical members of the liberal unions, had limited political influence before 1905. Indeed, the liberals were fortunate to escape the closer attention of the police, which was only achieved because the latter were over-worked, coping with the activities of the radical opposition as well as urban and rural unrest. Nevertheless, the liberals contributed to the momentum that was building up within the country for political change and were the main beneficiaries of the revolution in that year when one of their aims was achieved – a representative national body, the state Duma, was established.

The development of socialism and the emergence of the Social Revolutionary Party

Fig. 2 *Revolutionary activity in St Petersberg, in front of the Winter Palace, 1905*

By 1894, the slavophile and populist idea of a 'new Russia', based on the peasants, looked increasingly unlikely. However, ideas of '**agrarian socialism**' were revived after the Great Famine of 1891–92, which highlighted the need to reform the rural economy. Students began to champion a new-style Populism, taking inspiration from the defunct The Peoples' Will and favouring violent protest. Their activities culminated in the assassination of the Minister of Education, **Nikolay Bogolepov**, by a student named Pyotr Karpovich in 1901.

Agrarian socialism: taking estates from landowners and dividing the land between the peasants to be farmed communally

A CLOSER LOOK

The murder of Bogolepov, 1901

Pyotr Karpovich was a student rebel who had twice been expelled from Kazan University. His revenge killing won support from fellow students and as Bogolepov lay dying, several thousand people gathered in front of Kazan Cathedral in Karpovich's support. Although broken up by the police, with 60 injured and around 800 arrests, it provoked demonstrations in Moscow and an attempt on Pobedonostsev's life a month later by another student. On that occasion, the attempt failed.

The same year, the Social Revolutionary Party (SR) was founded as a rallying point for those who wished to appeal to the peasantry through a commitment to 'land socialisation' and decentralised government. Its most influential theorist was the intellectual, **Viktor Chernov** (1873–1952), a law graduate from Moscow and editor of the party journal, *Revolutsionnaya Rossiya* (*Revolutionary Russia*), but it was a fairly loose organisation comprising groups with a wide variety of views. Although the party never held a congress until 1906, its members broadly accepted Marxist teaching but combined this with populist ideas, thus favouring a specifically 'Russian' revolutionary programme.

The SRs put forward the view that the interests of peasants and workers – the so-called 'labouring poor' – were identical, and that they should therefore work together to destroy autocracy and bring about land redistribution. This emphasis on the peasantry and the concept of 'land socialisation' rather than 'land nationalisation' set them apart from the pure Marxists. Not surprisingly, they developed a wide national base, with a large peasant membership, but despite this, 50 per cent of their supporters were from the urban working class.

KEY PROFILE

Viktor Chernov (1873–1952) had been attracted to the populist cause and became engaged in revolutionary activity as a teenager. In 1894 he joined The People's Will and was arrested, spending some time in exile. He travelled to Switzerland in 1899 and was to provide much of the intellectual input into the founding of the Social Revolutionary Party in 1899. He went on to become the leader of the Socialist Revolutionaries in the Second Duma of 1907, and was Minister of Agriculture in the Provisional Government of 1917. After the Bolsheviks came to power, he settled in the USA.

A CLOSER LOOK

The activities of Yevno Azef

Yevno Azef (1869–1918) was a double agent working for the SRs and the Secret Police. He became involved in Marxism and was forced to live in exile in Germany, where he was recruited as an informer by the Okhrana. In 1899 he returned to Russia and became a member of the Social Revolutionary Party. He organised the arrest of the previous leader of its 'combat organisation' and took the position himself, using his influence to betray comrades and mastermind the murder of Plehve. He was exposed as a tsarist spy in 1908 and fled to Germany where he died in 1918.

CROSS-REFERENCE

Marxist teaching and populist ideas are described in Chapter 5.

The tactics of the Social Revolutionary Party were similar to the earlier populist organisation. They tried to stir up discontent in the countryside and strikes in the towns, and to disrupt government by political assassinations. In this they were quite successful, promoting a wave of political terrorism in the early years of the twentieth century. They carried out 2000 political assassinations between 1901 and 1905. These included the assassinations of two Ministers of Internal Affairs: Dmitri Sipyagin in 1902 and Vyacheslav von Plehve in 1904. The latter survived an attack in 1903 and two in 1904 before being killed by a bomb thrown into his carriage.

The party played an active part in the 1905 Revolution, developing a full programme in November 1905 and forming a separate combat organisation, which attracted many students, to carry out assassinations. Among their more spectacular 'successes' was the assassination of Prime Minister Stolypin in 1911. The SR maintained its campaign of killings and violence over the following years, but the Secret Police foiled some activities and was successful in infiltrating the movement at its highest levels. Some 4579 Socialist Revolutionaries were sentenced to death between 1905 and 1909, and 2365 were actually executed.

CROSS-REFERENCE

Plehve is profiled in Chapter 3, page 28, and Stolypin in Chapter 7, page 70.

ACTIVITY

Write a manifesto for the Social Revolutionary Party. Don't forget to include some comment on its heritage as well as its aims and preferred methods. When you have read the next section, you could produce a contrasting manifesto for the Social Democrats.

The influence of Marxism and the development of the Social Democratic Workers' Party

Industrial 'take-off' helped make Marxist theories more attractive to Russian intellectuals from the late 1890s. Georgi Plekhanov's Emancipation of Labour group grew (although Plekhanov himself remained in exile between 1880 and 1917 and played no active role within Russia) while a number of discussion circles, workers' organisations, illegal trade unions, and other groups were attracted by Marxist ideas. The socialism was common to both the Social Revolutionary Party and a new, Social Democratic Workers' Party (SD), which emerged in 1898 as an amalgam of various Marxist groups. However, despite sharing some basic principles, their approaches were to differ markedly.

CROSS-REFERENCE

The roots of Marxism in the 1870s and Marxist theory are outlined in Chapter 5.

Plekhanov is profiled in Chapter 5, page 47.

ACTIVITY

Read the sections in this chapter on the evolution of the Social Revolutionary Party and the Social Democratic Workers' Party. In the light of Mackenzie Wallace's arguments in Extract 2, make a chart to show the similarities and differences between the SRs and SDs.

EXTRACT 2

In the new heaven and the new earth of which the socialist dreams, all human beings are to be equally free and independent, all are to cooperate with brains and hands to the common good. What differentiated the groups from each other was the greater or lesser degree of impatience to realise the ideal. The radical socialists declared their ultimate aim to be the transfer of political authority from the autocratic power to the people and the complete reorganisation of the national life. They recognised that social reorganisation must be preceded by a political revolution. With so many opinions in common, it seemed at first that the SDs and SRs might unite their forces for a combined attack on the government; but apart from the mutual jealousy and hatred, they were prevented from coalescing, or even cordially cooperating, by profound differences both in doctrine and in method.

Adapted from Donald Mackenzie Wallace, *Russia*, 1961

CROSS-REFERENCE

Pyotr Struve moved to the liberal movement in 1903, as explained later in this chapter

In 1898, the **First Congress of the Russian Social Democratic Workers' Party** of the Soviet Union was held in Minsk, marking the launch of a new party welding these Marxist groups together. However, only nine delegates were present. They chose their name, elected a three-man Central Committee, and produced a manifesto (drawn up by Pyotr Struve), which asserted that the working classes had been, and were being exploited by their masters and that the future of Russia would be the product of the class struggle. The manifesto made it clear that the impetus for change had to come from the working men themselves.

A CLOSER LOOK

The First Congress of the Social Democratic Workers' Party

The congress was held in a private house at Minsk, 1–3 March 1898. The three-man committee comprised Stepan Radchenko from the Emancipation of Labour group, Boris Eidelman from a socialist organisation in Kiev, and Alexander Kremer, a leader of the Jewish labour union (bund) founded in 1897, which had sponsored the congress. Six meetings were held but because of the need for secrecy, no minutes were taken.

The congress was broken up by Okhrana agents who promptly arrested two of the newly elected committee. It was not a promising start, but in the years that followed, **Vladimir Ilyich Ulyanov (Lenin)**, who had been converted to Marxist ideas as a student from 1887, came to play a prominent part in the development of the party.

The Second Party Congress took place in 1903, commencing in Brussels, but subsequently moving to a small congregational chapel in Shoreditch, London. The 51 voting delegates considered a variety of propositions as to how the party should move forward, and were divided on a number of these. Lenin argued in favour of a strong disciplined organisation of professional revolutionaries to lead the proletariat. However others, led by **Julius Martov**, believed their task should be to develop a broad party with a mass working-class membership. While Martov saw members 'cooperating' with other liberal parties, Lenin wanted total dedication to revolution only. Lenin certainly did not have the overwhelming support of the majority at the beginning of the conference and it was only after a number of representatives withdrew that Lenin finally won the vote in favour of a more centralised party structure. Lenin then claimed that his supporters were the majority (in Russian 'the *bolsheviki*') whilst his opponents, led by Martov, and supported also by Trotsky, were dubbed 'the *mensheviki*' (the minority) – even though, overall, the reverse was actually true. Over the next few years there was continued argument and rivalry within the embryonic party about the nature, timing and organisation of the revolution that they were planning and the Bolshevik/Menshevik division hardened so that by 1906 there were effectively two separate Social Democratic Workers' Parties.

KEY PROFILE

Vladimir Ilyich Ulyanov (Lenin) (1870–1924) was a lawyer. He was attracted by Marxism and became leader of 'The Elders', a Marxist group meeting in St Petersburg. He wrote pamphlets and organised strikes among the factory workers but his activities led to his exile to Siberia. From 1901, he took the name Lenin, after the River Lena where he stayed. On his release, he went into exile in Switzerland. In 1902, he produced the pamphlet, 'What is to be done', arguing the need for 'revolution' rather than trade-unionism. He founded a revolutionary newspaper *Iskra* (*The Spark*) with Plekhanov and others, and helped develop a strong party network. However, his uncompromising attitude led the Social Democrats to split in 1903. Lenin remained in exile until 1917, except for a brief return to St Petersburg in October 1905.

Julius Martov (1873–1920) had helped found the Emancipation of Labour group and the SD movement. He contributed to the party journal *Iskra* and was editor, 1903–05, after breaking with Lenin. He favoured working through trade unions, cooperatives and soviets to destroy the government. He was not invited to join the Bolsheviks after October 1917 and his Menshevik group was banned in 1918. Martov was exiled in 1920 and died in Germany.

Fig. 3 *Lenin worked hard to win supporters for the Marxist cause*

KEY PROFILE

Lev Bronstein (Trotsky)
(1879–1940) became involved in
Marxist groups and strike activity
in his teens. He was imprisoned
and exiled to Siberia, but managed
to escape using a disguise and false
passport, for which he took the
name Trotsky, in 1902. He travelled
to London and became a friend
and associate of Lenin, although he
failed to support Lenin in the 1903
dispute. In 1905 he became Deputy
Chairman of the St Petersburg
Soviet, and was arrested, but once
more escaped abroad. He was in the
USA when revolution broke in 1917
and he hurried back to help lead it.

ACTIVITY

Write a letter from a delegate who
attended the 1903 conference to a
fellow revolutionary in Russia. Explain
what has happened, which side you
support, and why.

CROSS-REFERENCE

The events of 1905 are discussed in
Chapter 7.

The violence at the Lena goldfields
in 1912 is outlined in Chapter 9,
page 87.

A CLOSER LOOK

The split in the Social Democratic Workers' Party

The split in the party was to have major consequences for the future of
Marxism in Russia. In 1903–04, many members changed sides. Plekhanov
abandoned the Bolsheviks, whom he had supported, while **Trotsky** left the
Mensheviks in September 1904 over their insistence on an alliance with
Russian liberals. Between 1904 and 1917 Trotsky described himself as a 'non-
factional social democrat' and spent much of his time trying to reconcile the
different groups within the party. He clashed many times with Lenin and later
conceded he had been wrong in opposing Lenin on the issue of the party.

Table 1 The split in the SD party, 1903

Mensheviks	Bolsheviks
Awaited the bourgeois revolution that they believed had to precede the proletarian revolution	Suggested the bourgois and proletarian revolution could occur simultaneously
Believed the impetus had to come from the workers themselves	Felt that the party's job was to educate the workers to lead them through the revolution
Insisted that memberhip should be open to all and the party should work through the trade unions and other workers' organisations to raise workers' consciousness	Believed that membership should be restricted and that members should work within small cells that could escape police notice
Wanted to follow democratic procedures and feared the that approach of the Bolsheviks could lead to dictatorship	Favoured control in the hands of a Central Committee

The extent of opposition between 1905 and 1914

Trade unions

The 1905 Revolution exposed many tensions in tsarist society and brought
opposition to the fore. However, none of the emergent opposition groups
actually 'controlled' the activities of that year and although all sought to benefit
from it, the aftermath proved something of an anti-climax.

After the excitement raised by the 1905 Revolution, and the legalisation
of the trade unions, a reduction in working class discontent might have
been expected through better state-employer-worker relations. However,
despite some reforms, such as the 1912 Insurance law, the State continued
to fear independent working-class activity and, in particular, the potential
for revolutionaries to work through the trade unions. As a result, 497 trade
unions were closed down and 604 were denied registration between 1906 and
1910. Those that survived were mainly unions of the better-paid male skilled
workers, particularly in the metal trades.

From 1907, an economic depression and rise in unemployment combined
with the political clampdown reduced any opportunity for union action.
However, the shooting of unarmed demonstrators at the Lena goldfields in
April 1912 provided a new impetus. This followed the beginnings of economic
recovery from 1911, which gave skilled labour more bargaining power in the
market place. A new round of strikes ensued.

This trade union activity was mainly confined to St Petersburg and the
surrounding area where three quarters of the strikes took place; half in the
metal trades. However, they demonstrated the State's failure to pacify the

working class in 1905. The bitter resistance of employers (particularly those in the St Petersburg Society of Mill and Factory Owners) and the repressive measures taken to break strikes – fines, lockouts and blacklists – added to anger and opposition.

Nonetheless, the danger to the autocracy of the pre-war strike movement was less than it seemed. As well as being geographically limited, only 12 per cent of enterprises experienced a strike and even the General Strike in St Petersburg in the first half of July 1914 only brought out a quarter of the manufacturing labour force.

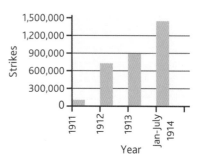

Fig. 4 *Strike activity in St Petersburg, 1910–13*

Other opposition groups

The moderate liberal opposition was largely appeased by the tsarist concessions in 1905–06 and tried to cooperate with the Duma system, in the hope of further constitutional evolution. Similarly, there was no single, strong opposition among the nationalities after 1905. Apart from the Poles and Finns, none wanted outright independence and, in the case of the Ukrainians and Belorussians, a combination of policies of assimilation and repression enjoyed success, delaying the emergence of an ethnic consciousness.

The revolutionary SR and SD parties were weakened by the exile of their leaders after 1905, as well as by the damaging split within the Social Democratic Workers' Party and the rivalry between the SDs and SRs. Ideological divisions within the parties were compounded by disagreements over the appropriate response to the 1905 defeat and the use parties should make of the 'legal' opportunities to work in and through the Duma. They also suffered from the activities of the Secret Police network whose agents were very effective in smashing revolutionary cells. The industrial depression from 1907, the lack of finance, and a shortage of secret printing presses made organisation difficult and none of the exiled leaders, including Lenin, exercised effective control over their parties within Russia.

Membership declined and neither SRs nor SDs succeeded in establishing national, regional or even all-city organisations. At best they maintained an 'underground' organisation in individual factories and workshops, where the leaders were local labour activists. Interestingly, these local revolutionary groups tended to cooperate irrespective of the ideological differences that absorbed the attention of their leaders in exile.

There was an apparent revival in Bolshevik fortunes in 1912–14, when they succeeded in taking over many legal labour institutions in both St Petersburg and Moscow from Mensheviks, and gained six workers' deputies in elections to the Fourth Duma. Their newspaper, *Pravda* (*The Truth*) was launched in April 1912 and enjoyed a much higher circulation than the Menshevik *Luch* (*The Ray*). The growing support for Bolshevik ideals was, however, quite limited. They had been helped in the Fourth Duma elections by an SR boycott. They enjoyed no success with army or navy and nothing

Fig. 5 *Nicholas II surrounded by petitions for reform in 1914; many problems remained unresolved*

CROSS-REFERENCE

For the role and functions of the Duma, look back to Chapter 7.

A CLOSER LOOK

In the Ukraine, nominal membership of the SDs fell from 20,000 in 1906 to 200 in 1912; and in Moscow from 7500 to 40 in same period.

came of their avowed promise to launch a general political strike, provoke mass street demonstrations and recreate a soviet of workers' deputies on the 1905 model.

Before 1914, opposition in Russia appeared weakened and demoralised. Most workers were politically apathetic, the trade unions failed to provide a broad popular base and labour protest was contained by repression and minimal concessions.

The coming of war in 1914 further diminished support for action as a patriotic fervour swept through all political groupings, save for the Bolsheviks. Lenin alone favoured defeat, believing it would bring Russia closer to the revolution he sought.

ACTIVITY

Research

In the fight against autocracy in the decade before 1914, a generation of political personalities emerged who were to be prominent in the later Bolshevik Russian State. These included: Chicherin, Litvinov, Tomsky, Voroshilov, Rykov, Kamenev, Zinoviev, Trotsky and Stalin. Choose one of these individuals and produce a file on this person — as might have been kept by the Secret Police. Don't forget to include a photographic record of past and present activity and some indication of why this person needed watching.

Summary

A number of differing strands of opposition emerged in Russia in the period 1894 to 1914. These included moderate liberals and radical SRs and SDs. While all sought to make capital out of the events of 1905, the tsarist concessions that won over some of the moderates left the left wing bitter but powerless in the face of repression. Nevertheless, radicalism survived and while little progress was made before 1914, it would not take much to bring political opposition out into the open again.

 PRACTICE QUESTION

Using your understanding of the historical context, assess how convincing the arguments in Extracts 1 and 2 are, in relation to the reasons why different types of opposition emerged in Russia in the years 1894 to 1914.

 PRACTICE QUESTION

'In the years 1894 to 1914, opposition movements achieved little.'
Explain why you agree or disagree with this view.

11 Political authority, opposition and the state of Russia in wartime

EXTRACT 1

Nicholas II leapt into the darkness of the Great War without anyone pushing him. The decisions of the European powers had consequences of massive significance. The Great War produced the situation that shattered the Romanov monarchy. It also made possible the Bolshevik seizure of power in October 1917. Except for the Great War, Lenin would have remained an émigré theorist scribbling in Swiss libraries, and even if Nicholas II had been deposed in a peacetime transfer of power, the inception of a communist order would hardly have been likely. The first three years of this military conflict, however, caused an economic and political disorder so huge that Nicholas II had to abdicate in February 1917.

Adapted from Robert Service, *Russia*, 1997

The political problems of tsardom in wartime

Fig. 1 *In 1914, Russia mobilised for war*

The Tsar's decision to go to war in 1914 was initially a popular one, supported by a wave of anti-German sentiment. Strike activity ceased, and extremists were imprisoned for their lack of patriotism. Having voted for **war credits**, the Duma dissolved itself, declaring that it did not want to burden the country with 'unnecessary politics' in war time. The Germanic 'St Petersburg' became the new Slavonic 'Petrograd' and a vast army was rapidly assembled, amazing the Germans by the speed with which this Russian 'steamroller' was able to get to the Eastern Front.

However, the spirit of national solidarity was dampened when initial victories gave way to defeat at the hands of the Germans in the disastrous Battle of Tannenburg in East Prussia, which left 300,000 dead or wounded in August 1914. Thousands were taken prisoner. A subsequent defeat at the Masurian Lakes in September forced the Russian army into a temporary retreat from East Prussia. Although the Russian troops were rather more successful in the south against Austria, it was soon clear that the war would not end in a quick victory, as had been hoped, and reports of military incompetence inflamed the simmering discontent in the Russian capital.

LEARNING OBJECTIVES

In this chapter you will learn about:

- the political problems of tsardom in wartime

- the economic and social problems created by the First World War

- opposition to the autocracy and the political collapse of February/ March 1917

- the development of Russia under the Dual Power of 1917.

KEY QUESTION

As you read this chapter, consider the following Key Questions:
- How was Russia governed and how did political authority change and develop?
- How did opposition develop and how effective was it?

ACTIVITY

1. Read Extract 1 carefully and identify Service's overall argument.
2. Summarise Service's argument in one sentence.
3. Which more specific arguments or views does Service advance?

KEY TERM

War credits: the raising of taxes and loans to finance war

Russian involvement in the First World War

Following Russia's defeat by Japan in the Far East in 1905, and agreements with Britain over Persia and Afghanistan in central Asia in 1907, Russian attention turned to the Balkan area. Encouraged by Pan-Slavist sentiment in St Petersburg, Nicholas backed Serbia, which sought to carve out a southern Slav nation. Following the dispute between Serbia and Austria-Hungary, which arose after the assassination at Sarajevo in July 1914, Russian mobilised in support of Serbia; it is possible that the Tsar believed that this would divert attention away from the discontent at home. Russia was rapidly drawn into war with Germany, Austria-Hungary's ally, and although Russia's allies, Britain and France, also fought against these 'Central Powers', Russia struggled alone on the Eastern Front.

CROSS-REFERENCE

Prince Lvov is profiled in Chapter 10, page 94.

Details about the Kadets, Octobrists and Progressives are in Chapter 7, page 68.

Wartime government and organisation

Even before the end of 1914, there were disputes over the organisation of the war effort. In July 1914, the tsarist government had set up 'military zones' within which all civilian authority was suspended, and the military assumed command. This, however, was opposed by the liberal *zemstva* who regarded the government as insensitive to the needs of the people and believed that civilians had a major part to play in running the war. For example, the government's decision to prohibit the sale of alcohol at the end of 1914 was both resented and evaded. Vodka was regarded as a near essential, especially in hard times, so peasants and workers simply distilled their own, while the government lost some valuable tax revenue from legal sales.

The *zemstva* established a 'Union of Zemstva' to provide the medical facilities which the State seemed to neglect. Another initiative came from factory owners and businessmen who established a Congress of Representatives of Industry and Business (which included representatives from the Duma and of workers) to help coordinate production.

In June 1915, existing *zemstva* and municipal dumas joined together to form the All-Russian Union of Zemstva and Cities, known as Zemgor. It was chaired by Prince Lvov and claimed the right to help the Tsar's government in the war effort, but it was never allowed any direct influence and, like the state Duma, soon turned into a liberal focus for discontent. Rather than working with the organisation, Nicholas blamed it for stirring up trouble.

In August 1915, some of the deputies (Kadets, Octobrists and Progressives) from the Fourth Duma, many of them also involved in the Congress of Representatives of Industry and Business, organised themselves into the 'Progressive bloc' and demanded that the Tsar change his ministers and establish a 'government of public confidence'. They were effectively asking for a constitutional monarchy, in which they would have a dominant voice. Had Nicholas II been a more astute man, he might well have seized this chance to institute political reform and transfer responsibility for the war effort to a civilian government. However, Nicholas was not prepared to contemplate such a move. Instead, in September, he suspended the sittings of the Duma and it remained officially closed until January 1917, although unauthorised meetings continued.

In September 1915, defeats in Galicia (on the Austro-Hungarian Front) led Nicholas II to make the disastrous decision to take on the role of Commander-in-Chief of the Russian Army and Navy and, 'with firm trust in Divine mercy and unshakeable confidence in ultimate victory', to travel to the front line. The move did nothing to help his cause. Although it had overtones of bravery and heroism, Nicholas had already lost the confidence and support of the Russian General Staff and did not possess the military experience to turn the war effort around. Instead, his new position simply made him appear yet more responsible for the varying disasters that befell his troops and the State, while distancing him even more from developments in Petrograd.

In the city, Rasputin began to meddle in political appointments and policy decisions, while there were rumours that Nicholas's German wife, Alexandra, was deliberately sabotaging the Russian war effort. Whether Rasputin was quite the evil influence some contemporaries made out, or simply the tool of political schemers, we can't be sure. Nevertheless, there were many changes of ministers in the 12 months after September 1915, including three or four changes in some ministries, and these were put down to Rasputin's influence. It was hardly surprising, therefore, that liberals and socialists began to lose patience and demand changes in government.

SOURCE 1

In September 1915, Zemgor declared:

On the path of victory there lies a fatal obstacle; an obstacle created by all the old vices of our political system; we mean irresponsible power, the absence of any link between the government and the country. A drastic change is required in place of our present governors. We must have men who enjoy the confidence of the nation. The work of the Duma should be resumed without delay.

Fig. 2 *Rasputin wielded great power over Nicholas and Alexandra. How does the cartoonist convey his views on this?*

The President of the Fourth Duma, Mikhail Rodzianko, and others warned Nicholas in vain of Rasputin's unpopularity and the damage he was doing the tsarist cause, but it would seem that Nicholas could not bring himself to take action against a person on whom his wife leaned so heavily. It was in an attempt to save the reputation of the monarchy that Prince Yusupov (a nephew by marriage to the Tsar) and his accomplice, Vladimir Purishkevich, who had referred to Rasputin as a 'filthy, vicious and venal peasant', invited Rasputin to an evening tea at the Yusupov Palace on 17 December 1916, and murdered him. The event came too late, however, and did little to quell the growing discontent.

A CLOSER LOOK

The murder of Rasputin, 1916

According to accounts of those not present at the time, but who knew those that were, Yusupov at first tried to kill Rasputin with poisoned cakes. When these had no effect (probably because his stomach was so well-lined after years of excessive drinking) he enticed Rasputin near him, to look at an Italian Renaissance crucifix. He fired twice into his ribs and Rasputin fell to the floor. Having checked there was no pulse, Yusupov went to get his car, ready to move the body. However, 12 minutes later, on returning to the room, he saw, to his horror, that Rasputin had half risen and was lurching towards him. He tore the epaulette from Yusupov's shoulder and yelled, 'You wretch! You'll be hanged tomorrow! I'm going to tell the Empress everything.' Yusupov ran from the room and called his waiting accomplices. They entered to find Rasputin gone. He had opened the door to the garden and was dragging himself away through the snow. Purishkevich fired a bullet into his neck and another into his body while Yusupov fetched a bronze candlestick and battered his skull. Finally they bound his body and threw him into the river – just to be sure that if he was not already dead, he would drown.

Nicholas seemed unaware of, or unconcerned about, political demands. His letters to Alexandra, whom he addressed with such terms of endearment as, 'my own lovebird', showed more anxiety about the children's measles than (as Alexandra wrote in a message on 25 February 1917), 'young boys and girls running about and screaming that they have no bread'. Nicholas reassured his wife that 'this will all pass and quieten down'.

The economic and social problems created by the war

The Russian economy quickly showed the strains of war. By Christmas 1914, there was already a serious shortage of munitions, and the prospect of a long war, requiring large numbers of men and munitions, was daunting.

ACTIVITY

Work in pairs to construct a diagram that shows the ways in which the war undermined Tsar Nicholas II's authority.

KEY QUESTION

- How and with what results did the economy develop and change?
- What was the extent of social change?

The army Chief of Staff informed the French ambassador in December 1914:

Our losses of men have been colossal, though if it were merely a matter of replacing wastage we could soon do so as we have more than 800,000 men waiting in our depots. But we're short of rifles to arm and train these men. Our magazines are nearly empty. The position is hardly less difficult as regards gun ammunition. Our entire reserve is exhausted. The armies need 45,000 rounds a day. Our maximum daily output is 13,000; we hope it will reach 20,000 by about 15 February. Until that date, the situation of our armies will not only be difficult but dangerous.

Military issues

Although the Russian government managed to mobilise around 15 million men between 1914 and 1917, mainly conscript peasants, it proved unable to provide for them. The problems of the early years grew steadily worse so that soldiers were sent to fight not only without suitable weaponry, but also lacking basic warm clothing and properly fitting, waterproof footwear. In 1914, the infantry had only two rifles for every three soldiers and in 1915 it was not unusual for Russian artillery to be limited to two to three shells per day. In these early years, the soldiers had to rely on the weapons of fallen comrades in order to fight at all.

The winter months of 1915–16 were relatively quiet for the Russians, allowing more time for training and the production of ammunition, and by the time of the **Brusilov offensive** in June 1916, most front line units had a reasonable complement of machine guns and artillery shells. However, by then the army had a serious lack of experienced officers since most been killed in the early stages of war.

A CLOSER LOOK

The Brusilov offensive

Named after General Brusilov, this was a Russian attempt to push westwards from the area of the Ukraine and break through the Austro-Hungarian lines. It succeeded in destroying the Austro-Hungarian armies, which had to rely on German reinforcements, but within three months it had ground to a halt, since the Germans, with their superior railway network, were able to move men forward more quickly than the Russians.

By the end of 1916, morale in the army had plummeted. Heavy casualties and the deteriorating economic and political situation within Russia itself led to 1.5 million desertions that year.

Internal problems

Spending on the war rose from 1,500 million roubles in 1914 to 14,500 million in 1918, but the real cost was far greater. The rural and industrial workforce was severely affected and although women and children took on some of the men's work, production slumped at a time when the country needed to to be producing more, not less, to feed and supply its armies. Poland, and other parts of western Russia, were overrun by the Germans, removing important industrial capacity. Naval blockades of the Baltic and Black Sea ports, together with the loss of overland routes to Europe, brought Russian trade to a virtual standstill.

Fig. 3 *Nicholas II encouraging his army officers*

A CLOSER LOOK

Some 15 million conscripts and volunteers were enlisted for military service between 1914 and 1917, although this represented only 9 per cent of the Russian population compared with 20 per cent in Germany and France.

In the countryside, some did well out of the war as conscription helped to relieve some of the population pressure, and those with horses or surplus grain could make money by supplying the military. However, in general, the prices offered by the government were low, tools and equipment were in short supply, and it was hard to find essential household goods. As a result, some hoarded what grain and foodstuffs they produced, exacerbating an already difficult situation.

Even when the grain was released for the market, inefficiencies of distribution meant that it did not always reach the town workers who desperately needed it. Railways had been taken over to transport men and goods to the front line, railway locomotive production halved between 1913 and 1916 and there were acute fuel shortages. Foodstuffs that should have found their way to the cities were left to rot beside railway sidings and huge cargoes of grain would be sent to the front line, leaving none for the desperate townsfolk. This made life hard for the town populations, which swelled as factories sought more workers for essential war industries. The recruitment drive meant that though armament manufacture improved in 1916, when rifle production doubled and heavy artillery production quadrupled, this was all at the expense of civilian needs.

In urban centres, particularly in Petrograd and Moscow, unemployment soared as non-military factories, deprived of vital supplies, were forced to close. Lock-outs and strikes, (some directly encouraged by the German government in a deliberate attempt to foster industrial unrest and undermine the Russian war effort) financially crippled what little industry survived. A 300 per cent rise in the cost of living, and rising death rates because of the workers' insanitary lodgings and the inadequacies of their diets, left thousands living on the brink of starvation. In such circumstances, in January 1917 30,000 workers went on strike in Moscow and 145,000 in Petrograd.

The opposition to the autocracy and the political collapse of February/March 1917

By the winter of 1917, the streets of Petrograd were tense with the pent-up frustrations of the unemployed, the starving and the desperate. A demonstration by 150,000 Petrograd workers on the anniversary of Bloody Sunday in January 1917 was a hint of things to come. The key events of February are shown in Table 1.

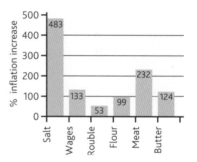

Fig. 4 *Inflation: percentage increase from pre-war figures*

ACTIVITY

Summary

Make a wall poster to illustrate the impact of the First World War on Russia. You will need to include political, economic and social factors. Find an illustration to accompany each theme.

KEY QUESTION

- Why did opposition develop and how effective was it?
- How did political authority change and develop?
- How important was the role of individuals and groups?

Table 1 Events of February 1917

Monday 14 February	Around 100,000 workers from 58 different factories go on strike in Petrograd. News that bread would be rationed from 1 March brings long round-the-clock queues and violent exchanges. The police, who struggle to keep order, are attacked.
Wednesday 22 February	20,000 workers are locked out of the Putilov Iron Works by the management after pay talks collapse. Workers in other factories go on strike in support.
Thursday 23 February **International Women's Day**	90,000 workers are on strike and 50 factories close. These workers join a traditional march of women from the Petrograd suburbs to the city centre along with militant students and women from the bread queues. The city falls into chaos with c240,000 out on the streets. Order is restored by a desperate police force in the early evening, although the day sees no loss of life.
Friday 24 February	200,000 workers are on strike and crowds overturn tsarist statues, wave red flags, wear red rosettes, shout revolutionary slogans calling for an end to tsardom and sing 'La Marseillaise'. There is no obvious organisation from any of the radical political parties, although some radicals distribute emblems and banners bearing political demands.
Saturday 25 February	250,000 people (over half the capital's workforce) are on strike and Petrograd is at a virtual standstill. Almost all the major factories and most shops are closed. There are no newspapers and no public transport. Violence escalates as Police Chief Shalfeev, in charge of the mounted police, tries to control the masses. He is set upon, dragged from his horse, beaten and shot. A band of civilians is killed by soldiers on the Nevskii Prospekt. However, late in the day, some Cossacks refuse to attack a procession of strikers when ordered to do so.
Sunday 26 February	Rodzianko, the Duma President, sends the Tsar a telegram: 'The situation is serious. The capital is in a state of anarchy. The government is paralysed; the transport service has broken down; the food and fuel supplies are completely disorganised. Discontent is general and on the increase. There is wild shooting in the streets. Troops are firing at each other. It is urgent that someone enjoying the confidence of the country be entrusted with the formation of a new government. There must be no delay. Hesitation is fatal.' Nicholas notes in his diary, 'That fat-bellied Rodzianko has written some nonsense to which I shall not even bother to reply.' His only response is to tell the Duma to stop meeting.
Monday 27 February	The Tsar orders Major-General Khabalov, Commander of the Petrograd military district, to restore order by military force. Soldiers are ordered onto the streets and around 40 demonstrators in the city centre are killed. However, a **mutiny** begins in the Volynskii regiment, where a sergeant shoots his commanding officer dead. 66,000 soldiers mutiny and join the protestors, arming them with 40,000 rifles. Police headquarters are attacked and prisons opened. Later in the day the Duma holds a meeting, despite the Tsar's orders, and sets up a 12-man provisional committee to take over the government. The army's High Command, which has already ordered troops to march to the capital to restore stability, change their minds and order them to halt and give support to the Duma committee. The same evening, revolutionaries set up the Petrograd Soviet, which also intends to take over the government. It begins to organise food supplies for the city.
Tuesday 28 February	Nicholas II leaves his military headquarters at Mogilëv and starts to make his way back to Petrograd. He sends a telegramme to Rodzianko, offering to share power with the Duma. The leader replies, 'The measures you propose are too late. The time for them has gone. There is no return.'

A CLOSER LOOK

International Women's Day

The first National Woman's Day took place in the USA in 1909. In 1910, around 100 women from 17 countries gathered for a socialist conference in Denmark and agreed to an annual women's day to campaign for female suffrage. Russian women, demanding peace, not war, observed their first International Women's Day on the last Sunday in February 1913. They were led by Alexandra Kollontai, who also helped to organise the women's march of February 1917.

The mutineers

Many of those ordered to shoot the demonstrators were themselves of peasant or worker background. They were were the young and newly

CROSS-REFERENCE

Alexandra Kollontai is profiled in Chapter 12, page 121.

enlisted, who had joined the Petrograd garrison to await the dreaded call to proceed to the front line. Furthermore their junior officers included men from the middle-ranking 'intellectual' class, rather than from the traditional 'noble' background. These were men who had joined the army from a sense of patriotism inspired by war. Their sympathies, like the sympathies of those they commanded, lay with the massses.

Under pressure from the soldiers and from mutineers at the Kronstadt naval base, the **Petrograd Soviet** agreed that each regiment should elect committees and send representatives to the soviet. The 'Order No.1' – a charter of soldiers' rights – was produced, promising the following:

- All units to elect a deputy to the soviet and agree to the political control of the Petrograd Soviet.
- The Military Commisssion of the Duma to be obeyed, only if it agreed with the soviet's orders.
- All weapons to be controlled by elected soldiers' committees – not officers.
- All soldiers to enjoy full citizens' rights when off duty – e.g. no requirement to salute or stand to attention.
- No honorific titles to be used for officers – only Mr General, Mr Colonel, etc.
- Officers are not to address soldiers in the 'ty' form (like 'tu' in French. This second person singular form was used to address children, pets and serfs).

Nicholas never returned to Petrograd. His train was diverted by rebellious railway workers and forced to stop at Pskov, 200 miles south of his destination. The Tsar was under pressure from the Chief of General Staff, General Alekseev, to resign. Alekseev had been reassured by an agreement on 1 March that the Petrograd Soviet would recognise a Provisional Government formed by members of the Duma, and suggested that the Tsar resigned in favour of his son, Alexei, with Nicholas's younger brother, Mikhail, acting as regent.

On 2 March, Nicholas agreed to their demand. However, fearing that Alexei's health was too delicate, he named Grand-Duke Mikhail as the new Tsar (even though he had not been consulted). He added that Mikhail should lead the country 'in complete union with the representatives of the people in the legislative bodies on principles to be established by them and to take an inviolable oath to this effect'.

By the time the members of the Duma committee reached Pskov on 2 March, the terms of Nicholas's abdication had already been agreed, although in the event Mikhail refused the offer of the throne.

The Tsar and his family were placed under house arrest, as were most of the members of the Tsar's Council of Ministers. Thus 304 years of the Romanov dynasty came to an end.

A CLOSER LOOK

Beyond Petrograd

Revolutionary disturbances spread beyond Petrograd – to Kronstadt naval base, Moscow and other industrial cities and rural areas. In cities, workers seized control of their factories, set up workers' committees and deposed their former bosses – sometimes dumping them in a nearby river! Everywhere, rebellious peoples set up their own elected regional assemblies and soviets. The army, technically under the command of the Petrograd Soviet, disintegrated into semi-independent bodies and soldiers' soviets without clear leadership

A CLOSER LOOK

Petrograd Soviet

Soviets had appeared in 1905 (see Chapter 7) and were literally 'councils'. They were not necessarily supportive of any one particular party and it was not originally a political term. Following the February 1917 Revolution, elected soviets sprang up in many cities and towns in Russia but the one in Petrograd, often known simply as 'The Soviet', was the most important. By 10 March it had 3000 members and because it was so large, most of its work was done by its 'executive committee', which was dominated by socialist intellectuals.

ACTIVITY

Why do you feel 'Order No.1' is regarded as 'revolutionary'?

ACTIVITY

Make a spider diagram to show why Tsar Nicholas II abdicated in Februrary 1917.

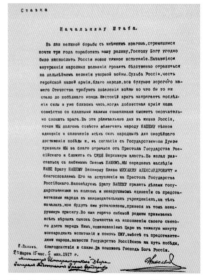

Fig. 5 *Nicholas II announces his abdication*

Creative thinking

Take on the role of one of the following groups of people and write your group's view of the events of February 1917, including their reaction to what happened, who or what they sought to blame or praise, and what their hopes for the future were:

- a soldier at the front
- a tsarist minister of noble rank
- a middle class member of the Duma
- a worker in Petrograd
- a peasant in western Russia.

Present your views to your class and decide which group would have been most/least hopeful for the future and why.

ACTIVITY

Pair discussion

Discuss with a partner: How far was the rising of February 1917 the work of the revolutionary opposition?

CROSS-REFERENCE

To read more about Prince Lvov, go back to Chapter 10, page 94.

KEY QUESTION

How was Russia governed and how did political authority change and develop?

ACTIVITY

The following were all prominent members of the Provisional Government. Find out what you can about one of them and prepare a short presentation for your group on his role and influence: Prince Lvov (Chairman); Pavel Milyukov (Foreign Minister); Alexander Guchkov (Minister of War); Alexander Konovalov (Minister of Trade) and Alexander Kerensky (Minister of Justice).

and coordination. In the countryside, peasants attacked landlords' properties and felled trees illegally. In the provinces such as Finland, Poland, the Ukraine and the Caucasus, national minorities declared their independence.

A CLOSER LOOK

The revolutionary opposition

Soviet historians (writing after the Bolsheviks came to power) interpreted the events of February 1917 as the result of the inevitable class struggle between the bourgeoisie-proletarian forces and traditional aristocratic forces of the urban workers in St Petersburg. They alleged that it was the Bolsheviks who inspired the revolution and the setting up of the Petrograd Soviet. However, rather as in 1905, when the revolution broke out, most of the revolutionary leaders, not only of the Bolsheviks, but also of the Mensheviks and Social Revolutionaries, were either in prison or in exile, in Siberia or abroad. The Bolsheviks were in no position to provide leadership and coordinate the risings of February 1917. The revolution itself would appear to have been largely spontaneous and the result of the peculiar circumstances of war. Furthermore, while it overthrew the Tsar, it did not overthrow all 'aristocratic forces'.

The development of Russia under the Dual Power of 1917

The Provisional Government

Grand-Duke Mikhail relinquished political authority to a hastily-convened 'Provisional Government', under Prince Lvov. Its members represented a cross-section of the influential elites and comprised those who had formerly favoured constitutional monarchy – liberals, moderate socialists and Kadets.

It was the original intention that the Provisional Government would, as its name suggests, be temporary and that elections would be held as soon as possible for a new Constituent Assembly, which would draw up a new constitution for Russia. Nevertheless, the Provisional Government was accepted as legitimate (thanks to Mikhail's blessing) by the old tsarist civil service, army officers and the police. It set itself up in the Duma chamber in the right wing of the Tauride Palace in Petrograd and so perpetuated its rule, although it never rejected the idea of elections at a later date.

The Petrograd Soviet

The mass of workers, soldiers and peasants regarded the Provisional Goverment as a self-appointed committee of the wealthy, tainted by their previous associations with tsardom. For them, the Petrograd Soviet was the more democratic organisation.

The Petrograd Soviet, which was dominated by Mensheviks and Social Revolutionaries, but also contained a small number of Bolsheviks, established its headquarters in the left wing of the Tauride Palace. It was primarily composed of radical socialist intellectuals and only 7 of the first 42 committee members were workers themselves, although it claimed direct democratic authority since its members were elected by the St Petersburg soviets. However, it seemed to lack the confidence needed to assume direct control and, thanks to some delicate negotiations by **Alexander Kerensky**, the only member of both the Provisional Government and the Soviet, an agreement to work together was reached which laid the foundations for the period of **Dual Power**. The Soviet made no attempt to demand land redistribution or the nationalisation of industry but accepted the Provisional Government's promises of:

- a general amnesty for political prisoners
- basic civil liberties
- the abolition of legal disabilities based on class, religion and nationality
- the right to organise trade unions and to strike
- that a Constituent Assembly would be elected.

To these, the Provisional Government added the promise in April that 'the power of the State should be based, not on violence and coercion, but on the consent of free citizens to the power they themselves created.' They allowed freedom of religion and the press, abolished the death penalty at the front, replaced the tsarist police force with a 'people's militia' and dismissed provincial governors, giving their work to the elected *zemstva*.

ACTIVITY

Consider the strengths and weaknesses of the Dual Power arrangement and complete the table below. Add to your chart as you read the next section.

Strengths	Weaknesses

The Dual Power in action

Rule by a mixture of liberals and radicals was never going to be easy. The Soviet's 'Order No.1' had said that the soldiers and workers should obey the Provisional Government, but only when the Soviet agreed with the Provisional Government's decisions and there were many points of disagreement in the early weeks.

While the Provisional Government tried to discipline **deserters** and restore order in towns and countryside, the Soviet encouraged peasants and workers to defy authority and assert their 'rights'. In addition, while the Provisional Government believed that the change of regime should lead to an all-out effort to 'win' the war, the masses had expected the political changes to being an end to wartime deprivation.

Workers' strikes and military desertions continued. Peasant disturbances affected 34 districts in March 1917 but this increased to 325 in July. Milyukov's announcement, in April 1917, that the government would continue fighting until a 'just peace' had been won, led to a massive anti-war demonstration in Petrograd forcing Milyukov and Guchkov to resign.

A CLOSER LOOK

Desertions

There had been 195,000 desertions between 1914 and February 1917, but between March and May 1917, there were over 365,000. Brusilov's major offensive in Galicia, in June, was undertaken in the hope of rallying the nation, but as the Russian advance was beaten back with heavy losses, anti-war sentiment grew stronger. Desertions reached a peak and the death penalty had to be reinstated as the only way of controlling the troops.

Milyukov and Guchkov were replaced by socialists from the Soviet. Viktor Chernov became Minister of Agriculture, Kerensky became Minister of War and two further Mensheviks were added to the cabinet. In July 1917,

KEY PROFILE

Alexander Kerensky (1881–1970) was a lawyer. He served in the Duma of 1912, sitting with the left-wing socialists. In February 1917 he joined the Social Revolutionaries and became a valuable link in the Dual Power from March, as both an SR representative on the Petrograd Soviet (where he was vice-chairman) and Minister of Justice in the Provisional Government. In May he became Minister of War, and in July, Prime Minister. He was deposed by the Bolsheviks in October and fled to France, and eventually to the USA.

KEY TERM

Dual Power: whereby Russia was governed by an alliance of the Provisional Government and the Soviet

A CLOSER LOOK

Local soviets

Local 'soviets' (councils) were established across Russia, by peasants, who seized land and tried to control their own affairs by factory workers, who demanded a say in the running of their factories, and by soldiers, who rejected their officers' authority. An 'All-Russian Congress of Soviets' met in Petrograd in June, with representatives from 350 towns, villages and military bases throughout Russia.

CROSS-REFERENCE

Viktor Chernov, the founder of the Social Revolutionaries, is profiled in Chapter 10, page 95.

Fig. 6 *General Kornilov reviewing his troops in 1917*

CROSS-REFERENCE

The extent of Bolshevik involvement in the July coup is discussed in Chapter 12, pages 112–113.

Turn to Chapter 12, page 113, to read more about the July Days

A CLOSER LOOK

Real wages

Real wages represent what 'money wages' can buy if money wages increase, but the cost of living increases more, then 'real wages' go down.

STUDY TIP

This is potentially a very big breadth question, so you will need to be selective in your choice of material. Make a list of developments (other than the First World War) which contributed to the political revolution of 1917. These may be economic, social and personal as well as political. Begin the essay by considering the ways in which the war contributed to political breakdown and change, and then balance that against the contributions of the other factors you have noted.

Prince Lvov was replaced as Chairman by Kerensky. Such changes alarmed the upper classes whose despair that the government had failed to protect their property, maintain order, or win the war was aggravated by its apparent shift to the left.

Street riots in July, known as the 'July Days' (which may or may not have been organised by the Bolsheviks) exacerbated their fears.

The hopes of the elites were consequently transferred to General Lavr Kornilov whom Kerensky had appointed as Commander-in-Chief of the army on 16 July. At the end of August, Kornilov ordered six regiments of troops to march on Petrograd – presumably intending to crush the Soviet and establish a military dictatorship. However, this attempted coup failed when Kerensky, who at first had supported Kornilov, panicked. Kerensky released imprisoned Bolsheviks and provided the Soviet with weapons from the government's armouries to halt Kornilov's advance. Kornilov's supply lines were cut and the coup leaders arrested.

ACTIVITY

Although it is difficult to be precise about the Kornilov coup because it was a secret plot and few written records exist, try to discover what you can about Kornilov and his plans, and discuss your ideas with the rest of your group.

By the summer of 1917, there was little support left for the Provisional Government. Food supplies were chaotic in the towns and although the government granted an eight-hour day, **real wages** fell rapidly in 1917 as prices rose. In January 1917 prices were 300 per cent of 1914 levels, by October they were 755 per cent. The early hope of the workers that unions and factory committees would be able to improve their lot was dashed in August when the right of factory owners to dismiss workers who went on strike was confirmed, and meetings of factory committees during working hours were forbidden.

The continuation of the war and the government's failure to redistribute land also lost it support in the countryside. The government claimed that such an important issue had to be left until after Russia had a democratically elected assembly; however the peasants took the law into their own hands and simply seized land anyway. Although an electoral commission was established in May, to arrange elections for November, suspicion that the 'bourgeois' government was deliberately delaying a move to greater democracy in order to preserve its own power was rife. The group that benefited most from this widespread disillusionment was the Bolsheviks.

ACTIVITY

Summary

Create a timeline chart of March–September with three columns. Use the first column for dates, the second for the key developments, and leave the third blank, to complete after you have read the next chapter. Record political developments in one colour and economic and social changes in another.

 PRACTICE QUESTION

To what extent was the First World War responsible for the political changes which had taken place in Russia by the beginning of October 1917? Answer with reference to the years 1894–1917.

The establishment of Bolshevik government

KEY QUESTION

As you read this chapter, consider the following Key Questions:
- How was Russia governed and how did political authority change and develop?
- How important was the role of individuals and groups?
- How important were ideas and ideology?

LEARNING OBJECTIVES

In this chapter you will learn about:

- the return of Lenin and the growth in Bolshevik support

- the Bolshevik seizure of power

- the consolidation of Bolshevik government by December 1917

- the opposition to Bolshevik government.

EXTRACT 1

The tsarist government's failings in the war and its weakness at home led to the self-destruction of the autocracy on a wave of discontent. Had the democratic February Revolution managed to hold, most likely, Russia today would be a great democratic state, rather than one that has disintegrated. Soon after returning from exile to Petrograd in April 1917, Lenin embarked on a course of violent seizure of power. His slogans, primitive and rabble-rousing, worked without fail. The Bolsheviks promised the war-weary, land-starved and hungry people, peace, land and bread and told them that to achieve this they must first stick their bayonets into the ground, abandon the trenches and go home, where they should seize their allotments. The power of Kerensky's Provisional Government melted like ice in the spring thaw. Meanwhile, the Bolshevik demagogues promised the gullible and ignorant peasants-in-uniform prosperity, land, bread, hospitals and liberty.

Adapted from Dmitri Volkogonov, *The Rise and Fall of the Soviet Union*, 1999

ACTIVITY

Evaluating historical extracts

What impression do you get of Lenin in Extract 1? Volkogonov is a modern Russian historian who has used soviet archives to provide a reappraisal of leaders such as Lenin. Consider his view as you read on. You will be invited to consider how convincing his views are in two questions given later in this chapter.

Lenin's return and the growth of Bolshevik support

Lenin returned to Russia from Switzerland on 3 April 1917. He was helped by the Germans who expected him to seize power and make peace. He had travelled in a railway carriage (which had been locked and sealed as it passed through Germany), from exile in Switzerland, through Germany to Sweden (neutral) and thence to Finland and Petrograd.

A CLOSER LOOK

The sealed train

Lenin travelled with 31 comrades on a German train from Gottmadingen on the Swiss boarder via Frankfurt, Berlin and Stockholm to Petrograd. The train had only one carriage and was sealed – insofar as there were no passport or luggage inspections carried out. Lenin had his own compartment, where he worked on his own. His fellow travellers used the corridor and the other compartments, and passed their time (to Lenin's annoyance), drinking and singing. Smokers were issued with a 'first class pass' that gave them priority in the use of the lavatory, which was the only place where smoking was allowed.

KEY CHRONOLOGY

April–September 1917

3 April	Lenin returns and the April Theses are compiled over the next few weeks
3 June	The first All-Russian Congress of Workers' and Soldiers' Deputies meet
2 July	Trotsky joins the Bolsheviks
3–4 July	The 'July Days' of anti-government demonstrations in Petrograd
5–7 July	Bolshevik leaders (including Trotsky) are arrested; Lenin flees to Finland
18 July	Kerensky becomes First Minister
27–30 July	Kornilov's coup fails and the Bolshevik Red Guards are given arms
September	Trotsky becomes Chairman of the Petrograd Soviet and the Bolsheviks command majorities in both the Petrograd and Moscow Soviets

Fig. 1 *Lenin's journey from Switzerland to Petrograd*

CROSS-REFERENCE

Turn to Chapter 10, page 98, for a profile on Trotsky.

Kamenev is profiled below, on page 114.

The Provisional Government is discussed in Chapter 11, page 108

Lenin greeted the crowds at the Finland Station in Petrograd, where he gave a rousing speech. The gist of his words were later written down in the so-called 'April Theses', although some of these were actually written in May, after Trotsky had also returned to Russia from the USA. They were published in the party's official newspaper, *Pravda*.

The April Theses demanded that:

- power should be transferred to the soviets
- the war should be brought to an immediate end
- all land should be taken over by the State and re-allocated to peasants by local soviets.

These demands have often been summed up as a demand for 'Peace, bread and land'. Lenin also stressed a policy of non-cooperation with the Provisional Government, giving rise to a further motto: 'All power to the soviets'. Adapting Marxist theory, Lenin argued that the Russian middle class was too weak to carry through a full 'bourgeois revolution' and that to allow the middle classes to continue in power was to hold the inevitable proletarian revolution back.

The initial reaction to his reappearance was mixed:

- Some Bolsheviks feared that Lenin had grown out of touch and that his radical proposals would do more harm than good.
- There were allegations that Lenin was in the pay of the Germans (to some extent true).
- The Mensheviks feared Lenin would undermine what they had been doing, and, by stirring up discontent, would provoke a right-wing reaction.
- Some thought Lenin's call to oppose the Provisional Government unrealistic since the Bolsheviks had only 26,000 members and were still in a minority among the socialists.
- The Bolsheviks were divided among themselves over whether to cooperate with the Provisional Government or not. (The first Bolsheviks in the capital, **Stalin** and Lev Kamenev, had supported the Provisional Government).

KEY PROFILE

> **Joseph Stalin** (1879–1953), the son of a Georgian cobbler, was one of the few leading Bolsheviks who could claim peasant roots. He had trained as a priest but was attracted by the Social Democratic movement in 1898 and expelled from his seminary in 1899. Over the following years, he was repeatedly arrested and exiled to Siberia, but he escaped several times – taking the name 'Stalin' (man of steel). He became a Bolshevik and helped to raise money by robbing banks. He was in Siberia from 1912 to 1917 but returned in 1917 and became the editor of *Pravda*. He played only a minor role in the October Revolution but was made Commissar for Nationalities because of his background. He eventually took the leadership after Lenin's death and established himself as a dictator within Russia.

However, Lenin gradually built support with his speeches – in which he claimed credit for much that was already happening, not least the peasants' seizure of land. By the end of April, Lenin had won over the majority of the Central Committee of the Bolshevik Party by sheer force of personality.

Winning wider support required persistence. When the the first 'All-Russian Congress of Soviets' met in Petrograd on 3 June, it passed a vote of confidence in the Provisional Government (recently augmented by left wing representatives) by 543 votes to 126. Nevertheless, Lenin won a key adherent when Trotsky finally decided to throw his full weight behind the Bolshevik cause at the beginning of July. Furthermore, Kerensky's determination to continue the war played into the Bolsheviks' hands, although the frustrations and disappointments of the workers, soldiers and sailors that boiled over in uncontrolled rioting in Petrograd during the '**July Days**' of 3–5 July threatened to undermine some of their 'good work'.

EXTRACT 2

On hearing of the (February) Revolution while still in Switzerland, Lenin exclaimed that Russia had become the freest country in the world. But the dazzling new developments – political amnesty, legalisation of all parties, fullest freedom for propaganda and agitation – were for him no reason to collaborate with and acquiesce in the new order. They were opportunities to put into action the concept of the revolutionary party that had been in his mind ever since he wrote 'What is to be done?' in 1902. On 4 April, Lenin produced his famous April Theses. No compromise with the Provisional Government – all power was to go to the soviets; no reunion with the Mensheviks – on the contrary, his party should change its name to Communist and help establish a new militant Marxist International devoted to world revolution.

Adapted from Adam B. Ulam, *A History of Soviet Russia*, 1976

CROSS-REFERENCE

The 'Dual Power' arrangement between the Provisional Government and the Petrograd Soviet, and the unrest that followed the February Revolution, are discussed in Chapter 11, page 109.

 PRACTICE QUESTION

Evaluating historical extracts

With reference to Extracts 1 and 2 and your understanding of the historical context, which of these two extracts provides the more convincing interpretation of Lenin's attitude to the political changes in Russia by 1917?

A CLOSER LOOK

July Days

Grain prices had doubled in Petrograd between February and June, following a poor harvest, and shortages of fuel and raw materials had forced 586 factories to close with the loss of 100,000 jobs. The workers wanted price contols but the government was frightened to act against the industrialists. Consequently, 20,000 armed sailors from Kronstadt joined workers and soldiers on the streets. They chanted Bolshevik slogans, such as 'All power to the soviets', attacked property, looted shops, and seized the railway stations and other key buildings. Some even invaded the Tauride Palace demanding that the Soviet take power.

STUDY TIP

Before attempting this question, find out a little more about Lenin and his ambitions, from whatever resources you have available. In answering this type of question you should show an understanding of the alternative interpretations in the extracts and should support a judgement from the historical evidence you have available. You may prefer to return to this question after reading the whole of this chapter – or an A level question follows on page 120.

Warrants for the arrest of Bolsheviks, who were blamed for stirring up the troubles, were issued and several, including Trotsky, were gaoled. It is unclear whether the rebellion was actually stirred up by Bolsheviks and Lenin, who had been on holiday when the rioting broke out, always claimed that the demonstrations were spontaneous. He immediately returned, but just as quickly fled in disguise into exile in Finland.

Troops loyal to the Soviet dispersed the crowds and the Soviet newspaper *Izvestia* denounced the role of the Bolsheviks, suggesting that Lenin was working in the pay of the Germans and against Russia's best interests. Bolshevik propaganda was burned and the offices of the Bolshevik newspaper *Pravda* closed. Lenin's reputation fell, for fleeing rather than leading, while other leaders languished in gaol.

On 8 July, Kerensky replaced Prince Lvov as Prime Minister and it might have appeared that the Bolsheviks' moment had passed.

Red Guards: these were not crack troops but were loyal, volunteer soldiers who had been recruited from the factory workers in the city; they included young and old alike

Lev Borisovich Kamenev (1883–1936) was the son of a Jewish railway engineer, who joined the Social Democrats in 1901. Arrested many times, he became a propagandist overseas until 1914, when he was arrested and deported to Siberia, where he met Stalin in 1915. He returned in April 1917 and edited *Pravda*, opposing the April Theses. With Zinoviev, he voted against an armed uprising in October 1917, preferring a coalition with the socialists. Nevertheless he was made a member of Lenin's Politburo and joined Trotsky at the Brest-Litovsk negotiations, making peace terms with the Germans in 1918. He was forced from power by Stalin, expelled from the party in 1932 and executed in 1936.

Grigorii Zinoviev (1883–1936) was of Jewish origin. He joined the Social Democratic party in 1901 and was a member of the Central Committee from 1907–27. He was close to Lenin in exile and returned with him in 1917 in the sealed train but then supported Kamenev against the October Revolution. Zinoviev was against the idea of the Bolsheviks seizing power on their own, and wanted to work with other socialist groups. He became the head of the party's Petrograd organisation. He too was expelled from the party by Stalin and was executed in 1936.

Fig. 2 *Red Guards in Petrograd in July 1917*

Their cause was saved by the 'Kornilov coup', when Bolsheviks were released from gaols and soldiers, sailors and workers again took to the streets, this time supposedly in defence of the Provisional Government. Kerensky even supplied them with arms and the Bolsheviks seized the opportunity to organise bands of workers commanded by their '**Red Guards**', a militia they had trained in secret.

The Bolsheviks were able to bask in the reputation of having been the only group to have opposed Kornilov consistently. Lenin sent orders from Finland urging his followers to keep up the pressure and 'Committees to save the Revolution' were set up throughout the country.

Consequently, Bolsheviks were elected in increased numbers to soviets throughout urban Russia and in the Duma elections in Moscow, Bolshevik support increased by 164 per cent between June and December. The Bolshevik membership, which had stood at 23,000 in February, had reached 200,000 by the beginning of October, by which time the party was producing 41 newspapers and maintaining a force of 10,000 Red Guards in the capital's factories. By September, when new elections were held to the Petrograd Soviet, the Bolsheviks won a majority, which together with their control of the Moscow Soviet placed them in a powerful position. On 21 September Trotsky even became Chairman of the Petrograd Soviet.

It looked as though Lenin's tactics were paying off, but it must be remembered that the Bolsheviks were not, at this time, a tightly organised or discplined group. They tended to go along with events rather than initiate change. From mid-September, Lenin (still in hiding in Finland) bombarded the 12-man Central Committee of the Bolshevik Party with demands to stage a revolution and seize power. However the Central Committee and, in particular its two most prominent members, **Grigorii Zinoviev** and **Lev Kamenev**, fearing that Russia was not yet economically ready for revolution, urged restraint and even burned some of Lenin's letters.

On 12 September, Lenin wrote claiming that 'history will not forgive us if we do not assume power now,' but three days later the committee voted against a coup. Kamenev and Zinoviev believed that they should not act before the results of the Constituent Assembly elections (the date of which was still indecided) were known, while Trotsky suggested they should work through the Petrograd Soviet and wait for the Congress of Soviets which was due to be convened on 26 October. He believed that, at this congress, they could win the support of all socialist parties for a Soviet government without having to resort to violence.

The Bolshevik Central Committee headquarters

The Central Committee of the Communist Party and the Petrograd Soviet had set up their headquarters in Petrograd's Smolny Institute, a former Convent School for the daughters of the Russian nobility. It stood adjacent to the picturesque Smolny Convent building and still bore the Imperial arms carved in the stone above the entrance. Within its 100 or so huge rooms, linked by vaulted corridors and lit by rare electric lights, the swarming throngs of workers and soldiers in their heavy boots must have looked hopelessly out of place. Everywhere were notices imploring cleanliness, and on the doors, which still bore enamel plaques with notices such as 'ladies' classroom no.2', newer handwritten signs such as 'Central Committee of the All-Russian Trade Unions' or 'Central Executive Committee' had been added.

This information comes from the article, 'Scenes at the Smolny Institute, 24 October 1917' by John Reed, an American journalist who was in Russia at the time. Reed's writings, and in particular his book, *Ten Days That Shook the World*, provide a valuable account of the momentous days surrounding the Bolshevik takeover of power.

The Bolshevik seizure of power, October 1917

October–December 1917

10 October	Lenin attends a meeting of the Bolshevik Central Committee and his call for a Bolshevik-led revolution is agreed
20 October	The Military Revolutionary Committee of the Petrograd Soviet meet for the first time
24–25 October	Armed workers and soldiers led by the Bolsheviks and organised by the Military Revolutionary Committee take over key buildings and communication centres in Petrograd
25–27 October	The remaining members of the Provisional Government are arrested by the Bolsheviks; the 'revolution' is announced at the second Congress of Soviets; the congress adopts Lenin's decree on peace and decree on land and appoints the first Soviet government, the Council of People's Commissars, with Lenin as Chairman
December	A Secret Police force – **the Cheka** – is established

ACTIVITY

Research

Try to get hold of John Reed's *Ten Days That Shook the World* and read about the events at first hand for yourself.

KEY TERM

Cheka: the name given to the Bolshevik Secret Police

Commissar: a representative appointed by a soviet, a government, or the Communist Party to be responsible for political indoctrination during and after the 1917 Revolution in Russia

On 7 October Lenin secretly returned to Petrograd to attend a meeting of the Central Committee and try to win them over in person to the policy of taking power immediately.

Kerensky was well aware that the Bolsheviks wanted to seize power. He responded by sending some of the more radical army units out of the capital. This provided an excuse for the Bolshevik-controlled soviet, which claimed that Kerensky was abandoning the capital to allow it to fall to the Germans, to set up a 'Military Revolutionary Committee' under Trotsky and Felix Dzerzhinsky on 9 October. This comprised 66 members – 48 of them Bolsheviks – and it appointed **commissars** to military units, to issue orders and organise weapons supplies. The committee controlled 200,000

ACTIVITY

Group discussion

Why do you think the members of the Central Committee were so reluctant to act in October 1917? One half of the group should deliver a speech, such as the one Lenin might have given to persuade the committee. The other half should listen, question and point out the problems.

Red Guards, 60,000 Baltic sailors and 150,000 soldiers of the Petrograd garrison. Its declared purpose was to control troop movements (in the face of a German threat). However, its existence also seemed justified by the fears that government ministers might support a right-wing coup.

On 10 October Lenin harangued the Central Committee of the Bolshevik Party all night and finally succeeeded (with a vote of ten to two) in persuading them that 'an armed rising is the order of the day'. (Zinoviev and Kamenev refused to agree and published their own views in a newspaper – *Novaia zhin* – declaring that, 'if we take power now and we are forced into a revolutionary war, the mass of soldiers will not support us.')

Kerensky tried in desperation to close down two Bolshevik newspapers and restrict the Military Revolutionary Committee's power. He even ordered that the bridges linking the working-class areas to the centre of Petrograd should be raised. However, Bolshevik propagandists suggested that his actions were a betrayal of the Soviet and an abandonment of the principles of the February Revolution, and used them as an excuse to act.

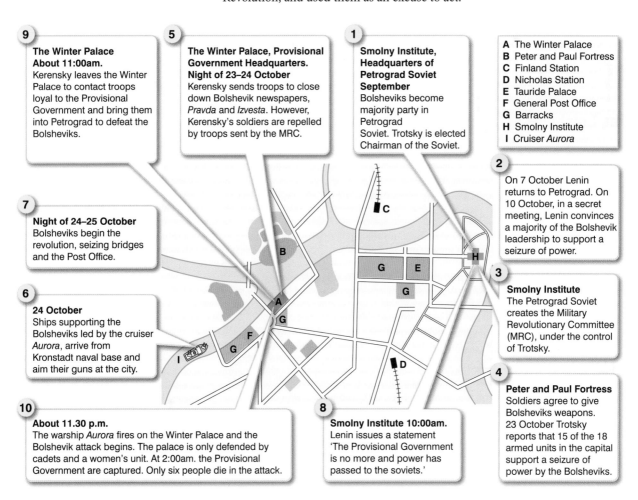

9 The Winter Palace About 11:00am. Kerensky leaves the Winter Palace to contact troops loyal to the Provisional Government and bring them into Petrograd to defeat the Bolsheviks.

5 The Winter Palace, Provisional Government Headquarters. Night of 23–24 October Kerensky sends troops to close down Bolshevik newspapers, *Pravda* and *Izvesta*. However, Kerensky's soldiers are repelled by troops sent by the MRC.

1 Smolny Institute, Headquarters of Petrograd Soviet September Bolsheviks become majority party in Petrograd Soviet. Trotsky is elected Chairman of the Soviet.

A The Winter Palace
B Peter and Paul Fortress
C Finland Station
D Nicholas Station
E Tauride Palace
F General Post Office
G Barracks
H Smolny Institute
I Cruiser *Aurora*

2 On 7 October Lenin returns to Petrograd. On 10 October, in a secret meeting, Lenin convinces a majority of the Bolshevik leadership to support a seizure of power.

7 Night of 24–25 October Bolsheviks begin the revolution, seizing bridges and the Post Office.

3 Smolny Institute The Petrograd Soviet creates the Military Revolutionary Committee (MRC), under the control of Trotsky.

6 24 October Ships supporting the Bolsheviks led by the cruiser *Aurora*, arrive from Kronstadt naval base and aim their guns at the city.

4 Peter and Paul Fortress Soldiers agree to give Bolsheviks weapons. 23 October Trotsky reports that 15 of the 18 armed units in the capital support a seizure of power by the Bolsheviks.

10 About 11.30 p.m. The warship *Aurora* fires on the Winter Palace and the Bolshevik attack begins. The palace is only defended by cadets and a women's unit. At 2:00am. the Provisional Government are captured. Only six people die in the attack.

8 Smolny Institute 10:00am. Lenin issues a statement 'The Provisional Government is no more and power has passed to the soviets.'

Fig. 3 *A map of Petrograd showing the Bolshevik takeover*

It therefore just remained for Trotsky, with his tremendous power and influence on the Military Revolutionary Committee, supported by fellow Bolshevik Yakov Sverdlov, to organise the final stages of the Bolshevik Revolution. Through the night of 24-25 October, with the support of the Petrograd Military Revolutionary Committee, and in the name of the Second Congress of Soviets, 5000 sailors and soldiers from Kronstadt moved into the city and Bolshevik Red Guards seized key positions around the capital. These included the telephone exchange, the post office, railway stations, the news agency, the state bank, bridges and power stations. Although they encountered some resistance at the main telegraph office, the troops on duty generally gave in without resistance. In the morning a further 3000 troops arrived.

Since Kerensky could not rely on the Petrograd troops to defend the Provisional Government, he left for the front – borrowing a car from the American Embassy and disguising himself as a nurse. He hoped to be able to make contact with loyal troops who would march to the city and defend it. The rest of the government met in an emergency session in the Winter Palace where on the evening of 25 October, as Red Guard soldiers and sailors surrounded the palace, a blank shot from the guns of the Battleship *Aurora* was heard at 9:40pm. This was the signal for the beginning of the Bolshevik attack. Further shots followed, including some from the Peter and Paul Fortress, the headquarters for the Military Revolutionary Committee, across the River Neva from the Winter Palace. However, only one shot hit the palace and most went into the river.

Fig. 4   *A soviet painting of the storming of the Winter Palace. In what ways is this picture an effective piece of Bolshevik propaganda?*

SOURCE 1

Semen Maslov, the Minister of Agriculture, who was one of those within the Winter Palace, recalled the events of 25 October:

At 7:00pm Nikolai Kishkin (appointed that day to control Defence) was handed a note signed by Vladimir Antonov (a Bolshevik) demanding the surrender of the Provisional Government and the disarming of its guard. The guard of the

Evaluating primary sources

How valuable is Source 1 for an historian studying the Bolsheviks' seizure of power?

Winter Palace was made up of some cadets, part of the Engineering School, two companies of Cossacks and a small number of the Women's Battalion. At around 10pm, a shot was fired in the palace, followed by cries and shots from the cadets. About 50 hostile sailors and soldiers were arrested and disarmed. In the meantime more and more sailors and soldiers arrived, until the guard seemed helpless.

At about 2:00 am, there was a loud noise at the entrance to the palace. The armed mob of soldiers, sailors and civilians, led by Antonov, broke in. They shouted threats and made jokes. Antonov arrested everyone in the name of the Revolutionary Committee and proceeded to take the names of all present. We were placed under arrest.

The October Revolution in Petrograd, whereby power passed to the Bolshevik Communists, thus proved a relatively small-scale affair. Trotsky claimed that 25,000–30,000 'at the most' were actively involved (this would mean around five per cent of all the workers and soldiers in the city) and this broadly tallies with other calculations based on the mobilisation of the Red Guards and others. There may have been 10,000–15,000 in the square in front of the **Winter Palace** on the evening of 25 October, but many would have been bystanders and not actually involved in the so-called 'storming'. The few surviving original photos suggest that forces were quite small. However, it suited the Bolsheviks to claim they were larger, as the legitimacy of their regime was based upon the fact that it emerged from a 'popular' revolution.

Much of Petrograd remained unaffected by the disturbances – trams and taxis ran as normal and restaurants, theatres and cinemas remained open. Even Trotsky had to admit that the revolution was essentially a series of 'small operations, calculated and prepared in advance'.

A CLOSER LOOK

The storming of the Winter Palace

In 1927, Sergei Eisenstein made a famous film entitled *October*, which perpetuated the myth that the storming of the Winter Palace was a heroic popular rising. The dramatic pictures of the masses breaking down the gates and storming in were entirely fictitious. In reality, when the *Aurora* fired, the Women's Battalion at the palace became hysterical and left, while the army cadets offered little resistance. Some Red Guards walked in through back doors and wandered around until they found the remaining members of the government. Furthermore, the discovery of the Tsar's wine cellar fuelled a frenzy of drunkenness.

KEY QUESTION

How important was the role of individuals?

ACTIVITY

Using Source 1 and the information in 'A Closer Look' above, list the ways in which the Bolshevik seizure of the Winter Palace was more shambolic than heroic. How far did the revolution of October 1917 differ from that of February 1917? Complete the following table:

	February 1917	October 1917
Participants		
Spontaneity		
Leadership		
Programme		
Actions		
Results		

Problems of interpretation

In the aftermath of the communist seizure of power, it suited Soviet historians to idealise Lenin's role and treat him as a hero. The British historians Edward H. Carr and Edward Acton also accepted the view that Lenin was the central directing force who won over the masses with his April Theses, built up Bolshevik membership and persuaded the Central Committee to take action in October. However, it was Trotsky who organised the Red Guard, took command in the Petrograd Soviet, dominated the Military Revolutionary Committee and organised the actual seizure of power. The British historian Robert Service has argued that Russia was heading for a socialist takeover anyway and that Lenin merely ensured that this was a Bolshevik takeover. Critics of the 'heroic Lenin' school argue that since he was absent for most of 1917, he simply reacted to events and was not the driver of revolution. They also point out that, when in Russia, he stayed in Petrograd rather than trying to create a truly 'Russian' revolution. If this interpretation is accepted, it might be felt that the Provisional Government's failures were more important than Lenin's leadership in bringing the Bolsheviks to power.

Another difficult issue concerns whether the October Revolution was, as Soviet historians suggested, a popular rising or whether, as Richard Pipes has claimed, it was, 'a classic coup d'état, the capture of governmental power by a small minority.' During the years of Cold War, Westerners tended to favour the latter interpretation but more recently some historians such as Sheila Fitzpatrick have adopted a more liberal view, accepting that there was, at least some radicalism and spontaneous rebellion which the Bolsheviks were able to exploit.

ACTIVITY

Research

Try to dip into the works and articles of different historians of the Russian Revolution and decide for yourself which interpretations you consider the most convincing. You will find some suggested books in the bibliography on page 237.

ACTIVITY

Complete the following table to summarise the reasons why the Bolsheviks took power in October 1917.

Weaknesses of the Provisional Government:	Strengths of the Bolsheviks:
Pollitical position:	Political manoeuvres:
Policies:	Policies:
Kerensky's mistakes:	Lenin and Trotsky as leaders:
Defeat in the First World War:	Pressure from workers and peasants:
Other factors:	Other factors:

EXTRACT 3

It simply would not have been credible, as an example to the rest of the world, for the Bolsheviks to have pretended, in a ruined and war-ravaged Russia, to light the path to the realm of plenty. Others, later, would no doubt blaze that trail; but the promise of the Russian Revolution, as conceived by Lenin, was more modest by far. It was no more than to fulfil the democratic revolution in the most radical way conceivable and thereby to ensure, in the future, the most favourable circumstances for the transition to socialism step by step with the international spread of the socialist revolution in the West. The revolution, as conceived by Lenin in 1917, was more modest in its objectives, more hybrid in composition, more ambiguous in its profession of socialist goals than many might have us believe.

Adapted from Neil Harding, *Lenin, Socialism and the State in 1917*, 1992

 PRACTICE QUESTION

Evaluating historical extracts

Using your understanding of the historical context, assess how convincing the arguments in Extracts 1, 2 and 3 are, in relation to the ambitions of Lenin and the Bolshevik Party.

The consolidation of Bolshevik government, October–December 1917

Fig. 5 *Lenin addressing the Second Congress of Soviets. How does the painter suggest that Lenin enjoyed widespread support?*

On 26 October 1917, the 670 delegates that had arrived for the Second All-Russian Congress of Soviets in the Smolny Institute held their first session. The Bolshevik action of the previous day was not universally approved and even the Bolsheviks, Zinoviev and Kamenev spoke out against the 'coup'. Irakli Tsereteli, the Menshevik leader, predicted that Bolshevik power would last no longer than three weeks, while the SR faction was split. Those on the left congratulated Lenin, while those to the right accused him of using violence to seize power illegally. Although 500 voted in favour of a socialist government, the Mensheviks and right-wing SRs were dismayed to find that the majority of seats for a new executive committee to carry this out went to Bolsheviks and more extreme left-wing SRs.

In protest, these 'moderates' walked out of the congress, leaving a Bolshevik and left-wing SR coalition in control. Their action simply played into the Bolsheviks' hands and Trotsky was able to shout at the retiring delegates the famous words, 'You're finished, you pitiful bunch of bankrupts. Get out of here to where you belong – in the dustbin of history.'

The executive committee established the 'Soviet of People's **Commissars**' or **Sovnarkom** as the new government. This was comprised exclusively of Bolsheviks, with Lenin as Chairman and Trotsky as Commissar for Foreign Affairs. It also included one female commissar, **Alexandra Kollontai**.

Lenin announced, 'We shall now proceed to construct the socialist order' and proceeded to introduce a series of decrees, designed to fulfil his promises of change and win support:

- 27 October: Decree on peace promised an end to war 'without annexation and indemnities'. (An armistice followed in November, accompanied by an official demobilisation process.)
- 27 October: Decree on land abolished private ownership of land and legitimised peasant seizures without compensation to landlords. (This reduced peasant support for the SRs and provided a breathing space for the consolidation of Bolshevik rule.)
- November: Workers' control decree gave workers the right to 'supervise management'.
- November: Nationality decree promised self-determination to the peoples of the former Russian Empire. (In December, Finland became an independent state, and an elected *rada* [parliament] was set up in the Ukraine.)
- November: New legal system of elected people's courts.
- November: Government outlawed sex discrimination and gave women the right to own property; decree against titles, all to become 'citizens'.
- December: Military decree removed class-ranks, saluting and military decorations from the army; officers were to be elected directly by the soldiers' soviets.
- December: Decrees on the Church nationalised Church land and removed marriage and divorce from Church control.
- December: Nationalisation of banks ended the private flow of capital.

Fig. 6 *The new Sovnarkom, 1917; all members were Bolsheviks*

The suppression of opposition to the Bolshevik government, October–December 1917

The establishment of control

Taking power in the name of the Congress of Soviets allowed the Bolsheviks to pose as the chosen representatives of the peasants and workers, but in reality their position was precarious and their support was still limited. Civil servants refused to serve under them and bankers refused to provide finance. It took them ten days to persuade the state bank to hand over its reserves, and then only under threat of armed intervention.

KEY TERM

Sovnarkom: the cabinet, made up of the important ministers who, between them, would run the country

A CLOSER LOOK

The word '**commissar**' was chosen to distinguish the new officials from the old bourgeois 'ministers', although they fulfilled the same function. Their full title became 'People's Commissar.'

KEY PROFILE

Alexandra Kollontai (1872–1952) came from an aristocratic background. She studied Marx, took part in Gapon's march in 1905, and joined the Bolsheviks in 1914. She was exiled but returned from the USA in March 1917, only to be arrested after the July Days. In government, Kollontai fought for the simplification of marriage and divorce, losing some favour with Lenin, but she became prominent under Stalin.

CROSS-REFERENCE

Stalin is profiled in Chapter 12, page 112.

Trotsky is profiled in Chapter 10, page 98

Lenin is profiled in Chapter 10, page 97

KEY QUESTION

- How did opposition develop and how effective was it?
- How did political authority change and develop?
- How important were ideas and ideology?

After his hasty departure, Kerensky had set up headquarters at Gatchina and rallied an army comprising 18 Cossack regiments and a small force of SR cadets and officers. Against this threat, the Bolsheviks looked weak. Many of the Petrograd garrison had returned to their homes in the countryside, and since Lenin had no direct contact with troops at the front, his forces were smaller in number than those of his opponents.

As he prepared to defend the city, there were ten days of fighting in Moscow between those who remained loyal to the Provisional Government and the Bolshevik revolutionaries. There was particularly heavy fighting around the Kremlin and many **Muscovites** were frightened to leave their homes. In Kiev, Kazan and Smolensk there was also strong resistance to the imposition of Bolshevik control. The railway and communications workers also went on strike in protest against the emergence of a one-party government.

This forced Lenin to agree to inter-party talks and, thanks to Bolshevik agitators who persuaded some of Kerensky's troops to defect, and a contingent of workers and soldiers who repulsed the rest on the outskirts of the city, the Bolshevik Revolution was saved.

By the end of the year the Bolsheviks dominated the major towns and railways, although large areas of countryside were still outside their control and it would take four more years of bitter civil war before the communists could claim full victory and military control of the country.

Lenin's promise to consider coalition with the other socialist parties was barely fulfilled. He only went as far as allowing left wing Social Revolutionaries to join Sovnarkom in December and it was made clear to them that they had to follow the Bolshevik lead. According to Volkogonov, he would 'brook no attempts to dilute or alter the absolute power the new regime represented'.

Other means of combating opposition

Lenin moved quickly to ensure Bolshevik control. His methods included:
- a propaganda campaign against political and 'class' enemies – particularly the *burzhui* (bourgeoisie).
- the closure of anti-Bolshevik newspapers
- a purge of the civil service
- the establishment the 'All-Russian Commission for the Suppression of Counter-Revolution, Sabotage and Speculation', in December 1917, more often known as the Cheka.
- leading Kadets, right-wing Social Revolutionaries and Mensheviks were rounded up and imprisoned in December.

Lenin's consolidation of control was so efficient that opponents could only pin their hopes on his promise of a Constituent Assembly. Elections for this began in November. These produced a 41.7 million turnout, but it was the SRs that won the most seats. Many votes had been cast without a full understanding of the political situation in Petrograd, but Lenin was appalled and declared that 'we must not be deceived by the election figures. Elections prove nothing.' Such a Constituent Assembly, comprising many political parties, he argued, was a mere remnant of bourgeois parliamentary democracy and to accept its rulings would be to take a step back in Russia's historical development.

KEY TERM

Muscovite: inhabitant of Moscow

ACTIVITY

Discuss with a partner what conclusions you would draw from Table 1.

Table 1 The Constituent Assembly elections

	Votes (in millions)	Number of seats	Per cent of vote
Socialist Revolutionaries	21.8	410 (including 40 left-wing)	53
Bolsheviks	10.0	175	24
Kadets	2.1	17	5
Mensheviks	1.4	18	3
Others	6.3	62	15

The Constituent Assembly was to meet for one day only – on 5 January 1918, after which Lenin dissolved it. Lenin believed that the Bolsheviks understood the needs of the proletariat better than the proletariat themselves understood them. Maxim Gorky wrote that Lenin had 'a ruthless contempt, worthy of an aristocrat, for the lives of ordinary individuals'. Even Rosa Luxemburg, a fellow revolutionary, expressed alarm. 'She feared that Lenin's policy had brought about, not the dictatorship of the working classes over the middle classes, which she approved of, but the dictatorship of the Communist Party over the working classes.'

ACTIVITY

Summary

Find the table you made at the end of Chapter 11. You should now be able to complete the third column with details of the Bolsheviks' growth through the months March-September 1917. On the back add a further timeline of Bolshevik rule October–December.

 PRACTICE QUESTION

'By the end of 1917, one autocracy in Russia had been replaced by another.' Assess the validity of this view.

STUDY TIP

To answer this type of question it is important to define autocracy. Try making a list of the key features of an autocracy and seeing to what extent they existed before 1917 (under the tsarist regime) and at the end of that year (under Lenin). Look for both change and continuity and, where possible, try to account for what happened.

3 The emergence of Communist dictatorship, 1917–1941

13 New leaders and ideologies

KEY TERM

Mandate: the authority to carry out a policy; this is usually given by the electorate to a party or candidate that wins an election

ACTIVITY

What impression does Extract 1 give of the importance of Marxist ideology for the Bolsheviks? According to Nettl, how does the Bolshevik interpretation of democracy differ from a Western interpretation?

KEY QUESTION

As you read this chapter, consider the following Key Questions:
- How did political authority change and develop?
- How important were ideas and ideology?
- How important was the role of individuals and groups?

EXTRACT 1

Lenin realised very well that the maintenance of Bolshevik power depended, in the short run, not on any objective measure of overall societal 'readiness' but on the twin immediacies of peace and land. Though the peasants and the disillusioned soldiers were not remotely interested in any sophisticated programme of socialism, they would support any government that fulfilled these promises. Here the Bolshevik understanding of democracy is crucial. Far from any programmatic platform on which the Bolsheviks could go forth and solicit electoral support, the Bolshevik view of democracy was action first and foremost – action which anticipated the expressed, or if necessary deduced, needs of the population: a commitment not a **mandate**. Such an understanding might be short on measurable criteria like majority votes, which bourgeois democracy valued so highly, but it was long on the unmeasurable but much more real links of action which bound leaders and the masses. The successful maintenance of power would be seen in continued popular commitment and support; the equivalent of being voted out of office would be successful counter-revolution.

Adapted from John P. Nettl, *The Soviet Achievement*, 1967

Fig. 1   *Propaganda poster from the Bolshevik era, showing Lenin*

Lenin's Russia; ideology and change

In the excitement and optimism that accompanied the 'revolution' of October 1917 and the establishment of a new Bolshevik government, issues of ideology were easily sidelined. The question of whether the manner of taking power conformed to the Marxist ideal became a side issue. Instead, the pressing need to retain and consolidate control led Lenin and the Bolsheviks to act first and 'justify' later.

In later years, Soviet historiography tried to explain and justify all that Lenin did, in the name of Marxism and the pre-determined logic of history. However at the time, such 'logic' was not always obvious and many of the key characteristics of the later Soviet state were the product of decisions taken as a result of circumstance.

Ideology and the end to war

Both Lenin and Trotsky had assumed that the Bolshevik seizure of power would spark similar revolutions elsewhere in Europe. They expected this particularly in Germany, which seemed ripe for revolution by all the economic, social and political criteria put forward by Marx. However, although they were ideologically committed to rousing the German workers and soldiers against their Imperial government, the Bolsheviks were simultaneously committed to pursuing peace with that government. This was despite knowing that peace would strengthen the Imperial government they wished to destroy.

This contradiction became acute when, following an **armistice** in November, Trotsky began peace negotiations in December 1917. The German Imperialist government demanded, as its price, large swathes of Russian territory. This split the Bolsheviks, with **Nikolai Bukharin** leading the 'revolutionary war group'. Protracted arguments followed in which practical necessity and the need for unity triumphed over pure ideology. Some Bolsheviks wanted to pursue the war, arguing that this was necessary to defend both socialism and Russia itself; but this would have been a betrayal of the promises that the Bolsheviks had made on seizing power.

Trotsky's solution was 'neither peace nor war' – retreating further if necessary while awaiting the revolution in the West. However Lenin took a more **pragmatic** view and argued for the acceptance of the German terms. After a long debate, the Treaty of Brest-Litovsk was signed on 3 March 1918 and ratified by an emergency Party congress. However, this was only after Lenin twice offered to resign. Trotsky spoke of sacrificing his deepest convictions in the interests of Bolshevik unity.

This decision was important for the future direction of the Soviet state. It set a precedent for future action by establishing that 'socialism at home' would take priority over the spread of international revolution. This commitment provided the intellectual foundation for Stalin's later 'Soviet-first' approach.

CROSS-REFERENCE

Look back to Chapter 5, page 44, where Marxist Theory is explained, and to A Closer Look on page 44.

Marxist ideas are outlined on page 127.

The October 1917 Revolution is discussed in Chapter 12.

KEY TERM

Armistice: a cease-fire

Pragmatic: dealing with matters realistically in a way that is based on practical rather than theoretical considerations

KEY PROFILE

Nikolai Bukharin (1888–1938) had joined the Bolsheviks in 1906, worked on *Pravda* in 1917 and entered the Politburo in 1922 as one of the 'younger generation'. He was very popular and an important theorist on the right of the Party. Although ousted by Stalin in the power struggle, he continued to work for the Party and contributed to the constitution of 1936. He was arrested in 1937, made to plead guilty in a show trial, and executed in March 1938.

The Treaty of Brest-Litovsk, March 1918

Fig. 2 *Map illustrating the territory lost by Russia under the Treaty of Brest-Litovsk in 1918*

Write and deliver a short speech that might have been made by Lenin, when he offered to resign. Make it clear why this peace with Germany is so important for the State and for the Bolsheviks. Consider how Lenin might reconcile his support for peace with his ideological beliefs.

Most of the territory on Russia's western border (including Finland, Estonia, Latvia and Lithuania, which became independent republics, and Poland, which became an independent state) was lost. Bessarabia was given to Romania (a German ally), and semi-independent governments were set up in Georgia, Belarus and the Ukraine. Russia lost a sixth of its population (62 million people) and two million square kilometres of land, including the area that produced almost a third of Russia's agricultural produce. Twenty-six per cent of Russia's railways lines and 74 per cent of its iron ore and coal supplies were taken.

Ideology and one-party government

Another ideological problem concerned the type of government that should be established in Bolshevik Russia. Before taking power, Lenin had suggested a conventional Marxist view that government would be in the hands of 'the people'. He used the slogan 'All power to the Soviets'.

SOURCE 1

In a speech in September 1917, Lenin said:

Power to the Soviets means the complete transfer of the country's administrative and economic control into the hands of workers and peasants, to whom nobody can offer resistance and who, through practice, through their own experience, will soon learn how to distribute land, products and grain properly.

Lenin suggested in *State and Revolution*, written shortly before the October Revolution, that 'the people' would readily see that a Bolshevik government ruled in their interests and would support it. He spoke of an expansion of democracy, with 'the people' managing their own affairs and a reduction in state bureaucracy.

In some ways, his early decrees, particularly those on land (October) and workers' control in factories (November) appear to support his theorising. However it is equally likely that he had little choice in this regard, since peasants were already seizing land and workers taking over factories. Furthermore these decrees did not actually help create the conditions necessary for 'socialism'.

CROSS-REFERENCE

For the decrees of October and November 1917, look back to Chapter 12, page 121.

EXTRACT 2

The Bolsheviks believed that one could give history a push, take over power, and create the conditions needed for the transition to socialism: an advanced level of industrial output; large-scale units of production, including those in agriculture; a powerful class-consciousness, and a disciplined industrial working class. But, the imperative necessity of preserving power made the Bolsheviks enact or tolerate policies and tendencies that clashed head on with the ideologically prescribed conditions for an orderly march toward socialism. Industrial production fell as workers' committees took over factories, often chasing out the managers. The Decree on Land enhanced the tendency to small-scale agricultural holdings. One need not discuss to what extent the Russian industrial worker of 1917–18 could be described as disciplined, able and willing to do everything in order to increase industrial production; the main prerequisite for laying down the material conditions for socialism.

Adapted from Adam Ulam, *A History of Soviet Russia*, 1976

ACTIVITY

What interpretation of the Bolshevik commitment to Marxist ideology is given in Extract 2?

The Petrograd Soviet, which had shared power with the Provisional Government in 1917 and in whose name the Bolsheviks had taken control, contained non-Bolshevik socialists, so Lenin sidelined it and formed the Bolshevik-only Sovnarkom. In doing so, Lenin showed that he had no intention of sharing power with other socialists: particularly, the Mensheviks and Social Revolutionaries, despite their shared Marxist heritage. Sovnarkom ruled by decree without seeking the Soviet's approval and the initiation of peace talks began without reference to the Soviet. While Sovnarkom met once or twice a day, the Soviet met increasingly less frequently. Its power was thus undermined, even though it continued to meet until the 1930s. The local soviets retained their importance, but they were brought into a new Bolshevik/Communist power structure.

Although Lenin agreed to allow some left-wing Social Revolutionaries to join Sovnarkom in November, following protests about the establishment of a purely 'Bolshevik' state, he was so hostile to any further suggestions of 'power-sharing' that Kamenev and Zinoviev (who favoured a broad socialist government) temporarily resigned. Once again there seemed to be a clash between the Marxist principle that power sprang from the people, and Lenin's determination to retain a dominant voice. Such determination meant that the Bolshevik state would be a one-party state.

CROSS-REFERENCE

The establishment of Sovnarkom is discussed in Chapter 12, page 121.

The new Bolshevik/Communist power structure is the subject of Chapter 14, page 135.

CROSS-REFERENCE

Kamenev and Zinoviev, two of the leading early Bolsheviks, are profiled in Chapter 12, page 114.

Lenin's resolution to avoid a socialist coalition government seems to fly in the face of both his ideological belief and the practical situation. Petitions from factory and army demanded a broad socialist government, and the railwaymen's strike in November demonstrated the strength of feeling for 'democratic government'. Even members of his own party favoured this. Lenin probably resisted because he feared other socialist leaders would not work with him personally and would dilute his own vision for the future.

CROSS-REFERENCE

To recap on the elections to the Constituent Assembly, look back to Chapter 12, page 122.

Lenin's determination was again seen in his dispersal of the Constituent Assembly in January 1918. When civilians demonstrated against his action, they were fired on and 12 were killed. Although such action appears to contradict the Marxist ideological principle of 'power to the people', in *State and Revolution* Lenin had written of the need for a strong party to provide for 'the dictatorship of the proletariat' and to crush any bourgeois attitudes or values that remained after the revolution. Thus, he was able to say with satisfaction that, 'The dissolution of the Constituent Assembly means the complete and open repudiation of democracy in favour of dictatorship. This will be a valuable lesson.'

Fig. 3 *The Bolshevik army marches through Red Square*

Lenin tried to claim that since the Bolsheviks were working in coalition with the Social Revolutionaries (although this was only the more radical left-wing of the party) it represented the 'people' and a higher form of 'democracy'. This shallow attempt at justification was shown up in the ensuing months, when the coalition government broke up, and the left-wing Social Revolutionaries walked out of Sovnarkom in protest at the Treaty of Brest-Litovsk. In March 1918 the Bolsheviks formally adopted the title of 'Communist Party' and from then on governed alone. All other groupings, whether former opponents or allies, were treated as 'enemies'.

Thus, the concept of the one-party state, with a ruling party incapable of sharing power with anyone outside the party, was established during the early months of Lenin's rule. It remains uncertain whether this concept was the product of the difficult situation in Russia in early 1918 or of Lenin's own stubborn belief that he alone could make a **utopian** Marxist state become a reality. However, the one-party state was to become a key principle of Soviet communism.

KEY TERM

Utopian: ideal or perfect

ACTIVITY

Group discussion

Half the group should find evidence suggesting that, in the first six months of his rule, Lenin was only interested in preserving his own power. The other half should find evidence that Lenin was genuinely trying to fulfil Marxist ideology. Choose two speakers to propose and oppose the motion that, 'Between October 1917 and March 1918, Lenin was more concerned with the preservation of his own power than the creation of a Marxist state.'

Ideology and the preservation of the Soviet state

The creation of the Cheka, in December 1917, confirmed Lenin's conviction that the 'dictatorship of the proletariat' would require the active repression of 'counter-revolutionary' enemies. His dismissal of the Constituent Assembly likewise supported his belief that 'revolutionary morality' justified strong action. Between 1918 and 1920, the new Communist State became even more firmly associated with 'terror' and repression as the Bolsheviks fought against their political enemies (from former tsarists to right-wing Social Revolutionaries) in a period of civil war.

This war had a huge effect on the development of the Party and State. The demand for obedience to the Party tightened; new central controls were brought in to manage the economy (known as War Communism) and deal with food shortages; and terror was used systematically to enforce the stringent new measures and eradicate opposition. By revealing the weaknesses of Bolshevik control, the years of civil war forced the adoption of a more centralised system of government.

'Central planning', the nationalisation of industry, and state control could be justified as the fulfilment of socialist principles, and many communists interpreted them that way, but they could equally be seen as a pragmatic reaction to crisis. Lenin's readiness to 'change course' after the war in 1921, allowing more capitalistic practices, would seem to reinforce that pragmatism was more important than ideology. It occurred when he was faced with revolt from workers and peasants who sought an end to wartime policies and the Kronstadt sailors, whose open revolt might be seen as symptomatic of working-class disillusionment. However, the issue of whether Lenin intended some capitalism to be permanent, or only temporary, was to cause a good deal of debate in later years.

Furthermore, Lenin's apparent change of heart had two other important consequences for the future of the Soviet state. Firstly, Lenin refused to admit any errors – and thus the concept that the Party could not, by definition, be

CROSS-REFERENCE

The civil war and its impact are discussed in Chapter 14, page 137.

The new central controls to manage the economy during the civil war were known as 'War Communism'; they are described in Chapter 15, pages 147–148.

The use of terror is discussed in Chapter 17, page 168.

The possibility of revolt from workers, peasants and the Kronstadt sailors is outlined in Chapter 15, pages 148–149.

Capitalism is defined on page 73.

KEY TERM

Faction: a group that shares similar ideas

CROSS-REFERENCE

Stalin's use of the ban on factions to defeat his rivals is covered on pages 129–130.

Commissar was the new communist title for 'minister'. For more on the role of commissar and the men who held these positions in the new Bolshevik government, return to chapter 12, page 121.

wrong was born. Secondly, Lenin successfully argued for a 'ban on **factions**' within the Communist Party, pointing out that Party unity was paramount in the difficult circumstances of 1921. Although this resolution meant little at the time, it was to assume much importance after Lenin's death, when Stalin used the ban to defeat his rivals.

The civil war years also saw one other major change in ideological commitment of the Communist government. Earlier support for 'national self-determination' for the ethnic minorities was abandoned and all independence movements were denounced as 'counter-revolutionary'. The demands for greater independence in Georgia from 1922 were brutally crushed (although against Lenin's wishes) on the orders of Stalin, who was a **Georgian** himself, and the People's Commissar for Nationalities.

A CLOSER LOOK

Stalin in Georgia

Georgia had been in the hands of Mensheviks during the civil war. When the Red Army advanced to establish control over the province, Lenin was assured by Stalin, as Commissar of Nationalities, that a massive Bolshevik uprising had occurred in Tbilisi and the Mensheviks had already been virtually overthrown by the Georgian people. However, both Lenin and Trotsky were appalled when they later heard that heavy fighting was taking place and that the people were supporting the Mensheviks and 'independence'; the Bolsheviks/Communists were therefore engaged in overthrowing an independent socialist régime by force of arms.

CROSS-REFERENCE

Read about show trials in Chapter 3 and in Chapter 17.

A CLOSER LOOK

Lenin's death

In August 1918, Lenin was shot in the neck by a Social Revolutionary named Fanya Kaplan, who claimed to be protesting against the Treaty of Brest-Litovsk. Lenin was badly wounded and although he recovered, in May 1922 he suffered the first of three strokes. The second, in December 1922, left him unable to speak and partially paralysed the right side of his body; the third, in March 1923 left him both mute and bed-ridden. Because of his incapacity, Lenin was largely distant from politics in the last year of his life. He died in January 1924.

Between 1921 and **Lenin's death** in 1924, many of the key features of the Soviet state in the Stalinist years became well established. A fierce attack on the Church (seen as a rival power source) began, censorship became more systematic, and the powers of the Secret Police were extended.

Nor was any mercy shown to political rivals once the years of civil war cooperation were over. Julius Martov, the Menshevik leader, left the country. The arrest of 5000 'for counter-revolutionary activities' destroyed this group as a political force. In 1922, a group of imprisoned Social Revolutionaries was given a 'show trial' and accused of plotting to assassinate Lenin. This resulted in 34 leaders being condemned, 11 executed and the party outlawed.

Although Lenin established many of the principles that underpinned the later Soviet state, at the time of his death, in 1924, it was still not clear quite what direction it would take. Lenin had combined ideology and pragmatism in order to survive, but from 1922 he became increasingly concerned about the state of the Party, the growing bureaucracy, and the future leadership. In the light of subsequent events, he was probably right to be so.

ACTIVITY

Look back through the chapter so far and write down all the basic principles of Soviet rule that appeared during the Leninist years.

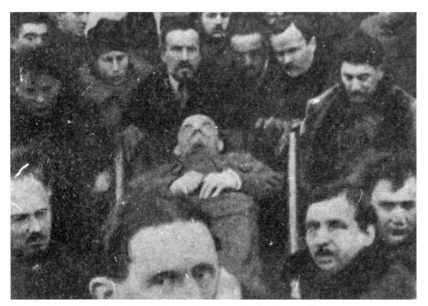

Fig. 4 *Members of the Central Committee carrying Lenin's coffin*

 PRACTICE QUESTION

To what extent did Lenin fulfil the revolutionary aims of the early Russian Marxists during his years as leader of Russia?

 PRACTICE QUESTION

Evaluating historical extracts

Using your understanding of the historical context, assess how convincing the arguments in Extracts 1 and 2 are, in relation to the importance of ideology in the emergence and consolidation of the Leninist state.

STUDY TIP

You will need to refer back to Chapters 5 and 10 in order to remind yourself of Marxist revolutionary ideas. As a young man, Lenin was influenced by Nikolai Chernyshevsky, whose novel *What is to be done?* inspired Lenin to write a tract with the same title in 1902. He was also influenced by Sergei Nechayev's *Catechism of a Revolutionary*. Using what you know of nineteenth-century Russian Marxism, try to assess whether Lenin fulfilled or neglected key principles.

STUDY TIP

You have already made notes on the interpretations contained in these extracts. You now need to ensure you consider how convincing the authors' arguments are. Don't forget to refer back to Chapter 12 for the 'emergence' of the Leninist state.

Stalin's rise; ideology and change

The power struggle and the emergence of Stalin

In December 1922, Lenin decided to dictate his 'Testament', in the form of a letter to be read to the Party congress on his death. Lenin did not nominate a future leader, but gave his critical opinion of other members of the **Politburo**: Grigorii, Lev Kamenev, Nikolai Bukharin and Trotsky. He particularly criticised Stalin, who had become the Party's first General Secretary in April 1922, partly because of the Georgian affair and partly because Stalin had insulted Lenin's wife, Krupskaya. Lenin referred to Stalin's 'personal rudeness, unnecessary roughness and lack of finesse' and suggested that 'comrades should think about a way of removing Stalin from his post'. This Testament was never read in public as intended, since the **Central Committee** decided among themselves to suppress it. This played into Stalin's hands.

KEY TERM

Politburo: the highest policy-making government authority under communist rule; it was the central policy-making and governing body of the Communist Party

Central Committee: elected by the Party congress and, in turn, elected the Politburo; the Politburo was therefore theoretically responsible to the Central Committee which directed all Party and government activities between each Party congress

CROSS-REFERENCE

Zinoviev and Kamanev are profiled in Chapter 12, page 114; Trotsky in Chapter 10, page 98; Stalin in Chapter 12, page 112 and Bukharin in Chapter 13, page 125.

A CLOSER LOOK

Stalin's insult

Stalin's wife, who worked as a secretary for Lenin during his illness, discovered that Lenin was in correspondence with Trotsky about future Party development, including the development of greater democracy. She informed her husband, but when Stalin tried to see Lenin, the latter's wife, Krupskaya, would not let him visit. In a telephone conversation with her, Stalin made a number of rude comments.

Leon Trotsky
Organised the October 1917 takeover; created the Red Army; hero of the civil war; member of Sovnarkom; regarded by Lenin as the 'most able' man in the Central Committee; believed in permanent revolution; joined the Bolsheviks in summer of 1917; a Jew; bourgeois background

Grigorii Zinoviev
Founder member of Bolshevik party; close associate of Lenin 1903-17; joined Kamenev to oppose timing of October Revolution; not a member of Sovnarkom; powerbase in Leningrad; a Jew; bourgeois background

Joseph Stalin
Old Bolshevik but not senior member until 1912; member of Sovnarkom; General Secretary of Communist Party from 1922; positions in Orgburo and Secretariat; peasant background

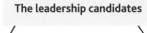

The leadership candidates

Lev Kamenev
Old Bolshevik and close associate of Lenin; had opposed timing of October Revolution; not a member of Sovnarkom; powerbase in Moscow; a Jew; bourgeois background

Nikolai Bukharin
Joined Bolsheviks 1906; not a senior member until 1922; theorist; described by Lenin as the 'golden boy'; some support in Moscow and among youth; son of a schoolmaster

Fig. 5 *The leadership candidates*

Stalin's emergence as leader of the Soviet Union followed a series of carefully crafted steps, as illustrated in Table 1.

Table 1 Stalin's route to leadership

Stage 1 1922–24	Dec 1922	A 'Triumvirate' alliance is formed between Zinoviev, Kamenev and Stalin, as the former seeks help to block Trotsky, who seems the most likely to succeed. Although Zinoviev and Kamenev share similar left-wing views on economic policy with Trotsky, they fear him because of his army support, arrogance and uncompromising personality.
	Apr 1923	At the 12th Party Congress (which Lenin is unable to attend) a new enlarged Central Committee of 40 members is elected; only three are strong supporters of Trotsky. Stalin uses his powers as General Secretary to build up supporters at local level, so ensuring that his nominees are elected to future congresses.
	Jan 1924	Lenin dies and Stalin gives Trotsky (who is travelling to the Black Sea, to recuperate from illness) the wrong date for Lenin's funeral; Trotsky is absent and Stalin gives the funeral oration. Stalin dismisses supporters of the Left Opposition.

Stage 2 1924–27	May 1924	Lenin's widow, Krupskaya, releases Lenin's Testament to the Central Committee shortly before the 13th Party Congress. Zinoviev and Kamenev argues against its publication (because it contains reference to their opposition in 1917) and Trotsky refuses to get involved. This aids Stalin.
	Nov 1924	In the congress Trotsky's speeches in favour of democracy and against the over-bureaucratisation of the Party are defeated by the Stalinist delegates and Zinoviev/Kamenev blocs. Trotsky does not appeal against the votes because of the ban on factions.
	Jan 1925	Trotsky publishes 'Lessons of October' showing how Zinoviev and Kamenev have (unlike himself) opposed Lenin on a number of issues. Stalin is not mentioned, which plays to his advantage. Stalin continues to bring in more supporters, forming majorities in committees.
	Dec 1925	Trotsky is forced from his position as Commissar of War.
	Jul 1926	At the 14th Party Congress, Stalin (whose policy of 'socialism in one country' is proving popular with Party members) supports Bukharin, on the right, claiming to share similar views on economic policy. Zinoviev and Kamenev attack Stalin and call for a vote of no confidence in him, but they lose every vote because the delegates are largely Stalinists. A new Central Committee and Politburo are elected with a Stalinist-Bukharin majority and Zinoviev is forced to step down as leader of the Leningrad Party in favour of Stalin's supporter, Kirov.
	Nov 1926	Zinoviev and Kamenev join Trotsky in the left-wing 'United Opposition', trying to appeal to the masses and organising demonstrations in Moscow. Stalin accuses them of 'factionalism' and Zinoviev is removed from the Politburo. Zinoviev and Trotsky are expelled from the Communist Party and Kamenev removed from the Central Committee. The United opposition collapses.
Stage 3 1927–29	Jan 1928	Trotsky is deported to a remote spot near the Chinese border; other defeated 'oppositionists' disperse elsewhere. Stalin announces a new 'left-leaning' economic strategy, which disagrees with that of Bukharin and his followers. Some of Trotsky's remaining supporters favour this approach and join Stalin.
	Sep 1928	In desperation, Bukharin contacts Trotsky and an alliance is considered, but rejected as supporters on both sides are hesitant. Stalin accuses both men of factionalism.
	Feb 1929	Stalin has Trotsky deported to Constantinople.
	Apr 1929	Bukharin is removed from his post as editor of *Pravda*.
	Nov 1929	Bukharin and his supporters, Rykov and Tomsky, are removed from the Politburo.
	Dec 1929	Stalin celebrates his fiftieth birthday as the undisputed Soviet leader.

The importance of ideology in the power struggle

Although various explanations have been given for Stalin's emergence as leader, ideological factors clearly played a part in the leadership struggle. From 1921, the communists had been split over economic policy, a vital element in Marxist Theory. Lenin's 'New Economic Policy' of 1921, which had allowed some private enterprise, had been controversial in that it conflicted with strict Marxist teaching. Whether or not Lenin intended this to be a temporary measure, to build the economy, as a precursor to full socialism was at the heart of the ideological debates of the 1920s.

1. While the 'left', as represented by Trotsky, Zinoviev and Kamenev, favoured abandoning the NEP, the 'right', led by Bukharin, Rykov and Tomsky supported its continuance. Stalin fluctuated from a left-leaning position to 1925, to temporary support for the right and the continuance of the NEP between 1925 and 1928, and back again to the left thereafter. This could suggest that he was a pure opportunist, although the last move could be accounted for by the bread shortages and high food prices of that year, rather than a lack of ideological principles.

2. To this was added another ideological issue. Despite the early expectations that revolution in Russia would trigger others, the Soviet Union remained the only Communist State in the 1920s. Nevertheless Trotsky still held to the line that the Russians should be working to stir up revolution elsewhere and that there should be 'permanent revolution' until a truly socialist society was created. Stalin, on the other hand had, by 1924, adopted the more pragmatic view that there could be 'socialism in one country' and that efforts should be concentrated on building a 'workers' paradise' in the Soviet Union as an example to the rest of the world. This less orthodox

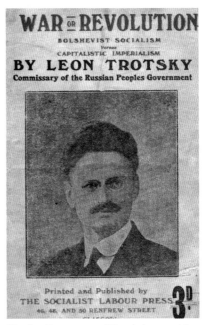

Fig. 6 *Front cover of Trotsky's pamphlet, 'War or Revolution'*

CROSS-REFERENCE

Lenin's 'New Economic Policy' of 1921 is discussed in Chapter 15.

CROSS-REFERENCE

For the change from elections to appointments and the growth of central control during the civil war, look forward to Chapter 14, page 139.

ACTIVITY

Undertake some further research into the key leadership contenders and the parts they played in the power struggle. Write a short speech, to be given by your personality at each of the three stages in the power struggle.

attitude appealed to those who favoured stability and feared the permanent revolutionary turmoil that Trotsky appeared to be advocating.

3. A further ideological issue concerned the nature of the leadership itself. Marx had not envisaged a single leader as necessary in a socialist state and there were elements within the Party who felt it was time to abandon the strong central leadership principle. They argued that this might have been justified in order to win the civil war, but was no longer necessary after 1924. Instead, they sought collective control, through a committee of equals. While this view had ideological justification, it was mainly advanced by those who feared the dominance of Trotsky and, in this way, the argument worked to Stalin's advantage. For most of the 1920s, Stalin's own ambition was grossly underestimated.

Whether we believe that Stalin was an opportunist who manipulated ideology, or a politician with genuine convictions, he certainly benefited from some of the principles laid down in the time of Lenin. The change from elections to appointments within the Party hierarchy, the ban on factions, and the growth of central control during the civil war provided the framework within which Stalin was able to rise to power.

ACTIVITY

Summary

Several key ideological principles have been considered in this chapter. Copy and complete the chart below to show the ways in which some Marxist ideas were (i) carried out and (ii) abandoned and changed, in the emergence of the Soviet state.

Ideological principle	Ways carried out	Ways abandoned or changed
International revolution		
Power in the hands of the people (decentralisation)		
Collective leadership		
No capitalism		
National self-determination for ethnic minorities		

STUDY TIP

Re-read Nettl's assessment in Extract 1 before you begin. This may provide some useful quotations to use in your answer. Remember that reference to what historians have written about a topic can be helpful in an essay, but only when you comment on the historians' views and either support or reject them with reference to your own knowledge.

 PRACTICE QUESTION

How important was ideology in the development of the Bolshevik state between 1917 and 1929?

14 The Communist dictatorship

The consolidation of Bolshevik authority; political developments 1917–24

EXTRACT 1

The totalitarian state had its origins in the civil war, when it was necessary to control every aspect of the economy and society. For this reason the Soviet bureaucracy ballooned spectacularly during the civil war. By 1920, 5.4 million people worked for the government. There were twice as many officials as there were workers in Soviet Russia and these officials were the main social base of the new regime. This was not a dictatorship of the proletariat but a dictatorship of the bureaucracy. The civil war became a model of success and shaped political habits until 1941. When Stalin spoke of a 'Bolshevik approach' or of doing things at a 'Bolshevik tempo' he had in mind the Party's methods in the civil war. From the civil war, the Bolsheviks inherited their cult of sacrifice; their military style of government with its constant 'battles' and 'campaigns' on 'fronts'; their insistence on the need to struggle permanently against the revolution's enemies, which they saw everywhere; and their utopian vision of the State as the maker of a new society.

Adapted from Orlando Figes, *Revolutionary Russia,* 2014

ACTIVITY

According to Figes in Extract 1, the period of civil war in Russia (which broadly lasted from 1918–20) was formative in creating a new style of government. Make a list of the ways in which Figes believes this occurred. See if you can add to your list from the knowledge you acquired in Chapter 13 and from what you read in this chapter.

KEY QUESTION

As you read this chapter, consider the following Key Questions:
- How was Russia governed and how did political authority change and develop?
- Why did opposition develop and how effective was it?
- How important were ideas and ideology?

The early months, 1917–18

The Bolsheviks survived the first months in power by a mixture of concession and ruthless action. They overcame the strikes and protests from the working classes in the cities (who favoured Soviet rather than Bolshevik rule) and by-passed the Soviet to establish a Bolshevik-dominated government headed by Sovnarkom. They prevented other political groups (except a few left-wing SRs) from sharing power and issued decrees designed to win support for the new regime. The Constituent Assembly was forcibly dissolved in January 1918 while the Treaty of Brest-Litovsk gave the government the peace it needed in order to survive, despite having been controversial even with the Bolsheviks.

LEARNING OBJECTIVES

In this chapter you will learn about:

- the consolidation of Bolshevik authority
- the evolving political authority of the Bolshevik/Communist State government under Lenin
- the political authority of the Communist State government under Stalin
- the development of Stalinist dictatorship.

KEY CHRONOLOGY

The consolidation of Bolshevik authority

1918 January Constituent Assembly meets and is dispersed

March Treaty of Brest-Litovsk

March Bolsheviks become the Communist Party with capital in Moscow

April/May Russian Civil War begins

July Murder of the Tsar and his family at Yekaterinburg in Urals; Constitution of Russian Soviet Federal Socialist Republic is adopted

1919 March Communist Party is reorganised: Party Secretariat, Politburo and Orgburo are established

1921 April 'Ban on factions'

1922 December Constitution of Union of Soviet Socialist Republics is adopted

1923 *Nomenklatura* system is adopted

1924 Death of Lenin

CROSS-REFERENCE

The Bolshevik activities summarised here are described in more detail in Chapters 12 and 13.

135

Fig. 1   *Lenin addressing the crowd in Red Square, Moscow*

Table 1   Early decrees of the Bolshevik state

Month	Decrees
October 1917	Maximum eight-hour day for workers Social insurance provides old age, health and unemployment benefits Ban on opposition press Decree on Peace Decree on Land
November 1917	Rights of the People of Russia Decree gives self-determination to minorities in Empire Abolition of titles and class ranks Workers' control of factories Abolition of old legal system Women given equality with men and right to own property
December 1917	Cheka established Banks nationalised Army placed under control of army soviet and soldiers' committees; officers to be elected and ranks abolished Marriage and divorce taken out of hands of Church Church land nationalised
January 1918	Workers' control of railways; creation of Red Army; Church and State separated
February 1918	Nationalisation of industry; socialisation of land

The 1918 Constitution

(RSFSR) was proclaimed in July 1918. This stated that supreme power rested with the All-Russian Congress of Soviets, which was made up of deputies from elected local soviets across Russia. The central executive committee of that congress was to be the 'supreme organ of power' – acting like a president. The congress was also made responsible for electing Sovnarkom for the purposes of the 'general administration of the affairs of the State'.

On the surface, the new constitution looked highly democratic. However there were limitations:

- The vote was reserved for the 'toiling masses'. Members of the former 'exploiting classes' (which included businessmen, clergy and tsarist officials) were excluded from voting or holding public office.
- In the election to the All-Russian Congress of Soviets, the workers' vote was weighted in the proportion of five to one against that of the peasants.
- While Sovnarkom was officially appointed by the congress, in practice it was chosen by the Bolshevik/Communist Party's Central Committee.
- The congress was only to meet at intervals – so executive authority remained in the hands of Sovnarkom.
- The structure was centralised and the real focus of power was the Party.

The Russian Civil War 1918–20

The greatest test for Bolshevik survival came in 1918, when anger at the concessions of the Treaty of Brest-Litovsk of March 1918 merged with the existing political opposition to create a force of '**Whites**'.

Russia's previous wartime allies, Britain, France and the USA, gave support to the Whites for various reasons:

- ideological – as capitalist nations they opposed the doctrine of communism
- the desire to force Russia back into the fight against Germany in the First World War
- to defend their own interests in Russia (since the Bolsheviks refused to pay back money borrowed in tsarist times and nationalised foreign-owned industries).

By the spring of 1918, an anti-Bolshevik Volunteer Army had been created in the south of the country, partly financed by Germany. In anticipation of the growing threat, the Bolsheviks moved their capital from Petrograd to Moscow in March 1918. However, the spark to war actually came from an outburst by the **Czech Legion** in western Siberia in May; three years of fighting followed.

Conflict with the Czech Legion

The Czechoslovak 'Army of Liberation', or the Czech Legion, had been formed from Czech nationalists in Russia during the war against Germany and Austria-Hungary. By 1918 it numbered 45,000 soldiers. In March 1918, the Bolsheviks gave permission for this army to travel eastwards, through Siberia, to continue the fight against their enemies on the Western Front. In May, as this force travelled along the Trans-Siberian Railway, some Bolshevik officials tried to arrest some of the soldiers and fighting broke out, as a result of which the Czech Legion seized the railway line through much of western Siberia and parts of eastern European Russia. With this, they abandoned their original plans, joined forces with anti-Bolsheviks and began to advance westwards towards Moscow.

Fig. 2 *The state coat-of-arms for the Union of Soviet Republics*

CROSS-REFERENCE

The Treaty of Brest-Litovsk, by which Russia withdrew from the First World War, is outlined in Chapter 13, page 126.

The Tsar and his family were murdered at Yekaterinburg in the Urals in July 1918. In theory, this was carried out by over-zealous local soviet officials, afraid that the Tsar would be rescued by the White armies and used as a figurehead. In practice, it is extremely unlikely that Lenin did not authorise these assassinations; their bodies were drenched in acid and thrown into a disused mine shaft.

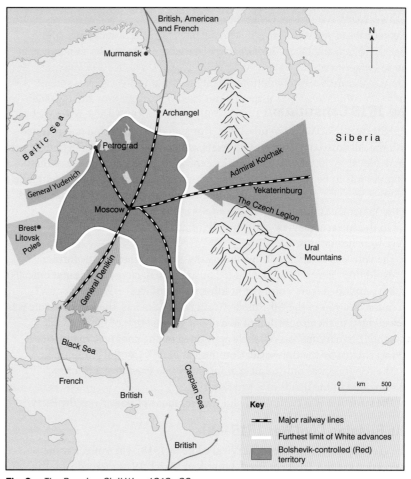

Fig. 3 *The Russian Civil War, 1918–20*

By the end of 1920, thanks primarily to the Bolsheviks' geographical advantages and superior organisation in the face of White division, most of the former Russian Empire was in communist hands. However this was at the cost of perhaps as many as ten million deaths from hunger and epidemic disease, as well as from military action.

Table 2 Reasons for Bolshevik victory

Geography	Unity and organisation	Leadership	Support	Other
The Reds commanded the hub of communications, the armaments factories and the most densely populated regions of central Russia (including Petrograd and Moscow). The Whites were widely dispersed in less-developed parts.	White generals operated independently and fought for different objectives. The Reds had a unified command structure.	The Red Army became a well-disciplined fighting force under Trotsky's leadership. The Whites had few competent commanders and ill-discipline was rife.	Although peasant support varied, generally Red land policies prevailed over the Whites' association with traditional tsarist policies.	Hostility to foreign involvement gave the Reds a propaganda platform. It did not greatly aid the Whites as foreign help was not extensive and was withdrawn after peace was concluded in the West.

The war continued into 1921 but as more of a nationalist struggle against Polish armies. The Poles invaded the western Ukraine, reaching Kiev in May 1920. Under direct orders from Lenin, Marshal Tukhachevsky mounted a successful communist counter-offensive against them. However, Lenin's hope that a communist revolution would break out in Poland and spread westwards into Europe was proved false. The Poles rose again and defeated the Red Army. This led to the Treaty of Riga (March 1921), which granted Poland self-rule along with Galicia and parts of Belorussia. The independence of Estonia, Latvia and Lithuania was also confirmed. Subsequently, this meant that Lenin's order to 'drive into Poland' was controversial, and split Bolshevik ranks.

The impact of the Russian Civil War on government and the Party

The Russian Civil War brought greater centralisation and Party control. The Party structure was based on annual congresses, elected by the mass membership (these met every year during Lenin's life) but actual policies and decisions were shaped by the Central Committee. In 1919, another body (theoretically a sub-committee), known as the Politburo, was created and this became the real centre for Party policy. The first elected Politburo of 1919 included Lenin, Trotsky and Stalin among its original members. Since these were also key government officials, the government increasingly became the instrument for carrying out policies made in the Politburo (of seven to nine men) and the Party Central Committee. Sovnarkom gradually met less frequently during the 1920s.

A CLOSER LOOK

An organisational bureau, the Orgburo, was also created in 1919 to supervise the work of local Party committees and supervise the permanent secretariat which was concerned with the day-to-day running of the Party.

Furthermore, it was decreed that the local soviets (the place where, in theory, the workers and peasants could show their voice in elections) should only consist of Party members. Added to this, Lenin's 1921 ban on factions meant that any decision taken by the Central Committee of the Communist Party had to be accepted by the whole Party, on pain of expulsion. This made it difficult to criticise Party decisions anywhere within the government structure.

The Party grew in complexity, and in April 1922 a new post of 'General Secretary' was created to coordinate its workings. This added another layer to the Party structure. This post was filled by Stalin, who was already acting as General Secretary, and was the only Party member to have a seat on the Politburo and the Orgburo. He was also a member of the secretariat.

In 1923, the introduction of the *nomenklatura* system added to the Party's domination. Official lists of c5500 key Party and government posts were drawn up, and appointments to these posts depended on the agreement of the Party Central Committee. This measure was intended to ensure that people in key positions were trustworthy. Thus a new loyal Party elite was created, to impose Party control. Those who wished to advance themselves enthusiastically sought positions. They were rewarded with special privileges, such as superior housing, in return for ensuring that central directives were obeyed without question.

Although Lenin spoke of '**democratic centralism**', the hold of the one-party state was therefore tightened.

CROSS-REFERENCE
Tukhachevsky is profiled in Chapter 17, page 175.

CROSS-REFERENCE
The Politburo and the Central Committee are both defined in Chapter 13, page 131.

Lenin's ban on factions is discussed in Chapter 13, page 129.

KEY TERM

Nomenklatura: a category of people who held key administrative positions in areas such as government, industry, agriculture and education, and whose positions were granted only with approval of the Communist Party in the region

A CLOSER LOOK

Democratic centralism

The communist idea of democracy was that because the workers and peasants elected members of their local soviets who, in turn, chose those who would sit on higher level soviets and the All-Russian Congress of Soviets; they thus exerted an influence on policy decisions. However, this was combined with centralism because the central authorities passed decisions down to the masses.

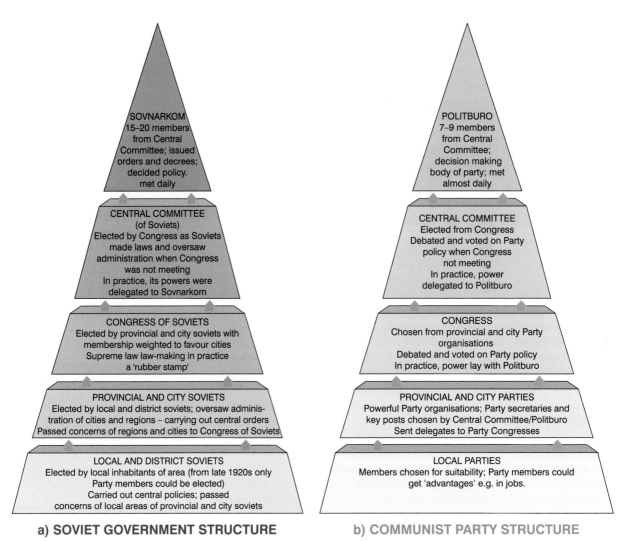

a) **SOVIET GOVERNMENT STRUCTURE**   b) **COMMUNIST PARTY STRUCTURE**

Fig. 4 *The parallel structure of Soviet government and the Party*

The impact of Civil War on the national minorities and the 1922 Constitution

The Civil War saw the communist government abandon its earlier support for 'national self-determination' as promised in the decree of November 1917. Although displays of national culture and native languages were permitted, independence movements were denounced as 'counter-revolutionary'. In 1922, demands from Georgia for greater independence were brutally crushed on the orders of Stalin, although his actions were condemned by Lenin.

The constitution was changed and the Union of Soviet Socialist Republics (USSR) was formally established in December 1922, replacing the RSFSR. In practice, the difference was minimal. Although Lenin prevailed over Trotsky in creating a federation of republics on a similar footing, rather than imposing direct control from Moscow which would have mirrored tsarist imperialism, the states which made up the union were kept under very strict control. The governments of the republics were regarded as regional branches of Sovnarkom which could, when necessary, be 'coerced' from the centre.

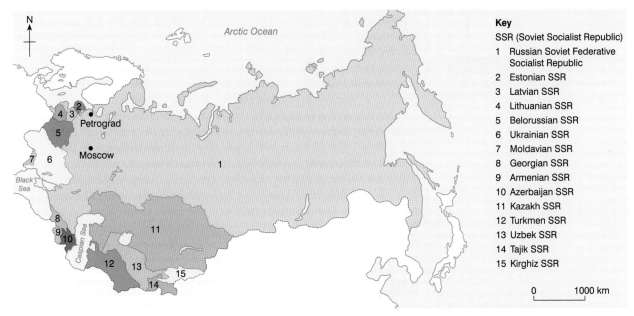

Key

SSR (Soviet Socialist Republic)

1 Russian Soviet Federative Socialist Republic
2 Estonian SSR
3 Latvian SSR
4 Lithuanian SSR
5 Belorussian SSR
6 Ukrainian SSR
7 Moldavian SSR
8 Georgian SSR
9 Armenian SSR
10 Azerbaijan SSR
11 Kazakh SSR
12 Turkmen SSR
13 Uzbek SSR
14 Tajik SSR
15 Kirghiz SSR

0   1000 km

Fig. 5   *The Union of Soviet Socialist Republics (USSR)*

The development of the Stalinist dictatorship

The political structure of the Communist State under Stalin

The structures established by Lenin – rule by one party and centralised control – were perpetuated and extended by Stalin who asserted an increasingly dominant personal influence. The Party continued to predominate over state institutions. Control was ensured through both the use of parallel structures at most levels, and the dual membership of Party and government offices held by trusted members of the *nomenklatura*. However, Stalin was increasingly concerned that the Party should reflect his wishes. Consequently, Party congresses were called less frequently – and none at all were summoned between 1939 and 1952.

Table 3   Party congresses 1924–52

May 1924	8 days
December 1925	13 days
December 1927	17 days
June-July 1930	17 days
January-February 1934	15 days
March 1939	11 days
October 1952	9 days

Through his position as General Secretary, Stalin controlled the more important appointments to the Party **'apparat'**. The *apparatchiki* in turn controlled the *nomenklatura*, which meant Stalin commanded vast patronage

CROSS-REFERENCE:

The Great Purges are discussed in Chapter 17, pages 174–75

over all of the important positions throughout Soviet society. Stalin preferred to work with personally selected committees rather than the full Politburo, and he used his power of appointment to build up the Party membership and develop an elaborate bureaucracy of loyal servants.

An expansion in Party membership began with the 'Lenin enrolment'. This took place in 1924–25, in commemoration of Lenin's death. The Party almost doubled its membership to one million. Further extensions increased the number of members to 1,677,910 by 1930 and 3,555,338 by 1933. Although there was a subsequent fall during the period of the Great Purges, there were still 3,399,975 members in 1940. Most new members tended to be drawn from the younger and less well-educated urban workers and ex-peasants who were less interested in ideological debate and more concerned with their own careers. They were often attracted by Stalin's more 'nationalist', energetic and sometimes brutal policies and knew that loyalty could bring benefits for themselves and their families. For the most part, they became firm supporters of the 'Stalinist' system and thus the structure of inequality, which had served their interests, became solidly entrenched.

A CLOSER LOOK

In *Revolution Betrayed* in 1936, Trotsky wrote that Stalin's power in the 1930s rested on a vast 'administrative pyramid' of five or six million Party officials, which needed to be swept away by a new proletarian revolution. Trotsky was certainly correct to identify the bureaucratised society that had emerged as a result of Stalinist centralisation. However, the bureaucrats were never to be swept away. Instead they became more entrenched and, ironically, the staunchest defenders of the Stalinist 'socialist order'.

The 1936 Constitution

In 1936, a new constitution, drafted by Nikolai Bukharin, was introduced, which Stalin claimed was 'the most democratic in the world'. It proclaimed the USSR to be a federation of eleven Soviet Republics (replacing the former seven). The All-Russian Congress of Soviets was replaced by a new 'Supreme Soviet' made up of the Soviet of the Union and the Soviet of Nationalities. Each republic also had its own supreme soviet. The new constitution promised local autonomy to ethnic groups and support for national cultures and languages ('nationalist in form, socialist in content'). It also promised four-yearly elections with the right to vote for all over eighteen (although this was raised to twenty-three in 1945) including the '**former people**' who had previously been deprived of voting rights. What is more, it was accompanied by an extensive statement of civil rights – such as freedom from arbitrary arrest and the right to free speech.

KEY TERM

Former people: dispossessed old elites who had no place in the new Russia

ACTIVITY

Look back to Chapter 14, page 137 at the details of the 1918 Constitution and draw parallel diagrams of the 1918 and 1936 Constitutions. (Note that the 1922 Constitution had made little difference to the 1918 Constitution.)

The new constitution did, indeed, look democratic and its main intention may have been to impress foreigners. In practice, the promised rights were largely ignored, and the central control exercised over the republics' budgets ensured the primacy of union laws and little real regional independence. Although the constitution acknowledged the right of any union republic to leave the union, when Party leaders in Georgia allegedly planned secession in 1951, they were purged.

Furthermore, elections were not contested so that the right to vote was merely to affirm a choice of representative. Moreover, the Supreme Soviet only met for a few days twice a year. This was said to be so that members could continue regular employment, but it meant that the body provided more of a sense of participation than any actual involvement in policy making. It was viewed by the Party as a forum for imparting decisions back to the localities rather than for electors to present their views to the centre.

'Stalinism' and the Stalinist dictatorship — the cult of personality

ДУХ ВЕЛИКОГО ЛЕНИНА И ЕГО ПОБЕДОНОСНОЕ ЗНАМЯ ВДОХНОВЛЯЮТ НАС ТЕПЕРЬ НА ОТЕЧЕСТВЕННУЮ ВОЙНУ... (И. Сталин)

Fig. 6 *Propaganda poster of Stalin, portrayed as the new Lenin*

From December 1929, and his fiftieth birthday celebrations, Stalin consciously developed his own cult, so promoting an image of himself that helped to inspire confidence during a period of rapid change. Stalin was universally portrayed as Lenin's true disciple and companion with slogans like, 'Stalin is the Lenin of today'. Portraits showed Marx, Engels, Lenin and Stalin in continuous progression, bringing enlightenment to the Russian people. Paintings, posters and sculptures were produced to glorify Stalin's role as the 'mighty leader', 'father of the nation', 'universal genius' and 'shining sun of humanity'.

The Stalin cult was fully established in the years 1933–39, although it did not reach its height until after the Second World War. *The History of the All-Union Communist Party* (or the 'Short Course') was published as the main historical textbook for all educational institutions in 1938. In this Stalin assumed a major role in the October Revolution, while Trotsky and other old Bolsheviks were portrayed as 'enemies of the people' or assigned to minor roles. Photographs were doctored to remove Stalin's enemies and show Stalin at the side of Lenin. This book had sold 34 million copies in the Soviet Union by 1948.

The adulation Stalin received was on a scale of intensity rarely seen before and, although it was 'manufactured', it also showed the strength of support he had acquired within the Soviet Union. Some praised him because they had benefited from his rule – or hoped to benefit in the future and needed to be assured of his patronage. However, for many, a very real sense of emotional attachment to Stalin reflected a very traditional sense of loyalty to the leader. Just as the peasantry had once shown unwavering loyalty to their Tsar, who could do no wrong, so Stalin was seen as a Father

ACTIVITY

1. Discuss with a partner: In what respects does Stalin deserve the title 'Red Tsar'?
2. Try to read Simon Sebag-Montefiore's biography of Stalin, entitled *Stalin: The Court of the Red Tsar,* which focuses on the years 1929–53, to get a fuller picture of Stalin in this period.
3. Some adjectives that might be used to describe the Stalinist dictatorship are nationalist, bureaucratic, undemocratic, centralised, repressive, coercive, uncompromising. Can you add any more?

to his people. Indeed he has been referred to as the 'Red Tsar'. Many were convinced that Stalin would look after their interests and that any problems within the system were the fault of lesser officials. He was regarded as a God-like figure and his portrait was carried and displayed in the manner of a religious icon.

ACTIVITY

Summary

The term 'Stalinism' is often used to describe the system of rule established by Stalin from the mid-1930s onwards but it is not an easy term to define. To develop a full picture of Stalinism, you will need to read Chapters 15–18 but, based on what you have learned about the development of political authority, you should already have some idea of what 'Stalinism' means.

Write a brief definition of Stalinism before reading the next section. When you have read further, you may want to change or add to your definition. As a group create a wall poster entitled, 'What is Stalinism?'

Summary

Government by 1941

EXTRACT 2

By 1941, the Soviet political system had been transformed. In 1934, Stalin's power derived from his position as head of the Party apparatus. Decisions flowed from the Politburo through the Party apparatus and then to the economic ministries, the Secret Police, the army and the various organs of government. By 1939, the Party apparatus could no longer control Stalin. Stalin had achieved a personal authority independent of any single institution. He had established his right to issue orders on his personal authority, using any bureaucratic channels he chose. In particular, he could act directly through the secret police against the party, the army or the economic ministries. Yet there was nothing to stop him acting through other institutions against the Secret Police.

Adapted from David Christian, *Imperial and Soviet Russia,* 1997

ACTIVITY

According to Christian in Extract 2, what powers did Stalin exercise? In what ways do Stalin's powers appear to differ from those exercised by Lenin in the early 1920s?

CROSS-REFERENCE

Stalin's enforced collectivisation is detailed in Chapter 15.

The NKVD and the Cheka are outlined in Chapter 17, page 169.

Yezhov is profiled in Chapter 17, where his role in the purges is outlined.

Malenkov is profiled in Chapter 21.

Although it is possible to see the 'Stalinist dictatorship' foreshadowed in the developments of the 1920s, the powerful coercive centralised state machine that Stalin had created by the mid-1930s was different from Leninist government in one very important respect. Stalin's rule was a personal rule, where he was above the Party and no longer dependent on it. The atmosphere of 'crisis' brought about by Stalin's enforced collectivisation and his new economic plans for industry helped to increase his power. So did the extensive propaganda that celebrated his image, his purge of the old elites, and his personal powers of patronage over a new, younger group of officials.

Stalin was not invincible, however. There was still a remote chance that others might act against him (he was, for example, outvoted in the Politburo in his plan to replace Nikolay Yezhov with Georgii Malenkov as head of the NKVD in 1937). Also, the inefficiency of the bureaucracy at local level was a limitation on what he might do. Nevertheless, Stalin's personal control after 1936 was sufficiently extensive for it to be referred to as a personal dictatorship.

Summary

PRACTICE QUESTION

Evaluating historical extracts

Using your understanding of the historical context, assess how convincing the arguments in Extracts 1 and 2 are in relation to the development of government in Soviet Russia between 1920 and 1941.

STUDY TIP

While Extract 1 concentrates on the impact of the civil war and Extract 2 is an overview from the perspective of 1941, both are concerned with why government developed as it did, offering two different arguments. You need to identify and comment on both, using your own knowledge of the context to evaluate the authors' views.

PRACTICE QUESTION

To what extent was the political authority exercised by Lenin and Stalin similar?

STUDY TIP

You will need to provide a definition of 'political authority' at the outset and remember to refer back to this in your essay. You should plan your answer by making a two-column list identifying the similarities and differences (or continuity and change) between the nature of political authority under Lenin and Stalin. Remember to give a judgement in your introduction, support it in your answer and repeat it in your conclusion.

15 Economic developments

LEARNING OBJECTIVES

In this chapter you will learn about:

- state capitalism and 'War Communism' under Lenin
- the New Economic Policy
- collectivisation under Stalin
- industrial development under Stalin, including the Five Year Plans

KEY QUESTION

As you read this chapter, consider the following Key Questions:
- How and with what results did the economy develop and change?
- How important were ideas and ideology?

EXTRACT 1

By 1921 Russia was ruined. The ruin had begun in the First World War. It grew in dimensions under the Provisional Government. The wild, initial experiments of the Bolsheviks were fast completing it. Fantastic inflation and hopeless deficits marked the abandonment of all conventional principles of exchange. Industry was more than five sixths gone. Transport had worn out most of its existing reserves and, in the failure of repair and production, except for military purposes it had broken down almost completely. Private trade had been suppressed at the outset, but in default of any adequate substitute, it continued illegally through the most curious channels. Not only the civil war and the foreign intervention, but the initial confiscation of all private property, even of foreigners, and the repudiation of government debts were entirely prohibitive of foreign trade. The fact that lay at the bottom of all other facts was, that during the civil war productive work had almost stopped, and the country was living on its reserves.

Adapted from Bernard Pares, *A History of Russia,* 1949

ACTIVITY

Evaluating historical extracts

Pares has some strong views about the impact of Bolshevik rule on the economy before 1921. Make a list of the factors which, according to Pares, had brought about Russia's 'ruin'. As you read the first section of this chapter, decide whether you agree with Pares. Do you feel that Lenin's handling of the economy could be excused or even praised in the years 1917–24? Draw up your own balance sheet.

KEY TERM

Socialist economy: one in which there is no private ownership and in which all members of society have a share in the State's resources

CROSS-REFERENCE

A definition of capitalism is in Chapter 7, page 73.

KEY TERM

Veshenka: this was the council responsible for state industry 1917–32 (its rival, Gosplan, is described in the section on the New Economic Policy, on page 149)

Nationalisation: taking businesses out of private hands and placing them under state control

The economy under Lenin

Lenin himself said 'Soviets plus electrification equals communism'. He understood that Russia had to modernise before the socialist ideal for which he had fought could be achieved. However in the early months of Bolshevik rule, there were many differing opinions as to how that '**socialist economy**' might be built.

State capitalism

Lenin's Decree on Land in October 1917 abolished private ownership of land, legitimising the peasant seizures and declared that all land belonged to the 'entire people'. Further decrees in November recognised workers 'control' over their own factories, so giving them the right to 'supervise management' through the establishment of factory committees, and similar committees were established for rural areas.

However, these early decrees really only legitimised processes that were already well underway and Lenin spoke out against the danger of moving towards 'socialism' too quickly. He seemed to envisage a long transition during which the first stage would be a form of 'state capitalism'. During this stage there would be a degree of state control but private markets would remain as an important feature of economic life.

In December 1917, **Veshenka** (the Council of the National Economy) was established to supervise and control economic development. However, Lenin remained cautious in the face of the demands of some in his Party that he should set about the **nationalisation** of industry.

Lenin's fears concerning peasants' and workers' control proved well-founded. Workers failed to organise their factories efficiently and output shrank at the time when it was most needed. Some workers awarded themselves unsustainable pay-rises, others helped themselves to stocks and equipment (there were cases of workers cutting slices of conveyor belt to make soles for boots) but mostly, they simply lacked the skills needed for successful management.

With more money than goods available, there was high inflation. This made peasants hoard produce, rather than sell for worthless money. So, the food shortages in towns, which were already affected by the loss of the Ukraine to the Germans, grew worse. The citizens of Petrograd were living on rations of just 50 grams of bread a day by February 1918 and elsewhere food riots threatened to undermine Bolshevik control.

CROSS-REFERENCE

The loss of the Ukraine to the Germans as a result of the Treaty of Brest-Litovsk is outlined in Chapter 13, page 126.

War Communism

Fig. 1 *Poster from 1919 reads, 'Stand Up for Petrograd!'*

In the spring of 1918, when faced with yet another 'grain crisis', Lenin took the further step of expanding the State's 'right to grain' by beginning a programme of **food requisitioning**. He also encouraged the establishment of collective or cooperative farming, hoping that if peasants pooled their resources they would farm more efficiently; but only a tiny minority of households complied. A food-supplies policy was set up in May 1918 which organised detachments of soldiers and workers from the large towns into the countryside to ensure that grain was delivered to the State. Officially, the peasants were paid a fixed price, but grain, livestock carts and firewood were often brutally confiscated, leaving the peasants with scarcely enough to live on, while the requisitioning detachments kept a share of what they collected as a reward.

The peasants were divided into three categories. The poor and moderately poor were regarded as allies of the urban proletariat but the 'grasping fists' – the *kulaks*, who had made personal wealth from their farming – were labelled 'enemies of the people' and had their entire stocks seized. Such measures brought misery to rural areas and peasants resisted where they could. They hid their crops, grew less, and murdered members of the requisition squads. The Cheka had to be used extensively to make the policy work at all.

KEY TERM

Food requisitioning: this involved taking grain and other foodstuffs from the peasants at a fixed rate in order to supply the urban workers and soldiers; the rate took no account of harvests or local conditions

CROSS-REFERENCE

Read about the Cheka in Chapter 12.

To recap on the Putilov Iron Works, look back to Chapter 8, page 76.

A CLOSER LOOK

Rations and barter

Under the system of barter, goods were exchanged without using money. A worker might, for example forfeit his meat rations in order to obtain a surplus of eggs, then exchange these eggs for cooking utensils. Petty traders exploited the system by supplying 'black market' goods. Rationing was also used to discriminate against the 'former people' (nobility, bourgeoisie and clergy) who received the lowest rations.

ACTIVITY

Design your own propaganda poster for War Communism – either for a town or the countryside. Try to inspire the workers or peasants to support the policy.

A CLOSER LOOK

The Tambov revolt

The requisitioning squads arrived in Tambov in August 1920, when the peasants had almost no reserves after a poor harvest. Led by Alexander Antonov, a 70,000-man Peasant Army was formed and the struggle continued until June 1921. This revolt spread across large swathes of south-eastern Russia.

At the same time, the railways, banks, merchant fleet, power companies and the Putilov Iron Works were all nationalised. With the increasing demands posed by the civil war, the number of nationalisations multiplied. The first entire industry to be nationalised was sugar in May 1918, followed by oil in June. By November 1920 nationalisation was extended to nearly all factories and businesses. The workers lost the freedom they had formerly enjoyed and professional managers (often the very same 'specialists' who had recently been displaced from factory ownership) were employed by the State to reimpose discipline and increase output. Working hours were extended and ration-card workbooks (for food, clothing and lodging) were issued, replacing wages. Internal passports were also introduced to stop employees drifting back to the countryside.

Under this draconian system, which became known as War Communism, all private trade and manufacture were forbidden. Some saw this as the transition to a socialist economy since money was no longer the main agency of exchange and lost its value in favour of a system of barter. Indeed, the political commissars that were attached to each Red Army unit made it their business to indoctrinate the soldiers with Marxist Theories that justified the harsh economic measures

While War Communism was, in some ways, an extension of the class warfare to destroy 'bourgeois attitudes' already seen in the early months of Bolshevik rule, there is no evidence that Lenin had originally planned to radicalise the economy so quickly. Trotsky initially opposed War Communism and put forward his own mixed socialist/capitalist scheme in 1920, but when this was rejected, he accepted the measures and spoke of building communism by force. It is easy to see that War Communism existed to ensure that the Red Army was supplied with munitions and food by the towns but whether there was more to it is unclear; it is an issue that has vexed contemporaries and historians alike.

In practice, War Communism created more problems than it solved. As transport systems were disrupted by the fighting and management struggled to get factories working efficiently, production declined. By 1921, total industrial output had fallen to around 20 per cent of its pre-war levels and rations had to be cut. Diseases such as cholera and dysentery were rife and a typhus epidemic swept through the cities and caused the death of more than three million in 1920. Some workers went on strike, which only made matters worse. Others ignored the passport system and braved the armed guards stationed on the city boundaries to flee to the country in the hope of finding food. (By the end of 1920 the population of Petrograd was 57.5 per cent lower than the level of 1917. In Moscow it was 44.5 per cent lower.) However, those who fled were to be disappointed.

The combination of harsh requisitioning and the attack on the *kulaks* in the countryside had reduced grain supplies to dangerous levels. There was an acute food shortage by 1920, as insufficient grain was planted. A third of land had been abandoned to grass and cattle and horses had been slaughtered in their thousands by hungry peasants. When the harvest of 1921 produced only 48 per cent of that of 1913, there was widespread famine. Millions died from malnourishment and disease. Russia's population, which had stood at 170.9 million in 1913, had fallen to 130.9 million by 1921. Conditions were so bad that there were even reports of cannibalism and trade in dead bodies.

Demands for economic change

The famine brought a new outbreak of peasant revolts, the worst being in the **Tambov** province, 300 miles south-east of Moscow. Some 100,000 Red Army troops had to be deployed to deal with the troubles and there were brutal reprisals, particularly against those accused of being *kulaks*. Poison gas was even used to deal with those who hid in the forests.

Fig. 2 *Victims of famine in the Volga region of Russia in 1921; the severity of the famine caused scattered outbreaks of cannibalism*

The food crisis and a reduction by a third in the bread ration in several cities, including Moscow and Petrograd, brought further strikes and riots. Workers protested against factory discipline, and a lack of union representation in factories and support for other socialist parties revived. **Martial law** was declared in January 1921, but even some regular soldiers refused to take action and the Cheka had to be used to crush the demonstrations.

The most alarming revolt, as far as the government was concerned, came from the 30,000 sailors stationed in the Kronstadt naval base. The Kronstadt sailors had been the most loyal supporters of the October Revolution. However, in March 1921, they sent a manifesto to Lenin demanding an end to one-party communist rule. The Red Army was sent five miles across the ice (supported by an artillery force on land and Cheka men to the rear in case any soldier tried to desert) to crush the rebels. They took 15,000 rebels prisoner and the leaders were shot. Lenin denounced the sailors as 'White Traitors', but the incident had shaken him, particularly coming at the point when the Tambov revolt was reaching its peak.

These troubles also caused divisions within the Bolshevik party itself. The 'Workers' Opposition' group was set up under Aleksandr Shiyapknikov and Alexandra Kollontai and argued for greater worker control and the removal of managers and military discipline in factories. They strongly opposed those in the Party (which, from 1920 included Trotsky) who wanted to continue and intensify War Communism.

Lenin claimed that the Kronstadt revolt was 'the flash which lit up reality better than anything else', but it was probably the coincidence of the many troubles of 1921 that persuaded him that a change of economic direction was necessary.

The New Economic Policy (NEP)

Gosplan was formally established, by a Sovnarkom decree in February 1921, to advise on a New Economic Policy, which Lenin formally announced at the 10th Party Congress in August 1921. This was supported by Bukharin, Zinoviev and most of the leadership, but many rank and file Bolsheviks saw this 'NEP' as an ideological betrayal.

Although state control of transport, banking and heavy industry, such as coal, steel and oil, continued, the NEP allowed for the private ownership of smaller businesses (usually through cooperatives and trusts) and permitted private trade.

KEY TERM

Martial law: an extreme measure involving the use of military force; military leaders are used to enforce the law and normal civil liberties are suspended

CROSS-REFERENCE

Alexandra Kollontai is profiled in Chapter 12, page 121.

KEY TERM

Gosplan: the State General Planning Commission (1921–91), with headquarters in Moscow and additional branches in each Soviet republic; helped coordinate economic development and, from 1925, drafted economic plans, however this brought it into conflict with Veshenka (see page 146 of this chapter)

Fig. 4 *A Soviet propaganda poster, which reads, 'We are on the threshold of changing from an agrarian nation into an industrial nation.'*

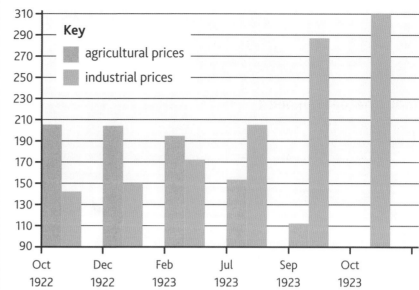

Fig. 3 *The 'scissors crisis' – what does this diagram show about the effects of the NEP?*

Rationing was ended and industries had to pay their workers from their profits. This ensured the efficient use of resources. There was an end to the requisitioning of grain and although peasants were still required to give a proportion of their produce to the State, as a form of tax, they were permitted to sell any surplus.

The NEP got the economy moving again, although the peasants responded more quickly than the town workshops and industrial cooperatives. This produced a 'scissors crisis', as Trotsky called it, in 1923, whereby a huge increase in grain supplies brought down food prices in the towns, but a lack of industrial goods for peasants to buy in exchange encouraged them to hold back their supplies. Consequently, the government capped industrial prices and replaced the peasants' quotas with money taxes from 1923. This forced the peasants to sell.

The crisis was short-lived and by 1926, the production levels of 1913 had been reached again. This brought with it better living standards, an end to the revolts and disputes, and some favourable trade agreements with Britain and Germany. A money economy and private wealth returned as '**Nepmen**' traders flourished by buying grain and selling industrial goods around the country, and the *kulak* class re-emerged.

The economy under Stalin

EXTRACT 2

The Bolsheviks' second industrial revolution began in 1928. It was this which ultimately gave the Soviet Union its modern character, the basic image and the various associations implied by the term, 'Soviet Communism'. In one sense, the second revolution completed the work of Lenin and the old Bolsheviks. Where they had imposed a new philosophy, a new instrument of rule and a new group of leaders on an ancient, predominantly peasant society, Stalin and his new Bolsheviks reached right down to eliminate every cranny of conservatism with their plans of steel and concrete and their irresistible claim to be fulfilling Marxist orthodoxy. By the time Stalin died the Soviet Union had been completely transformed.

Adapted from John P. Nettl, *The Soviet Achievement*, 1967

Draw a Venn diagram showing War Communism in one circle and the NEP in another, and complete it with details of each. Show their individual characteristics as well as the features that were common to both economic strategies.

How important was the role of individuals and groups?

Industrial development

Disputes over the continuation of the NEP lay at the heart of the leadership struggle between 1924 and 1929. During this period, Stalin's own views appeared to change – or at least evolve – so that, by 1927 he was ready to embark on a new strategy. The evolution of policy in these years is summarised in Table 1.

Table 1 Economic policy, 1925–27

1925	14th Party Congress (the 'industrialisation congress') called for 'the transformation of our country from an agrarian into an industrial one, capable by its own efforts of producing the necessary means.'
1926	NEP was maintained although concerns were raised as more investment was needed to drive industry forwards.
Dec 1927	15th Party Congress – announcement of the end of NEP and the beginning of the First Five Year Plan for rapid industrialisation, known as the '**Great Turn**'.

The Great Turn

This was the move from the NEP to the Five Year Plans and collectivisation of agriculture. This entailed a move to central planning, making the government responsible for economic coordination. This is sometimes called a '**command economy**'. It was believed that the new industrial growth would build self-sufficiency and lead to a truly 'socialist' state.

The struggle for power after Lenin's death and Stalin's establishment of his leadership are the subject of Chapter 13.

Stalin's 'Great Turn' was driven by a number of economic factors, quite apart from his political desire to establish his leadership. By 1927, the NEP was failing to produce the growth that many leading communists sought, and a war scare in the late 1920s made them particularly nervous. They wanted to increase the USSR's military strength and develop its self-sufficiency, so that it was less reliant on foreign imports. Furthermore, to move towards true 'socialism' it was essential to develop industry and not have a State dependent on peasants and the grain harvest. It also suited Stalin's personal style to have strong central control over the economy, known as 'central planning'.

Stalin chose to advance his economic programme for industry through a series of 'Five Year Plans', which set targets for the chosen industrial enterprises to attain. These targets were usually very ambitious; they were intended to force managers and workers to devote their maximum effort to the programme. The launching and fulfilment of these plans were accompanied by much propaganda. Since failure to achieve a target was deemed a criminal offence, all those involved in administering and carrying out the plans went to great lengths to ensure that the reported statistics showed huge improvements – often way above the targets originally set. Thus, corruption and faulty reporting was built into the system from the outset.

The First Five Year Plan, 1928–32

The aims of the First Five Year Plan were to:
- increase production by 300 per cent by setting targets for growth
- develop heavy industry (coal, iron, steel, oil and machinery)
- boost electricity production by 600 per cent
- double the output from light industry such as chemicals production.

The publicity surrounding the launch of the plan provoked an enthusiastic response. Such was its success that Stalin claimed that the targets were met in four years rather than five. However this was probably due to 'over-

Magnitogorsk

This was a brand new industrial centre situated in the Urals that was intended to showcase socialism in action. A gigantic steel plant was built there and a town of 150,000 people was created from nothing. This new industrial base was designed to be the home of the new 'socialist man' – dedicated to his work and the Party. Here, workers lived in communal barracks beneath imposing pictures of Lenin and Stalin and were subject to constant lectures and political discussions.

CROSS-REFERENCE

Stalin's purges and their impact are the subject of Chapter 17.

ACTIVITY

Make a diagram to show the economic achievements and failures of the first three Five Year Plans. Provide a paragraph of conclusion giving your view on the plans' successes.

enthusiastic' reporting by local officials, keen to show their loyalty and effort. In reality, none of the major targets was actually met, although major investment brought some impressive growth. Electricity output trebled, coal and iron output doubled, and steel production increased by a third. New railways, engineering plants, hydro-electric power schemes and industrial complexes such as **Magnitogorsk** sprang up.

However, despite Stalin's claims, the targets for the chemical industry were not met and house-building, food-processing and other consumer industries were woefully neglected. There were too few skilled workers and too little effective central coordination for efficient development. As well as this, smaller industrial works and workshops lost out in the competition from the bigger factories.

The Second Five Year Plan, 1933–37

The aims of the Second Five Year Plan were to:
- continue the development of heavy industry
- put new emphasis on the light industries, such as chemicals, electrical and consumer goods
- develop communications to provide links between cities and areas of industry
- boost engineering and tool-making.

The plan had some success, particularly during the 'three good years', 1934–36. The Moscow Metro was opened in 1935, the Volga Canal in 1937 and the Dnieprostroi Dam producing hydro-electric power, that had just been completed in 1932, was extended with four more generators to make it the largest dam in Europe. Electricity production and the chemical industries grew rapidly and new metals such as copper, zinc and tin were mined for the first time. Steel output trebled, coal production doubled and by 1937, the Soviet Union was virtually self-sufficient in metal goods and machine tools. In 1936, the focus of the plan changed slightly as a greater emphasis was placed on rearmament, which rose from 4 per cent of GDP in 1933 to 17 per cent by 1937.

Nevertheless, oil production failed to meet its targets and despite some expansion in footwear and food-processing, there was still no appreciable increase in consumer goods. Furthermore, an emphasis on quantity, rather than quality, which had also marred the First Five Year Plan, continued.

The Third Five Year Plan, 1938–42

The aims of the Third Five Year Plan were to:
- focus on the development of heavy industry (given a renewed impetus because of fear of war)
- promote rapid rearmament
- complete the transition to communism.

Again heavy industry was the main beneficiary, with some strong growth in machinery and engineering, although the picture varied across the country and resources were increasingly diverted to rearmament, on which spending doubled between 1938 and 1940. This had an adverse effect on other areas. Steel production stagnated, oil failed to meet targets, causing a fuel crisis, and many industries found themselves short of raw materials. Consumer goods were also relegated, once again, to the lowest priority.

The biggest problems with the Third Five Year Plan were the dearth of good managers, specialists and technicians following Stalin's purges, an exceptionally hard winter in 1938, and the diversion of funds into rearmament and defence. Furthermore, the plan was disrupted and finished early because of the German invasion of 1941.

CROSS-REFERENCE

'Command economy' is explained in A Closer Look on The Great Turn on page 151.

```
┌─────────────────────────────────────────────┐
│            Central planning                   │
│     Command economy and its pressures         │
└─────────────────────────────────────────────┘
                      │
                      ▼
┌─────────────────────────────────────────────┐
│   Priorities in planning were established by  │
│              the Party                        │
│  Output targets and labour norms were laid    │
│              down                             │
└─────────────────────────────────────────────┘
                      │
                      ▼
┌─────────────────────────────────────────────┐
│  Instructions were passed down through        │
│  bureaucratic layers to industrial managers   │
│  Managers were required to 'balance the       │
│  books'; paying for fuel, raw materials and   │
│  labour from their enterprise's income        │
└─────────────────────────────────────────────┘
                      │
                      ▼
┌─────────────────────────────────────────────┐
│  Failure to meet targets was a criminal       │
│  offence                                      │
│  Managers who failed to meet targets could    │
│  find themselves accused of 'wrecking'        │
└─────────────────────────────────────────────┘
                      │
                      ▼
┌─────────────────────────────────────────────┐
│  Bonuses were paid to enterprises that        │
│  exceeded targets                             │
│  Managers had to pay 'extra' to workers who   │
│  exceeded norms rather than using bonuses     │
│  for further investment                       │
└─────────────────────────────────────────────┘
```

Fig. 5 *The key features of the central planning system*

Agricultural change

Fig. 6 *Dinner time during harvest season on a collective farm in Russia*

KEY TERM

Petty-bourgeois: a term used in a derogatory way to suggest the peasants were middle class or 'bourgeois' in outlook, thinking only of themselves and how they could make personal profits

CROSS-REFERENCE

Read about the *Kulaks* in the time of Tsar Alexander II in Chapter 2, page 15.

A CLOSER LOOK

Kulaks

Under Stalin, a *kulak* was defined as a peasant that owned two horses and four cows or more. However, the term was often extended and interpreted in an arbitrary way by local officials.

KEY TERM

Kolkhoz: a collective operated by a number of peasant families on state-owned land, where peasants lived rent-free but had to fulfil state-procurement quotas; any surplus was divided between the families according to the amount of work put in, and each family also had a small private plot

Changes in agricultural organisation were seen as a prerequisite for rapid industrialisation. Surplus grain was needed for export, to enable the purchase of industrial equipment and to feed a growing industrial workforce, yet the peasants were still not producing enough by 1927. Furthermore, ideological beliefs favoured a more socialist system in the countryside. Critics of the free market created by the NEP believed that the system was working to the advantage of the peasants over the industrial workers and that the peasants (with their '**petty-bourgeois** attitudes') were holding back the move to true socialism.

Stalin's 'Great Turn' involved a move towards collective farming – a form of cooperative farming where all the agricultural workers were employed on large 'factory-farms', delivering quotas of grain and other food products to the State. Collectives, it was hoped, would provide for more efficient farming, give more opportunity for mechanisation, make grain collection easier and 'socialise' the peasants.

Key events in the late 1920s are shown in Table 2.

Table 2   Key events, 1920s

1926	Despite a good harvest, the requisition of grain produces only 50 per cent of what is expected. It is suspected that grain is being hoarded. This leads to increased taxes on 'kulak speculators' and Nepmen.
1927	Grain procurement crisis; again the state collections are low and food crises in the expanding industrial towns threaten industrial development.
Dec 1927	15th Party Congress – the 'collectivisation congress' – Stalin argues in favour of strengthening cooperative farms, increasing mechanisation and supporting voluntary collectivisation.
1928	Continuing problems lead to rationing in cities. The 'Ural-Siberian method' of grain requisitioning (supported by Stalin) involves the forcible seizure of grain and the closing down of markets. This brings unrest in rural areas.
1929	The Ural-Siberian method is used throughout most of the Soviet Union bringing the NEP to an end. In December, Stalin launches forced collectivisation.

Collectivisation Stage 1, 1929–30

Stalin believed that some of the grain procurement problems had been caused by the *kulaks* or richer peasants, who understood how to make money by holding back supplies. Consequently, in December 1929, Stalin announced that he would 'annihilate the *kulaks* as a class'. The Red Army and Cheka were used to identify, execute or deport *kulaks*, which were said to represent four per cent of peasant households. In reality, around 15 per cent of peasant households were destroyed and c150,000 richer peasants were forced to migrate north and east to poorer land. Not surprisingly, some tried to avoid being labelled as *kulaks*, by killing their livestock and destroying their crops, but this only added to rural problems.

In January 1930, Stalin announced that 25 per cent of grain-farming areas were to be collectivised that year. Collectivisation went hand-in-hand with the destruction of the *kulaks*, whose treatment was designed to frighten poorer peasants into joining the '*kolkhoz*' collectives. The secret police, army and Party work brigades, sent from the cities, were all used to force the peasants into accepting the new arrangements. By March 1930, 58 per cent of peasant households had been collectivised through a mixture of force and propaganda, and even Stalin accused Party members of becoming 'dizzy with success'. The speed of collectivisation had created such hostility, that a brief return to voluntary collectivisation was permitted until after the harvest had been collected that year, but numbers immediately began to fall back and by October 1930, only around 20 per cent of households were still collectivised.

A CLOSER LOOK

The speed of collectivisation

The phrase 'dizzy with success' comes from an article, published by Stalin on 2 March 1930, in which he shifted the blame for the hostility to collectivisation on to local officials, whom he accused of being over-eager in their duties. The speech led to a slow-down in the collectivisation process.

Collectivisation Stage 2, 1930–41

A new drive to collectivisation began in 1931, proceeding at a slower pace and accompanied by the establishment of 2500 machine tractor stations (MTS) to provide seed and maintain and hire machinery to the *kolkhozes*. These MTS also had a secondary purpose: to ensure that quotas were collected and to control the countryside by dealing with troublemakers.

On the surface, the drive to collectivisation looked successful but there were massive problems with its implementation:

- 'Dekulakisation' was not only inhumane, it also removed c10 million of the most successful farmers.
- Grain and livestock was destroyed (25–30 per cent of cattle, pigs and sheep were slaughtered by peasants 1929–33). Livestock numbers did not exceed pre-collectivisation until 1953.
- Unrealistic procurement quotas led to peasants being forced to hand over almost all their grain in some areas. Grain output did not exceed pre-collectivisation levels until after 1935.
- The collectives were often poorly organised. The Party activists who helped establish them knew nothing of farming; there were also too few tractors, insufficient animals to pull ploughs (as they had been eaten by the peasants) and a lack of fertilisers.
- In October 1931, drought hit many agricultural areas. Combined with *kulak* deportations, this brought a severe drop in food production and by the spring of 1932, famine appeared in the Ukraine – and spread to parts of the northern Caucasus. The period 1932–33 saw one of the worst famines in Russian history (and in some areas it continued to 1934).

By a law of August 1932, anyone who stole from a collective (and this could mean taking a few ears of corn) could be jailed for ten years. (This was subsequently made a capital crime.) Further decrees gave ten-year sentences for any attempt to sell meat or grain before quotas were filled, and internal passports were brought in to stop the peasants leaving the collectives. Not surprisingly, the peasants referred to collectivisation as a 'second serfdom'.

Although peasants were supposed to receive a share of the profits of their collective farm, these profits were non-existent and peasants saw little incentive to work hard. Their only interest was their private plots, where they could grow goods to sell in the market place and since the food was desperately needed, the government allowed this to continue. It has been estimated that 52 per cent of vegetables, 70 per cent of meat and 71 per cent of milk in the Soviet Union was produced this way.

Table 3 Percentage of collectivised households

Year	Collectivised households (%)
1931	50
1934	70
1935	83
1936	90
1941	100

A CLOSER LOOK

State responsibility for starvation

Despite the drop in grain production, the State continued its requisitions. Government policy therefore contributed to the deaths from famine and historian Robert Conquest believes that it was a deliberate policy to take unrealistic grain quotas in areas that opposed collectivisation – particularly the Ukraine – thus condemning millions of peasants to starvation.

Overall the State seemed to achieve its purposes in promoting collectivisation. The industrial workforce was fed and exports of grain increased, while many peasants escaped the countryside to swell the workforce in the towns. Nevertheless, such achievements were at the expense of the peasants themselves who, at best, endured an upheaval that destroyed a way of life and, at worst, were forced to starve and die in the interests of 'economic socialisation'.

Summary

Between 1917 and 1941, the organisation of the Soviet economy went through a number of stages:

- state capitalism 1917–18
- War Communism 1918–21
- NEP 1921–28
- central planning, with the Five Year Plans and enforced collectivisation 1928–41.

By 1941, the USSR had a 'command economy', tightly run by the State. To achieve this, the personal interests of many groups of people had been sacrificed.

 PRACTICE QUESTION

How successful were Soviet leaders in creating a socialist economy in the years 1917–41?

 PRACTICE QUESTION

Evaluating historical extracts

Using your understanding of the historical context, assess how convincing the arguments in Extracts 1 and 2 are, in relation to the transformation of the Soviet economy under communist rule.

16 Leninist/Stalinist society

EXTRACT 1

'Bolshevism has abolished private life,' wrote Walter Benjamin on a visit to Moscow in 1927. The revolution did not tolerate a private life free from public scrutiny. There were no party politics but everything people did in private was 'political', from what they read and thought to whether they were violent in the family home – and as such were subject to the censure of the collective. The ultimate aim was to create a transparent society in which people would police themselves through mutual surveillance and the denunciation of 'anti-Soviet' behaviour. The constant public scrutiny drove people to withdraw into themselves and live behind a mask of soviet conformity to preserve their own identity. They learned to live two different lives – one in public, where they mouthed the language of the revolution and acted out the part of loyal Soviet citizens; the other in the privacy of their own homes, or the internal exile of their heads, where they were free to speak their doubts or tell a joke.

Adapted from Orlando Figes, *Revolutionary Russia 1891–1991*, 2014

ACTIVITY

In this chapter you will be encouraged to reflect on how the communists set about trying to change society and the extent to which they succeeded. Figes gives one view of the impact of the Bolshevik revolution on society in Extract 1. Summarise his view and, as you read the chapter, try to find evidence of both the positive and negative impact of communism for all levels of society.

Class issues

The classless society

Since Marxism teaches that society evolves through class struggles, it is not surprising that the Bolshevik revolution was accompanied by an active campaign against the 'class' enemies of the proletariat, in whose name the revolution was fought. These were collectively known as the ***burzhui*** and they were subject to rough treatment. With the official abolition of the 'class hierarchy' in November 1917, titles and privileges disappeared and everyone became a plain 'citizen' or '*grazhdanin*', while Party members could be addressed as '*tovarishch*' (comrade). Those identified as former nobility or bourgeoisie were not allowed to work, were forced to undertake menial tasks, such as road-sweeping, and had their houses requisitioned and turned into ***kommunalka*** for the workers.

This class warfare was extended to rationing during the civil war. Allocations depended on 'work-value', with workers and soldiers receiving the most, essential civil servants and professionals, such as doctors, a lower rate and *burzhui* barely enough to survive on. Some managed to get through by selling their possessions but sometimes middle-class girls turned to prostitution.

There was something of a reprieve in the class battle when the NEP was brought in, in 1921. This more capitalist policy was an admission that Soviet Russia still needed bourgeois 'specialists' in the interests of economic growth. It did not, however, halt the campaign against the bourgeois 'way of life'

LEARNING OBJECTIVES

In this chapter you will learn about:

- 'class' and the new communist society
- the position of women and young people in communist society
- issues of religion and ethnicity
- communist propaganda and cultural change.

KEY QUESTION

As you read this chapter, consider the following Key Questions:

- What was the extent of social and cultural change?
- How important were ideas and ideology?

KEY TERM

Burzhui: this term was used against aristocrats, priests, merchants, landowners, officers, employers and the 'well-dressed'; anyone considered a hindrance to worker or peasant prosperity might be condemned as a 'bloodsucker', a 'bourgeois parasite' or a 'non-person'

A CLOSER LOOK

Kommunalka

A *kommunalka* was a communal dwelling. Lenin drafted a plan to 'expropriate and resettle private apartments' shortly after the revolution. Building committees were allocated to housing blocs who reallocated space within them, according to family size. Typically, two to seven families shared a hallway, kitchen and bathroom, while each family had its own room, serving as a living/dining room and bedroom.

CROSS-REFERENCE

For Lenin's New Economic Policy (NEP) look back to Chapter 15.

(known as *byt*) and with Stalin's decision to halt the NEP, class-based attacks (as mirrored in dekulakisation and the purges of the industrial managerial class) continued in earnest through the 1930s and beyond.

The communists wanted to create a new 'socialist man'; the type of man (or woman) who was publicly engaged and committed to the community. This 'socialist man' would have a sense of social responsibility and would willingly give service to the State – in the factory, on the fields or in battle. In all policies, both in the time of Lenin and of Stalin, there was always this agenda. Whether it was in land reorganisation or the building of new industrial city complexes, the outcome had to be an environment in which the 'socialist man' could flourish; one where the community took precedence over the individual.

Fig. 1 *Workers in a mechanical engineering factory in the USSR*

The proletariat

'**Proletarianisation**' was an important step in the creation of the 'socialist man' and yet life was far from paradise for the workers. After a brief spell of 'worker-power', both in the factories and on the land in the early months of Bolshevik rule, labour discipline was tightened and that early 'freedom' never returned. During the civil war, internal passports were issued to stop workers leaving their employment. By 1921 workers could be imprisoned or shot if they failed to meet targets and unions became a means of keeping the workers under control.

The harsh living and working conditions experienced in Leninist times persisted throughout the NEP. If anything they got worse in Stalin's early years, as peasants were herded into the collectives and more emigrated to the towns – almost doubling the urban labour force by 1932. The drive for industrialisation brought a seven-day working week and longer working hours. Arriving late or missing work could result in dismissal, eviction from housing and loss of benefits. Damaging machinery or leaving a job without permission was a criminal offence and strikes were illegal.

KEY TERM

Proletarianisation: to turn the mass of the population into urban workers; it was believed that the masses had to be proletarians in order to create a socialist – and ultimately, communist – state, which meant ridding society of selfish capitalist attitudes and developing a cooperative mentality in both town and countryside

CROSS-REFERENCE

The temporary increase in powers to the workers under early Bolshevik rule is discussed in Chapter 13.

From 1931, the introduction of wage differentials, bonuses, payment by the piece (designed to increase productivity) and opportunities for better housing to reward skills and devoted application, produced a more diverse proletariat. Workers were allowed to choose their place of work and could therefore move to improve their lot, while disciplinary rules were eased. Huge propaganda campaigns, including the **Stakhanovite movement**, increased 'socialist competition', which, in turn, produced a new 'proletarian elite'. More peasants moved to towns, more town workers became managers and more children of workers benefited from the increased educational opportunities that Stalinist Russia offered.

A CLOSER LOOK

The Stakhanovite movement

Aleksei Stakhanov was a miner who, in August 1935, extracted, in 5 hours 45 minutes, the amount of coal (102 tonnes) normally expected from a miner in 14 times that length of time. He was therefore hailed as an example of how human determination and endeavour might increase productivity. Competitions were arranged for others to emulate Stakhanov's achievement and by December the number of broken records had entered the world of make-believe and filled two volumes. The 'Stakhanovite movement' became a way of forcing management to support their workers so as to increase production; failure to fulfil targets (which were increased on average by ten per cent in 1936) meant managers might be branded 'saboteurs' and removed.

Stalin's industrialisation drive thus produced new opportunities for social advancement. In addition, his purges (which hit hardest at the intellectuals and white-collar workers) reduced the numbers competing for jobs and created plenty of vacancies 'at the top'. In 1933, Stalin could announce, 'life has become better, comrades, life has become more joyous'. Nevertheless, the realities of daily life remained grim throughout this period. Living conditions in the countryside remained primitive, while, in the towns, workers had to live in extremely cramped communal apartments and cope with inadequate sanitation and erratic water supplies. Public transport was over-crowded, shops were often empty and queues and shortages were an accepted feature of life.

Although real wages increased during the Second Five Year Plan, they were still lower in 1937 than they had been in 1928 – and in 1928 they had been little better than in 1913. Rationing was phased out in 1935 but market prices were high. Furthermore while those in positions of importance in the socialist system (for example, Party cadres), could obtain more goods more cheaply, this was not the case for ordinary workers, whose living standards stagnated and may even have fallen slightly in the last years before the war.

The effects of social change on women

One of the greatest social changes to take place after 1917 was a change in the position of women. Soviet propaganda extolled the new 'liberation' which communism, with its doctrine of equality, offered, although as was so often the case, the propaganda did not tell quite the full story.

Early policies

The role of the predominantly peasant women before the revolution had primarily been to attend to household tasks and children, although they had also been expected to play their part in farming and the small-scale domestic economy. They had been without legal privileges and, for example, had no inheritance rights.

CROSS-REFERENCE

Stalin's purges are the subject of Chapter 17.

Real wages are defined in Chapter 11, page 110.

A CLOSER LOOK

Government attitudes towards workers became harsher again in 1939–40 as the prospect of war loomed. Discipline was again tightened: being 20 minutes late for work became a criminal offence. A decree of 1940 ended the free labour market: skilled workers could be directed anywhere, others needed permission to change jobs. Social benefits were cut and fees introduced in secondary schools and higher education.

In Muslim areas, the minimum age of marriage (which was 18 years in European Russia) was raised to 16, bride money was banned and campaigns were launched against traditional practices such as wearing the veil and polygamy.

Fig. 2 *A poster from the 1920s depicting the muscular, plainly dressed women who helped to build Soviet Russia*

Fig. 3 *A poster from the 1930s that reads, 'Tractors and creches are the engines for the new village.'*

The revolution changed all this. In November 1917, the new government decreed against sex discrimination and gave women the right to own property. Further decrees followed:

- Church influence was removed by recognising only civil marriage.
- Divorce was made easier and less expensive.
- In 1920, abortion was legalised, to protect against the high mortality rates produced by illegal abortions.
- Free contraceptive advice was provided.
- A new family code in 1926 gave women in 'common law' marriages, the same rights as those who underwent the civil ceremony. In 1928, wedding rings were banned.

Women were not only given the right to work in paid employment; they were expected to work – and indeed most did. This is where the advertised 'equality' disguised reality because most women found themselves not only working on the land or, increasingly, in factories and offices, but also coping with attending to all the household tasks and the family's needs – which meant spending a considerable number of non-working hours in food queues. Girls were given the same educational rights as boys, which enabled a minority to obtain qualifications and careers not previously open to women. But for most the double burden of work and home made for a grim life of constant toil.

Stalinist policies

In the 1930s, Stalin reverted to more traditional policies. This was driven by several factors, including a fall in population growth – not helped by the purges nor by living conditions on the collectives and in the *komunalki*; and also fears of war. The 'family' became the focus of a new propaganda wave, in which Stalin was presented as a father figure and ideal 'family man', and divorce and abortion were attacked. The importance of marriage was re-emphasised, wedding rings were reintroduced and new-style wedding certificates were issued. Even in films and art, women were portrayed in a new way – less the muscular, plainly dressed women who had helped to build Soviet Russia in the 1920s, than the more feminine family woman with adoring children.

From 1936, a number of measures were introduced which reversed the earlier changes:

- Large fees were introduced to deter divorce, with the added penalty that men would be expected to contribute 60 per cent of their income in child support.
- Adultery was criminalised (and the names of male offenders published in the press).
- Contraception was banned and only permitted on medical grounds.
- Financial incentives were offered for large families. Tax exemptions were granted for families of six or more and there were bonus payments for every additional child to ten in the family.

Despite the new emphasis on family life, and encouragement for women to give up paid employment when they married, many continued to work. The number of female industrial workers grew from 3 million in 1928 to 13 million in 1940, and 43 per cent of the industrial workforce was female by 1940. Numbers of women in education also doubled over this period and large numbers of women worked on the collective farms. A growth in the provision of state nurseries, crèches and canteens, as well as more child clinics, all helped women to cope with work and family, although, on average, women earned 40 per cent less than men and the higher administrative posts were mostly held by men.

Furthermore, the divorce rate remained high (37 per cent in Moscow in 1934) and there were still over 150,000 abortions to every 57,000 live births. Indeed, although the encouragement to traditional marriage meant that in 1937, 91 per cent of men and 82 per cent of women in their thirties were married, the years 1928 to 1940 saw a falling rate of population growth.

Young people

Fig. 4 *A meeting of Komsomol members, the All-Leninist Union Young Communist League*

Education

Education was seen as crucial in building a socialist society and Lenin set up the Commissariat of the Enlightenment, which provided for free education at all levels in coeducational schools. The old secondary *gimnazii* were abolished and replaced by new secondary schools which combined general education with vocational training. At both primary and secondary level traditional learning was combined with physical work. During the 1920s, most schools abolished textbooks and examinations. This was largely because there were insufficient textbooks written within a communist framework; however, a fair amount of freedom, creativity and individualism was permitted and physical punishment was banned.

Under Stalin, some of these more liberal trends were reversed. Although, for the less able, increasing amounts of 'practical' work – linking to the Five Year Plans – were encouraged, the bulk of expansion at secondary and higher level involved more formal teaching so as to develop the skills needed in a modern industrial society. Many schools became the responsibility of the collective farms or town enterprises while the universities too were seen as agencies for delivering economic growth and put under the control of the economic planning agency, Veshenka.

The quota system, whereby a high proportion of working-class children were given places at secondary school, was abandoned in 1935 and selection reappeared for all, including non-proletarians. For the selected, a rigid academic curriculum, formal teaching, report cards tests and uniforms permitted young people to obtain a strong academic education. Sometimes this took place in single-sex schools. The core subjects were reading, writing and science with 30 per cent of time devoted to Russian language and literature, 20 per cent to Maths, 15 per cent to Science and 10 per cent to Soviet-style History. Nationalism was promoted and military training introduced into middle and higher schools and universities in the years before the war.

The Stakhanovite movement also extended to the teaching profession and teachers were encouraged to set high targets for themselves and their students. However, if students failed to do well, teachers could be blamed and purged.

CROSS-REFERENCE

Veshenka, the economic planning agency, is described in Chapter 15, page 146.

ACTIVITY

Write a 'history worksheet' on the October Revolution, presenting the subject matter in the way it might have been taught in a Soviet school in the Stalinist era.

Teachers and university lecturers were closely watched and could be arrested if they failed to live up to the expected principles.

By 1941, the Soviet experimentation had produced marked educational improvements. Some 94 per cent of the 9–49 age groups in the towns were literate and 86 per cent in the countryside, while at university level, the USSR was turning out particularly strong science graduates. Furthermore, education had proved itself a vehicle for social mobility, even though the numbers of working-class students reaching university and the higher classes at secondary level fell when the quota system was abandoned.

Youth organisations

A Russian young communist league (RKSM) was formed in 1918 for those aged 14–21, and this was extended in the early 1920s to become the youth division of the Communist Party. Lenin's wife, Krupskaya, who had been made Commissar for Education, took a particularly active role in these developments and in the establishment of a junior section in 1922, the Pioneers, for children from ten years old. In 1926, the youth organisation was renamed '**Komsomol**' and the age range extended to include children from 10–28 years. However, only six per cent of eligible youth had joined at this stage and it was not until the Stalinist era that the organisation began to have a more influential role and more widespread membership.

The organisation taught communist values. Smoking, drinking and religion were discouraged, while volunteer social work, sports, political and drama clubs were organised to inspire socialist values. Young Pioneer Palaces were built, which served as community centres for the children and summer and winter holiday camps were organised free of charge.

There were close links with the Party, to which it became directly affiliated in 1939. Members took an oath to live, study and fight for the Fatherland 'as the great Lenin has instructed' and 'as the Communist Party teaches me', and they helped to carry out Party campaigns and assisted the Red Army and police. *Komsomolskaia Pravda* was published as a youth newspaper, encouraging young people to protect family values and respect their parents. It also promoted sexual abstinence.

Membership of Komsomol and the Young Pioneers demanded full-time commitment, but also offered a chance for social mobility and educational advancement. The uniform, with its red neckerchief and rank badges, singled these young people out and helped smooth their educational path.

Of course, not all young people wanted to become involved in these youth movements. Some were more interested in Western culture. Their tastes lay in cinema, fashion and jazz – despite the regime's condemnation of such preoccupations as 'hooliganism'. Some simply opted out, but there were also a number of small secret 'oppositional' youth organisations. However direct confrontation between these organisations and state authorities was rare.

Religion

Marx had described religion as 'the opium of the people', used to justify the power of the upper classes over the people. However, Lenin did not see the Church as a threat and allowed freedom of religious worship after the October Revolution. He accepted that the largely atheistic Bolshevik minority were surrounded by an overwhelmingly Christian Orthodox majority and that toleration was the best policy.

Nevertheless, a good deal of propaganda was used to applaud the secular society and changes took place in the position of the Church within the State. Church lands, for example, were seized in 1917, when private ownership of land was declared illegal and, in accordance with educational policies, Church schools and seminaries were taken over by the State. The decree on civil marriage and the civil registration of births, marriages and deaths was

KEY TERM

Komsomol: the All-Leninist Union Young Communist League, the youth division of the Communist Party which was represented in its own right in the Supreme Soviet

CROSS-REFERENCE

The decree on civil marriage is outlined above, on page 160.

followed by the official separation of Church and State in 1918. From 1921, the teaching of religion in schools was forbidden. Churches became the property of those who worshipped in them; monasteries became state property and were turned into hospitals, schools, prisons and barracks.

Deprived of rations, hundreds of priests lost their lives during the years of War Communism. Although the peasantry retained strong religious beliefs, there was little concern for the fate of such priests, who were attacked in the propaganda as repressors of the people. **The Patriarch of the Orthodox Church**, Tikhon, was arrested in 1922 for his opposition to the direction of government policy. He was to have undergone a show trial, but instead, he chose to recant and accept the religious changes. As a result he was released and, on his death in 1925, given a state funeral. His successor, Sergius, was less accommodating and spent his first two years in office in jail. He was released in 1927, on signing a document promising to stay out of politics in return for state recognition of the Orthodox Church. This agreement had to be accepted by all priests.

The Church suffered a good deal from desecration. Church bells were seized during the civil war, officially to be melted down and the metal sold to raise funds for famine relief, while diligent communist officials had a field day in exposing the Church's sacred relics as fakes, and keen members of Komsomol ransacked churches to show their commitment to socialist teaching. In 1923, a newspaper, 'The Godless' was founded and in 1925, its supporters founded the League of the Godless to coordinate anti-religious propaganda. It tested Bible stories against scientific knowledge and spread atheistic literature, but the government remained wary of its activities and preferred to weaken the hold of religion by less explicit means.

Christian festival days disappeared when New Year's Day replaced Christmas and May Day replaced Easter as holidays with public celebrations. In 1929, worship was restricted to 'registered congregations' only and from 1932, the introduction of an 'uninterrupted six-day work week' prevented a 'holy day' of church attendance.

Stalin's 1936 constitution criminalised the publication or organisation of religious propaganda, although priests regained the right to vote (which they had lost in 1918).

As with the Orthodox Christians, in the early years of Bolshevik rule, Muslims were treated leniently. However, during and after the civil war, Muslim property and institutions (land, schools and mosques) were confiscated and their Sharia courts were abolished. This produced a split within the Islamic Church with the 'New Mosque' movement taking a pro-Soviet line. Pilgrimages to Mecca were forbidden from 1935, the frequency of prayers, fasts and feasts reduced and the wearing of the veil forbidden. This led to a backlash in some of the central Asian Muslim communities where traditionalists murdered those who obeyed the Soviet injunctions. Many Muslim priests were imprisoned or executed.

The anti-religion drive also extended to Buddhists and the Armenian and Georgian Churches. In each case, while the power of the Church as an institution was broken, faith remained strong. By 1941, nearly 40,000 Christian churches and 25,000 Muslim mosques had been closed and converted into schools, cinemas, clubs, warehouses, museums and grain stores. Nevertheless, there was plenty of evidence of strong religious belief – and this was possibly strengthened by the attacks during the period of collectivisation and the purges. In 1937, 57 per cent of the population defined themselves as believers.

National minorities

The Bolsheviks had come to power with the support of the ethnic minorities, to whom they had promised national self-determination – a pledge fulfilled by their decree of November 1917. However, this encouraged separatist movements, particularly in Finland, the Baltic and the Caucasus. In December

A CLOSER LOOK

The Patriarch of the Orthodox Church

The office of Patriarch of the Orthodox Church, abolished by Peter the Great in the eighteenth century, was revived in 1917. The Patriarch was elected by a Church Council and the office was intended to strengthen the Church at a time of uncertainty.

A CLOSER LOOK

The working week

Between 1929 and 1940 Sunday itself was abolished (providing six days in the week, each with a sixth of workers having a day off). However this was very unpopular and disruptive to family life and the workplace as well as Church services.

CROSS-REFERENCE

To recap on the Georgian uprising and Stalin's response, look back to Chapter 13.

A CLOSER LOOK

Deportations before 1941

The deportations mostly consisted of internal, forced migrations. These started with the Finns (1929–31 and 1935–39) and Poles from Belorussia, the Ukraine and European Russia (1932–36). In 1937, Koreans in the far east of Russia were deported while Stalin divided central Asia into five separate republics and forced the migration of Muslim ethnic groups, to weaken any loyalty to a single Muslim state. After the annexation of the eastern part of the Polish republic, 1.45 million people in the region were deported during 1939–41, of which 63.1 per cent were Poles and 7.4 per cent were Jews. The process was repeated in the Baltic republics, while Romanians and the Volga Germans were deported in increasing numbers in 1941.

A CLOSER LOOK

The invasion of eastern Europe and the Baltic republics

Under the terms of the Nazi-Soviet 'Non-Aggression Treaty' (generally known as the Nazi-Soviet Pact) of August 1939, a secret protocol granted the Soviet Union a sphere of influence in the Baltic states, Finland, eastern Poland and Bessarabia. These were effectively the territories the Empire had lost in 1917. Assured of Russian neutrality, Germany invaded Poland from the west on 1 September and shortly afterwards the Red Army entered Poland from the east. Troops were accompanied by NKVD agents to carry out arrests and executions. The Soviet Union subsequently invaded the Baltic states (Latvia, Lithuania and Estonia) and, with more difficulty, Finland. These territories were incorporated into the Soviet Union.

1917, Finland opted to become an independent state, whilst an elected *rada* (parliament) was set up in the Ukraine.

Whether or not to force the integration of the minorities provoked heated debate within the Party. In this, Lenin stood by his principles throughout, although in the difficult circumstances of the civil war, the regime could not afford to lose the Ukraine or Georgia (and Stalin did not hesitate to repress harshly the attempts at independence in his native province.)

Nevertheless, all the major nationalities, including the Jews, were given separate representation within the Communist Party and in 1926, Soviet Jews were given a special 'national homeland' settlement in which they could maintain their cultural heritage. This was in part of the far eastern province, which became an autonomous republic in 1934. By 1941, about a quarter of that region's population was Jewish. Furthermore, the early communists promoted literacy campaigns which encouraged the use of national languages and, with the abolition of all anti-Semitic laws in 1917, Yiddish became an acceptable language, although Hebrew, with its religious connotations, did not.

However, Stalinist policy in the 1930s veered towards greater centralisation and less tolerance of the ethnic groups as he sought to create a single 'Soviet identity'. Nationalism meant Russian nationalism and the leaders of the different republics that formed the USSR were purged as 'bourgeois nationalists' if they deviated from the path laid down in Moscow. From 1938, learning Russian became compulsory in all Soviet schools. Moreover, Russian was the only language used in the Red Army. So, despite the propaganda which proclaimed the 'family of nations', embracing a variety of different peoples, the Russians were firmly at the head.

Stalin began his **deportations** of non-Russians (which were to become more common in the war years) in the 1930s. This decade also saw anti-Semitic attitudes revive, especially in rural areas during the campaigns against 'saboteurs'. When two million Jews were incorporated into the Soviet Union in 1939-40, as a result of the **invasion of eastern Poland and the Baltic republics,** many rabbis and religious leaders were arrested in these areas.

However, the Stalinist state remained officially opposed to racial discrimination and inter-marriage was welcomed as a way of assimilating the different national groups. Indeed, most of the campaigns of the period were politically, rather than racially motivated.

Propaganda

Fig. 5 *A propaganda poster from 1936, which reads, 'Thanks to a dear Stalin for a happy childhood!'*

Lenin understood the value of propaganda and used it to particularly good effect in the civil war. Posters, film and the arts were all employed to win converts to socialism. For barely literate peasants, the power of the striking representation or of the simply repeated message was understood as an effective means of mobilising support.

Stalin too, relied heavily on his propaganda machine to harness support for his collectivisation and industrial policies. Pictures full of happy, productive workers reinforced the socialist message and heroes, such as Stakhanov, were extolled as role models to copy. The exploits of Soviet aviators and Arctic explorers were given wide publicity in the press and stories of model citizens (such as the young Pavlik Porozov who denounced his father as a *kulak* and was killed by angry relatives) were praised as examples of sacrifice in the socialist cause.

Every new initiative was 'sold' as the inspiration of the all-knowing leader and pictures and posters often showed Karl Marx, Freidrich Engels, Lenin and Stalin in continuous progression, bringing enlightenment to the Russian people. Stalin thus reinforced his own position through the associations made between himself and Lenin. These were further emphasised by slogans like, 'Stalin is the Lenin of today'. Peasants even created a 'red corner' of the great leaders in their homes, in the same way that they might have created a saints' corner in tsarist times.

A 'cult of personality' grew enormously under Stalin. Lenin had never sought cult status, but it occurred, after his death, largely through the efforts of Stalin, who wanted to appear his disciple. By the later 1920s, Lenin was being treated like a god, whose words held the answer to all Russian problems. Stalin even insisted (against Lenin's widow Krupskaya's wishes) that his body be embalmed, and Lenin's tomb was turned into a shrine. The word 'Lenin' appeared everywhere as roads, cities and squares were re-named after him – most famously, Petrograd became **Leningrad**.

Once Stalin was well established in power, he consciously developed his own cult. His self-promotion was an important aspect of his consolidation of power.

Cultural change

In the early years after the October Revolution, cultural enterprise flourished in the new, freer atmosphere the Bolsheviks brought. Although Lenin was personally a traditionalist, freedom of expression was encouraged, provided that art was not used to express counter-revolutionary sentiments. This stimulated artistic creativity and innovation and the 1920s became known as the 'silver age' of Russian literature and poetry. The world of music also enjoyed new experimentation, inspired by the revolutionary spirit of the era.

This was all to change under Stalin who viewed cultural pursuits in much the same way as he viewed pure propaganda. Literature, art, architecture, sculpture, the theatre, film and music alike were all considered only valuable and legitimate if they supported socialist ideology and the creation of the 'new socialist man'. 'Art for its own sake' had no place in the Soviet state and writers were expected to be 'engineers of the human soul'. The creativity of the 1920s thus gave way to conformity in the 1930s.

From 1932, all writers (whether of newspapers, magazines, plays, novels or poems) had to belong to the 'Union of Soviet Writers' while similar bodies were established for musicians, filmmakers, painters and sculptors. These exerted control over both what was created and who was allowed to create, for non-membership meant artistic isolation with no opportunity for commissions or the sale of work. Individual expression was deemed politically suspect.

The new norms demanded adherence to the doctrine of 'social realism'. According to the writers' union this meant, 'the truthful, historically concrete representation of reality in its revolutionary development.' In simpler terms, it meant that writers (and all other artists) were not to represent Soviet life exactly as it was at that time; they were to show what it might become (and was moving

CROSS-REFERENCE

Stakhanov's heroic achievements in the field of industry are described earlier in this chapter, on page 159.

KEY QUESTION

How important were ideas and ideology?

A CLOSER LOOK

Leningrad

In 1924 Petrograd – formerly St Petersburg – was again re-named and became Leningrad.

ACTIVITY

Choose a social group that you wish to target and create your own Stalinist propaganda poster.

CROSS-REFERENCE

Read about Stalin's 'cult of personality' in Chapter 14.

KEY QUESTION

- What was the extent of cultural change?
- How important was the role of individuals and groups?

Andrei Aleksandrovich Zhdanov
(1896–1948) was a former
Bolshevik, who had worked his way
up through Party ranks to replace
Sergei Kirov as Party Secretary in
Leningrad in 1934. He became a
member of the Politburo in 1939 and
led the defence of Leningrad against
the German Army in 1941–44. In
1946, he was appointed to direct
cultural policy and he promoted the
Zhdanovschina (see Section 4). He
died suddenly in 1948; there were
rumours that Stalin had deliberately
had him removed but there is no
actual evidence for this.

CROSS-REFERENCE

Shostakovich and his work during
Stalin's rule is mentioned in
Chapter 19, page 192 and
Chapter 20, page 198.

towards) in the future. In this way people were to be led to appreciate 'socialist
reality' and to see the reflection of the future in the present. Literature and art
were to be used to show how the 'march to communism' was inevitable.

The frame of reference for writers was laid down by **Andrei Zhdanov**
in April 1934 at the first congress of the Union of Soviet Writers. However,
the principles applied to all art forms. Works were expected to glorify the
working man, and particularly communities working together and embracing
new technology. The messages conveyed were to be uplifting, optimistic and
positive. It was an era of happy endings.

The mid-1930s also saw a ruthless attack on the avant-garde. In 1936, for
example, *Pravda* published a damning critique of Dmitry Shostakovich's opera
Lady Macbeth of Mtsensk, under the headline, 'Chaos instead of Music'. Stalin
had recently heard this modernist work and, despite the popularity the opera
had enjoyed since the premiere in 1934, the composer was accused of 'leftist
distortions'. Although Shostakovich himself avoided arrest, a theatre director
who spoke in his defence was seized, brutally tortured by the NKVD and shot;
the director's wife was also stabbed to death.

While new artistic endeavour was constrained by political demands, there was
also much interest in Russian works of the nineteenth century. Although Soviet
culture was designed to be for the 'ordinary people' (the proletariat), there was no
attempt to create a new 'proletarian culture' which was in any way distinct from
the 'upper class/bourgeois' culture of the pre-revolutionary era. So, the great
works of the nineteenth century were much read, seen, heard and copied, since it
was believed that the 'ordinary people' could understand and relate to these. The
Stalinist era thus brought solid and imposing classical forms in **architecture** and
recognisable 'real' subject matter in painting. Landscape art was revived as a
favoured medium – particularly scenes that showed nature being tamed by Soviet
industrial endeavour. In music, there was a return to the Russian classical
composers Glinka and Tchaikovsky; in literature, to Pushkin and Tolstoy.

Fig. 6   *One of the 'Palace of the Soviets' designs*

Architecture

The transformation of Moscow epitomised socialist realism in
architecture. The style was monumental. Lenin's mausoleum
'shrine' on Red Square 'parade ground' stood in the shadow
of the Kremlin, on which, in 1935, five red stars replaced the
Imperial eagles which had never been removed. The new Moscow
Metro, also opened in 1935, had stations designed as 'palaces
of light'; symbols of 'all-victorious socialism'. Mosaic designs,
marble-pattern floors and stained-glass panels were designed to
inspire pride and reverence. The grandest design of all (but one
that was never completed) was for the 'Palace of the Soviets'. It
was intended as the tallest building in the world, topped with a
gigantic statue of Lenin.

Folk culture was also promoted. Traditional peasant arts and crafts were
praised and museums of folklore were set up. Folk choirs and dancing troupes
appeared, supposedly representing a Russian 'national culture' and performing
in folklore festivals. The theme tied in well with Stalin's commitment to

'national' values, and praise for Russia's great heritage, but in practice, much of this was pure modern invention.

Summary

By 1941, the communist dictatorship brought profound changes to society. Some groups benefited, some lost out, but perhaps the biggest change was that 'society' and 'culture' became part of the broader political framework. Individuals were no longer able to live their own lives, unimpeded by the State. Ideology and state directives affected everyone.

EXTRACT 2

Only by destroying the very basis of the old society and providing a universal structure of literacy, by controlled mobilisation into a social environment dominated by crude perspectives of production, could the basis of a new society be created. But, for ordinary people, life was grim and grey. The pressures must, at times have seemed well-nigh intolerable. At the bottom of the process of industrialisation, life is hard under any system, but even more so when all the basic received certainties of life – religion, friendship, traditions – are being questioned and changed at the same time. Some people even thought nostalgically of pre-war Russia, though, of course, they did not dare say so. This was, above all, a period of dislocation, of movement into new regions and towns. The Party was everywhere. You learned to trust no one. The naturally open nature of the Russians gradually became enclosed in the new official culture of silence.

Adapted from John P. Nettl, *The Soviet Achievement*, 1967

 PRACTICVE QUESTION

Evaluating historical extracts

Using your understanding of the historical context, assess how convincing the arguments in Extracts 1 and 2 are, in relation to society in the Soviet state before 1941.

 PRACTICE QUESTION

To what extent was a new Soviet society created in USSR in the years between 1917 and 1941?

ACTIVITY

Research

1. Find out more about the artists, musicians, writers and others that lived and worked in Russia before the Second World War.
2. Find a copy of *And Quiet Flows the Don* by Mikhail Sholokhov. This is a love story written in 1934, which describes the relationship of two Russian peasants who are trying to support the establishment of communism in Russia. Reading this would greatly enhance your interpretation of the Soviet Union in this period.

ACTIVITY

What impression does Nettl give of communist society in Russia? Look back at Extract 1. How far do the views of Nettl and Figes agree?

STUDY TIP

Use the notes you have already made on Extracts 1 and 2 to address this question. Remember to evaluate the arguments in each.

STUDY TIP

One way to approach this essay would be to define what 'Soviet society' means – at least in theory – and an argument which balances the ways in which the key ideas of a Soviet society were achieved against the ways they were not. You may want to emphasise change in some areas more than others and you should try to explain why this was so.

LEARNING OBJECTIVES

In this chapter you will learn about:

- opposition and Lenin's consolidation of power

- the Red Terror and faction in the Leninist period

- opposition to Stalin and his reaction in the early 1930s

- the Kirov affair and the Great Purges.

KEY QUESTION

As you read this chapter, consider the following Key Questions:

- Why did opposition develop and how effective was it?
- How was the Soviet Union governed and how did political authority change and develop?
- How important was the role of individuals and groups?
- How important were ideas and ideology?

CROSS-REFERENCE

The walk-out of the Soviet Congress of October 1917 by the Mensheviks and Social Revolutionaries is described in Chapter 12, page 120.

Pressure by the railway workers to establish a coalition government is outlined in Chapter 12, page 122.

The dismissal of the Constituent Assembly is covered in Chapter 13, page 128.

EXTRACT 1

While he was still in Switzerland, Lenin envisaged a 'Red Terror' in the months following a successful revolution. This would have the effect of both weeding out the new regime's enemies and deterring any fresh enemies from raising their heads. In the first week after the October Revolution, the Red Guards were the main means of keeping order, but they were inadequate for this task and had little time to spread terror among the bourgeoisie. For this reason the Cheka was established. All over the country, the Cheka executed, sometimes after torture, anyone suspected of counter-revolutionary activity. It could never be deemed an intelligence service, for most of its operatives were unintelligent, and frequently illiterate. But by killing or imprisoning every possible suspect, it did ensure that among each hundred innocent victims would be one or two genuine and dangerous enemies of the regime. For this reason it can be said to have been successful in its main aim.

Adapted from John N. Westwood, *Russia since 1917*, 1980

ACTIVITY

1. With reference to what you have learned in the earlier chapters of this section, define which 'opposition' groups Westwood is referring to with the following descriptions:
    a. the 'new regimes' enemies'
    b. 'fresh enemies'
    c. 'the bourgeoisie'
    d. 'counter-revolutionaries'
2. What is Westwood's overall view in Extract 1?

Faction and opposition in the 1920s

Opposition and the consolidation of power

From their earliest days in power, the Bolsheviks faced three types of 'opposition':

- from other political groups both on the right and left of politics
- from their many opponents throughout the Empire – from former tsarist officers to capricious peasants who were ultimately to resist the regime militarily
- from the ideological 'opposition' (more often perceived than real), the bourgeoisie, and upper classes of society against whom the Bolsheviks had fought.

Political opposition in Petrograd itself was the first concern. The Menshevik and SR opposition in the Soviet Congress of October 1917 destroyed themselves by their walkout, leaving the Bolsheviks with a monopoly of power. On 27 October, Sovnarkom banned the opposition press, and ordered the arrest of Kadet, Menshevik and SR leaders. Over the next month, the Bolsheviks skilfully avoided pressure (from striking railwaymen) for a coalition government. So many political prisoners were put in the capital's gaols that criminals had to be released to accommodate them.

The establishment of the Cheka, under 'Iron' **Felix Dzerzhinsky** in December 1917, was a sign of the new regime's determination to destroy its opponents. Combined with the dismissal of the Constituent Assembly and the extension of the Red Army to deal with rebellion, it soon became clear that the Bolshevik state would do all in its power to destroy all enemies, be they political, military or ideological.

The Cheka from 1918

In 1918, the Cheka established its Moscow base in the Lubianka (former insurance company) building. This housed a prison, leading to the joke that it was the tallest building in Moscow, since Siberia could be seen from its basement. The Cheka controlled units of the Red Guard and military. Most provinces had their own Cheka branch, with officials reporting directly to Lenin and the Politburo. From 1922, the Cheka was renamed the GPU and in 1923, the OGPU (Joint State Political Directorate). From 1934 to 1943, it was placed under the control of the NKVD (the People's Commissariat for Internal Affairs). It was therefore often referred to itself as the NKVD.

KEY PROFILE

Felix Dzerzhinsky (1877–1926) was a Pole from Lithuania who had once intended to become a Jesuit priest. He became involved in Marxist groups as a student and spent many years in tsarist prisons. He welcomed Lenin in 1917, became a Bolshevik, played a part on the military revolutionary committee in the October Revolution and was rewarded with the directorship of the Cheka, to which he transferred some of his early religious fanaticism. He held this post until his death.

The consolidation of Bolshevik power was accompanied by a form of 'class warfare', which was intended to intimidate and exact revenge on the middle and upper classes. Bourgeois property was confiscated, social privilege ended and discriminatory taxes levied on the *burzhui* – the 'enemies of the people'. Ideological opponents as much as political ones were arrested, exiled or executed.

The Red Terror

The civil war of 1918–21 was the culmination of the Bolshevik fight against opposition forces. It also brought a new wave of coercion against both real and 'assumed' enemies, thus creating the 'Red Terror'.

In August 1918, the attempt on Lenin's life provided the excuse for a frenzied written attack on the 'bourgeois', while the Cheka rounded up thousands on whom this label might be pinned. Confessions and the names of 'accomplices' were obtained by torture, and so began a 'terror' that left hardly any group untouched.

In September 1918, Sovnarkom gave the Cheka authority to find, question, arrest and destroy the families of any suspected traitors. Yakov Sverdlov, chairman of the Bolshevik Central Committee, spoke of 'merciless mass terror against all opponents of the revolution!' All remaining Social Revolutionaries and Mensheviks were branded traitors and 500 were shot in Petrograd alone.

The Red Terror escalated because local Cheka agents, keen to show their zeal, often took matters into their own hands. They sought incriminations and discovered 'hidden' opposition. Victims ranged from the Tsar and his family, shot on 17 July 1918, to ordinary workers suspected of 'counter-revolution' because they had associated with a 'class enemy' or had the misfortune to have neighbours who bore a grudge. Merchants and traders (black marketeers, hoarders and Nepmen), professors, prostitutes and peasants (particularly those branded as '*kulaks*') all suffered, as did their families, friends and sometimes entire village. Priests, Jews, Catholics and, to a lesser extent, Muslims were also persecuted. Around 8000 priests were executed in 1921, for failing to hand over valuable Church possessions, which were supposedly required for the relief of famine victims.

Some were executed immediately and it has been estimated that between 500,000 and a million people were shot in the 1918–21 period. Others might be tortured and/or sent to labour camps, where many died as a result of the physically demanding work they were expected to perform while living on meagre rations.

CROSS-REFERENCE

The term *burzhui* is explained in Chapter 16, page 157.

The assassination attempt on Lenin is outlined in Chapter 13, page 130.

A CLOSER LOOK

Political opposition came to an end in 1921, when 34 SRs were given 'show trials', and made to admit their crimes in public and denounce others. Both the SRs and Mensheviks were outlawed as political organisations that year.

CROSS-REFERENCE

The assassination of the Tsar and his family is covered in Chapter 14, page 137.

ACTIVITY

Write a Cheka report on a successful arrest

A CLOSER LOOK

Torture

The Cheka used extraordinary violence against their victims. In Kharkov, they put victims' hands in boiling water and kept topping it up until the blisters became so bad, the skin started to peel off. In Kiev, a cage full of rats was placed around the victim's body. This was heated, thus driving the rats to eat their way through the victim's body to escape.

CROSS-REFERENCE

To recap on the 'Workers' Opposition' look back to Chapter 15, page 149.

Alexandra Kollontai is profiled in Chapter 12, page 121.

The 'ban on factions' is discussed in Chapter 13, page 129.

Faction and control

By 1921, Lenin's concerns had turned to the opposition 'within' his Party. In 1920–21 there were some serious disagreements about political and economic policy and groups such as the 'Workers' Opposition' under Aleksandr Shlyapkinov and Alexandra Kollontai had been set up, demanding that workers had more control over their own affairs. Lenin believed such dissension was weakening the Party and was determined to restore Party unity. His 'ban on factions' of 1921 meant that all Party members had to accept the decisions of the Central Committee. Anyone who opposed was threatened with expulsion from the Party. The opportunity for debate and challenge was thus removed and, in the highly centralised, authoritarian, one-party state that emerged from the years of civil war, opposition became virtually impossible.

ACTIVITY

Group discussion

How successful was Lenin in dealing with opposition to his rule? Divide into two groups. One group should find evidence of success, and the other of failure or 'flawed' methods that might lead to future problems. Present your views and try to reach an overall conclusion.

Opposition to Stalin and the purges

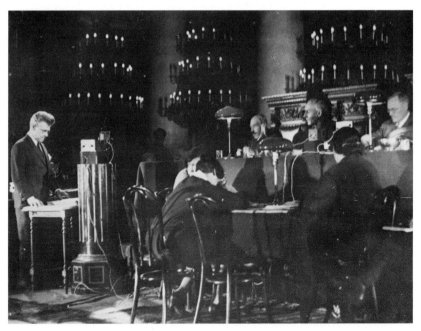

Fig. 1 *Lenoid Ramzin, left, confesses to being a wrecker during the trial of the Industrial Party. This was the first Stalinist show trial.*

Stalin and opposition to 1932

Stalin's rise to the leadership position gave him plenty of opportunity to show his skill in out-manouvring and defeating those who opposed him. He extended the use of terror and class warfare, as practised by Lenin, to enforce collectivisation through the destruction of the *kulaks* and maintain his Five Year Plans for industry. He accomplished this by sending 'bourgeois managers', specialists and engineers, whom he accused of machine-breaking and sabotage, to labour camps.

The **Shakhty show trial** of 1928 was a clear indication of Stalin's determination to find a scapegoat for the chaos caused by his own economic policies, while delivering the message that the regime had to maintain its vigilance against those who were set to destroy it. This heralded an 'industrial terror' which deprived hundreds of 'bourgeois specialists' of their jobs and, often, lives. Critics within Gosplan were removed and further trials took place throughout the Soviet Union. In the 'Industrial Party' show trial of November 1930, a group of industrialists were accused of sabotage. In the 1933 Metro-Vickers trial, British specialists were found guilty of wrecking activities.

By 1929, Soviet prisons could no longer cope with the numbers of *kulaks*, bourgeois specialists, wreckers, saboteurs and other 'opponents' that arrived and **Genrikh Yagoda** was commissioned to investigate ways in which the prison population could be put to better use. His proposal involved building on the corrective-labour camps established by Lenin by creating a series of new camps, of c50,000 prisoners each, in remote areas of the north and Siberia, where diamonds, gold, platinum, oil, nickel, coal and timber were all to be found. By offering minimum '**per capita**' funding and imposing economies of scale it was believed these '**gulags**' (an acronym for Main Administration of Corrective Labour Camps and Colonies) could contribute to economic growth, while at the same time offering appropriate 'correction' for the prisoners. The camps were to be placed under the direct authority of the OGPU (the political police until 1934, when the NKVD took control). By then, they housed a million people.

Fig. 2 *Prisoners working in a gulag*

A CLOSER LOOK

The White Sea Canal

One major gulag project was the construction of the White Sea Canal, joining the Baltic Sea and the White Sea, which was dug (cheaply) with no

CROSS-REFERENCE

Stalin's defeat of his opponents is described in Chapter 13.

Stalin's enforcement of collectivisation in agriculture and implementation of the Five Year Plans in industry is the subject of Chapter 15.

A CLOSER LOOK

The Shakhty and other show trials

In 1928, 53 engineers at the Shakhty coal mine in the northern Caucasus were accused of 'counter-revolutionary activity' after there was a decline in production there. They were given a 'show trial' in which they were forced to confess. Five were executed and 44 received long prison sentences.

KEY PROFILE

Genrikh Grigoryevich Yagoda (1891–1938) joined the Bolsheviks in 1907 and became a member of the Cheka in 1920. He was a deputy chairman of the OGPU, 1924–34 and from 1930 was in charge of the labour camps. In 1934, he joined the Central Committee and was put in charge of the Commissariat of Internal Affairs (NKVD), into which the Secret Police was absorbed. He may have engineered the murder of Kirov. He prepared the first show trial in 1936, but was dismissed in September 1936 and replaced by Yezhov. He was arrested in 1937, accused of being a member of a 'Trotskyite' conspiracy. He was convicted, sentenced to death on 13 March, and shot.

KEY TERM

Per capita: per head or 'for each person'

Gulags: 'economic colonies' – a way of exploiting the prison population to boost economic growth; millions of prisoners were used to dig mines and canals, build railways and clear forests

ACTIVITY

Read *One Day in the Life of Ivan Denisovich*, by Aleksandr Solzhenitsyn, to get a greater understanding of life in a gulag.

CROSS-REFERENCE

Bukharin is profiled in Chapter 13, page 125. He had stood for the Continuance of the NEP, along with Tomsky and Rykov, against Stalin's preference for enforced collectivisation in the power struggle. This is also explained in Chapter 13, page 133.

KEY PROFILE

Sergei Kirov (1886–1934) had been an early recruit to the Social Democrats. He had supported the Bolsheviks and played an active part in the revolution and civil war. He joined the Central Committee in 1923. Although a moderate, he had supported Stalin in the leadership struggle and replaced Zinoviev as Party Secretary in Leningrad in 1926. He was a good speaker and popular with Party members.

KEY TERM

Purge: literally a 'cleaning out of impurities'; this term was used to describe forcible expulsions from the Communist Party in the 1920s but in the later 1930s it came to mean the removal of anyone deemed a political enemy

ACTIVITY

Extension

Find out more about Stalin's family (Svetlana Alliluyeva, Vasily Dzhugashvili, Yakov Dzhugashvili, Artem Sergeev,) particularly his second wife, Nadezhda Alliluyeva, and his daughter, Svetlana, whose memoirs provide us with a lot of information about Stalin.

more than axes, saws and hammers in freezing cold temperatures. Some 100,000 prisoners were employed on this task in 1932, but 25,000 died in the 1931–32 winter. It was opened by Stalin in a blaze of publicity in 1933, but since it was only 12 feet in depth, it actually proved useless to bigger shipping.

The crisis of 1932

In November 1932, Stalin's wife, Nadezhda, committed suicide. She left a note criticising Stalin's policies and showing her sympathy for Stalin's political enemies. According to Orlando Figes this 'unhinged' Stalin, who now felt that even those closest to him could be betraying him behind his back – saying one thing but believing another. The suicide, which was reported to the public as death from appendicitis, came at the end of a bad year. In 1932 there had been famine in the countryside and a spate of workers' strikes in the industrial towns, primarily driven by economic factors, but also bringing voiced criticisms of the five year plan and Stalin's leadership.

Stalin's position was far from secure. His old opponent, Nikolai Bukharin, had been re-elected to the Central Committee in June 1930; the same year as some of those who had formerly supported Stalin in the leadership struggle against Bukharin were expelled for criticising the way collectivisation was being carried out.

In 1932, two opposition groups emerged within the Party elite. An informal group of 'old Bolsheviks', which included Leonid Smirnov, was discovered to have held meetings at which they had debated Stalin's removal. They were quickly arrested by the OGPU and Smirnov expelled from the Party. A second group was led by Martemyan Ryutin, (former Moscow Party Secretary and a 'rightist') and their criticisms became known as the 'Ryutin Platform'. They disapproved of Stalin's political direction and personality and some of their papers were found in Nadezhda's room. Ryutin even sent an 'appeal', signed by a number of prominent communists, to the Central Committee urging Stalin's removal. Ryutin and his circle were arrested and it has been suggested that Stalin called for their immediate execution but was over-ruled the Politburo and, in particular, by **Sergei Kirov**, the Leningrad Party Secretary. If true, this again shows the precariousness of Stalin's position at this time. Nevertheless, 24 were expelled from the Party and exiled from Moscow, while several other 'old Bolsheviks', including Zinoviev and Kamenev, were also expelled and exiled, simply for knowing of the group's existence and failing to report it to the police. Ryutin was sentenced to ten years in prison. He was shot, on Stalin's orders, in 1937.

If Nadezhda's suicide had not already 'unhinged' Stalin, the Ryutin affair certainly did. In April 1933, he announced a general **purge** of the Party and over the next two years, he conducted a paranoid struggle in which over 18 per cent of the Party membership were branded 'Ryutinites' and purged. Most of these were relatively new Party members whose loyalty Stalin felt unsure of; he thought them mere 'careerists'.

The Kirov Affair, 1934

At the 17th Party Congress in 1934, which coincided with the tenth anniversary of Lenin's death, Stalin announced that the 'anti-Leninist opposition' (by which he meant those that had opposed his own policies and leadership) had been defeated. Bukharin, Alexei Rykov, Mikhail Tomsky, Karl Radek (a former supporter of Trotsky) and others who had challenged Stalin in the leadership struggle, all admitted their 'errors' to give the impression of unity at the top.

However, in the elections to the Central Committee, Stalin received c150 negative votes (although only three were officially recorded). A split opened up between those who wanted to maintain the pace of industrialisation, and others within the Politburo, including Kirov, who spoke about stopping forcible grain seizures and increasing workers' rations. It is unlikely that Kirov set out to challenge Stalin as he was very close to the leader. Nevertheless, only two of the Politburo firmly supported Stalin (**Vyacheslav Molotov** and **Lazar Kaganovich**), while Kirov received a long, standing ovation for his speech advocating a more moderate approach.

A further issue which also arose from the 17th Party Congress was the abolition of the title of 'General Secretary'. Stalin and Kirov, along with Andrei Zhdanov and Kaganovich, were all given the title 'Secretary of Equal Rank'. Stalin may have supported this, in order to spread the responsibility for the economic crisis; but it meant, in theory at least, that Stalin was no more important than the other secretaries.

CROSS-REFERENCE

For the Zhdanovshchina, see Chapter 20, page 197.

Zhdanov, another Bolshevik member and supporter of Stalin, is profiled in Chapter 16, page 166.

Fig. 3 *Stalin and Kirov*

KEY PROFILE

Lazar Moiseyevich Kaganovich (1893–1991) had been a Bolshevik since 1911. From 1924, he was responsible for Party patronage and helped Stalin defeat his political rivals. He rose quickly in the Party administration and by 1930 was a full member of the Politburo. He supported collectivisation and brought the Moscow regional Party organisation firmly under Stalin's control (1930–35).

Vyacheslav Mikhailovich Molotov (1890–1986) had joined the Bolsheviks in 1906 and become secretary of the Central Committee in 1921. He supported Stalin in the leadership struggle and in 1926 was promoted to the Politburo. He took control of the Moscow Party Committee, purging it of its anti-Stalin membership in 1928–30, and in 1930 was made chairman of the Council of People's Commissars – a post he held until 1941. He replaced Litvinov as the Soviet Commissar of Foreign Affairs in May 1939, and negotiated the Nazi-Soviet Pact in August. He held various diplomatic posts after the war.

Kirov was murdered in December 1934. The circumstances were suspicious and Stalin (who may well have been implicated) was quick to claim that this was part of a Trotskyite conspiracy, led by 'Zinovievites', to overthrow the Party. A decree was published a day after the assassination, giving Yagoda, head of the NKVD, powers to arrest and execute anyone found guilty of 'terrorist plotting'. Around 6500 people were arrested under this law in December.

A CLOSER LOOK

Kirov's murderer

Kirov was shot in the neck by Leonid Nikolayev as he approached his office in the Leningrad Party headquarters on 1 December 1934. Nikolayev was a disgruntled Party member (once expelled, but reinstated), whose wife may have been having an affair with Kirov. However, he was not linked to the left opposition and when questioned, Nikolayev suggested the NKVD 'knew' all about the murder. Kirov's bodyguard and some NKVD men were mysteriously killed in a car accident before they could give evidence and although some leading NKVD men were sentenced for failure to protect Kirov, their terms were short and their treatment lenient. In 1938, Yagoda pleaded guilty to allowing Nikolayev to reach Kirov, although since Yagoda himself was then on trial, this may have been said under duress.

Fig. 4 *Lazar Moiseyevich Kaganovich*

ACTIVITY

Write a press report on Kirov's murder for:

a. *Pravda* (the official communist newspaper)

b. a Trotskyite paper, published abroad.

KEY QUESTION

How important was the role of individuals and groups and how were they affected by developments?

CROSS-REFERENCE

The Soviet Constitution of 1936 is outlined in Chapter 14, page 142.

KEY TERM

Homogeneous: forming a whole of the same type

KEY PROFILE

Nikolai Ivanovich Yezhov (1895–1940) was nicknamed 'the dwarf' because he was only five feet [1.5 metres] tall. He joined the Communist Party in March 1917, and became a political commissar in the Red Army in the civil war. He became a close associate of Stalin and in 1934 became a member of the Central Committee. In September 1936, he succeeded Yagoda as NKVD chief and carried out the Yezhovshchina, (ruthless elimination of Stalin's enemies or alleged enemies). By 1938, he was under suspicion and was replaced by Lavrenti Beria. He was arrested in April 1939 and shot in 1940. He implicated many family members and friends in his confession and hundreds of these were also killed.

In January 1935, Zinoviev, Kamenev and 17 others were arrested and accused of instigating terrorism, and sentenced to between five and ten years imprisonment. Some 843 former associates of Zinoviev were also arrested in January/February 1935. During the course of that year, 11,000 'former people' were arrested, exiled or placed in camps and 250,000 Party members were expelled (after investigation by the NKVD) as 'anti-Leninists'. There was also a purge of Kremlin employees (from cleaners to librarians) to uncover reputed 'foreign spies'. Abel Yenukidze, chairman of the Central Committee and a high-ranking communist, was even expelled for helping 'oppositionists' find employment in the Kremlin. Stalin's old civil war comrade, Grigory Ordzhonikidze, also died in mysterious circumstances.

The Great Purges, 1936–38

While Stalin was creating a new, and seemingly more liberal, constitution for the Soviet Union in 1936, he was also busy preparing for a new purge; one that would be more far-reaching than ever before. In Extract 2, Volkogonov gives one interpretation of why Stalin thought the purge necessary.

EXTRACT 2

Stalin was driven by a powerful need to 'win'. He was obsessed by the idea of 'overtaking' everyone, of 'racing forward'. He was trying to outrun the natural course of events. People, however, change slowly. Soviet society, Stalin maintained, still harboured countless members of the old middle classes, former officers, unreconstructed members of the pre-1917 political parties, covert saboteurs and spies, and the 'sharpening of the class struggle' was at hand. The system needed a general purge from which it would emerge stronger and more **homogeneous** and hence be able to speed up the transition to the second phase of communism. The creation of a new constitution and the act of 'clearing' the social field for its operation were thus closely interconnected. For the Stalinist system to function, permanent purge was a necessity. The entire period of Stalin's rule was a bloody one, though the 1930s saw the worst excesses. The population, silent except when told to shout the slogan of the day, was made to expose and 'uproot' a seemingly endless succession of hostile groups.

Adapted from Dmitri Volkogonov, *The Rise and Fall of the Soviet Empire*, 1998

ACTIVITY

1. List the reasons for the launching of the Great Purge, as given in Extract 2.
2. Summarise Volkogonov's interpretation in Extract 2 in your own words.

In August 1936, a show trial involving Zinoviev, Kamenev and 14 others took place. Its purpose, like that of others which followed, was not only to gain confessions and convictions, but to 'prove' the existence of political conspiracies. All 16 were found guilty of involvement in a Trotsky-inspired plot to murder Stalin and other Politburo members. All were executed – together with 160 'accomplices'. A month later, Yagoda was replaced by **Nikolai Yezhov** as NKVD chief, as it was claimed Yagoda had not been active enough in uncovering this 'conspiracy'.

In January 1937, a further show trial of 17 prominent communists was staged. These included Radek and they were again accused of plotting with the exiled Trotsky, to sabotage industry and to spy. After giving their 'confessions', 13 were sentenced to death. Yezhov also accused Bukharin of having known about the conspiracy; when Bukharin refused to confess, he was expelled from the Party and arrested.

In May/June 1937, eight senior military commanders, including **Mikhail Tukhachevsky**, all of whom were 'heroes' of the civil war, were arrested, tortured and made to sign false confessions. They were tried in secret, in a military tribunal, convicted of espionage and of participating in a 'Trotskyite-Rightist anti-Soviet conspiracy', and shot. This was followed by a further purge of military personnel. Of the 767 of the High Command, 512 were executed; 29 died in prison, 13 committed suicide and 59 were placed in jail. A substantial number in military intelligence were also executed or imprisoned, although around a quarter of these were reinstated by the middle of 1940.

The third and largest major political show trial took place in March 1938, when 21 Bolsheviks were interrogated and Bukharin, Rykov and Yagodha and 13 others were sentenced to be shot for conspiring with the 'Trotsky-Zinoviev terrorist organisation' to assassinate leaders, conduct espionage and carry out acts of sabotage. Bukharin made the mistake of trying to defend himself, and while admitting to general charges added, 'whether or not I knew'. This only infuriated his accusers and he was shot, along with 16 others.

A CLOSER LOOK

Historiography of the Great Purges

Whether or not there had been genuine opposition to Stalin at this time so as to justify such extreme action is still unclear. John Arch Getty in *The Road to Terror* (1999), produced evidence that Trotsky was in contact with middle-ranking communist officials between 1930 and 1932 and that it is perfectly possible there was a Trotsky/Zinoviev alliance to oust Stalin. However, the scale of the purges and terror went far beyond the likely number of oppositionists associated in such a conspiracy, even if it did exist.

The Yezhovshchina, the purge of ordinary citizens, 1937–38

In 1937–38, the Great Purges merged with the Yezhovshchina, named after Yezhov, head of the NKVD, as terror was spread down from the Party hierarchy into the Soviet institutions and ultimately into every town and village. Thousands, from all sections of society, were terrorised, executed or sent to labour camps. Increasingly, this 'Great Terror' was directed at ordinary citizens. The persecution reached its height in mid-1937 and lasted until December 1938 when Yezhov was replaced by Lavrenti Beria.

In July 1937, a Politburo resolution condemned 'anti-Soviet elements' in Russian society and an arrest list of over 250,000 was drawn up, including artists, musicians, scientists and writers, as well as managers and administrators. A quota system was established and each region was expected to find a proportion of oppositionists.

Surveillance was everywhere. Ordinary citizens were encouraged to root out 'hidden enemies' – to check up on fellow workers, and even watch friends and family for signs of 'oppositional thoughts'. The NKVD maintained a strict vigilance, employing 'reliables' in offices, universities and factories. Everyone lived in fear of a knock on the door since the arrests were continuous and random. Many Soviet citizens died in prison. Table 1 summarises the range of victims that suffered in the Great Terror. Many were shot; others were sent to the gulags.

KEY PROFILE

Mikhail Nikolayevich Tukhachevsky (1893–1937) came from an aristocratic family and had fought for Russia in the First World War. He was captured by the Germans in 1915 and, after four escape attempts, succeeded on his fifth. He joined the Bolshevik party and the Red Army, rising rapidly through its ranks. He became Soviet Minister for Defence in 1934 and Marshall of the USSR. In May 1937 he was suddenly arrested on Stalin's direct order and accused of planning an anti-Bolshevik plot. He was convicted of espionage and high treason and executed in June 1937. Tukhachevsky's wife was jailed and executed in 1941; his mother and one sister died in prison. Three other sisters managed to survive prison, but their husbands were executed as well as Tukhachevsky's two brothers.

Table 1 Victims of the Great Terror and Yezhovshchina

Those purged:	What happened to them:
Leading Party members	Around 70 per cent of the members of the Central Committee at the 17th Party Congress were arrested and shot. Of 1966 delegates to the congress, 1108 were arrested. Old Bolsheviks on both the left and right of the Party were removed through show trials. The Party members were encouraged to criticise and denounce others, leading to local as well as high-level Central Party purges.
Minority nationalities	Leaders of national republics were charged with treason or other offences and removed. In Georgia, two state prime ministers, four out of five regional Party secretaries and thousands of lesser officials lost posts. Around 350,000 people from minority ethnic groups were put on trial, including 140,000 Poles.
Armed Forces	Eight senior generals, three out of five marshalls, all eleven war commissars, all eight admirals (and their replacements) were shot. All but one of the senior airforce commanders, approximately 50 per cent of the officer corps in all three services and a substantial number in military intelligence were also tried; many were shot.
Managers, engineers and scientists	High proportion of managers, leading physicists and biologists lost their positions, some were executed.
NKVD	Yagoda and more than 23,000 NKVD men were put on trial; most were shot.
Peasants and industrial workers	Although it is difficult to differentiate the victims of purges from the victims of famine, *kulaks* represented around 50 per cent of all arrests and more than half of the total number of executions.
Relatives of the purged	Colleagues, subordinates, relatives, wives, children, friends and associates of the purged were also liable to be arrested, and deported or shot.

ACTIVITY

Pair discussion

Assess the results of the purges for Stalin and for the USSR. Do you think they would strengthen or weaken the communist regime?

The end of the purges

Although purges of Stalin's opponents continued until well into the Second World War, the pace slowed down after the end of 1938. The Yezhovshchina had threatened to destabilise the State and both industry and administration had suffered. Consequently, Stalin used Yezhov as a scapegoat, accusing him of excessive zeal, and in November he was replaced by his deputy, Beria.

The 18th Party Congress declared that the 'mass cleansings' were no longer needed. Around 1.5 million cases were reviewed: 450,000 convictions were quashed, 128,000 cases were closed, 30,000 people were released from gaol, and 327,000 were allowed home from the gulags. Yezhov himself was arrested and shot in February 1940. The same year a hired assassin murdered Trotsky in Mexico. This meant that almost all the old Bolsheviks who might have had a greater claim to leadership than Stalin had been removed.

By the end of the purges, Stalin was in a position of supreme power. His political rivals had gone, while the quashing of sentences and release of so many prisoners helped restore faith in the system and its leader. Yezhov was generally viewed as the cause of the troubles and faith in Stalin remained as high as ever. He had absolute control over the Party and a subservient populace.

ACTIVITY

Summary

Create a summary chart to illustrate stages in the development of communist control and terror, as follows

Stage	What happened
Control 1917–18	
Red Terror 1918–24	
Power struggle 1924–28	
Stalin's early years 1928–34	
Kirov Affair and its aftermath 1934–36	
Great Purges and Yezhovshchina 1936–38	
Final phase 1938–41	

ACTIVITY

With reference to Extract 3, how does Brown explain the purges? What impression does he give of Stalin?

EXTRACT 3

Some of the earlier purges were a logical consequence of the choice of the Soviet leadership not to embrace universally recognised democratism, but to impose its will, and many harsh policies, on the population by dictatorial decree. Other purges, including those of Party workers and of the officer corps of the Red Army, went well beyond the logic of communist rule. Stalin was both a true believer in the strand of Leninism he had himself developed, and a disordered personality who, as Lenin recognised too late, should never have had great political power placed in his hands. As Stalin grew older, he became increasingly paranoid. Chronic suspicion, a love of power (behind a façade of modesty) and bloodthirsty vindictiveness became ever more prominent features of Stalin's personality. Stalinism thus became a distinctive form of communism, one whose excesses had devastating consequences for Soviet society and whose extremes incorporated much more than was required to maintain a Communist Party in power.

Adapted from Archie Brown, *The Rise and Fall of Communism*, 1994

 PRACTICE QUESTION

Evaluating historical extracts

Using your understanding of the historical context, assess how convincing the arguments in Extracts 1, 2 and 3 are, in relation to the communist use of terror between 1917 and 1941.

 PRACTICE QUESTION

How successful were the communist leaders in crushing opposition in the years 1917–41?

STUDY TIP

Extracts 1, 2 and 3 present varying ideas about why the communist leaders resorted to terror. You should consider the arguments presented and support or challenge them with reference to your contextual knowledge. A summary conclusion will help you to stress how 'convincing' each extract is.

STUDY TIP

Don't forget that both Lenin and Stalin faced a range of different 'oppositional forces'. You might like to suggest that some of the opposition they faced was real, but that other elements were imagined. Nevertheless, you should look at both leaders' successes and failures and try to draw some overall conclusion about the extent of success.

18 The Soviet Union by 1941

LEARNING OBJECTIVES

In this chapter you will learn about:

- the political state of Stalinist Russia by 1941

- the strengths and weaknesses of the Soviet economy

- the impact of Stalinism on Russian society

- the condition of the Soviet Union in June 1941.

CROSS-REFERENCE

The NEP (Stalin's New Economic Policy) is described in Chapter 15, page 149

KEY QUESTION

As you read this chapter, consider the following Key Questions:

- How was the Soviet Union governed and how did political authority change and develop?

- How important were ideas and ideology?

- How important was the role of individuals and groups?

EXTRACT 1

Stalin always portrayed his revolution as a continuation of the Leninist tradition, the belief that the Party's collective will could overcome all adverse contingencies, as Lenin himself had argued during the October seizure of power. And in a way Stalin was correct. His drive towards industrialisation, sweeping aside the market and the peasantry, was in essence no different from Lenin's own drive towards Soviet power which had swept aside democracy. One could argue that the centralised command system was itself an inevitable outcome of the contradiction between a commitment to a proletarian dictatorship and an overwhelmingly peasant country. Soviet Russia's international isolation, which stemmed directly from the October Revolution, reinforced the argument of the Stalinists that the 'peasant-cart-horse pace' of industrialisation under the NEP would be much too slow for Russia to catch up with, and defend itself against the West.

Adapted from Orlando Figes, *A People's Tragedy*, 1996

ACTIVITY

Evaluating historical extracts

There has been much debate about the extent to which 'Stalinism' was the natural continuation of 'Leninism'. In this chapter, you will be encouraged to reflect on the meaning of Stalinism in Russia before the Second World War. Begin by noting Figes' argument in Extract 1. To what extent, and for what reasons, does he suggest there was a continuity between Leninism and Stalinism?

The political condition of the Soviet Union

One-party centralisation

Fig. 1 *Crowds carrying placards with pictures of Stalin and his generals*

By 1941 Stalin led a highly centralised and authoritarian one-party state. Some of the foundations for this can certainly be seen in the Leninist years. Lenin had always favoured single-party rule. He had, for example, fought against coalition government in 1917 and had forced the closure of the Constituent Assembly in 1918. Lenin's Constitution only permitted the existence of one party – the Communist Party – and from 1918, in the circumstances of civil war, the Party increased its dominance over the institutions of the State.

Although Marxist doctrine had talked of the State 'withering away', Stalin not only upheld it, he went further than Lenin had ever done, extending one-party domination and redefining centralisation. Although Stalin's new constitution of 1936 included democratic structures such as universal suffrage, it was made clear that the Communist Party and its institutions were the only bodies that could put candidates up for election. This reinforced Stalin's intent to preserve the one-party state.

The structure of government still provided for parallel appointments in both the government and Party hierarchy, but the *nomenklatura* system of privileges that was used to reward loyal officials had the effect of concentrating decision-making into a much smaller number of hands. Furthermore, the ultimate source of all authority was increasingly concentrated in the hands of Stalin, rather than the Party. This meant that, from the mid-1930s, he no longer depended on the Party, and was able to avoid calling Party congresses.

Centralisation meant that all power emanated from Stalin himself, working with individuals or small groups. Stalin seldom left Moscow and disliked mass meetings. Indeed, he added to his own 'mystique' by restricting those who he had direct access with. It has been said that the commissars trembled at meetings of Sovnarkom as Stalin paced up and down behind his colleagues. Within the Stalinist state, no independent institutions were permitted to emerge; no rival power centres were countenanced; and, where possible, younger officials, dependent on Stalin's favour, were placed in positions of authority.

It has sometimes been suggested that the Soviet Union changed from a 'one-party state with a powerful leader' to a 'personal dictatorship' in the 1930s. However, it must be remembered that Stalin relied on the workings of a highly bureaucratic structure and that, in some respects, the policies he pursued actually weakened his own control. The purges, for example, may have emanated from the centre, but they acquired a drive and momentum of their own in the hands of local officials. There was plenty of corruption within the ranks too; lying, falsifying statistics and presenting inaccurate reports were endemic. Local officials would often protect one another against central demands and at the lower levels of administration, non-compliance with central orders was widespread.

Attacks on opposition

Another characteristic of the Communist State was its intolerance of opposition. Lenin had created the Cheka and developed a prison camp system to deal with both his ideological and political enemies. As well as attacking the SRs, Mensheviks and *burzhui*, he carried out non-violent purges of his Party leading to the expulsions of 150,000 Party members in 1921. Furthermore, he introduced a ban on factions in 1921.

Stalin, again, extended and intensified Leninist intolerance. He continued Lenin's ideological 'class warfare' – mostly directed at the *kulaks* and bourgeoisie. Also, his political attacks were far more brutal than anything seen under Lenin. Within the circumstances of the one-party state he attached those within the Communist Party whom he saw as potential

CROSS-REFERENCE

Stalin's new democratic structures, including universal suffrage, are discussed in more detail in Chapter 14, page 139.

Nomenklatura was first introduced by Lenin in 1923, but was developed by Stalin. Read more about how this system worked in Chapter 14, page 139.

Stalin's purges in politics are the subject of Chapter 17, page 170.

ACTIVITY

In the 1920s, Stalin claimed to be Lenin's disciple (follower); by the early 1930s, he portrayed himself as Lenin's equal, stating that 'Stalin is the Lenin of today'. By the later 1930s, he portrayed himself as the 'father of the nation'. What does this suggest about political change under Stalin? Find a propaganda poster online, which illustrates this idea.

KEY QUESTION

Why did opposition develop and how effective was it?

Fig. 2 *Skulls of people shot during the Stalinist purges, found in mass graves*

CROSS-REFERENCE

The exploitation of labour in the gulags is discussed in Chapter 17, page 171.

ACTIVITY

Look back at Sections 1 and 2: what similarities can you identify between tsarist autocracy and Stalinism?

KEY QUESTION

- How and with what results did the economy develop and change?
- What was the extent of social and cultural change?

ACTIVITY

Evaluating historical extracts

What impression of Stalin's leadership of USSR do you get from Extract 2? Select three short quotations which support this view.

CROSS-REFERENCE

Look back to Chapter 15 for more on the central planning system.

Fig. 3 *Oil fields in Baku, Azerbaijan*

enemies and rivals. No leading Bolshevik or Party member lost his life from political vindictiveness, nor was made to stand up and give a public 'confession' of his crimes by Lenin. During the Stalinist purges the OGPU and NKVD arrested millions of ordinary citizens and 600,000 Party members were executed.

The 'correction camps' developed into gulags providing slave labour and, as with so many aspects of Stalinist rule, persecution was on a far more monumental scale. Yet, even Stalin could not exert perfect control. There is plenty of evidence of rural hostility, and the welcome which some Soviet citizens (particularly from the ethnic minorities) gave to the invading Germans in 1941, speaks for itself.

Economic and social position

Extract 2 gives another interpretation of Stalin's rule

EXTRACT 2

It is no accident that the Soviet industrialisation drive was managed by one of the most powerful, coercive and centralised state systems of the twentieth century. Building on Russia's autocratic political culture, Stalin created a modernised autocracy of immense power. Collectivisation helped remilitarise the Party and led to a rapid expansion of the police and of the labour camp system. The atmosphere of crisis created by collectivisation, the purges and fears of foreign attack generated a paranoid mood which strengthened the leadership by making any form of opposition look like treachery. The huge mobilisational effort of the 1930s achieved much, though at great human cost. It turned the Soviet Union into a great military and industrial power, and generated a surprising amount of popular support. Yet it also created new forms of legal and economic inequality that undermined the idealistic claims of Soviet socialism. Whilst its economic achievements were immense, the brutal methods of Stalinism did much to discredit the ideals of socialism.

Adapted from David Christian, *Imperial and Soviet Russia*, 1986

The Stalinist economy

By 1941, Stalin's Five Year Plans had transformed Russia into a highly industrialised and urbanised nation, while all Russian farms had been collectivised and the free market brought to an end. Although Soviet claims and statistics were often exaggerated, an impressive transformation had taken place since 1917 – and even more so since 1928. In 1926, 17 per cent of the population lived in towns, but by 1939, 33 per cent did so. By 1940, the USSR had overtaken Britain in iron and steel production and was not far behind Germany.

By developing heavy industry, transport and power resources, Stalin helped lay the foundation for the ultimate Soviet victory in the Second World War. Coal and oil production were vastly stepped up in the Third Five Year Plan; nine aircraft factories were constructed in 1939; and between 1938 and 1941, spending on rearmament rose from 27.5 billion roubles to 70.9 billion roubles.

However, there were crucial weaknesses. Economic development was uneven and although there was a massive growth in heavy industry, consumer production had been so neglected that consumer goods were scarcer in 1941 than they had been under the NEP. The quality of goods was also poor, even though labour productivity had increased. The bureaucrats were so set on meeting their exaggerated targets that nothing else mattered to them. The central planning system was inefficient and organisation at local level was at times chaotic and not helped by Stalin's purges of specialists and managers.

Furthermore, in 1941 the nation was still producing less grain than under the NEP. A major crop failure in 1936, which produced a yield even smaller than that of 1941, weakened the nation's reserves. There was insufficient attention paid to modern farming techniques and limited use of agricultural machinery. Even when available, modern agricultural equipment was sometimes neglected because there were insufficient trained individuals to service and repair it.

Stalinist society

Stalin's economic programme had also brought major social change to the USSR. Communist control in the countryside had grown stronger as something of the socialist 'communal' values had been put in place. Peasants were living and working in the *kolkhoz* and firmly under the supervision of the Party officials. They were also watched by the NKVD units stationed at each Motor Tractor Station. Increased urbanisation and the massive expansion of town populations had also helped create a far stronger working class 'proletariat' – the backbone of the Communist State.

A new 'mass culture' was being developed. Through education, propaganda, the leadership cult, public celebrations, arts, culture and the show trials, it was claimed that the fulfilment of socialist values was well underway. It may be hard to measure, but it can be stated with some confidence that 'Stalinism' never entirely reshaped public opinion in USSR. According to the modern historian Robert Service, interviews with Soviet citizens who fled the USSR during the Second World War have suggested that although there was support at this time for state welfare policies and strong government, as well as pride in Soviet achievements, there was also a feeling of resignation to life's hardships, mingled with hope that one day things might get better.

The quality of life did not increase substantially under Stalin. In the Leninist era, the demands of the Russian Civil War had made poor living standards excusable. Under Stalin, the low rations, poor housing and lack of consumer goods were much less so. Internal passports (reintroduced in 1932) restricted freedom of movement; there was strict censorship, and propaganda was everywhere. Mass organisations and movements mobilised the people, particularly the youth, and even the churches were held in close check.

CROSS-REFERENCE

The exploitation of peasants in the *kolkhoz* is discussed in Chapter 15, page 154.

The NKVD is outlined in Chapter 17, page 169.

CROSS-REFERENCE

The show trials are discussed in Chapter 17, page 171.

EXTRACT 3

Stalin shaped a system founded on an unbeatable, universal ideology, a Party consisting of legions of bureaucrats, a single and almighty leader who was virtually an earthly God, a vast military machine and total political surveillance by 'punitive organs'. The anonymous crowd was wrapped in a blanket of ideology and used as an obedient tool. As for the Party, it was, as Stalin put it in a speech, 'a kind of order of sword-bearers within the Soviet state' and the Party held the masses in its grip. As Stalin said, ' no important political or organisational issue is decided by our soviet or other mass organisations without directional instruction of the Party.' The individual, in other words, was no more than a tiny cog in the machine that executed the dictator's will.

Adapted from Dmitri Volkogonov, *The Rise and Fall of the Soviet Empire*, 1999

ACTIVITY

According to Extract 3, what is Volkogonov's interpretation of Stalin's rule in USSR? Does he have similar or different views from Figes and Christian in Extracts 1 and 2?

What emerged in the 1930s was a very different type of society from the socialist ideals of the October Revolution. Rather than a classless society, there was a hierarchical society dominated by a privileged elite organised around the Party and *nomenklatura*. The urban and rural working classes, no longer exploited by capitalist employers, were instead ruthlessly driven by their Soviet masters and instead of 'withering away' the State had become more formidable, extensive and brutal.

PRACTICE QUESTION

Using your understanding of the historical context, assess how convincing the arguments in Extracts 1, 2 and 3 are, in relation to Stalin's rule in Russia by 1941.

The Soviet Union by June 1941

Fig. 4 *Russian troops roll towards the battle front, June 1941, to defend Soviet territory from German troops on the first day of Hitler's Operation Barbarossa*

As the 1930s drew to a close, a new challenge faced the Soviet Union: an expansionist Nazi Germany. However when the invasion came, on 22 June, Stalin was caught by surprise. Although he could not have been entirely unaware of the impending attack, and defence spending had increased from 16.5 per cent in 1937 to 32.6 per cent in 1940, he had ignored intelligence reports and seems to have miscalculated as to when the Germans would turn east.

The Soviet Union was not ready for war in 1941. The purges of the Red Army between 1936 and 1938 had removed most senior officers and sapped the strength of the army. Soviet fighting capacity had also been affected by inadequate training and those who had promoted more advanced military theories, such as Mikhail Tukhachevsky, an exponent of massed tank operations, had all been removed. A lack of military initiative had already been seen in the Winter War with Finland in 1939–40, when no commander dared try anything new. Furthermore, Stalin had re-established the 'dual command' of military units; bringing back the political commissars which had been abandoned in the late 1920s. This move had increased Party control yet hindered actual combat capabilities.

Economically, despite the move towards rearmament in the Third Five Year Plan, there were deficiencies in the quantity and quality of equipment. Most Soviet aircraft, tanks and guns were of old design and the reconstruction of the navy had been slow, with Stalin insisting on the development of traditional battleships and cruisers rather than aircraft carriers. Stalin's industrial drive had certainly made the Soviet Union stronger than it would have been ten years earlier – by 1941 the Soviet Union was producing 230 tanks, 700 military aircraft, and more than 100,000 rifles per month. However, because of the increased expenditure on the military, there had been insufficient investment in the collective and state farm system, which was still not producing enough to feed the population.

Psychologically, too, the Soviet Union was unprepared for the fight. Having withdrawn anti-fascist propaganda and praised 'Soviet-German friendship' since 1939, Soviet troops were suddenly expected to fight their former allies.

Stalin may therefore be criticised for failing to prepare his country adequately for attack, and the results of this were seen in the ease with which the German forces overran Soviet territory in the first months of war.

A CLOSER LOOK

Hitler and the USSR

The establishment of Nazism in Germany in 1933 had worried the Soviet Union. Hitler wanted *Lebensraum* (living space) in the east and the Soviet Union tried to reach an agreement with the Western powers to restrain Nazi expansionism. However, British and French appeasement of Germany confirmed Soviet suspicions that they were happy to see an attack on the communist USSR. Consequently, the Nazi-Soviet Pact with Hitler was agreed in August 1939, by which Hitler advanced into Poland (so beginning the Second World War) while Soviet troops seized eastern Poland, the three Baltic provinces and the Romanian province of Bessarabia (now Moldova). They also took Finland after the Winter War of 1939–40. Stalin knew, however, that the pact would only buy time.

ACTIVITY

Summary

Make a chart to show the strengths and weaknesses of the Soviet Union on the eve of war in 1941.

A LEVEL PRACTICE QUESTION

To what extent did the USSR of 1941 fulfil Lenin's vision of a 'Socialist Utopia'?

CROSS-REFERENCE

There is more information on the Nazi-Soviet Pact with Hitler in Chapter 16, page 164.

ACTIVITY

Copy and complete the table below, contrasting Leninism and Stalinism. Was there more continuity than change? Explain your answer.

	Leninism	Stalinism
Political		
Economic		
Social		

STUDY TIP

It's useful to start your response to this type of question with a definition of Lenin's vision of a 'Socialist Utopia'. Try to think of four or five different themes to discuss and consider ways in which these had been fulfilled, partly fulfilled, neglected, or ignored. Try to provide some balanced discussion as well as conveying a judgement.

19 Stalinism in wartime

KEY QUESTION

As you read this chapter, consider the following Key Questions:

- How was the Soviet Union governed and how did political authority change and develop?
- How important were ideas and ideology?
- How important was the role of individuals and groups?

KEY TERM

Absolute monarch: a monarch who wields unrestricted political power over the State and its people

A CLOSER LOOK

Stalin had killed a large proportion of senior officers in the purges of 1937–38. In the first weeks of the Second World War, Stalin authorised the shooting of more officers for 'cowardice' when they failed to prevent the advance of the Germans. Even senior officers who brought bad news were liable to be arrested.

EXTRACT 1

Immersed as he was in an atmosphere of spy-mania of his own making, Stalin was clearly unable to evaluate the various kinds of information arriving in the Kremlin on the eve of the war. Nor was there the possibility of sober collective judgement while he was the subject of such total adulation. He believed that his judgement and wishes coincided with the real needs of the Party and the country which he ruled like an **absolute monarch**. The appalling suffering inflicted on the Soviet people in the war was no less the result of German force and treachery than of major mistakes by the Soviet leadership. Apart from the damage caused by dismissing vital and, as it transpired, accurate intelligence, flawed strategic thinking compounded the disaster. Stalin exacerbated the already extreme violence of war by pursuing his customary methods of ruling. He was extricated from his disastrous miscalculations, not only by the unprecedented self-sacrifice of the Soviet people, but also by the mass terror applied to those who wavered or lost heart.

Adapted from Dmitri Volkogonov, *The Rise and Fall of the Soviet Empire*, 1999

ACTIVITY

Evaluating historical extracts

In Extract 1, what is Volkogonov's opinion of Stalin as a war leader? What arguments does he use to justify his opinion? As you read this chapter, try to find evidence that both supports and challenges Volkogonov's view.

A CLOSER LOOK

The Great Patriotic War 1941–45

In June 1941, the Germans launched a three-pronged attack – known as Operation Barbarossa – on the USSR: to Leningrad in the north, Moscow in the centre, and Kiev and Rostov-on-Don in the south. Although initially successful, they failed to capture Moscow and the Red Army launched a successful counter-offensive. In 1942, the Germans concentrated their efforts on an attack on the Caucasus oil fields to the south. This encompassed an attack on Stalingrad, which the Soviets repulsed in early 1943. A monumental tank battle at Kursk in the summer of 1943 confirmed that the initiative had passed to the Soviets who subsequently drove the Germans back, finally reaching Berlin in 1945.

Operation Barbarossa launched the invasion of the Soviet Union, without any declaration of war, on 22 June 1941. Three German battle groups made amazingly rapid advances. They overran eastern Poland and the Baltic States in the north and penetrated deep into Ukraine, capturing more than a million prisoners. By the end of September 1941 the complete defeat of the USSR appeared imminent. Then came stiffening Soviet resistance and the onset of winter; the German advance was halted short of Moscow.

Fig. 1   *Operation Barbarossa: the German invasion of the Soviet Union, 1941*

KEY CHRONOLOGY

1941:

June	Operation Barbarossa – the German invasion of the USSR
September	Beginning of the siege of Leningrad
November	The Battle for Moscow
December	Zhukov's counter-offensive

1942:

September	Beginning of the siege of Stalingrad

1943:

February	End of the siege of Stalingrad
July	Battle of Kursk

1945:

May	Red Army takes Berlin; Germany surrenders

Russia at war: political authority and opposition

The launch of Operation Barbarossa (the German invasion of the USSR), on the night of 21/22 June 1941, appeared to take Stalin by surprise. Although his military intelligence agents – as well as the British Government – had warned of an imminent attack, and the build-up of German forces near the Soviet border should have provided a warning, nevertheless Stalin seemed shocked and confused when the attack actually came. Indeed, his initial reaction was to suggest that someone contact Hitler in Berlin because he suspected the troop advance to be a 'limited act of provocation'.

Stalin had never expected the Nazi-Soviet Pact to be long-lasting and it is generally assumed that he made the deal in order to win a 'breathing space' during which to build up Soviet defences. However, the country was still far from prepared for war by the summer of 1941.

Wartime leadership

Stalin met his Politburo immediately and his first wartime order was to demand that the German air force be destroyed and the invading forces annihilated. However, he left the public announcement of hostilities to Vyacheslav Molotov, possibly because he could not bring himself to make it. Molotov was thus left to inform the nation (through the loudspeakers set up on the main streets of Soviet cities) that a German invasion was underway. He ended with the stirring words: 'Our cause is just, the enemy will be smashed, victory will be ours.'

The onset of war brought the need for a clearly defined structure of governmental and military authority. Whether Stalin was affected by depression or whether he deliberately took time to plan his strategies, this took over a week to establish. Table 1 shows the sequence of events.

A CLOSER LOOK

The German 'blitzkrieg' ('lightning' attack) on the USSR began at 3:00am on the Sunday morning of 22 June 1941, when three million soldiers with 7184 artillery guns, 3580 tanks, and 740,000 horses poured into the USSR, supported by the Luftwaffe (German air force). This was the largest invasion force in history and it left the Soviet forces in chaos. By 28 June the Germans had captured Minsk and forces were heading for Moscow and Leningrad.

Table 1 Events of June/July 1941

1941	Changes in authority	Details and significance
23 June	Stavka (Supreme Military Command) is established	Responsible for all military planning. Consisted of: • all marshalls of the Soviet Union • the Chief of General Staff • heads of the various military services
27 June	Stalin withdraws to his *dacha*, creating confusion	Stalin is not seen or heard in public for ten days
30 June	State Defence Committee (GKO) set up by Politburo	Civilian body responsible for organisation and coordination; exercises absolute authority over all Party, state, military and other organisations and directs the wartime economy. Marshal Voroshilov is removed from military command to serve on this Small group of five (expanded to eight from February 1942)
30 June	Stalin responds to visit by Politburo members	Stalin agrees to return to Moscow and agrees to restructuring
1 July	Stalin reassumes authority as Head of Government and as leader in both Stavka and the GKO	Coordination is aided by right of GKO members to attend Stavka meetings
3 July	Stalin makes first public wartime address	Stalin calls for unity: 'the issue is one of life and death for the people of the USSR; the issue is whether the peoples of the Soviet Union shall be free or fall into slavery'
20 July	Stalin assumes overall military command	Stalin becomes 'the supreme war leader'

From July 1941, all authority, both political and military, rested with Stalin. His speech of 3 July was the first of many designed to establish his leadership and unite the nation, rekindling patriotism and mollifying those who had opposed his policies in the 1930s. Interestingly, in this and subsequent war speeches, Stalin appealed to his people's love of their country and played on the threat to their culture, rather than the threat to socialism. The people fought for Russia, not communism.

Stalin's authority was not questioned and his speeches and actions were crucial in bolstering morale. As the Germans came dangerously close to Moscow in October, Stalin ordered the evacuation of the government to Kuibyshev on the Volga. However, in a display of resistance, he insisted that the Red Square parade, held annually on the anniversary of the revolution, should take place as normal.

After the disastrous opening to the war, Stalin also understood the need to let his military commanders plan campaigns. The running of the war was increasingly left to the General Staff, although if military leaders displayed incompetence they were removed, no matter how close they had once been to Stalin. Marshals Voroshilov and Budyenny (both former civil war commanders) for example, were replaced by men of talent brought back from gulags where they had been sent during the Terror. Stalin also came to rely heavily on **Georgi Zhukov**, who successfully defended Moscow in November 1941 and ultimately led the Soviet troops to Berlin in April 1945.

Wartime opposition

Although there was no outright opposition to Stalin's authority within the USSR, not all Russians were supportive and the NKVD never abandoned its vigilance. Hitler had nurtured some hope that the invasion would spark an anti-Stalinist revolt. He was disappointed in this, but in the wake of the invasion, large numbers of those in national minority areas, particularly Estonia, Lithuania, Belorussia and the Ukraine, welcomed the German soldiers as liberators after the harsh Stalinism of the 1930s. Thousands in these areas became collaborationists. Some acted as '*Hilfswillige*', others fought. The Russian Liberation Movement under Andrey Vlasov, for example, was formed in the Ukraine. This became a division of the **Waffen-SS** and at its peak had 50,000 soldiers, fighting against their former Red Army comrades. Probably over a million (including 250,000 Cossacks) joined Hitler's side but, as Slavs, many were only allowed to perform lesser jobs.

Fig. 2 *Army General Andrey Vlasov*

KEY QUESTION

- Why did opposition develop and how effective was it?
- How important was the role of individuals and groups?

A CLOSER LOOK

Nazi ideology worked to the German disadvantage in harnessing the support of the non-Russian nationalities. It was inconceivable to the Nazis that mere Slavs should be allowed to fight alongside Aryans, and the Germans failed to capitalise on potential support. When the Nazis entered Belorussia in 1941, they were initially welcomed but Nazi brutality (a policy to kill 75 per cent and condemn the rest to slavery) produced one of the largest **partisan** units in the Soviet Union. There was even a bomb-making factory, run by Jews, hidden in the Naliboki Forest.

In the greater part of unoccupied USSR, winning the war relied, in some measure, on the continuation of pre-war 'terror tactics' – both for the army and for the civilian population. When the Germans threatened Stalingrad in July 1942, Stalin issued order 227, 'Not One Step Backwards'. Any soldier who fell behind or tried to retreat was to be shot on sight, and more than 150,000 were sentenced to death under this order. Penal battalions were created from those who broke discipline and were thus labelled 'cowards'. They were sent to the front to undertake the most dangerous jobs, such as clearing minefields, and supposedly to 'redeem' themselves. Casualty rates of c50 per cent were normal for such groups. 'Blocking units' equipped with machine guns were also added to the NKVD units in the rear of action, to prevent desertion or retreat.

EXTRACT 2

One cannot disregard Stalin's positive contributions. First, for many Soviet citizens, he became a symbol of national unity, an embodiment of the spirit of resistance. Certain of his speeches and writings are said to have rallied the people and given invaluable boosts to their morale. Second, so great was the Terror that he inspired at the highest levels of Party and State that a rebuke from him, let alone a threat, could elicit impressive performances from factory managers and generals alike. Finally, although Stalin committed military blunders throughout the war, he improved as a strategist — not least because he became aware of his own professional limitations. Unlike Hitler, he encouraged strategic debate and did not hesitate to solicit or accept advice. The Stalinist system did help the USSR win the war.

Adapted from Gregory Freeze, *Russia, a History*, 1997

KEY TERM

Hilfswillige: those 'willing to help' the Germans; they served in a number of roles including drivers, cooks, hospital attendants, ammunition carriers and messengers

Waffen-SS: an armed wing of the Nazi Party, which served alongside the regular army

Partisan: a member of a military force behind the front line opposing the control of the area by the enemy

ACTIVITY

Evaluating historical extracts

Look carefully at Freeze's argument in Extract 2. Summarise his views in one sentence. Look back at Extract 1. In what ways does Freeze agree and disagree with that extract?

Although a narrower question than is usual, you will have an opportunity here to evaluate the arguments about Stalin's wartime leadership. As always, assess the historians' views by applying your own contextual knowledge.

Fig. 3 *A propaganda poster from 1944 reads, 'Are you doing your share of the work to rebuild Leningrad?'*

KEY TERM

Scorched earth policy: destroying anything useful to the enemy before retreating; Stalin ordered both soldiers and civilians to deny the German troops basic supplies as they moved eastwards

A **LEVEL** **PRACTICE QUESTION**

Evaluating historical extracts

Using your understanding of the historical context, assess how convincing the arguments in Extracts 1 and 2 are, in relation to Stalin's leadership in the Great Patriotic War.

The political, economic and social impact of the war

Political impact

Since the multinational nature of the Empire was seen as a potential threat to state security, Stalin took action to prevent political disintegration. As early as August 1941, he dissolved the Volga German autonomous republic and sent its peoples (even those who had Communist Party membership) to the east. Elsewhere, he relied on the deportation of 'suspect' ethnic groups. The Karachai, the Kalmyks, the Chechens, the Ingushi, the Meskhetians and the Crimean Tartars, for example, were all deported away from their homelands. Around 1.5 million people in total were forced to uproot. In what was, in many ways, an extension to the purges, they were often brutally treated and only two thirds survived the journey to Kazakhstan, Uzbekistan, Kirgizia and Siberia.

The war also brought a change to the composition of the Communist Party. To win the war, Stalin had addressed former grievances of army officers, for example by downgrading the role of the political commissars attached to the army units and bringing back special badges of rank. He had also put an emphasis on the political education of the troops. The result was that increasing numbers of the military chose to join the Party.

During the war over 5 million candidate members and 3.6 million new members joined the Party. Of these, 3.9 million candidate members and 2.5 million members were members of the army and navy. By 1945, a quarter of those in the armed forces were communists and 20 per cent were members of Komsomol. So, whereas in June 1941, only 15 per cent of the military had been in the Party, they formed around half its membership by 1945.

Overall, the war helped to strengthen belief in the communist system. Although nationalism had been emphasised over the Marxist struggle in the course of campaigns, by May 1945, Stalin could declare that the war had shown the superiority and resilience of the socialist system. It was a victory for communism over fascism and was thus hailed as a vindication of both Stalin and the Stalinist system.

Economic impact

KEY QUESTION

How and with what results did the economy develop and change?

Hitler had intended to seize Russian farmland and industry in the wake of his invasion and use it to German advantage. By the end of 1941, it looked as though he had achieved something of his ambition. The German-occupied Soviet territory contained 63 per cent of the country's coal, 68 per cent of its iron, 58 per cent of its steel, 45 per cent of its railways and 41 per cent of its arable land. However, with the establishment of a wartime economy on 30 June 1941, the Soviets had already taken measures to ensure their economic survival.

A '**scorched earth**' policy had rendered much of the farmland useless. Moreover, 1523 entire Soviet factories together with their workers were transplanted from western Russia and the Ukraine to areas in the east (the Urals, Siberia, Kazakhstan and Central Asia) in the months between July and November 1941. The industrial growth that had already taken place in these areas during the Five Year Plans was also capitalised upon, with production geared to needs of the military. New railways were built or redirected and the industrial bases rapidly linked to the front line.

Managing a wartime economy proved easier for the USSR, with its existing centralised, planned economy, than for than its Western allies. People's Commissars were established to supervise the different sections of wartime production, such as tanks, aircraft and guns, while compulsory state orders allowed for changes to take place in a very short timeframe. The whole population was harnessed for war and rigorous labour controls ensured maximum production

National expenditure was redistributed so that, by the end of 1942, the military share of budget had risen from 29 per cent to 57 per cent and munitions manufacture was 76 per cent of all production. Most spending was focused on the giant heavy industrial complexes in the Urals where, in total, 3500 new industrial enterprises were built during the course of the war. New furnaces were constructed at Magnitogorsk in just eight months, and at Chusivaya in seven months. The Engels plant in Zaporozhye started production 20 days after it was moved.

CROSS-REFERENCE

The social impact of the war is discussed later in this chapter, on page 190.

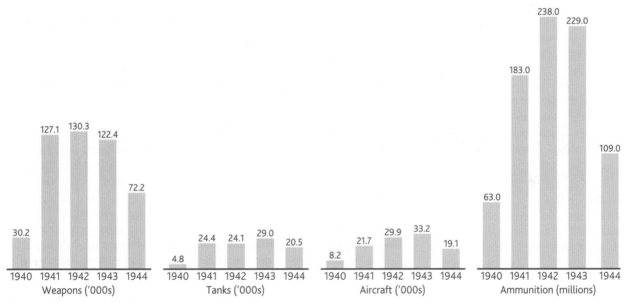

Fig. 4 *Units of Soviet military production, 1940–44*

By mid-1943, industrial output not only exceeded that of Germany but the quality of the weapons produced was also superior. The T-34 tank, Katysusha rocket launcher and Yak-1 fighter aircraft are reckoned to have been among the best weaponry produced during war.

Food problems took longer to solve, particularly since the grain harvest of 1942 was only a third of that of 1940. However, survival was ensured by strict rationing and demanding quotas on collective farms, although to maintain morale and incentive, peasants were allowed to keep private plots and to sell their produce. Farm output was maintained by women, elderly men and children, while those in the towns and cities were strongly encouraged to cultivate any patches of soil for vegetables.

Although the bulk of needs was met through domestic production, the Russian economy was helped by considerable foreign aid, although this was never advertised to the Soviet people, who were encouraged to believe that their efforts were ignored by the West.

- The UK and the USA supplied essential war materials which the USSR had limited production of, such as lorries, tyres and telephones. These were either carried in British ships to Murmansk, or sent overland from Iran.
- In total 17.5 million tons of military equipment, vehicles, industrial supplies, and food were shipped from the West to the USSR, 94 per cent coming from the USA.
- Under the **Lend-Lease** scheme of 1941, 11 billion dollars of aid was provided by USA.
- The USA supplied the USSR with 6430 planes, 3734 tanks, 104 ships, 210,000 vehicles plus essential raw materials and 5 million tonnes of food. By the end of the war, 427,000 of 665,000 vehicles in USSR came from overseas.

KEY TERM

Lend-Lease: a programme under which the USA supplied the USSR (and other nations) with food and wartime material between 1941 and August 1945; the aid was free, although sometimes it was expected that major items (such as ships) would be returned after the war

Social impact

KEY QUESTION

- What was the extent of social and cultural change?
- How important was the role of individuals and groups?

The announcement of the German invasion saw recruitment stations flooded with volunteers keen to fight for the Motherland. Around 120,000 signed up in Moscow alone. Some volunteers believed they were following the tradition of the pioneers that fought in the civil war; others fought for their community and locality, and this was particularly true of the citizens of Leningrad, Stalingrad and Moscow. The panic induced by the German attack helped to reunite Russian society and provide the cohesion that had been threatened in the 1930s.

Soldiers and workers

The central authorities also stepped in to 'manage' society, particularly recruitment and the deployment of labour, in the same way that they directed agriculture and industry. Everything was to be subordinated to the sheer necessity of survival.

In December 1941, a new law was introduced, which mobilised all undrafted workers for war work. All men aged 16 to 55 years and women aged 16 to 45 years were required to devote themselves to the war effort. White-collar workers were sent to munitions factories; pensioners were encouraged to return to work; and students were asked to undertake part-time work.

Overtime became obligatory and holidays were suspended. The working day was increased to 12 hours, the average working week was 70–77 hours, and it became normal for workers to sleep in their factories. Factories were placed under martial law and discipline was tightened. This meant severe punishments for negligence, lateness or absenteeism. Unauthorised absence from work was classed as desertion, punishable by death. Clearly, the harsh conditions suffered in the 1930s helped in the acceptance of such measures and probably helped to provide some of the resilience displayed in the war years.

Discipline in the army was also tightened. Not only was it an offence to be taken captive; while a soldier was in captivity his family's military ration cards were confiscated. Indeed, service in the army was tough in every respect. For Stalin, the lives of Red Army soldiers were expendable in the interests of the 'greater good' and 8.6 million soldiers were killed between 1941 and 1945 – an average daily rate that was twice that of the allies. Such, largely male, losses naturally had a disastrous effect on the ability of families 'back home' to survive.

ACTIVITY

Design a Soviet poster that might have been produced to inspire workers/peasants or soldiers to greater effort in wartime. Use the poster in Figure 6 (page 193) as an example to inspire your own design.

Living conditions

Fig. 5 *Two women collect the remains of a dead horse for food in 1941*

The Soviet people also suffered a chronic food shortage. Over a quarter of the estimated 25 million deaths suffered by the USSR during the war were caused by starvation. A comprehensive rationing system (which favoured the military) was maintained but the allowances were often pathetically low. The allies provided tinned spam, which was often a lifesaver, and rations were only given to those who turned up for work.

Added to this were acute housing and fuel shortages, so that health problems escalated. Some found themselves refugees, fleeing the German advance; others were left fighting for survival in the besieged cities; and yet more were forced to leave their homes and accept tough living conditions alongside their newly relocated factories in the east. Here, the priority was always factory-building first, accommodation second, and through the bitter winter of 1941–42, thousands were forced to live in improvised huts and tents.

To maintain supplies, **gulag labour** was used. Many of those deported to the camps (in particular prisoners of war, collaborators and ethnic minority groups) built airports, landing strips and roads in the most inhospitable of conditions, as well as producing vital war supplies. The death rate in the labour camps in 1942 was 25 per cent, but slave labour was regarded as endlessly renewable.

Propaganda and culture

Stalin played on the connotations of the 'Great Patriotic War' to harness society for the war effort. The people were encouraged to sacrifice themselves in the interests of 'Holy Mother Russia' against the godless invaders and 'child-killers'. Posters bore words such as 'Everything for Victory', 'Long live our Motherland, Her freedom, Her independence! Death to the German invaders!' The non-Russian nationalities were told to 'join in with your Russian brothers – the home of the Russian is also your home'. Deeply patriotic and violently anti-German letters were published in *Pravda*, to inspire heroism and self-sacrifice. One wrote, 'We must not say "Good morning" or "Goodnight". In the morning we must say "Kill the Germans" and at night we must say "Kill the Germans". We want to live and in order to live we must kill the Germans.' In 1943, the Internationale (the socialist anthem) was even replaced by a new nationalistic song of the Motherland.

A CLOSER LOOK

Gulag 'slave-labour' produced around 15 per cent of all Soviet ammunition and a large proportion of uniforms, as well as extracting coal and oil, precious metals and raw materials – mostly from Arctic regions. Read more about gulags in Chapter 17, page 171.

CROSS-REFERENCE

For a Key Profile and the denunciation of Shostakovich, see Chapter 20, page 198.

ACTIVITY

Listen to the 'Leningrad' Symphony by Shostakovich and try to find out more about what the composer was trying to convey in his music; you might also like to read some Soviet war poetry in translation.

Artists enjoyed more freedom in the interest of fostering an atmosphere of national reconciliation, and previously banned individuals were allowed to work again, so long as they avoided direct criticism of Marxist-Leninism. For example, Anna Akhmatova, a poet, broadcast patriotic verse on the radio.

Musicians gave concerts. Maria Yudina, a concert pianist, was flown into Leningrad during the siege (1943) where she performed both live and on the radio with poetry recitals in the intervals. Shostakovich was reprieved and composed his Symphony No.7 'Leningrad', which was performed at the height of the siege on 9 August 1942. The brass players had to be given extra rations to enable them to perform. The stirring music was relayed on loudspeakers in the city and elsewhere, and hailed as a denunciation of fascism, although Shostakovich later claimed it was a denunciation of all dictatorships.

Churches

There was a respite in the persecution of the Churches, which were reopened. The Russian Patriarch, whose position had been abolished by the Tsars, was restored and clergy were released from the camps, although priests and bishops were officially vetted and had to swear an oath to the Soviet state. Stalin wanted to use the Church to lift morale and strengthen the people's resolve, so attendance was encouraged. Services became patriotic gatherings with sermons and prayers calling for victory and defiance of the Germans, and praising the great leader, Stalin. Priests blessed troops and tanks and reinforced feelings of devotion to the Motherland. However, the Church was not allowed any real autonomy and all Christian denominations were placed under the control of the Orthodox Church, which to some extent, turned religion into an arm of the government.

Women and the family

The war brought a reaffirmation of the importance of the family. In July 1944, new measures were introduced to try to combat the falling birth rate and the deaths brought about by the war. Taxes were increased for those with fewer than two children, restrictions on divorce were tightened, abortion was forbidden, the right to inherit family property was re-established, and mothers of more than two were made 'heroines of the Soviet Union'. Such measures undermined earlier communist attitudes to women and female communist organisations were allowed to collapse, as they were not of use to war production or defence.

CROSS-REFERENCE

Attitudes to women earlier in Stalin's rule are discussed in Chapter 16, pages 159–160.

ACTIVITY

Make a chart to illustrate the differences in policies regarding women and the Churches before and during the war years.

Women's burdens increased in wartime as they became essential members of the workforce and were expected to raise large families. By 1945, over half of all Soviet workers and more than four fifths of land workers were female. Local defence units and fire wardens were recruited from women. Over half a million women also fought in the Soviet armed forces as pilots, snipers and even tank commanders. One legendary female, Lyudmila Pavlichenko, was recorded as killing 309 Germans before her own death in June 1942. Others risked their lives as partisans. Without their effort, the USSR could not have survived and yet they received little reward; in fact women's pay rates fell between 1930 and 1945.

Partisans

Some Soviet citizens and Red Army soldiers found themselves left behind the German lines in the rapid advance of 1941, and thus were forced to live in occupied territory. Some formed partisan groups, using guerilla tactics to harass the enemy and sabotage operations. By 1943 there were an estimated 300,000 such partisans and probably a million or more by 1945. Many of them were women. One such, Zoya Kosmodemyanskaya, was made a 'Hero of the Soviet Union' for her refusal to betray her comrades when caught by Germans as she cut telephone cables. Pictures of her tortured body – executed and dumped in the snow by the Nazis – became forceful propaganda pictures in wartime.

It was not only the partisans themselves that were liable to be the victims of harsh punishments at German hands. Many thousands of innocent villagers were also massacred in reprisals because of partisan activity.

The effect of war on Stalin, the government and the people

The final stages of war

As the Red Army pushed westwards in 1944–45, it liberated the nations of central and eastern Europe from German control and imposed its own authority over them instead, turning them into satellite states: a buffer against future invasion of USSR. In Poland, Stalin allowed German forces to crush Warsaw before the Red Army occupied the country, and then installed a pro-Soviet provisional government. Soviet armies occupied Czechoslovakia, Hungary and Germany. By May 1945, when the Soviets took Berlin, and the Germans surrendered, the USSR had become the leading power in Europe.

Stalin

Stalin's reputation soared in wartime. He turned into a national superhero and was held in greater awe than ever before. So, while doubts about his leadership had been tentatively whispered before the hostilities, it was scarcely possible to even consider such betrayal by 1945. Paintings portraying him as the great wartime leader soon adorned all public buildings.

However, despite his personal triumph, Stalin emerged apparently more paranoid at the end of the war than before it. His suspicions of real or imagined enemies had grown. This paranoia was most apparent in his attitude to returning prisoners-of-war, whom Stalin regarded as tainted with Western values, purely because of their survival in Western camps during the war. Many of these were transferred directly from German to Soviet labour camps. Any collaborationist Soviet citizens who had fought for Germany against the USSR were immediately executed and their communities were made to suffer. The Cossacks, for example, were virtually wiped out in retribution for their support of German armies. Other servicemen returning to USSR from abroad were interrogated by the NKVD in 'filtration camps'. Those believed to have potentially subversive views were sent to the gulags. Those with a good war record were given access to higher education and rapid promotion to better jobs.

Government

Politically, the war was seen as a triumph for the Stalinist system, which Stalin claimed had 'proved its unquestionable vitality'. It helped to make the Soviet government a popular 'nationalist' government and in international terms, the Soviet Union emerged from war with a reputation as a great military power. It not only retained all the regions it had occupied under the Nazi-Soviet Pact, it also took more, creating a band of satellite states in eastern Europe.

Such achievements might have reduced the need for authoritarian government and a relaxing of internal discipline. However, the 66-year-old Stalin was in no mood for change. Victory was portrayed as a victory for the system, not the people. To Stalin it vindicated direct, coercive mobilisation and justified his belief that the USSR could solve its own problems. He had

Fig. 6 *A propaganda poster reads, 'Glory to the Victorious Warrior!'*

CROSS-REFERENCE

Key profiles for Kaganovich and Molotov are in Chapter 17, page 173.

Read more about Anastas Mikoyan in Chapter 20.

KEY PROFILE

Andrei Andreyev (1895–1971) was of peasant extraction and had joined the Bolsheviks during the First World War. He rose to become a member of the Politburo from 1932, leaving in 1952, when he became deaf. He served as Commissar for Agriculture in 1949 and helped prepare accusations in the Leningrad case (see page 200). He opposed any criticism of Stalin and lost all his positions in 1953.

Table 2   The impact of the war

Civilian deaths	19 million
Soldiers killed	9 million
Towns destroyed	1200
Villages destroyed	70,000
Railways destroyed	65,000 km
Hospitals destroyed	40,000
Kolkhozes wasted	100,000

STUDY TIP

To answer this question, you will need to look back at the key developments that had occurred in Soviet society in the Stalinist years before 1941, and then contrast these with the developments in 1941–45. You could for example approach this question thematically, looking for example at men, young people and women, religion and the Church, national minorities, propaganda, and cultural change.

no desire to run the USSR any differently from the pre-war days. He himself retained the two key posts of Head of Government and Party Secretary and he chose very much the same men to serve in his Politburo as in 1939 – Vyacheslav Molotov, Kliment Voroshilov, Lazar Kaganovich, Anastas Mikoyan, **Andrei Andreyev** and Nikita Khrushchev. In this way, the last years of Stalin's life saw a return to the methods of the 1930s.

People

The Russian people endured some terrible suffering in wartime, as exemplified in the statistics in Table 2.

At the end of the war, 25 million people in the western provinces had nothing but wooden huts to live in and many of the achievements of the 1930s had been destroyed.

However, despite the deaths and material damage, the war years were in some ways easier years for the Soviet people, as they offered ordinary people more opportunity for individual initiative and helped to bring State and people closer. The sense of collective endeavour for their country, their government and Stalin, gave new hope of change when war was over. The comradeship among soldiers helped to spread new liberal thinking – especially as they saw more of the West – and army officers emerged from the war at forefront of the movement for greater liberalisation.

Soviet society was also opened to Western influence in wartime in a way that had not been possible in the isolationist 1920s and 1930s. Links with Western allies and the Lend-Lease scheme, as well as the movement of soldiers in the later years of war, opened the eyes of ordinary Soviet citizens and helped to disprove the propaganda image of the drab and dismal West. Hollywood films, Western books, Western music (especially jazz) and Western goods found their way into the USSR and restaurants and commercial shops appeared. Such developments also gave hope that a more open society might emerge from the war. In reality, the years between 1945 and 1953 were among the most bleak of the entire Stalinist period.

Summary

The Second World War, beginning for USSR in 1941, had immense political, economic and social consequences. The Soviet armed forces rallied and the Soviet economy was restructured and survived. Government became even more personal and autocratic and Stalin emerged as a superhero. For the Soviet people, the war brought extreme hardship and control. Used to suffering in the 1930s, the people of the Soviet Union fought for sheer survival, but as the promise of victory grew closer, so too did their hopes of change in the future.

 PRACTICE QUESTION

With reference to the period 1928–45, to what extent did the Great Patriotic War change the development of Soviet society?

20 Political authority 1945–53

The years after 1945 witnessed one of the grand illusions of modern history. The Soviet Union had emerged from the Second World War as the greatest military power in Europe and it proceeded to turn itself into one of two global superpowers. To all outward appearances it was unimaginably strong. At the same time its internal processes were decomposing – here was an armoured dinosaur that was dying on its feet. Stalin's last years brought no relief to the long night of fear and suffering. Speculation that age and victory would mellow him proved unfounded. The same old gang of Stalin's pre-war cronies clung to power. The same mixture of terror, propaganda and collective routine kept the Soviet peoples down. The gulags kept up the same regular motions of mass arrests and slave labour. There is strong evidence to suppose that Stalin was preparing another great purge when he died. Yet, in those years the Soviet Empire expanded to its greatest extent and news of Stalin's death caused tens of millions to weep.

Adapted from Norman Davies, *Europe*, 1996

LEARNING OBJECTIVES

In this chapter you will learn about:

- political authority, government and 'High Stalinism'
- the revival of terror and the destruction of 'supposed opposition'
- the cult of personality
- the power vacuum on Stalin's death.

ACTIVITY

Evaluating historical extracts

In Extract 1 Norman Davies presents two contrasting views of post-war USSR. Identify these. In this chapter you will be invited to consider the validity of these views. Look for evidence that supports each view.

KEY QUESTION

As you read this chapter, consider the following Key Questions:

- How was the Soviet Union governed and how did political authority change and develop?
- How important was the role of individuals and groups?

Political authority and government to 1953 – High Stalinism

The years that followed the end of the Second World War are often referred to as the period of 'High Stalinism'. It was during these years that Stalin's authority over State and Party, as well as the cult of personality that had grown up around him, reached its pinnacle. Stalin's leadership was undisputed. As the great hero of the Second World War, basking in the glory of success and presiding over a **world superpower**, he could rule more or less as he chose to while those around him competed for the privilege of fulfilling his will.

A CLOSER LOOK

World superpower

By the end of the war, the USSR had grown larger, with the annexation of new territory (as promised by the Nazi-Soviet Pact). Within the next four years it was to establish a series of Soviet satellite states in Poland, Czechoslovakia, Hungary, Romania, Bulgaria and Eastern Germany. Soviet participation in the wartime summit meetings broke its outcast status of pre-1939 and made it one of the arbiters of post-war Europe. Its role in victory and its new military strength (reinforced by the Soviet possession of an atom bomb in 1949) gave the USSR a new ascendancy.

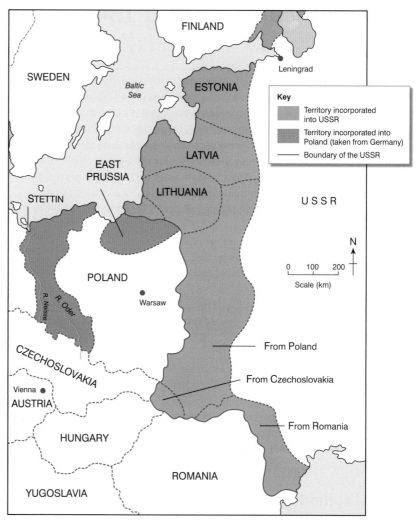

Fig. 1 *Soviet territories gained after Second World War*

Political High Stalinism

Stalin's approach to post-war government was 'back to the future'. Wartime developments worried Stalin. Increased Party membership under lax wartime rules had made the Party unwieldy and potentially unreliable, while the reputation of the Soviet military was left too high for his liking.

Wartime institutions were therefore dismantled and the GKO (State Defence Committee) was dissolved on 4 September 1945, its functions returning to the various commissariats. The military hierarchy was also downgraded. Stalin personally took the role of Minister of Defence and high-ranking officers were moved into inferior posts. The most notorious of these moves was the demotion of Marshal Zhukov, who was seen as a potential rival for popular adulation. He was sent to the military command at Odessa, losing his position on the Central Committee of the Party.

Other major figures of the war years were played off, one against the other. When Andrei Zhdanov returned to the Party Secretariat in Moscow and challenged the policy of Stalin's closest war time aide, Georgi Malenkov (who favoured removing industrial plant from Germany to USSR), an investigation under Mikoyan was set up which condemned Malenkov's actions. Malenkov subsequently lost his position as Party Secretary and Zhdanov became Stalin's closest adviser – launching the Zhdanovshchina.

CROSS-REFERENCE

Malenkov is profiled in Chapter 21, where his role in the power struggle following Stalin's death is discussed in more detail.

Zhdanov is profiled in Chapter 16, page 166.

The Zhdanovshchina is discussed on page 197.

However, a further disagreement occurred over foreign policy, with Zhdanov and his supporters favouring the Berlin blockade of 1948 while Malenkov argued for a more moderate path. Malenkov was reappointed to the Party Secretariat and Zhdanov's supporters were demoted. Zhdanov himself died the same year.

By such manipulations, Stalin's personal dominance was assured. Although the Central Committee met in March 1946 and elected a new Politburo, Secretariat and Orgburo, which met regularly, Stalin continued to hold the reins of power in his position as Head of Government and Head of the Party. He relied increasingly on his private secretariat to bypass both government and Party and exert direct central authority.

Not only did the Party no longer have any real supervisory role over the government, its regular institutions were also undermined in this period. Party congresses, which should have met every three years, were not held between 1939 and 1952, and only six full meetings of the Central Committee were convened during this time. The Politburo was reduced to an advisory body, which awaited instruction on the 'official' line from Stalin or his spokesman, and much of the decision-making took place in small ad hoc gatherings, between Stalin and those privileged enough to be in his inner circle.

Recruitment to the Party fell back from the war years. Still, by 1952, it had nearly 7 million members, while Komsomol had around 16 million. These new members were once again recruited from 'administrative' ranks in industry, the government and education, rather than from peasants and manual workers as had occurred in wartime. Indeed, a campaign had to be launched to raise the ideological level of the little-educated military recruits. However, the 'old guard' of those who had been driven to join the Party because of their personal commitment to the ideals of Marxism was replaced by a new-style Party member. The 'new men' who came to dominate local politics accepted the Party as a way of life and, having been brought up in a period of shifting political priorities, were cautious and careful – both in their Party positions and in their personal lives. They waited to receive official policy rather than helping to formulate it. They became faceless bureaucrats, unwilling to act unless they were assured of the backing of higher authority.

By destroying Party autonomy, Stalin thus reduced it to a mere chain of command. Its earlier dynamism gave way to a rigid bureaucratic structure, duplicating the official governmental structure.

ACTIVITY

The 'faceless' Russian bureaucrats that emerged in this period were caricatured by George Orwell in *Animal Farm* (1945) and *1984* (1949). Try to read one of these novels and give a short presentation to your class on Orwell's allegories.

 PRACTICE QUESTION

To what extent did political authority and government change under Stalin?

Cultural High Stalinism

KEY QUESTION

- How important were ideas and ideology?
- What was the extent of social and cultural change?

STUDY TIP

To answer this question you will need to look back at earlier chapters and trace the changes that had occurred since the 1920s. Take care, however, that you do not produce a piece of narrative. Instead look at the different elements of government and try to write thematically.

Complementing Stalin's unparalleled authority in government were new controls over intellectual life. The period became known as the Zhdanovshchina, as it was Andrei Zhdanov who launched a cultural purge in 1946. Possibly fearing the result of the increased Westernisation of the war years, the movement stressed conformity to socialist ideals and promoted

Fig. 2 *The Russian poet Anna Akhmatova*

CROSS-REFERENCE

The poet Anna Akhmatova is introduced in Chapter 19.

To recap on socialist realism in the 1930s, look back to Chapter 16, page 165.

KEY PROFILE

Dmitry Shostakovich (1906–75) was renowned internationally as a composer. He wrote 15 symphonies, numerous chamber works, and concerti, but largely under the pressures of government-imposed standards. His relationship with the authorities was chequered. He taught in both the Leningrad and Moscow academies but fell from favour in 1936 over his opera *Lady Macbeth of Mtsensk* in 1936 although his Symphony No.7 of 1941 was an inspiration during the siege of Leningrad. After his second denunciation of 1948, his teaching activities were terminated. His 'Leningrad' Symphony is detailed in Chapter 19, page 192.

the cult of Stalin. Everything Western was condemned as bourgeois and decadent; all things Russian were regarded as superior and uplifting.

The Zhdanovshchina began with a purge of two literary journals published in Leningrad. The first, *The Adventures of a Monkey*, by the satirist Mikhail Zoshchenko, was condemned because the monkey was perceived to be anti-Soviet. The second, a journal of Anna Akhmatova's poetry, was described as 'poisonous'. The publishers of these works were purged and their authors expelled from the Union of Soviet Writers. Thereafter, neither was able to persuade anyone else to print their writings. Even the staff of the *Literary Gazette* who had printed a portrait of Akhmatova the previous year were condemned. Boris Pasternak was also condemned for his 'apolitical poems' and his mistress, Olga Ivinskaya, was sent to a gulag.

Socialist realism again became the norm in literature, art, music and film. **Dmitry Shostakovich** was accused of 'rootless cosmopolitanism' and Sergei Prokofiev was criticised for 'anti-socialist' works. His income was severely curtailed and he was forced to compose Stalinist pieces. Eisenstein was criticised for his film *Ivan the Terrible* because he portrayed the Tsar's bodyguards as thugs rather than a 'progressive army'. All these –and other condemned artists – were forced to make public recantations of their errors in order to continue working.

Literary scholarship was condemned for suggesting that Russian literature had been influenced by Western thinking while the works of Dostoevsky were removed from sale as it was felt his heroes lacked socialist qualities. Instead novels, plays and films that denigrated American commercialism, conveyed the treachery of the West, or extolled Russian achievements, including almost obligatory praise of Stalin, were favoured. Anti-Semitism also flourished; many Jewish drama and literary critics disappeared and the last Jewish newspaper was closed down. Indeed, Nazi atrocities were portrayed without mentioning Jews.

Scholarship that did not conform to official Marxist interpretations was dismissed. In 1948 Zhdanov restated his support for the theories of the environmentalist Lysenko whose ideas had been condemned by biologists before the war. The study of Maths, Physics and Chemistry was also governed by Marxist principles. Stalin became involved in spurious theories about the language that would be used once the socialist revolution was complete – and in 1950 decided in favour of Russian. He also published his own views on economic theory in 1952, which no one dared challenge.

Western influence was completely blocked. Non-communist foreign papers were unobtainable, foreign radio transmissions were jammed, only a few 'approved' foreign books were translated into Russian (and sometimes abridged), only pro-Soviet foreign writers and artists were allowed to visit the USSR and very few Soviet citizens were allowed to go to the West.

ACTIVITY

Compose a piece that would have been acceptable in the Zhdanovshchina – perhaps a poem, article or artwork in praise of Stalin. (You might like to read the section on the 'cult of personality' at the end of this chapter before attempting this.)

The revival of terror and the destruction of 'supposed opposition'

KEY QUESTION

- Why did opposition develop and how effective was it?
- How important was the role of individuals and groups?

High Stalinism was also characterised by a revival of terror. Stalin demanded an excessive isolationism from the non-Soviet world during these years. This was partly out of concern for national security at a time of emerging Cold War, but also because of an obsessive fear of ideological contamination. Stalin's harsh treatment of returned prisoners-of-war and his purge of former army officers bore witness to his paranoia, and even the relatives of those who had spent time outside the USSR were considered suspect.

Within the USSR, and particularly in the areas newly incorporated into it, vigilance was needed to ensure unwavering loyalty. A careless word or brief contact with a foreigner could land a person in a gulag and the Party, police, **procuracy**, friends and colleagues were all possible instruments whereby an individual might be singled out and subsequently condemned. In February 1947, a law was passed outlawing hotels and marriages to foreigners. Restaurants and embassies were watched by police for Soviet girls who met foreign men.

At the head of the security apparatus was Lavrenti Beria who, as well as being deputy Prime Minister, was also a full member of the Politburo. He was largely responsible for a vast expansion in the gulag system and his dreary and sadistic personality cast a long shadow over the USSR.

The NKVD was itself strengthened and reorganised under two separate ministries. The MVD (Ministry of Internal Affairs) controlled domestic security and the gulags, while the MGB (Ministry of State Security – the forerunner of the KGB) took charge of counter-intelligence and espionage. Although the Terror was not as great as in the 1930s, tens of thousands were arrested annually in these later years and convicted of 'counter-revolutionary activities'. In total, around 12 million wartime survivors were sent to the labour camps, suffering appalling conditions.

Dealing with 'opposition'

Fig. 3   *Stalin, with Vyacheslav Molotov to his right and Nikolai Yezhov to his left, at the Moscow-Volga Canal Embankment in 1937*

Stalin dealt with those who had already fallen from favour by removing them from history. Their very existence was written out of the history books and Stalin manipulated the science of photography using airbrushing and other techniques to remove the old, disgraced Bolsheviks. The Great Soviet Encyclopaedia was full of such altered images.

CROSS-REFERENCE

Stalin's treatment of prisoners-of-war and his purge of former officers are discussed in Chapter 19, page 193.

KEY TERM

Procuracy: (in Russian, *Prokuratura*) was a government office responsible for ensuring all government ministries and institutions, as well as individual officials and citizens, obeyed the law; this 'watchdog of legality' largely enforced communist orders

ACTIVITY

You can learn more about the altering and censoring of photographs in David King's book *The Commissar Vanishes: The Falsification of Photographs and Art in Stalin's Russia* (1997).

Fig. 4 *In this manipulated version of Fig. 3, Stalin is pictured with Molotov at the Moscow-Volga Canal Embankment (after Yezhov was tried and executed, his likeness was removed from the original picture)*

The Leningrad Case, 1949

In 1949, Stalin decided to take a stand against the 'Leningrad party', which had always shown some independence in its views and actions, and some of whose members had been promoted to senior positions in Moscow during the time of Zhdanov's ascendancy. On the basis of false evidence, several leading officials were arrested, including the Head of Gosplan and Voznesensky, an economic reformer who held a position in the Politburo. (After Stalin's death it was found that four of those arrested, including Voznesensky, were executed.)

Anti-Semitism

Although Stalin had initially favoured the creation of a Jewish state in Palestine at the end of the war, when Israel turned out to be pro-USA, he reverted to his former anti-Semitic stance, fearing that all Jews within the USSR were potential enemies. This feeling was reinforced by the arrival of the Israeli ambassador to the USSR, Golda Meir, in 1948. She was enthusiastically cheered by Soviet Jews wherever she went. The director of the Jewish theatre in Moscow, Solomon Mikhoels, was mysteriously killed in a car accident in 1948 – almost certainly arranged by the MVD. The Jewish wives of Politburo members Molotov and Kalinin were arrested in 1949 and a new campaign against 'anti-patriotic groups' was launched the same year, mainly affecting cultural areas and the universities.

CROSS-REFERENCE

Beria is profiled in Chapter 21, page 204, where his role in the post-war government is discussed in greater detail.

The Mingrelian Case (Georgian purge) 1951–52

In 1951 a purge was launched in Georgia, directed against the followers of Lavrenti Beria, the head of the NKVD. They were accused of collaboration with Western powers. Beria was himself of Mingrelian ethnic extraction and, although many aspects of this purge remain unclear and it was still in progress when Stalin died, it seems likely that the 'Mingrelian Case' was aimed at weakening the authority of Beria. (It did, however, also have some anti-Semitic overtones.)

The Doctors' Plot, 1952

A new conspiracy was 'discovered' when Lydia Timashuk – a female doctor in the Kremlin hospital and part-time MGB informer – wrote to Stalin two days before Zhdanov's death in 1948, accusing nine highly-placed doctors of failure to diagnose and treat Zhdanov professionally. At the time, nothing was done, but in 1952, Stalin reopened the file and ordered the arrest of the doctors, accusing them of a Zionist conspiracy to murder Zhdanov and other members of the Soviet leadership. Stalin put it about that Jews, in the pay of the USA and Israel, were using their positions in the medical profession to harm the USSR and had infiltrated the Leningrad party association, the MGB and the Red Army.

Stalin threatened his Minister of State Security, Nikolai Ignatiev, with execution if he did not obtain confessions, and hundreds of doctors were arrested and tortured. However, the purge went still further. Thousands of ordinary Jews were also rounded up and deported from the cities to the remote regions of the USSR where a new network of Labour camps was rapidly established. Anti-Jewish hysteria was also whipped up by the press, so that non-Jews feared to enter hospitals and shunned all Jewish professionals.

The nine named doctors were duly condemned and sentenced to execution, but before this could take place, Stalin died. The news must have brought relief to those at the top who seemed to be lined up as the victims of yet another purge – Beria, Mikoyan, Molotov and Kaganovich.

Stalin's cult of personality after 1945

Stalin suffered a mild stroke in 1946 and this may have been responsible for his increasing paranoia in the post-war years. His reclusiveness and irrational behaviour seemed at odds with his wartime leadership, but it is equally likely that these personality traits were always present and simply became stronger in old age. Nevertheless, none of this prevented, and may indeed have fostered, an even greater public adulation of their leader.

Building on his reputation as the saviour of Russia in wartime, Stalin was accorded a god-like status. He was portrayed as the world's greatest living genius, equally superior in all areas, be it philosophy, strategy or the economy. This image was carefully cultivated in newspapers, books, plays, films, radio and speeches and it became customary for the first and last paragraphs of any academic article or book to be devoted to Stalin's genius or interest in the subject matter. A 1948 biography of Stalin exalted him as the modern Lenin and leading Marxist theoretician and others were denigrated in order to show Stalin's superior powers.

Even though Stalin had not visited a peasant village or *kolkhoz* for 25 years and spent most of his later years at his *dacha* [country house] or Black Sea home, he was portrayed as a 'man of the people' who knew what everyone was doing and thinking. In reality, he relied on films and written papers for his knowledge and was probably misled by his own propagandists. On his seventieth birthday, newspapers were entirely given over to his praise and in Red Square in Moscow, a giant portrait of Stalin was suspended in the sky, illuminated by halo of searchlights.

Towns vied to use Stalin's name (Stalingrad, Stalino, Stalinsk, Stalinabad and Stalinogorsk) although the proposal to rename Moscow Stalinodar was not carried out. Stalin prizes were introduced for artistic or scientific work (to counter-balance the Western Nobel prizes). The great leader enjoyed everlasting ovations and his photos were airbrushed to remove the pockmarks from his face. Monuments to him appeared all over the USSR. Special workshops were even established to produce standard models for gigantic Stalin statues; deluxe models were made in copper.

ACTIVITY

The novel *The Betrayal* by Helen Dunmore conjures up the atmosphere of suspicion in Stalin's last years, with particular reference to the vulnerability of the doctors. This is a sequel to another excellent novel, *The Siege*, in which the story unfolds against the backdrop of conditions in Leningrad during the war years. Although fiction, both books are of value in helping to understand conditions in these periods.

A CLOSER LOOK

After Stalin's death, the doctors were re-examined and released, although two had already died – probably under torture. Timashuk was made to hand back her 'Order of Lenin' awarded for her vigilance and some members of the MVD (although not Ignatiev) were executed for falsifying evidence.

KEY QUESTION

How important was the role of individuals?

CROSS-REFERENCE

Read about the cult of personality in Chapter 14, page 143.

ACTIVITY

1. Discuss with a partner: Would it be correct to refer to the 'cult of personality' as another branch of Stalinist government?
2. Search online for examples of Stalin statues, monuments and other depictions of his cult, and create a Stalin poster for display.

The power vacuum on Stalin's death

Despite his unpredictable outbursts, Stalin became increasingly frail in his last year of life, spending much of his time watching films and enjoying all-night drinking sessions with his wartime cronies. He made no attempt to groom a successor, although he finally called a Party congress in October 1952 at which his subordinates, Malenkov and Khrushchev, delivered the main speeches. Stalin's request to be relieved of his position as Party Secretary because of his advanced age was rejected by delegates unsure of his intentions. Equally bewildering was Khrushchev's announcement that the Orgburo was to be abolished and the Politburo replaced by an enlarged **Presidium**. This was seen as a hint of preparations for another purge.

Stalin's death in March 1953 left a nation politically demoralised. While there were hysterical public displays of grief, and crowds queued to see his embalmed body which was laid in state in the Hall of Columns within the Party Congress Hall in Moscow, another political leadership struggle was underway between the prominent members of the ruling 'troika' – Lavrenti Beria, Georgii Malenkov and Vyacheslav Molotov.

CROSS-REFERENCE

Khrushchev is profiled in Chapter 21, page 204, where his rise to power following Stalin's death is described in more detail.

KEY TERM

Presidium: Stalin re-named the Politburo as the Presidium in 1952 and this name was retained until 1966; the Politburo/Presidium was nominated by Stalin, rather then elected, during his time as leader (see page 131 for details of the Politburo)

ACTIVITY

Evaluating historical extracts

What is Freeze's view of Stalin? Identify some key words or expressions that help convey this view. Freeze advances three possible motives for Stalin's behaviour in his final years. In the light of what you have read in this chapter, which would you most agree with?

EXTRACT 2

Stalin was accorded god-like veneration in the post-war years: he was the hero of plays and the subject of folksongs; symphonies and odes were composed in his honour; canals and dams were dedicated to his name. Orators praised him as 'the father of the peoples' and 'the best friend of all children'. Rapturous enthusiasm greeted his every pronouncement. However gratifying, universal adulation did not relax Stalin's vigilant concern for his personal power. In the last years of his reign, the tyrant took pains to keep his closest associates in a constant state of poisonous antagonism and mutual suspicion. It is not known whether his motivation was authentic fear of conspiracy, belief in the efficacy of divide and rule or mere perversity. Even as a corpse Stalin brought calamity: 500 people were trampled to death in Moscow because of poor security on the day of his funeral.

Adapted from Gregory Freeze, *Russia, a History*, 2009

Summary

The years 1945 to 1953 saw Stalin's authority reach new heights. Such was his influence that this period is often referred to as 'High Stalinism'. Politically, Stalin was supreme, but this did not end his concern to eliminate all ideas and actions that reflected an independent and possibly oppositional line. Hence the 'Zhdanovshchina' brought an intense persecution of artists and intellectuals, while a revival of terror kept the wider population in check. The more Stalin's own position was exalted, the harder it became for anyone to question him, or for a potential successor to emerge.

STUDY TIP

Extracts 1 and 2 consider the 'High Stalinism' of the period 1945 to 1953 but your should evaluate the arguments with reference to the broader theme of Stalinist authority, paying attention to how these authors explain what happened after the Great Patriotic War.

 PRACTICE QUESTION

Evaluating historical extracts

Using your understanding of the historical context, assess how convincing the arguments in Extracts 1 and 2 are, in relation to Stalin's authority in the USSR by 1953.

21 Khrushchev and reaction to Stalinism, 1953–64

EXTRACT 1

At first sight it seems strange that the man who came to bury the personality cult in the Soviet Union should display a much more distinctive personality than Stalin ever had. Stalin's beginnings had been obscure, his period of power monumental, his statues martial and stiffly **avuncular**. His contact with people had always been carefully stage-managed and had been as unspontaneous as befits a ruler protected and exalted by a bureaucracy. Khrushchev was entirely different. He had few pretensions as an interpreter of Marxism-Leninism and left to others the task of aligning his practical policy with the official ideology. Unpredictable in his personal behaviour, he played the role of a man of the people with verve and humour; his spontaneous slogans and jokes reeked of the farmyard and peasant household. Agriculture was also his pet political preoccupation. But he transformed its problems into simple and direct imagery, not into blankets of pseudo-Marxist reasoning.

Adapted from John Peter Nettl, *The Soviet Achievement*, 1967

ACTIVITY

Evaluating historical extracts

In Extract 1, Nettl contrasts Khrushchev and Stalin. Create a two-column chart and record the comparisons made between the two leaders. As you read this chapter, and subsequent chapters, try to decide whether you agree with these comparisons and what evidence you could cite to support or refute them.

Khrushchev's rise to power

KEY CHRONOLOGY

The leadership struggle
1952:

October	Presidium begins debate on succession
1953:	
March	Stalin dies; Malenkov takes leadership as Chairman of Council of Ministers and General Secretary of the Party, but a week later is replaced as General Secretary by Khrushchev and a collective leadership is established
June	Beria is arrested
December	Beria is executed
1954	Khrushchev launches his Virgin Lands Scheme
1955:	
Feb	Malenkov is replaced by Bulganin as Chairman of Council of Ministers
1957:	
June	Anti-Party group tries to oust Khrushchev, but fails and is purged
October	Zhukov is dismissed
1958:	
March	Bulganin is forced to resign

LEARNING OBJECTIVES

In this chapter you will learn about:

- Khrushchev's rise to power
- Khrushchev's policies and ideology, and de-Stalinisation
- changes in politics and the Party.

KEY TERM

Avuncular: kindly and friendly towards others, especially those younger or less experienced

KEY QUESTION

As you read this chapter, consider the following Key Questions:
- How was the Soviet Union governed and how did political authority change and develop?
- Why did opposition develop and how effective was it?
- How important was the role of individuals and groups?

Fig. 1   *Georgi Malenkov*

Fig. 2   *Lavrenti Beria*

Georgi Malenkov (1892–1988) was part of the five-man Defence Council during the war, which managed the Soviet Union's war effort, particularly military supplies. In 1946, Stalin appointed him as deputy Prime Minister and he became a full member of the Presidium. He was one of Stalin's favourite *apparatchiki* – Stalin liked to talk about 'old-times' with him even though Malenkov's political leanings were towards reform. He exercised a brief period of leadership after 1953 but was expelled from the Presidium in 1957, and from the Party in 1961.

Nikita Sergeyevich Khrushchev (1894–1971) was of peasant origins and had worked for the Communist Party in Kiev and Moscow in the early 1930s, gaining a reputation for efficiency. From 1935 he was Secretary of the Moscow Regional Committee where he organised the building of the Moscow underground. From 1938–47, he was in the Ukraine, assisting in the military operation at Kursk. He entered the Politburo in 1939 and in 1947 and was chosen to supervise agricultural production. He went on to become First Secretary of the Communist Party 1953–64.

Lavrenti Beria (1899–1953) had made his career in the communist Secret Police and had replaced Yezhov as head of the NKVD, following Yezhov's purge in 1938. An intelligent but ruthless and opportunistic man, his powers increased in the war years and he was rewarded with a position as deputy Prime Minister in 1941 and Politburo member in 1946.

ACTIVITY

Create a diagram featuring these contenders for power, together with a brief statement on their strengths and weaknesses as candidates in the power struggle.

CROSS-REFERENCE

The replacement of the Politburo by the new Presidium is covered in Chapter 20, page 202.

Vyacheslav Molotov is profiled in Chapter 17, page 173.

The Mingrelian Case (Georgian purge) is outlined in Chapter 20, page 200.

Even as Stalin was dying, the newly created and enlarged Presidium that had replaced the Politburo at the nineteenth Party Congress in 1952 was in session and debating the succession.

It was announced on 6 March 1953 that Georgi Malenkov would combine the roles of Secretary of the Party's Central Committee and Chairman of the Council of Ministers, but within a few days his rivals had forced him to step down as Party Secretary and concentrate instead on his governmental role. This was a significant development, as his post was taken by Nikita Khrushchev. A collective leadership was subsequently created with Vyacheslav Molotov, the Foreign Minister, and Lavrenti Beria, formerly Malenkov's ally and head of the MVD, all exerting considerable influence.

Khrushchev immediately began appointing his own protégés to important Party posts and although underestimated by the others as a serious contender for power, built himself a strong support network in the Party's administrative machinery.

In the following weeks, Beria emerged as the leader who was most anxious to depart from Stalinist policies. He advocated the release of all but the most dangerous political prisoners, took a moderate line in foreign policy, denounced the Mingrelian purge and sought to scale back on some of Stalin's more costly construction projects. The popularity of his pronouncements as well as the power of his office caused alarm at the top.

Malenkov and other Presidium members including Khrushchev conspired against him and arranged Beria's arrest at the hands of the military in June 1953. An anti-Beria campaign was conducted in the press and he was accused of 'criminal anti-Party and anti-State activities'. He was secretly tried and executed on 24 December 1953. His supporters were also purged.

Policy differences caused further splits. The leadership was divided on foreign policy, industrial and agricultural policy and the role of the Party. Malenkov, who placed government above Party, attempted, with Molotov's backing, to use his influence to launch a 'new course'. He wanted to change collective farm policy, reduce peasant taxes and put more investment into consumer goods. Against this, Khrushchev, who placed Party before government, offered his own set of policy proposals. He offered a less radical proposal for the parallel development of heavy and light industry and sold himself as an agricultural expert, launching his Virgin Lands Scheme early in 1954. The early successes of this scheme helped to rally the Party behind him.

In February 1955 Malenkov found himself isolated and was therefore forced to step down as Chairman of the Council of Ministers. He took the new and relatively unimportant role of Minister for Power Stations. He was succeeded by Nikolai Bulganin, one of a number that Khrushchev had been promoting in the state ministries over the preceding years.

Khrushchev and Bulganin acted as joint leaders until 1958, although there was an attempt to unseat Khrushchev in 1957 when they were on a visit to Finland. A majority in the Presidium voted for Khrushchev's dismissal but Khrushchev insisted the matter be put to the Central Committee. Before this convened, Khrushchev ensured those favourable to himself were brought to Moscow to vote in his favour. He also benefited from the support of Marshal Zhukov, who had been brought back into power as deputy Minister for Defence and thus brought Red Army support. Zhukov spoke out against Malenkov, Molotov and their supporter Kaganovich.

The plotters, who became known as the 'anti-Party group', were duly outvoted by the Central Committee and accused of conservatism and involvement in the purges of the 1930s. They were expelled from the Central Committee and sent to jobs far from Moscow, while Zhukov and other supporters were rewarded with seats in the Presidium.

However, Khrushchev was not content to be reliant on others. In October 1957 Zhukov was dismissed and a propaganda campaign against him accused him of hindering Party work in the army and creating his own personality cult. In March 1958, Bulganin was accused of encouraging the anti-Party group and forced to step down and Khrushchev took over as General Secretary of the Party. Thus the two top jobs – in Party and in government – were combined once more.

Policies and ideology, and de-Stalinisation

In June 1955, the government announced a meeting of the first Party congress since Stalin's death. It would be the twentieth and would meet on 25 February 1956.

Before it took place, Khrushchev had already begun to reverse Stalinist policies. Those accused in the Doctors' Plot were released, Beria, the police and the gulag system had all been attacked, and a cultural 'thaw' was underway. The congress offered an opportunity to explain the change in direction, but so doing was not easy.

CROSS-REFERENCE

For Khrushchev's Virgin Lands Scheme, look ahead to Chapter 22, page 215.

ACTIVITY

Create an illustrated storyboard to show how Khrushchev established his power between 1953 and 1958.

KEY QUESTION

- How important were ideas and ideology?
- How important was the role of individuals and groups?

CROSS-REFERENCE

To recap on the 'Doctors' Plot' look back to Chapter 20, page 201.

Fig. 3 *A crowd of people surround the demolished head of a statue of Stalin*

Most of the Presidium welcomed the dismantling of the Stalinist Terror apparatus, but many had been involved in the purges and did not welcome a re-opening of the past. They were uneasy at the thought of delegates debating Stalin's rule and thus Khrushchev, who was determined to speak out, was persuaded to do so only in a 'closed session'. This was to be held in secret and none of the 1400 delegates was allowed to ask questions. In preparing his speech, Khrushchev used material that had been assembled by a special commission of the Central Committee into abuses under Stalin.

In his speech, entitled, 'On the Cult of Personality and its Consequences', Khrushchev delivered a blistering attack on Stalin, accusing him of responsibility for the purges, terror, torture, mass arrests, executions and the gulags, causing 'tremendous harm to the cause of socialist progress'. He quoted from Lenin's testament to illustrate Lenin's view of Stalin and accused Stalin of betraying Leninist principles (also implying that Malenkov and Molotov were his accomplices). He blamed Stalin for the murder of Kirov, called for the rehabilitation of Trotsky and questioned Stalin's war leadership.

The speech was met by resounding applause. Although it was supposedly held in secret and was never published in the USSR, copies were soon sent to foreign parties and its content soon filtered down through the Party ranks in the USSR. Some younger communists, such as the 31-year-old Mikhail Gorbachev, demanded that those responsible for Stalinist 'crimes' should be brought to justice, but Khrushchev quietly avoided comment on such suggestions.

Although the '**Secret Speech**' condemned matters such as autocratic leadership, the undermining of the Party, the brutal suppression of Party members and the mishandling of the war, which affected the Soviet ruling elites, it paid limited attention to the purging of ordinary soviet citizens and accepted economic controls, strong leadership, a single Party and the elimination of factions as perfectly legitimate. In short, the speech tried to justify a good deal of continuity, while distancing the leadership from Stalinist mistakes. There was no wish to incriminate those, like Khrushchev himself, who had benefited from the Stalinist system.

CROSS-REFERENCE

Kirov's murder is described in Chapter 17, page 173 .

A CLOSER LOOK

Khrushchev's speech inspired uprisings in favour of reform in Tblisi, Georgia (Stalin's birthplace), and in the satellite states of Poland and Hungary. Khrushchev's support for the use of force to crush these risings shows the limitation of his reformist principles.

EXTRACT 2

After decades of adulation for Stalin, communists had to come to terms with the fact that Stalin was, to put it bluntly, a mass murderer. Some refused to believe it and held that Khrushchev's 'Secret Speech' must be a forgery. In 1961, however, Khrushchev went on to attack Stalin in the open session of the 22nd Party Congress, thus putting an end to any doubts about the authenticity of his 1956 speech. What he did not do at either of those de-Stalinising congresses was to call into question the political system which had allowed Stalin and the Secret Police to get away with their atrocities. Khrushchev himself at times wavered in his anti-Stalinism, partly as a result of pressure from more conservative colleagues, but more because of his own worries about a loosening of Party control. He remained an ideologically convinced communist who actually agreed with Stalin on many matters.

Adapted from Archie Brown, *The Rise and Fall of Communism*, 2010

ACTIVITY

Evaluating historical extracts

To what extent does Extract 2 support the view that Khrushchev was totally committed to de-Stalinisation? Explain your answer.

Political and Party change

Stalin's death brought changes in the balance of power within the Soviet Union. Under Stalin, both Party and state governmental institutions had become mere 'rubber-stamping organisations', dependent on one man. As a result of the leadership struggle they assumed a renewed importance as centres for debate and decision-making. Initially, a third institution – the police – competed with them for influence. However, with Beria's arrest and execution in 1953, the police found themselves again, as in 1934, under the authority of the Party and government. The coercive machinery of the Stalinist era was dismantled and the Secret Police apparatus reduced in size. Political amnesties and a partial revival of an independent judicial system marked a move away from police influence in state matters.

The Party gained most from Beria's fall. Since Khrushchev was First Secretary, he was able to use his influence in the Party in his struggle for power. When he sought the support of the Central Committee in 1957 to defend his position in the face of a challenge in the Presidium, he was returning to the traditional hierarchy of power, as advocated by Lenin, whereby the smaller institutions were directly responsible to their parent bodies.

Khrushchev thus helped to restore the position of the Party back to something like that which it had enjoyed in the 1920s. However, there were two other goals sought by Khrushchev from 1957, which sometimes contradicted the Party's ascendancy:
- democratisation – this would involve weakening the traditional bureaucracy to give more responsibility to the people
- decentralisation – this would give more initiative to the localities.

Measures and actions which sought to fulfil the twin goals of democratisation and decentralisation included:
- In 1962 the Party was split into urban and rural sections at all levels.
- New rules were issued, limiting how long Party officials could serve.
- Membership was expanded: from 7 million in 1956 to 11 million in 1964 (from 3.6 per cent to 4.8 per cent of the population). This brought more working-class members, broadening the Party's popular base, while reducing the power of the higher level bureaucrats.
- The role of the local soviets was augmented and comrade courts to handle minor offences were revived.
- Non-Party members were encouraged to take supervisory roles and some were invited to Party congresses.

KEY QUESTION

- How was the Soviet Union governed and how did political authority change and develop?
- How important were ideas and ideology?
- How important was the role of individuals and groups?

CROSS-REFERENCE

Economic decentralisation is covered in more detail in Chapter 22, page 210.

- Khrushchev visited villages and towns – showing a personal desire for first-hand contact with the people.
- Economic decentralisation was pursued, moving some power from central Moscow ministries to provincial authorities.

The autocratic terror state of Stalin disappeared in this era, to be replaced by a central government system that was similar to that of the mid-1920s. However, although the Party again became the dominant political institution, and its dominance limited the influence of the Secret Police and its own leader, nevertheless, other policies in this period took power away from the centre and attempted to weaken the position of the entrenched bureaucracy which propped up the Party structure.

ACTIVITY

Summary

The struggle for power after Stalin's death was largely about the political direction that the USSR should take. Although Khrushchev established his ascendancy before his de-Stalinisation speech, his reforming ideas had already attracted a good measure of support and, while the speech proved divisive it clarified the path that he intended to follow. Based on what you have read in this chapter, write and deliver a speech, in which Khrushchev gives his views on the future direction of government and political authority.

ACTIVITY

What is Hosking's view of Khrushchev in Extract 3?

EXTRACT 3

Khrushchev was a figure symptomatic of his time. Both agent and beneficiary of Stalin's Terror, he came to power disillusioned with Stalin's methods, and thirsting, like most of his countrymen, for a more stable and secure existence. In his attitude and modes of operation, however, he was a prisoner of the system which had produced him. He saw the world in absolute terms, and in any given situation he was sure there was one 'correct' solution which would solve all problems, provided it was applied by the exercise of the leader's willpower. To establish good rapport with the ordinary people he convinced himself that he had their support, and that therefore opposition to him was sly, elitist and illegitimate. Political resistance could be overcome; the Party, led by him, was always right. In essence a moderate, he approached problems like an extremist and thus blocked his own progress.

Adapted from Geoffrey Hosking, *Russia and the Russians*, 2001

STUDY TIP

Look at each extract carefully and note the key points made by each author about the change in the style of leadership. Although you are not required to identify similarities and differences, you might wish to allude to these in a short conclusion in which you should give your overall view.

 PRACTICE QUESTION

Using your understanding of the historical context, assess how convincing the arguments in Extracts 1, 2 and 3 are, in relation to changes in the style of leadership from Stalin to Khrushchev.

Economic and social developments

EXTRACT 1

Khrushchev was no ideologist, but a pragmatic activist who took his Marxism largely for granted – and dug industriously in Lenin's collective works whenever he felt the traditional need for theoretical justification. His over-riding passions were agricultural improvement and commitment to industrial growth. It was in these terms that he saw socialist competition with the capitalist world and the triumph of communism. At the 21st Party Congress in January 1959, he made extravagant promises about the economic future, both in terms of consumption and in the context of comparison with the United States. At the 22nd Party Congress, the new programme of the Communist Party, which had not been touched since 1919, provided a cautious, but nonetheless determined projection into a fully communist future. In 1964, he was speaking openly of making consumer goods and agricultural investment the top priority. He was willing to pin his reputation on the success of these policies. But the facts were against him.

Adapted from John Peter Nettl, *The Soviet Achievement*, 1967

ACTIVITY

Evaluating historical extracts

What impression of Khrushchev do we get from Extract 1? In this extract, Nettl speaks of Khrushchev's ambition, but writes that 'the facts were against him'. As you read this chapter, try to compile a list of the sort of 'facts' Nettl was thinking of.

Industrial development

Industrial development under Stalin, 1945–53

The USSR faced huge economic strains after the Second World War, which had destroyed 70 per cent of its industrial capacity and severely reduced the workforce. Not only had the Soviet economy to be revived, the USSR faced a huge defence budget as it policed its new 'satellite states' and met the costs of the emerging Cold War. Lend-Lease came to an abrupt end, and, in 1947, Stalin refused to allow territories under Soviet influence to receive US **Marshall Aid**. Instead, he established **Cominform** to counter Western propaganda and **Comecon** to link the Eastern European countries that formed the Soviet bloc economically.

A CLOSER LOOK

After the war, the USSR established communist governments in the occupied eastern European countries (Czechoslovakia, Poland, Hungary, Romania, Bulgaria and Eastern Germany) turning these into Soviet 'satellite states' that were politically, economically and militarily reliant on the USSR. This helped to create tensions between the communist East – the 'Soviet bloc' – and the capitalist West, headed by the USA. Such tensions led to a period of 'Cold War' in which each side tried to control the other's influence.

LEARNING OBJECTIVES

In this chapter you will learn about:
- the development of industry
- the development of agriculture and the Virgin Lands Scheme
- social change
- cultural change.

KEY QUESTION

As you read this chapter, consider the following Key Questions:
- How important were ideas and ideology?
- How and with what results did the economy develop and change?

KEY TERM

Marshall Aid: financial aid, offered by the USA from 1947, to assist European economic recovery

Cominform: the communist information bureau, established 1947, to disseminate propaganda and establish Soviet control over all communist parties; it was feared by the West but had a limited effect outside the Soviet bloc

Comecon: The Council for Mutual Economic Assistance, established in 1949 to coordinate the economic growth of countries inside the Soviet bloc

Fig. 1 *Concrete workers restoring the dam of the Dnieper power plant*

KEY CHRONOLOGY

Economic developments under Khrushchev

1956	Sixth Five Year Plan
1957	Moves towards decentralisation
1959	Seven year plan and establishment of Supreme Economic Council
1961	Seventh Five Year Plan

The redistribution of industry in the war years was to provide a broad base for industrial recovery since the expanded eastern industrial areas permitted the exploitation of new sources of raw materials and energy. Nevertheless, the rebuilding of the devastated (and formerly occupied) western areas was also essential. To meet Soviet needs, Gosplan coordinated two more Five Year Plans following the same target-setting methods that had been used before the war, as outlined in Table 1.

Table 1 The Fourth and Fifth Five Year Plans

Fourth Five Year Plan, 1946–50		
Aims	**Detail**	**Results**
To 'catch up' with the USA To rebuild heavy industry and transport To revive the Ukraine (a third of all expenditure was allocated here)	Use of extensive reparations from East Germany Maintenance of wartime controls on labour force – long hours, low wages, high targets, female labour 'Grand projects' – canals and HEP plants	The USSR became 2nd to the USA in industrial capacity Most targets in heavy industry met Production doubled and urban workforce increased from 67 to 77 million (1941–52) By end 1947, Dnieper Dam power station in action again Industrially stronger than pre-war

Fifth Five Year Plan, 1951–55		
Aims	**Detail**	**Results**
Continuation of development of heavy industry and transport Post-1953, under Malenkov, consumer goods, housing and services received stronger investment	Continuation of Fourth Five Year Plan but resources diverted to rearmament during the Korean War (1950–53) After Stalin's death, Malenkov reduced expenditure of the military and heavy industry	Most growth targets met National income increased 71 per cent Malenkov's changes met opposition resulting in his loss of leadership in 1955

Industrial development under Khrushchev, 1953–64

Economic issues were one of the most hotly debated areas during the leadership struggle after 1953. Initially, Khrushchev opposed Malenkov's proposal to move the economic focus away from heavy to light industry (and, in return, Khrushchev's agricultural proposals were criticised by Malenkov).

Nevertheless, once firmly established in power, Khrushchev introduced industrial changes which went some way to changing the rigid Stalinist planning system that he inherited and also took steps towards developing new industrial areas.

Decentralisation and industrial planning

Although the USSR had seen some impressive economic growth under the Stalinist system, by 1953 that growth was slowing down. There were several issues with the Stalinist system:

- Ministers in Moscow (who were often out of touch with the situation on the ground) set different industrial targets for each enterprise. (Such a system was complex enough in itself, but as the number of enterprises had increased and the products which they supplied to one another required increasingly complex planning, it began to break down.)

- There were too few administrators to make the system work properly.
- Enterprises were judged and given bonuses according to their success in fulfilling their output targets. However, exceeding targets would mean that the targets were raised the next year, so managers preferred to 'play safe', hide the productive capacity of their enterprises and avoid too much innovation and improvement.
- Another disincentive to modernisation was the way the output targets were assessed, which was usually by weight. As a result heavy goods were favoured over lighter ones, regardless of whether this was what consumers wanted!
- Since resources were not being efficiently used, increasing amounts of capital investment were needed even to stand still – and even more was needed to maintain growth.

The changes that Khrushchev introduced in industry were not all his own ideas, but he implemented them with a new energy and drive, helping to break some of the past constraints. The Sixth Five Year Plan was launched in 1956, but its targets were over-optimistic and the plan was abandoned after two years. Nevertheless an important step forward took place in 1957, which helped to move the Soviet economy towards a degree of decentralisation.

- Sixty Moscow ministries were abolished.
- The USSR was divided into 105 economic regions, each with its own local economic council (*sovnarkhoz*) to plan and supervise economic affairs.

This reform had an ulterior political motive in that it removed Malenkov's men (in the central ministries) and extended Khrushchev's patronage network in the localities. In addition, by moving the management of industry into the hands of local republic and district Party officials,

SOURCE 1

Khrushchev hoped to cut unnecessary bureaucracy and win credit for 'communism' and the 'socialist' way, which was under threat of being discredited by the economic problems; he made this clear when he said:

We must help the people to eat well, dress well and live well. You cannot put theory into your soup or Marxism into your clothes. If, after 40 years of communism, a person cannot have a glass of milk or a pair of shoes, he will not believe that communism is a good thing, no matter what you tell him.

Even with the decentralisation measures in place, there still needed to be a degree of 'central planning' in Moscow. State committees and a new Supreme Economic Council were therefore set up to supervise a new seven year plan, announced in 1959.

ACTIVITY

With reference to Chapter 15 and what you have read here, copy and complete the following table with your own ideas.

	Advantages	Disadvantages
Centralised economy		
Decentralised economy		

Fig. 2 *A replica of Sputnik II, the spacecraft that took a dog – Laika – into orbit*

Industrial change

The seven year plan of 1959 had an emphasis on improving standards of living for ordinary people, with a 40-hour week and a 40 per cent wage rise promised by 1965. The targets it laid down were merged into a Seventh Five Year Plan (1961–65). Both were trumpeted with the slogan 'Catch up and overtake the USA by 1970' and there was a slight shift in priorities from the old heavy industries to the previously-neglected 'modern industries':

- vast expansion of chemicals industry – especially in fields of plastics, fertilisers and artificial fibres
- housing factories to produce prefabricated sections for new flats
- increased production of consumer goods
- greater exploitation of USSR's resources – natural gas, oil and coal – and building of power stations.

Expanding Soviet communications and technology was also a major focus throughout the Khrushchev period and impressive displays of Soviet technology amazed the world at the Brussels World Fair in 1958.

- Many railway lines were electrified or had engines converted to run on diesel. In addition, the network was greatly expanded.
- Air transport was expanded and the Aeroflot corporation was subsidised to offer cheap long-distance passenger travel – often undercutting the railways. (It was said that a peasant could afford to buy an air ticket to travel 200 miles to Moscow to sell his produce in a Moscow market, and still make a profit!)
- In 1957, the USSR launched the Earth's first artificial satellite (Sputnik); the same year, Sputnik II took a dog – Laika – into orbit; in 1959 a red flag was placed on the moon and pictures of the 'dark side' of the moon were taken.
- In 1959, the icebreaker *Lenin* was launched. This was the world's first civil nuclear-powered ship.
- Russian space science made continuous advances. A test flight brought two dogs back to Earth alive and in April 1961 Yuri Gagarin became the first human in space; in 1963 Valentina Tereshkova became the first female cosmonaut.

Results of industrial change

Statistically, Khrushchev would appear to have been very successful, as shown in Table 2.

Table 2 Industrial output 1955–65

	1955	1958	1965
Coal (million tons)	391	496	578
Electricity (billion kWh)	170	235	507
Tractors (thousands)	314	415	804
Woollen fabric (million square metres)	316	385	466
TV sets (thousands)	495	979	3655
Refrigerators (thousands)	151	360	1675
Retail – including food (millions of roubles)	50.2	67.2	104.8

Khrushchev's ambition was, however, rather greater than his achievement. His decentralisation measures actually just added another layer of bureaucracy and his system was rapidly abandoned in 1965, shortly after his fall from power. Standards of living certainly improved but there were still severe limitations to the quality of life.

Heavy spending on armaments and the space race distorted the economy and although the USSR narrowed the gap between its own economic growth and that of the USA, it came nowhere near to overtaking its rival. Indeed, from 1958, Soviet industrial growth began to slow down significantly. Having been over 10 per cent per annum for the previous decade, it fell to 7.5 per cent in 1964. Moreover, the decline was particularly marked in consumer industries, which enjoyed only a 2 per cent growth in 1964. Furthermore, while the Soviet Union certainly marked itself out as a leader in the space race, this was only by some excessive risk-taking (Laika, the first creature sent into space in 1957, died in orbit) and while Soviet rocketry was good, its instrumentation was unsophisticated and inferior to that of the USA.

The gap between those industries that the State supported and others also widened. It is often pointed out that when the USSR opened its first 'supermarkets', the shop assistants used abacuses rather than cash registers.

Developments in agriculture

Agriculture under Stalin, 1945–53

Soviet agriculture had been left in a desperate state by the war. The 'scorched earth' policy had destroyed western regions and only a third of farms were left operational. The 1945 harvest produced less than 60 per cent of pre-war harvests and 1946 saw the worst drought experienced since 1891. Two thirds of the agricultural labour force had gone, many animals had been destroyed, there were few horses left, and there was little agricultural machinery. Consequently, the two post-war Five Year Plans tried to promote revival, as outlined in Table 3.

> **CROSS-REFERENCE**
>
> Improvements in living standards are discussed later in this chapter, on page 217.

> **ACTIVITY**
>
> With reference to the period 1945–64, create a diagram to illustrate the ways in which Khrushchev promoted industrial development.

Table 3 Agriculture and the Five Year Plans

Fourth Five Year Plan, 1946–50		
Aims	**Detail**	**Results**
To force the *kolkhozes* to deliver agricultural products To revive the wheat fields of the Ukraine (although more investment went to industry here) To 'transform nature' and revitalise barren land	Massive state direction: high quotas for grain and livestock/low peasant wages Higher taxes on produce from private plots and private land absorbed in the war returned to *kolkhozes* Tree plantations, canals and irrigation ditches to make more land usable Followed ideas of scientist **Trofim Lysenko**	State procured 70 per cent of 1946 harvest, leaving peasants with little Output of *kolkhozes* increased (and food rationing ended 1947) but not to 1930s levels Incentives remained low Almost a half of output came from private plots Lagged behind industry Lysenko's ideas perpetuated inaccurate theories which held farming back
Fifth Five Year Plan, 1951–55		
Aims	**Detail**	**Results**
Continuation of the Fourth Five Year Plan's aims plus Khrushchev's initiative to develop 'virgin lands' and build 'agrocities' from 1953	High procurement levels maintained Expansion of agriculture in formerly uncultivated areas	Agricultural production still behind industry and not yet to level of 1940 (For assessment of 'virgin lands' and 'agrocities' see pages 215)

Trofim Denisovich Lysenko
(1898–1976) was a biologist and
agronomist who rejected traditional
genetic theories and claimed that
externally-caused changes to
an organism such as plants and
seeds could be inherited by future
generations of the same plant.
Hence he advocated cold-treating
seeds to increase grain yields.
He was favoured by Stalin and
promoted to Director of Institute of
Genetics (replacing the respected
biologist, Nikolai I. Vavilov,
who was sentenced to 20 years'
imprisonment). No one dared
contradict him and he remained the
leading 'authority' until 1964.

Table 4   Livestock 1929–50

Year	Horses (millions)	Cattle (millions)	Sheep/goats (millions)	Pigs (millions)
1929	34.6	67.1	147.0	20.4
1945	10.5	47.0	69.4	10.4
1950	15.3	65.3	121.5	31.2

ACTIVITY

What conclusions can be drawn from Table 4?

Agriculture under Khrushchev, 1953–64

Fig. 3   *Khrushchev with a Ukrainian farmers' collective*

Khrushchev prided himself on his agricultural expertise. Coming from a
peasant background himself, he enjoyed spending time in the countryside,
talking with the peasants in an 'earthy' language which at least suggested
(and probably meant) he was interested in farming matters.

As early as 1953 Khrushchev told the Central Committee that the
limitations of agricultural production under Stalin had been concealed by
unreliable statistics and that, in practice, grain output and the number of
livestock being reared had been less than in the last years of tsarist Russia.
Stalin's encouragement of particular farming methods was also criticised as
counter-productive, although Khrushchev continued to favour some whose
ideas were scientifically dubious, such as Trofim Lysenko. Khrushchev
therefore increased investment and put forward a number of proposals for
change. As with industry, he placed the implementation of reforms in the
hands of the local Party organisations. The Ministry of Agriculture's powers
were thus reduced so that it became little more than a consultative and
advisory body.

Several changes were introduced to incentivise peasants to produce more:
- the price paid for state procurements of grain and other agricultural goods
  was raised (grain prices rose c25 per cent between 1953 and 1956)
- state procurement quotas were reduced
- taxes were reduced (and made payable on plot size rather than what the
  peasant owned, for example, livestock)
- quotas on peasants' private plots were cut
- peasants who did not possess animals were no longer to be required to
  deliver meat to the State

- collectives were allowed to set their own production targets and choose how to use their land.

Other changes were designed to increase production:

- increase in the numbers of farms which were connected to the electricity grid (previously most were without electricity although some had their own diesel generators)
- a 1962 campaign for the increased use of chemical fertiliser
- increases in the use of farm machinery, which the collectives were able to buy from the Machine Tractor Stations (then disbanded in 1958 – which suited the peasants who had formerly had to pay for the loan of equipment in goods – and turned into repair stations)
- encouragement to merge collectives to create larger farms. The result was that the number of collectives was halved 1950–60 and the number of 'state farms' (generally double the size of the collectives) was increased. These were used in particular to develop previously uncultivated 'virgin lands'.

The Virgin Lands Scheme

Khrushchev believed that one way to increase production was to cultivate grazing lands in western Siberia and northern Kazakhstan that had not previously been put under the plough.

When the first scheme in 1953 proved successful, the cultivated area was extended and a huge campaign was launched to attract farmers to settle in these parts. Members of the Soviet youth movement, the Komsomol, were also encouraged to spend time on the new farms, helping to build settlements, put up fences, dig ditches and build roads. By 1956, 35.9 million hectares of 'virgin land' had been ploughed for wheat; the equivalent of the total cultivated area of Canada.

Khrushchev's other campaigns

Khrushchev also launched several campaigns for new crops, particularly maize. He thought this would be the answer to the USSR's food shortages, since it produced a high tonnage per hectare and not only could it be used for human consumption, it also provided good animal fodder. Indeed, after he visited the USA in 1959, he encouraged the production of cornflakes (made of maize). He even staged a campaign against private cows – many of which were 'voluntarily' transferred to the collectives.

Another idea involved the creation of 'agrocities' (*agrogoroda*) – huge collective farm/towns. This was an attempt to replicate urban conditions of work and living on the land and so destroying the old, conservative, rural villages, making for greater efficiency. However, this never got beyond the visionary stage.

Results

Table 5 shows the increase in agricultural production, although the figures conceal some marked variations within the different time periods.

Table 5   Average production, in millions of tons

	1952	1953–56	1957–60	1961–64
Cereals (excluding maize)	82	99	120	132
Meat	5.2	6.3	8.2	9.1
Milk	36	42	59	63

The statistics look impressive, although Khrushchev's target of 180 million tons of cereals was not met. Nevertheless, they again hide a more complex picture.

A CLOSER LOOK

Khrushchev often made announcements that were taken at face value. When, for example, he condemned the *Travopolye* (crop rotation system) keen local officials urged peasants to plough up their grassland; when Khrushchev praised legumes, some grain fields were turned over to beans and clover.

ACTIVITY

Create a poster to advertise one of Khrushchev's campaigns. Try to include some appropriate slogans, which reflect Khrushchev's interests and ambitions.

When goods were in short supply, prices in the cities, of course, went up. In a protest in Novocherkassk in 1962, against high food prices, crowds broke into the city's soviet headquarters building. Some 24 people were killed when troops were called in to disperse the rioters (although this was not made public knowledge until 30 years later).

Pair discussion

In pairs, consider which saw the greater improvement in the years 1945–64: industry or agriculture. Justify your conclusions to the rest of the class.

The new measures failed to encourage the peasants to put more effort into their work on the collectives and state farms. Although there was some attempt to increase the amount of time the peasants spent on communal farming (as opposed to their own private plots), the latter continued to provide about half the peasants' income and to contribute over 30 per cent of the produce sold in the USSR. This was despite the fact that private plots represented only around 3 per cent of the total cultivated area.

Furthermore, the new pricing system proved a failure because state officials kept altering the prices, so farmers found it difficult to plan ahead. Frustrations at the low prices the State paid for products and the interference of Party officials in farm management brought plenty of grumbling, and sometimes had the effect of reducing peasant output.

Even the selling of tractors to collectives was less effective than it might have been, because there were too few farmers capable of carrying out repairs, and peasants were not prepared to pay the repair stations to service the machinery.

Khrushchev's 'grand schemes' also had their problems. The Virgin Lands Scheme was much less successful in the longer term than it seemed at first. Climatic conditions had not been taken into account, and the land was worked so intensively, and without any rotation of wheat with other crops, that land erosion took place and the soil rapidly became infertile. A particularly bad harvest in 1963 did not help matters but, embarrassingly for Khrushchev, the USSR was forced to import grain as a result – some from North America.

Similarly the over-enthusiasm of local officials to meet with favour by growing maize, growing legumes, or ploughing up grassland was not always agriculturally sound. There was only a limited rise in milk production when cows were transferred to the collectives while crops, such as maize, were often grown in unsuitable soil and sometimes to the detriment of much-needed wheat. In any case, Khrushchev's cornflakes did not go down well with a population more used to buckwheat porridge.

Khrushchev was the first USSR leader to show such an interest in agriculture and he also made a huge effort to integrate rural areas into the Party structure, increasing rural representation within the Party at both the local and a more senior level. The Soviet-controlled press devoted many pages to exalting the new initiatives and commenting on the carefully massaged statistics. However, despite all the effort, results were really very mixed. Khrushchev's USSR was, in reality, a time of too many different initiatives, carried out with insufficient thought.

Social developments

- How important were ideas and ideology?
- What was the extent of social and cultural change?

Social change under Stalin, 1945–53

Neither the Fourth nor Fifth Five Year Plans substantially improved standards of living for the ordinary Russian people:

- Peasants were squeezed by the quota system and lived on an income that was less than 20 per cent of an industrial worker.
- In the towns, diets were poor and housing, services and consumer goods were all in short supply.
- The working week remained at its wartime levels with a norm of 12 hours per day.

- Wage differentials meant higher rations for Party officials.
- In a continuation of the Stakhanovite programme, workers could be relocated to wherever they were needed.
- Women were expected to make up for the war dead (and in the building trade represented a third of all workers).

By 1950, real household consumption was only a tenth higher than in 1928. Furthermore a 90 per cent devaluation of the rouble in 1947 wiped out savings. There was some attempt under Malenkov to give increased priority to clothing, housing and social services from 1953, but much still needed to be done.

Social change under Khrushchev, 1953–64

EXTRACT 2

Having defeated his most dogmatic opponents, Khrushchev was eager to be associated with movement to a new stage of Soviet society. The programme, endorsed by the 22nd Party Congress on 31 October 1961, declared that the Soviet Union had become a 'state of the whole people'. It was no longer a dictatorship of the proletariat. This was the last authoritative document to take entirely seriously the building of a communist society. Its final words were, 'Thus the Party solemnly declares: the present generation of Soviet people shall live in communism'. The projection was that a communist society would be built by 1980. In the meantime the role of the Party would become greater rather than diminish. The Khrushchev era was one of profound contradictions but he retained some human warmth and was a true believer in the goal of a human world communism.

Adapted from Archie Brown, *The Rise and Fall of Communism*, 2009

Whatever his motivation, Khrushchev committed himself to improving the living standards of the Soviet people. Through his de-Stalinisation campaigns and economic reforms, he certainly accomplished something of this aim. Consumer goods such as radios, televisions, sewing machines and refrigerators became more widely available, for example, and small quantities of imported foreign goods also began to enter the shops, although they always sold out very quickly. There were some ambitious new housing initiatives too, including the construction of prefabricated flats to alleviate overcrowding.

Taxation changes also helped. In 1958, compulsory voluntary subscriptions to the State were abolished, and both the bachelors' tax and that on childless couples were removed. Pension arrangements were improved and even peasants became eligible for a state pension.

Hours of work were reduced with the introduction of the 40-hour working week, and a wage equalisation campaign saw an increase in the wages of the lowest paid. This helped along the path towards greater social equality and the wage differentials between the highest and lowest paid in the USSR were indeed lower than those in any other highly industrialised country. Factory trade unions were also given more responsibilities and this enabled them to take a more active role in employment negotiations.

Better and more widely available education, continued improvement in medicine and welfare services and technological improvements which brought better transport also made the workers' lot a happier one.

However, privileges still remained in the form of non-wage payments, access to scarce commodities, health care and holidays for those at the higher level of the political hierarchy. These undermined any claim that Khrushchev's USSR was an equal society. Although cars became more common in the early

Fig. 4 *Fashion magazines from Soviet Latvia, 1953*

ACTIVITY

Evaluating historical extracts

1. Look back at the explanations of Marxist ideology in Chapters 5 and 12. How do the developments explained in Extract 2 relate to Marxist Theory?
2. From what you know, how accurate was the 1961 declaration?
3. What is Brown's view of Khrushchev?

Table 6 Ownership of consumer goods, 1955–66 (per 1000 people)

	1955	1966
Cars	2	5
Radios	66	171
Refrigerators	4	40
Washing machines	1	77
Sewing machines	31	151
Televisions	4	82

ACTIVITY

Create a chart to illustrate the positive and negative aspects of social change under Khrushchev. Allow space to add comments on the quality of life and cultural change after reading the next section of this chapter.

KEY QUESTION

- What was the extent of cultural change?
- How important was the role of individuals and groups?

CROSS-REFERENCE

The Zhdanovshchina and Stalin's cult of personality are covered in Chapter 20, pages 197 and 201 respectively.

KEY TERM

'The thaw': this comes from a novel of the same name (*Ottepel* in Russian) by Ilya Ehrenburg, published in 1954; it tells of a woman who finds the courage to leave her husband – a tyrannical factory manager and 'little Stalin'

1960s, for example, they were generally beyond the reach of 'ordinary' citizens and reserved for Party officials. Furthermore, although living standards were better than in earlier years, they were significantly lower than in most industrialised states, while the quality of consumer goods was poor.

The quality of life and cultural change

Quality of life and cultural change under Stalin, 1945–53

The post-war years had seen the grim 'Zhdanovshchina' during which censorship had grown tighter, the ethnic minorities had suffered, and freedom of cultural expression was non-existent. Despite the adulation he received, Stalin's paranoia had cast a grim shadow over social life breeding an atmosphere of fear and secrecy.

Social life and cultural change under Khrushchev, 1953–64

De-Stalinisation was accompanied by a '**thaw**', which brought a greater personal freedom for Soviet citizens.

Restrictions on the reading of foreign literature, on listening to foreign radio broadcasts and, to some extent, on what could be written or said, were lifted. A limited number of citizens were allowed to travel abroad. Cultural and sports tours were arranged and televisions showed international performances by companies such as the Bolshoi and Kirov Ballet and the Moscow state circus, as well as by sports teams such as the Moscow Dynamos football team.

Khrushchev also realised the economic potential of international tourism, and established 'Intourist' through which foreigners could visit the USSR and witness Soviet achievements at first hand. For ordinary citizens, and particularly for young people, seeing Westerners at close range was a transformative experience which opened new horizons.

Fig. 5 *Visitors dancing with Russians at the World Festival of Youth*

Greater contact with Western culture – either directly (for example at the World Festival of Youth, staged in Moscow in 1957, and attended by 34,000 people from 131 different countries) – or through radio and television broadcasts brought a new source of discontent with the rigidity of Soviet life. Young people saw the dress, music and behaviour of Westerners as exciting and 'modern'. Jeans, rock and roll, jazz, make-up, greased hair, 'slang' and

Tarzan movies all entered Soviet youth culture. There was even a Soviet version of the 'Teddy Boys' – the *stiliagi*.

Changes in youth attitudes brought more incidents of petty vandalism and hooliganism, while in the universities there were incidents of students boycotting lectures or the communist dining rooms in protest against controls. According to a survey carried out by Soviet authorities in 1961, the majority of young people were cynical about the ideals of the October Revolution and were more motivated by material ambitions. Since 55 per cent of the population was under 30 years of age, this was a serious threat to the system.

Changes in elitist culture

Khrushchev tried to reinforce the distance travelled since the harsh Stalinist era and rehabilitated some of those persecuted in the Zhdanovshchina. The composer Shostakovich, for example, and the writers Akhmatova, Bebel, Pilnyak and Zoschchenko were permitted to work again.

Vladimir Dudinstev, who wrote about a Soviet engineer whose creativity was stifled by the industrial bureaucracy in *Not by bread alone* in 1956, is an example of a writer who thrived on the new freedom. Aleksandr Solzhenitsyn is another. He was released from labour camp and allowed to publish *One Day in the Life of Ivan Denisovich* in 1962, in which he described conditions in the gulag. Both books, which were highly critical of Stalinist times, achieved impressive sales; the latter sold a million copies in six months. Books by Western writers such as Graham Greene, Ernest Hemingway and A.J. Cronin were also permitted to be sold in the USSR for the first time.

However, artists and writers did not enjoy complete freedom. Khrushchev's own tastes were conservative. He disliked 'modernism' in literature and art and was quite outspoken and critical after a visit to a Moscow art gallery displaying modernist works in 1962. Nevertheless, 'culture' was not judged solely by his personal taste. Artistic endeavour was, as it always had been, measured by its commitment to 'social responsibility'.

Artists and writers constantly tested the boundaries, forcing the Party (which was much happier setting economic targets than trying to arbitrate on cultural matters of which it often knew little) to judge what was permissible and what not. Works that went further than criticising the Stalinist system and, instead, challenged the very basis of communism or the Soviet State, were as firmly outlawed as ever.

Boris Pasternak, for example, was not allowed to publish *Dr Zhivago*, a personal drama of lives destroyed by the Civil War, completed in 1955. He therefore had to resort to smuggling it out of the country and having it printed in Italy in 1957. It immediately became an international bestseller, earning Pasternak the Nobel Prize for Literature in 1958. However, the writer was hounded within the USSR. He was expelled from the Soviet Union of Writers, heavily criticised in *Pravda* and prevented from travelling to receive his prize. Ivan Dzyuba and Paul Litvinov were similarly attacked for their criticisms of the Soviet system and prevented from publishing.

The Churches

Khrushchev revived the socialist campaign against the Churches – both Orthodox and other sects as well as the Islamic faith. Atheism was brought into the school curriculum, children were banned from church services from 1961 and it was forbidden for parents to teach religion to their children. All higher learning institutions had to deliver a mandatory course on 'the foundations of scientific atheism'.

CROSS-REFERENCE

For the restrictions imposed on Shostakovich and Akhmatova under Stalin, look back to Chapter 20, page 198.

ACTIVITY

Try to find and read some of the literature that was printed in the Khrushchev era – and some that was not. Solzhenitsyn and Pasternak would be good starting points.

A CLOSER LOOK

Boris Pasternak's impact

Pasternak refused his Nobel Prize and wrote two 'apologies' to *Pravda*. He died of lung cancer shortly afterwards in 1960 and his funeral turned into an embarrassing political demonstration. Huge crowds turned out and one of his banned poems was read.

ACTIVITY

Dudinstev said his aim had been to expose Soviet officials who had become 'enemies of the people' by inhibiting individuals and sapping the strength of the revolution. Pasternak, on the other hand, was seen as questioning the October Revolution by showing its destructive effect on the lives of the intelligentsia. Based on such information, compile your own list of the rules that might have been issued as to what was, and was not, acceptable.

KEY TERM

Seminary: a training college for priests

A CLOSER LOOK

The **pilgrimage** monastery of Pochaev Lavra suffered harassment and persecution. The local soviet confiscated its fields and an apiary of 100 beehives in 1959 and forbade restoration work in 1960. Pilgrims might be beaten or removed by the militia at night. Some monks were forcibly incarcerated in a mental hospital, some were declared 'infectious', 13 were conscripted into military service and others were kidnapped and returned to their villages. By 1962, only 36 of the original 146 remained although international outrage prevented the monastery's complete closure.

There was a mass closure of monasteries, convents and Orthodox churches, reducing the latter from 22,000 in 1959 to just under 8000 by 1965. All the remaining **seminaries** were shut down. Churches were often turned to secular use and became town museums (with an emphasis on the triumph of socialist values) or community centres.

Pilgrimages were banned and extensive regulations were imposed on the holding of services and ringing of church bells. Clergymen who criticised atheism might be forced into retirement, arrested or sent to labour camps. Devout individuals might also be imprisoned for their beliefs, their children removed and their jobs lost.

Ethnic minorities

The greater air of liberalism also failed to reach the ethnic minorities. Although Khrushchev himself was a Ukrainian, he made no moves towards greater independence for the nationalities. The Party doctrine, as reformulated at the 22nd Party Congress of 1961, stated that the ultimate aim was for ethnic distinctions to disappear and a single common language be adopted by all nationalities in the Soviet Union. He spoke of 'rapprochement' (*sblizhenie*), greater unity and the fusion of nationalities.

Furthermore, while Khrushchev vehemently denied being an anti-Semite and had a Jewish daughter-in-law, he was strongly against permitting Jews to have their own schools and complained that Soviet Jews preferred intellectual pursuits to 'mass occupations' such as the building trades and metal industry. He also refused to allow Jews to emigrate to the new state of Israel created after the Second World War.

Summary

The death of Stalin in 1953 and the subsequent de-Stalinisation of 1956 marked a major shift in the USSR's economic, social and cultural development. Post-war economic reconstruction was carried through in the same centrally-driven way as the Soviet Union fought the war, with the people's needs placed well below those of the State as a whole. The years of High Stalinism also saw a high degree of social-cultural control, so Soviet citizens continued to live in a state of fear, wary of their neighbours and continually anxious lest they cross the authorities. From 1953, a somewhat more relaxed environment was in evidence, with a drive towards raising living standards and improving the quality of life. Not all plans succeeded and not all areas saw the same degree of reform, yet overall, by 1964, the USSR had become a rather easier place to live in and its citizens had some hope for the future well-being of their families.

STUDY TIP

Take each extract in turn and consider the arguments that their authors put forward. It is a good idea to identify the overall view conveyed by each extract, and then look at the underlying ideas. Use your own knowledge to explain and comment on these. Complete your answer with an overall conclusion as to whether you find these two extracts convincing or not.

 PRACTICE QUESTION

Evaluating historical extracts

Using your understanding of the historical context, assess how convincing the arguments in Extracts 1 and 2 are, in relation to Khrushchev and reform in the Soviet Union.

Opposition and the fall of Khrushchev

LEARNING OBJECTIVES

In this chapter you will learn about:

- opposition to Khrushchev from cultural dissidents

- opposition to Khrushchev from hardliners and reformers within the Communist Party

- Khrushchev's fall from power.

EXTRACT 1

Khrushchev is a suspect figure. The reasons for this distrust are several and they vary with different kinds of people. In the first place Khrushchev has given Soviet society a thoroughgoing shake-up, and people rarely like being shaken up. He has upset and offended at one time and another almost every group in the Soviet Union except for the very poor. In the second place, with all this activity, more often than not high-handed rather than ruthless, he has not made himself respected. He talks too much; he clowns in public; he has committed monumental blunders; he is widely thought to be insufficiently aloof and withdrawn to be the fit ruler of the mighty Soviet state. Time and again the reasonable, reasoning language adopted by Khrushchev and his followers has been shattered by spurts of the old familiar gutter language, chilling in its ferocity. Thus, Marshal Zhukov, Malenkov and also Molotov were accused in the language of the gutter. The operation against Pasternak was brought down to cesspool level. However, in the teeth of bitter resistance from the entrenched reactionaries, the Soviet Union has moved to better days.

Adapted from Edward Crankshaw, *Khrushchev's Russia*, 1959

KEY QUESTION

As you read this chapter, consider the following Key Questions:
- Why did opposition develop and how effective was it?
- How important were ideas and ideology?
- How important was the role of individuals and groups?

ACTIVITY

1 In Extract 1, what is Crankshaw's view of Khrushchev's leadership?
2 How does Crankshaw explain the existence of suspicion and opposition in the Soviet Union in the time of Khrushchev?
3 Can you find examples, either in this or earlier chapters, to support the views given in Extract 1 as to why Khrushchev was not more respected?

Opposition from cultural dissidents

Fig. 1   *A crowd at the unveiling ceremony of a monument dedicated to the satirical poet Vladimir Mayakovsky in Moscow, 1958*

The harsh censorship of the Stalinist years had largely ended the Russian tradition of criticism through the medium of literature and the arts (as formerly seen, for example, in the writings of Tolstoy). However, under Khrushchev, with the return of greater intellectual and artistic freedom, there emerged a new group of 'cultural dissidents' who used the arts to convey political messages.

Such dissidents were primarily committed to greater democracy, human rights and the rights of the nationalities. Sometimes their protest also stemmed from religious feeling or expressed grievances against the violation of artistic freedom. Theirs was not an outright physical opposition but it was worrying to the authorities, nevertheless.

Publishing

The written word, and in particular poetry, was a favourite medium by which to express political views. Some writers sought to evade Soviet censorship by publishing their work abroad. This was known as *tamizdat*. It was hoped that the substance of such works would be relayed back to Soviet citizens through foreign broadcasts. The publication of Pasternak's *Dr Zhivago* overseas would be one such example.

Others used *samizdat*, laboriously duplicating material by hand or by typewriter using carbon paper, or possibly by finding printers prepared to run a press illegally at night. Copies would then be circulated by personal contact. However, such activity was high risk and brought the danger of imprisonment and the labour camps.

Dissident literature was also spread through underground societies, including 'The Youngest Society of Geniuses', a student group set up in the mid-1960s. This produced a journal, *The Sphinxes*, which contained collections of prose and poetry.

Poetry

On 29 June 1958, a monument to Vladimir Mayakovsky (1893–1930), a satirical poet who had criticised the Stalinist system, was unveiled in Moscow. The event was marked by impromptu public poetry readings. This sparked a series of regular readings known as the 'Mayak' (lighthouse) in Mayakovsky Square. These became very popular and were attended by students and members of the intelligentsia. However, in 1961, some of the regular attenders were arrested for subversive political activity. The action cost **Vladimir Bukovsky**, a biology student, his university place and drove him to become a fully committed dissident, while Eduard Kuznetsov, who was accused of publishing *samizdat* and charged with 'anti-Soviet agitation and propaganda', was to spend seven years in prison.

Magazines

A number of 'dissident' magazines were also established. Alexander Ginzburg (1936–2002), the editor and publisher of a Moscow *samizdat* poetry magazine called *Syntaxis*, was arrested in 1960. He was sent to labour camps on three separate occasions, between 1961 and 1969, for exposing human rights abuses and demanding reforms. He also tried to smuggle writings abroad in order to increase external pressure on the USSR. Other dissident publications included *Boomerang*, edited by Vladimir Osipov from 1960 and *Phoenix*, edited by Yuri Galanskov from 1961. Even *Novy Mir*, an official publication, changed its political stance and adopted a more dissident position in the early 1960s. In November 1962 this magazine became famous for publishing Solzhenitsyn's *One Day in the Life of Ivan Denisovich*.

The authorities took steps to restrict this spread of unwarranted material in 1961, when 130,000 people were identified as leading an

KEY TERM

Tamizdat: printing banned writings abroad

Samizdat: dissident activity whereby individuals reproduced works that would not pass the censor, and distributed them

CROSS-REFERENCE

The publication overseas of Pasternak's *Dr Zhivago* is discussed in Chapter 22, page 219.

KEY PROFILE

Vladimir Bukovsky (b. 1942) was studying Biology at Moscow University when, in September 1960, he and friends became involved in the Mayakovsky Square poetry readings. His 'Theses on the Collapse of the Komsomol', in which he portrayed the USSR as an 'illegal society' brought him to the attention of the authorities. He was interrogated and thrown out of university in 1961. In May 1963 he was convicted for possessing anti-Soviet literature and confined to a psychiatric hospital until February 1965. He went on to be major cultural dissident, fighting against such practices under Brezhnev.

'anti-social, parasitic way of life'. These were intellectuals whose writings were considered hostile to the regime, and who were prevented from obtaining employment by the State. Some avoided imprisonment by taking unskilled jobs such as street sweepers, which still gave them time to pursue their writing, but others were sent to labour camps or mental hospitals. Further campaigns followed. In 1963, **Joseph Brodsky**, who became a Nobel laureate in 1987, was charged with 'social parasitism' and sentenced to five years exile in Archangel.

Music

Music also produced its cultural dissidents and, just as writers used *samizdat* to self-publish, so musicians made illegal recordings known as *Magnitizdat* – on reel-to-reel tape recorders. Tapes were passed between friends, allowing forbidden musical styles and song lyrics to spread quickly in the 'underground'. Jazz, 'boogie-woogie', rock 'n' roll, soul music and Western pop were all disseminated in this way.

Yuliy Kim was typical of the musicians who reacted to political events in their song writing. He associated with the dissident movement in Moscow and wrote a song cycle called 'Moscow kitchens' which told how subversive thought was passed around in free discussions in the capital's kitchens.

Soviet 'nonconformist art' which broke free from the shackles of Soviet realism also brought dissident painters. The limitations to the 'thaw' which had marked the coming of Khrushchev became apparent in 1962, when Khrushchev attended the Manezh Art Exhibition at which several nonconformist artists were exhibiting. He engaged in an argument about the function of art in society but this only had the effect of encouraging the dissident painters to pursue their art in private, challenging official artistic reality.

Major Soviet nonconformist artists of the period include Oleg Vassiliev and Ilya Kabakov, both of whom worked 'officially' as children's book illustrators for part of the year, thus allowing themselves the time and freedom to pursue 'underground art'. Erik Bulatov was a conceptual artist who founded the 'Sretensky Boulevard Group' (named after the street where they met and where they discussed and displayed their work); this included Vassilev and Kabakov. Other members of the group included Edik Steinberg, Viktor Pivovarov and Vladimir Yankilevsky, who had been one of the exhibitors at the Manezh Art Exhibition. Unlike the dissident writers, however, the artists were largely able to escape persecution. Most managed some 'legal' work and it would seem that the authorities of the period found their activities less potentially damaging to the regime.

A few cultural figures expressed their opposition to the Soviet regime by seizing the opportunities, provided by Khrushchev's more open relationship with the West, to defect. One of the best known of these was the ballet-dancer **Rudolf Nureyev** who had becoming a leading dancer with the Kirov Ballet when, on an overseas tour in 1961, he defected in Paris.

Opposition from within the Party – hardliners and reformers

Not all members of the Communist Party were content with the way the USSR was led under Khrushchev. His rise to power saw a struggle between those who believed in liberal reform, such as Bulganin, and hardline conservative pro-Stalinists such as Molotov, Malenkov and Kaganovich.

Fig. 2 *Rudolf Nureyev with Margot Fonteyn*

ACTIVITY

Choose a cultural area that interests you and research a cultural dissident from the pre-1964 period. You could provide an illustrated presentation to the rest of your group.

CROSS-REFERENCE

Khrushchev's victory over the vote against him and the expulsion of the anti-Party group from the Presidium are covered in Chapter 21, page 205.

Fig. 3 *Aleksandr Solzhenitsyn, who wrote One Day in the Life of Ivan Denisovich, about life in a gulag, was rehabilitated in 1957*

KEY TERM

Rehabilitated: a prisoner who is declared not guilty of the for which they were punished, and thus eligible for full state rights again; however, there was no apology or compensation and many were posthumously rehabilitated

ACTIVITY

Which posed the greater threat to the survival of the Soviet state – the opposition of the hardliners or the demands of liberal reformers and cultural dissidents who wanted to bring greater change? Divide in two groups. Each should prepare a speech to support one or the other side. Having delivered these speeches, take a class vote.

Although Khrushchev succeeded in establishing Bulganin and himself in the top jobs in February 1955, the hardliners could not forgive his attack on Stalin in 1956 and tried to oust him in 1957. This opposition group fought Khrushchev less because of his policies and reorganisation than out of a desire to restore 'Stalinism'. The reformers, on the other hand, spoke in his favour through fear of a return to the old regime and police rule.

Khrushchev survived by appealing to the wider Central Committee over the vote against him in the Presidium and the expulsion of the 'anti-Party' group from the Presidium was a victory for the reformers over the hardliners. It was not until Khrushchev had dismissed Zhukov and thus put the Red Army in its place, however, that total victory was achieved.

ACTIVITY

Re-read the section on Khrushchev's rise to power in Chapter 21 and complete the table below. You may like to research further into some of the key personalities among the hardliners and reformers.

	Hardline Stalinists	Reformers
Examples	Molotov, Malenkov, Kaganovich, Vorosjilov	Khrushchev, Bulganin, Kirilenko, Mikoyan, Suslov
What they believed in		
When and how they tried to assert their views		
Consequences		

Treatment of political opposition

The treatment of political opposition was less harsh than in Stalin's day. At the top, politicians were demoted, but generally not shot. Molotov became ambassador to Mongolia; Malenkov became director of an HEP station in Kazakhstan; and Kaganovich was made director of the Sverdlovsk cement works.

At a lower level, as well as an improvement in treatment, the political prison population was reduced. By 1955, a quarter of a million appeals from political prisoners had been considered by the Soviet Procuracy, but only four per cent had been released. However, within a few months in 1956, eight to nine million former or present political prisoners were **rehabilitated**. In total, around two million returned from the gulags and prison colonies, and another two million from special settlements between 1953 and 1960. By 1957 only two per cent of the Soviet prison population were political prisoners.

However, combined with his de-Stalinisation speech, Khrushchev's more lenient treatment of political opponents bred further dissent. While the cultural dissidents and intelligentsia saw this as an opportunity to discuss and debate issues such as multi-party elections and full human rights and freedoms, the hardliners and loyalists were vocal in their opposition. These were most marked in Georgia, Stalin's birthplace, where there were violent nationalist demonstrations in Tblisi, 4–10 March 1956.

Outright opposition among ordinary Soviet citizens was minimal. Having been conditioned by the Stalinist Terror, most ordinary people remained silent. However, this is not to say that there was no dissent.

EXTRACT 2

Although Khrushchev rehabilitated millions, he punished only a handful of Stalin's intimates for the abuses of power he regularly condemned. His evasiveness had the effect of maintaining public distrust of politicians. People did not feel grateful to Khrushchev for long. Material and social conditions had got better, but life in general remained hard – and the political, economic and cultural order was still extremely authoritarian. Khrushchev, in his frequent lengthy speeches, showed that he underestimated the depth of popular grievances. The authorities could still maintain their one-party, one-ideology state, but they were unable to secure acquiescence in their more mundane demands on a daily basis – and the extent of non-collaboration was worrisomely broad in a society wherein no social, economic or cultural activity was officially considered innocent of political implications. Non-compliance rather than direct resistance was the norm and many social malaises survived.

Adapted from Robert Service, *Russia*, 1997

Khrushchev's fall from power

In April 1964, **Leonid Brezhnev** gave Khrushchev's seventieth birthday speech and loudly praised him for all his devotion and various achievements. There was even a special ceremony in the Kremlin, when Khrushchev was presented with various honours including the 'Hero of the Soviet Union' gold medal. However, just a few months later, he was ousted in a coup orchestrated by Brezhnev, Nikolai Podgorny and Mikhail Suslov.

Khrushchev was on holiday in Pitsunda, Georgia on the Black Sea in October 1964. Here, he received an urgent telephone call from Brezhnev summoning him to an emergency meeting of the Presidium. He initially ignored this, but, sensing opposition, returned to Moscow on 13 October. He was taken straight to a meeting of the Presidium where several of his former supporters voiced their criticisms of him. At first, Khrushchev tried to interrupt, but he seemed genuinely surprised by the degree of hostility towards him. He refused to resign, but he was denied access to the media, which might have enabled him to whip up popular support to resist his attackers. (Two of his supporters – the editor of *Pravda* and the head of the state radio – were 'out of Moscow'.)

The following day, a resignation paper was presented to Khrushchev and he had little option but to sign. He sat for a time in silence and then left. He was not present on day three, when Suslov stood up to read a damning list of his shortcomings, and resolutions were passed by which Brezhnev became First Secretary and Alexei Kosygin became Premier.

A public announcement was made that Khrushchev had resigned through 'advanced age and ill health'. This was partly to appease the international community. Within the USSR, *Izvestia* (edited by Khrushchev's son-in-law) was suppressed on the day the resignation was announced, so only *Pravda* and the radio announced his retirement.

Only weeks later, however, *Pravda* denounced Khrushchev for his 'hare-brained schemes, half-baked conclusions, hasty decisions, unrealistic actions, bragging, phrase-mongering and bossiness'.

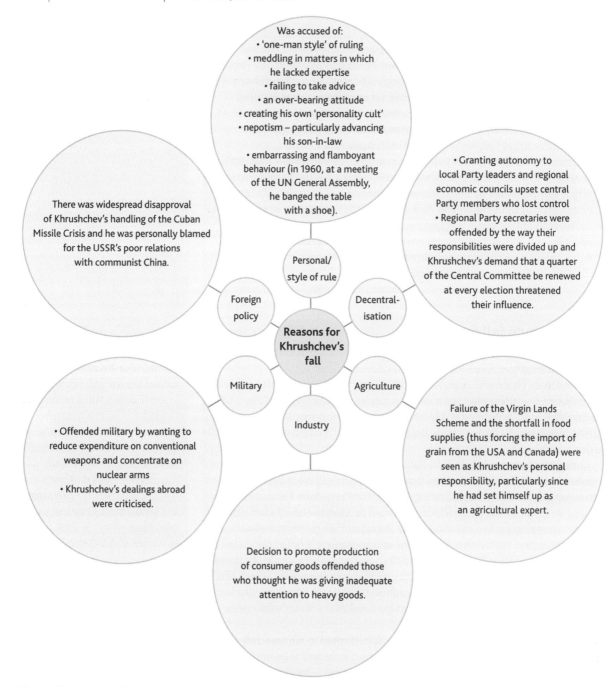

Fig. 4 *Reasons for Khrushchev's fall*

A CLOSER LOOK

The Cuban Missile Crisis

In 1962, the USA discovered that Khrushchev was supplying nuclear weapons to Castro in Cuba. They placed a 'quarantine' around Cuba and ordered Soviet ships heading for the island to turn back. After tense negotiations, the ships withdrew; an apparent victory for US diplomacy.

A CLOSER LOOK

Khrushchev's son-in-law

Alexei Adzhubel, Khrushchev's son-in-law, had a lively personality and was clearly given special favours. He was made editor of *Izvestia* and had a direct telephone line to Khrushchev's office in the Kremlin; he was elected to the Central Committee; he was used to speak to foreign diplomats in preference to the dour Foreign Minister, Andrei Gromyko. The final straw for Khrushchev's opponents came when Khrushchev arranged a visit to Western Germany in 1964 through his son-in-law, ignoring the state bureaucracy.

EXTRACT 3

Khrushchev had alienated and annoyed many of the administrators and Party officials who had been directly affected by his reforms: civil servants sent to the country, agricultural experts hauled over the coals and subjected to a torrent of contradictory changes, the armed services with a vested interest in a rich flow of military expenditure, the Party traditionalists for whom the priority of heavy industry in any Soviet investment programme was sacred. At a more profound level there were the basic diehards who questioned Khrushchevism as a whole – the idea of a halfway house in the retreat from Stalinism. He was concerned to emphasise the return of Party control over policy and administration, but at the same time was not prepared to articulate a genuinely collective policy from the bottom up. His insistence on rational and effective working seemed to be in flat contradiction to his own tendency to interfere in everything and make decisions off the top of his head. He became something of an **anachronism** in the post-Stalin Soviet Union; what was wanted now was the benefits of Khrushchevism without Khrushchev.

Adapted from John P. Nettl, *The Soviet Achievement*, 1967

Khrushchev was granted a personal pension and lived in obscurity outside Moscow writing his memoirs, which were published in Europe and the USA in 1970. He died in 1971, aged 77 but he received no state funeral, nor were his ashes interred in the Kremlin.

PRACTICE QUESTION

Using your understanding of the historical context, assess how convincing the arguments in Extracts 1, 2 and 3 are, in relation to opposition to Khrushchev within the USSR.

Summary

Khrushchev faced opposition from cultural dissidents who wanted to see further change to the Soviet system, particularly in relation to human rights, and from hardliners within the Communist Party who longed for a return to the stability of Stalinism. Although Khrushchev was generally supported by reformers, some believed he had not gone far enough, or weakened his own reforms with rash initiatives. By 1964 he had alienated a wide variety of different interest groups who combined to force him from power. Nevertheless, it was clear that times had changed; he was not shot, but allowed to retire on a pension.

PRACTICE QUESTION

'The opposition faced by Khrushchev in the years 1953–64 was far less than that faced by Stalin in the years 1928–41.' Assess the validity of this view.

KEY TERM

Anachronism: something or somebody that is 'out of its time' – seeming to come from a past era

ACTIVITY

How many different types of 'opponents' to Khrushchev can you identify in Extract 3?

ACTIVITY

Write an obituary for Khrushchev, providing a balanced appraisal of his domestic contributions to the USSR 1953–64.

STUDY TIP

You will need to consider the views and arguments of each author about the real or supposed opposition from different groups. Evaluate each in turn with reference to your contextual knowledge, and offer a judgement.

STUDY TIP

You will need to re-read Chapter 17 and reflect on the material in Section 3 of this book before attempting this breadth essay. You could for example plan your answer thematically. This could include a comparison of party political opposition; opposition from other elites (including the cultural elites) and opposition from the 'ordinary people'.

24 The Soviet Union by 1964

LEARNING OBJECTIVES

This chapter will provide a summary of the USSR in 1964 by reflecting on:

- the political condition of the Soviet Union

- the economic condition of the Soviet Union

- the social condition of the Soviet Union.

KEY QUESTION

As you read this chapter, consider the following Key Questions:
- How important were ideas and ideology?
- How important was the role of individuals and groups?

Fig. 1 *Khrushchev in 1964*

CROSS-REFERENCE

Command economy is explained in Chapter 15, page 151.

EXTRACT 1

What was it that Khrushchev wanted? First of all, of course, he wanted power. But the whole course and tenor of his career, and the general bias of his character suggests consistently and strongly that he was not one of those who sought power for the sake of power: he wanted power obviously because he liked it, but still more he needed it in order to get things done. What he wanted done was nothing less than the transformation of the Soviet Union into a prosperous and enlightened society, always within the framework of the Leninist idea, fit to hold up her head in the company of other prosperous and enlightened countries: more than this to surpass all others. Progress has not been even and there have been many sharp backslidings, but over the years it has been steady enough.

Adapted from Edward Crankshaw, *Khrushchev's Russia*, 1959

ACTIVITY

Edward Crankshaw offered this view of Khrushchev's aims in 1959. Note down what he identifies as the leader's aims and as you work through this chapter, consider whether you feel Khrushchev fulfilled these and whether progress had been made by 1964.

The period 1941–64 was one of instability and change. After the tough Stalinist post-war period, reforming governments, led initially by Malenkov but for most of the period by Khrushchev, dismantled parts of the 'Stalinist system' and began to redistribute some of the wealth generated by Soviet industrialisation to the ordinary Soviet citizens. This chapter is concerned with an appraisal of the Soviet Union by 1964 – politically, economically and socially.

The political condition of the Soviet Union

Stalin had made himself central to the workings of the Soviet political system; and no more so than in the post-war era, when despite his advancing years an aura of god-like authority was created, perpetuating the belief that he was the font of wisdom and no decision could be taken without him. His death in 1953 thus left a political vacuum; it also left an expectation of change. The years before 1964 were partly spent filling that political vacuum and establishing a new-style leadership backed by the authority of the Party rather than resting on the sheer force of the individual. They were also spent attempting to steer the system away from the autocratic and coercive practices of the Stalinist era.

However, such changes could never be absolute. The Party elite had risen to power under the Stalinist system and they had good cause to want to perpetuate their control over the State and its resources, since these provided the material privileges on which their lives and careers depended. The preservation of the one-party state and command economy was thus never in question, but trying to establish limited reform within this context was not easy and this may help to explain why the process of reform was half-hearted and erratic.

ACTIVITY

In order to assess the political condition of the USSR in 1964, create a table like the one below. Look back at the chapters in this section and complete the right hand column with details.

Political condition, 1964	Detail and examples
Structure and power of the Party	
Authority, leaders and those at the top	
Political ideology	
Political opposition	

The economic condition of the Soviet Union

The Stalinist era had created a large industrial base for the Soviet economy and, despite the destruction wrought by the war, much had been accomplished to rebuild that economy by 1953. Stalin's successors were thus in the favourable position of being able to make some redirection of resources away from heavy industry and armaments towards consumer goods, housing and agriculture. Changing the workings of the centralised command economy, which had always had a strong heavy industry base, created new problems for the planners and led to an expanded bureaucracy. The USSR also developed technologically in the post-war period with the acquisition of nuclear weapons and huge advances in rocketry perpetuating the reputation of the Soviet Union as a great military power.

Stalinist industrial and agricultural development had been wasteful of resources – particularly human labour. The challenge after 1953 was to stimulate greater productivity without relying on increases in labour or the exploitation of new materials – neither of which was capable of increasing indefinitely. Khrushchev attempted a limited degree of decentralisation in an attempt to incentivise, and he made an increase in agricultural productivity levels his personal crusade. However, his campaigns were not always well thought through; such improvements as there were relied more on the increased use of land than on real improvements, and there was no significant increase in the output from either factories or farms. By 1964, no solution to the major issue of how to sustain economic growth had been found.

KEY QUESTION

- How and with what results did the economy develop and change?
- How was the Soviet Union governed and how did political authority change and develop?
- Why did opposition develop and how effective was it?

Fig. 2 *A Soviet postage stamp depicting agriculture in 1964*

ACTIVITY

Reproduce the table below. Look back at the chapters in this section and complete the right hand columns with details of the positive and negative aspects of the economy in 1964.

Economic condition, 1964	Positive detail	Negative detail
Economic planning and the command economy		
State of heavy industry		
State of 'newer' industry and technology		
State of agriculture		

The social condition of the Soviet Union

EXTRACT 2

The less coercive government that emerged in the 1950s negotiated a new 'social contract' with Soviet society. Of course, there was no formal negotiation. However, the government was very sensitive to popular demands and keen to prevent popular discontent. The unspoken contract negotiated during these years allowed the government to keep its monopoly on political power, to maintain tight controls on travel and the media and to control economic planning. In return, the government began to raise material living standards, while guaranteeing full employment and an extensive, if low grade network of social services. Under this contract, Soviet consumers began to reap the benefits of their immense efforts during the industrialisation drive.

Adapted from David Christian, *Imperial and Soviet Russia*, 1986

Soviet living standards began to rise rapidly in the 1950s and consumers began to reap some of the benefits of industrialisation. The improvements generated a mood of optimism and made it look as though the USSR might be really building a 'better' society. However, beneath the surface there were still massive problems that had not been solved.

Fig. 3 *An exhibition of Russian consumer goods*

ACTIVITY

Look back at the chapters in this section and complete the table below.

Social condition, 1964	Positive detail	Negative detail
Living standards/material position including housing		
Living standards/quality of life		
Cultural freedom		
Political opposition		

ACTIVITY

Summary

The state of the USSR by 1964 is clearly a complex one. There had certainly been a number of positive changes since 1941, but there were also major weaknesses which Khrushchev, for all his reforming zeal, had not touched. Create your own diagrammatic profile of the USSR in 1964. You might like to add some illustrations, quotations and statistics to provide a full picture.

EXTRACT 3

Khrushchev's achievements were undeniable, especially in the ending of the Terror and the raising of the general standard of living. But further improvement was not forthcoming and Khrushchev's futurological boasts, his idiosyncratic bossiness and his obsessive reorganisations had taken their toll on the patience of practically everyone. He was a complex leader. At once he was a Stalinist and anti-Stalinist, a communist believer and cynic. Yet it must be remembered that his eccentricities in high office also resulted from the immense, conflicting pressures upon him. Unlike his successors, he was willing to try to respond to them by seeking long-term solutions. But the attempted solutions were insufficient to effect the renovation of the kind of state and society he espoused. Reforms were long overdue. His political, economic and cultural accomplishments were a great improvement over Stalin. But they fell greatly short of the country's needs.

Adapted from Robert Service, *Russia*, 1997

 PRACTICE QUESTION

Evaluating historical extracts

Using your understanding of the historical context, assess how convincing the arguments in Extracts 1, 2 and 3 are, in relation to changes to the Soviet Union by 1964.

STUDY TIP

Look for the overall argument in each extract and comment on this, before considering any subsidiary arguments. Remember to use your own knowledge of the context to assess how convincing each authors' arguments are.

 PRACTICE QUESTION

To what extent did conditions of living for ordinary people in the Soviet Union improve in the years 1941 to 1964?

STUDY TIP

To answer this question you will need to reread the relevant chapters of this section on both Stalin and Khrushchev. In your opening paragraph it would be helpful to define 'conditions of living' by referring to both material possessions and physical welfare as well as the personal and artistic freedoms that represent the quality of life. You may want to argue that some aspects of 'conditions of living' improved, while others did not.

Conclusion

KEY QUESTION

Throughout the course of your study
you have been considering the
following six Key Questions:
- How was Russia governed and how
  did political authority change and
  develop?
- Why did opposition develop and how
  effective was it?
- How and with what results did the
  economy develop and change?
- What was the extent of social and
  cultural change?
- How important was the role of
  individuals and groups?
- How important were ideas and
  ideology?

In 1855, Alexander II and his ministers would scarcely have been able to picture the USSR of 1964. Secure in the knowledge that the Romanov dynasty had the weight of nearly 250 years behind it, they would have been hard pressed to imagine a Soviet State in the hands of a son of a coalminer who claimed to rule in the name of the Communist Party on behalf of the workers. Yet, beneath this vast change, there were still elements with which Alexander II would have been familiar: a malfunctioning economy; opposition among the intelligentsia; demanding national minorities; social uncertainty and a peasant/working class whose lives were controlled by those in authority.

The modernisation of the sprawling state which began in Alexander II's reign eventually led to the USSR's super-power status in the postwar period. However, in trying to transform the autocracy into something resembling a modern western state, Alexander II released forces of opposition which were destined to grow and destroy the Tsardom. Like his successors, Alexander III and Nicholas II, Alexander II frequently found himself having to choose between encouraging reform and modernisation by relaxing the controls of the autocratic state and maintaining firm political control in order to protect that state from the forces that were threatening it. Alexander III swayed towards the path of repression while Nicholas II wavered between repression and reform, but in the end the tsarist autocracy was unable to maintain itself. The changed society that resulted from the industrialisation drive from the 1890s, combined with the pressures of war from 1914, served to bring the autocracy tumbling down in February 1917.

Tsardom fell when the military refused to obey orders and abandoned their ruler. It was a lesson that later Communist rulers would never forget.

By the autumn of 1917, Lenin, Trotsky and other Bolshevik leaders found themselves in a position to force through the revolution for which they had been striving for years. It might have taken the form of a coup rather than a spontaneous proletariat rising, but the outcome was the same; it established the Bolshevik/Communists in command of Russia and opened the way to a new Communist future.

However, no sooner had the ideologically driven Bolsheviks assumed control than they had to compromise their ideals to retain power. Lenin replaced the tsarist Okhrana with the Communist Cheka, abolished the freedom of the press, abandoned many hard-won civil rights and ruled by decree. In his determination to repress the national minorities, prevent a tsarist comeback and ensure the permanence of one-party Soviet power, he plunged the country into a bloody civil war. During this time a strong central government direction, backed by coercion, was established – a form of government which still remained in 1964, albeit with some change after 1953.

The Communist State established by Lenin was taken further along the path to an oppressive dictatorship by Stalin whose long domination of power – from c1928 to 1953 – created a state in his own image. Not without cause was he termed the 'Red Tsar'. On the positive side, Stalin drove the Soviet economy forward, giving it the basis for its post-Second World War ascendancy. However, to support this drive he resorted to extreme political repression – purges, terror and the total control of social life and culture. Such measures brought the 'Red Terror' of the 1930s and the Stalinist dictatorship of the war and post-war years. He may have led the people to victory in the 'Great Patriotic War' but the outcome of that war brought more, rather than less oppression.

The period from 1953 to 1964 saw some unravelling of this 'Stalinism' and a belated attempt to return, in part, to the ideals of the early revolutionaries who had fought in the name of the people to provide them with a better future. However, by the 1960s, it was becoming all too obvious that pure Socialism was more elusive than its protagonists might have believed and despite Khrushchev's measures of reform, the truly 'Communist State' was as remote in 1964 as it had been in 1917 or 1928.

Throughout the years from 1855 to 1964, two concerns predominated in the minds of the Russian/Soviet leadership – strengthening their state's economy and achieving great power status while maintaining their own political control. Both aims were achieved, although leaders came and went. However, these aims were fulfilled at the expense of the ordinary Russian/Soviet people, who were only just beginning to enjoy the fruits of their sacrifices in 1964. Downtrodden and repressed by the tsarist autocracy, they were 'bribed' from 1917 by the Bolshevik/Communist promise that the end justified the means, but by 1964, the end seemed as remote as ever.

Glossary

A

absolute monarch: a monarch who wields unrestricted political power over the State and its people

agrarian socialism: taking estates from landowners and dividing the land between the peasants to be farmed communally

anti-Semitic: being prejudiced against and persecuting Jews

apparat: the Party 'apparatus' or administrative system

autocratic: having no limits on a ruler's power

B

Black Hundreds: nationalist gangs, devoted to 'Tsar, Church and Motherland'

bureaucracy: a system of government in which most of the important decisions are taken by state officials rather than by elected representatives

burzhui: anyone considered a hindrance to worker or peasant prosperity

C

capital accumulation: building up money reserves in order to invest

capitalism: private enterprise, which includes making money out of a 'capital' investment

Central Committee: elected by the Party congress and, in turn, elected the Politburo between each Party congress

Cheka: the name given to the Bolshevik Secret Police

civil servant: someone working for the government

civil society/institutions and rule of law: a society where all members enjoy the protection of laws, which are applied equally and fairly, while organisations exist in which the people of the country can express their views and influence decisions

closed court session: a trial held in secret to which no observers were permitted and where no reporting was allowed

Comecon: the Council for Mutual Economic Assistance, established in 1949 to coordinate the economic growth of the Soviet bloc

Cominform: the communist information bureau, established in 1947 to disseminate propaganda and establish Soviet control over all communist parties

command economy: making the government responsible for economic coordination

conscription: compulsory enlistment of a person into military service

constitution: set of rules by which a country is governed

constitutional monarch: a monarch who rules in conjunction with an elected assembly and whose powers are limited by that assembly

cottage industry: work done in the worker's own home or a small workshop

D

Dacha: a second home in the country, often used by Russians in the summer

democratic centralism: communist idea of democracy whereby members of the local soviets were elected who, in turn, chose those who would sit on higher-level soviets and the All-Russian Congress of Soviets

Dual Power: whereby Russia was governed by an alliance of the Provisional Government and the Soviet

Duma: an elected governing assembly

E

edict: (Russian, *ukaz*) an official order issued by a person of authority

electoral colleges: in a system of electoral colleges, individuals vote for others who then cast votes on their behalf

emancipation: freeing from bondage

F

former people: dispossessed old elites who had no place in the new Russia

G

General Strike: a strike that involves all workers so that the country is brought to a standstill

Gosplan: the State General Planning Commission (1921–91); helped coordinate economic development and, from 1925, drafted economic plans

Great Turn: the move from NEP to the five-year plans and collectivisation of agriculture entailed a move to central planning and a 'command economy'

gulags: economic colonies where millions of prisoners were used to dig mines and canals, build railways and clear forests

H

Holy Synod: a group of bishops, which forms the ruling body of the Orthodox Church

I

indirect voting: a citizen elects a delegate to vote in the general election on their behalf

Intelligentsia: the more educated members of Russian society, including writers and philosophers with both humanitarian and nationalist concerns

internal market demand: the desire and ability to buy the products of manufacturing within the country

K

kolkhoz: a collective operated by a number of peasant families on state-owned land

komunalki: communal family dwellings formed of formerly private apartments that were resettled shortly after the revolution

Komsomol: the All-Union Leninist Young Communist League, the youth division of the Communist Party which was represented in its own right in the Supreme Soviet

kulak: a prosperous landed peasant

L

landowning elite: those who owned land and who were a privileged minority in Russian society

Lend-Lease: a programme under which the USA supplied the USSR (and other nations) with food and wartime material between 1941 and August 1945

M

mandate: the authority to carry out a policy; this is usually given by the electorate to a party or candidate that wins an election

martial law: an extreme measure involving the use of military force; military leaders are used to enforce the law and normal civill liberties are suspended

military colony: where the conscripts lived (with their families) and trained, all under strict military discipline

mir: a peasant commune

mortgage: involves borrowing money by providing a guarantee

N

national ideology: a belief in the strength of one's own country, language and traditions

nationalisation: taking businesses out of private hands and placing them under state control

Nepmen: speculative traders who bought up produce from the peasants to sell in the towns, and consumer items in the towns to sell in the peasant markets – making a profit on both transactions

nomenklatura: a category of people who held key administrative positions in areas such as government, industry, agriculture and education, appointed by the Communist Party in the region

O

Orthodox Church: following a split in the Christian Church in the eleventh century, the Eastern Orthodox Church developed its own beliefs and rituals

Over-Procurator: appointed by the Tsar from the laity, this was the highest Church official

P

Pan-Slavism: a belief that Slav races should be united

partisan: a member of a military force behind the front line opposing the control of the area by the enemy

Party of St Petersburg Progress: a loose title given to the more liberal nobles and officials who frequented the salons of the Tsar's aunt, or gathered around his brother

patriarchal: fatherly; in Russia, the male had almost unlimited authority over his family

payment in kind: payment in goods or services, such as accommodation, rather than money wages

petty-bourgeois: derogatory term for peasants who were middle class or 'bourgeois' in their outlook, thinking only of themselves and how they could make personal profits

pogrom: an assault by one ethnic group on another; after 1881 it gained the special connotation of an attack on Jews

polarised: opposite 'extremes', such as the North Pole and the South Pole

police state: a state in which the activities of the people are closely monitored and controlled for political reasons

Politburo: the highest policy-making government authority under communist rule

pragmatic: dealing with matters realistically in a way that is based on practical rather than theoretical considerations

Presidium: Stalin re-named the Politburo as the Presidium in 1952; this name was retained until 1966

Procuracy: (Russian, Prokuratura) a government office responsible for ensuring all government ministries and institutions, as well as individual officials and citizens, obeyed the law

proletariat: urban working class

proletarianisation: to turn the mass of the population into urban workers

provincial: living away from the capital

pud: a Russian measure of weight

purge: getting rid of those regarded as 'impure' i.e. believed to hold different political views

reaction: implies actions and policies that are backward looking in an attempt to restore the past

Red Guards: paramilitary voluntary soldiers serving the Bolsheviks to January 1918, when they were reorganised into the Red Army

redemption payment: serfs were required to pay money in exchange for their freedom

Russification: forcing everyone within the Russian Empire to think of themselves as 'Russian', by enforcing the Russian language and culture

S

samizdat: dissident activity whereby individuals reproduced works that would not pass the censor, and distributed them

scorched earth policy: destroying anything useful to the enemy before retreating

seminary: a training college for priests

serf: a person who was the property of the lord for whom he or she worked

show trial: a trial that took place in front of the general public, usually for 'propaganda' purposes

socialism: the political and economic theory that the means of production, distribution, and exchange should be owned by the community as a whole and that people would work cooperatively together

socialist economy: one in which there is no private ownership and in which all members of society have a share in the State's resources

socialist: person who believes that society should be egalitarian

Soviet: workers' council; the one in Petrograd (known as the Petrograd Soviet) was the most important

Sovnarkom: the cabinet, made up of the important ministers who, between them, would run the country

T

tamizdat: printing banned writings abroad

Tsar: the title by which the Russian 'emperors' were known

V

Veshenka: the Council of the National Economy

volost: a peasant community consisting of several villages or hamlets

W

war credits: the raising of taxes and loans to finance war

Whites: the forces ranged against the Bolshevik 'Reds'

Bibliography

Books for students

Corin, Chris and Fiehn, Terry, *Communist Russia under Lenin and Stalin,* Hodder, 2002

Evans, David and Jenkins, Jane, *Years of Russia, the USSR and the Collapse of Soviet Communism*, Hodder, 2nd ed., 2001

Laver, John, *The Modernisation of Russia 1856–1985,*Heinemann, 2002

Lee, Stephen J., *Russia and the USSR*, Routledge, 2005

Lynch, Michael, *Reaction and Revolutions:Russia 1881–1924*, 3rd ed., Hodder, 2005

Murphy, Derrick and Morris, Terry, *Russia 1855–1964*, Collins, 2008

Oxley, Peter, *Russia 1855–1991: From Tsars to Commissars,* Oxford University Press, 2001

Todd, Allan, *The Soviet Union and Eastern Europe 1924–2000*, Cambridge University Press, 2012

Waller, Sally, *Imperial Russia, Revolutions and the emergence of the Soviet State 1853-1924*, Cambridge University Press, 2012

Books for teachers and extension

Brown, Archie, *The Rise and Fall of Communism*, Vintage Books, 2010

Christian, David, *Imperial and Soviet Russia,* Palgrave Macmillan, 1986

Cranksjaw, Edward, *The Shadow of the Winter Palace*, Penguin, 1976

Falkus, Malcolm E., *The Industrialisation of Russia, 1700-1914*, Palgrave Macmillan, 1972

Figes, Orlando, *A Peoples Tragedy: The Russian Revolution,1891–1924,* Pimlico, 1997*

Figes, Orlando, *Revolutionary Russia, 1891-1991*, Penguin, 2014*

Fitzpatrick, Sheila, *The Russian Revolution*, 3rd ed., Oxford University Press, 2008*

Freeze, Gregory, *Russia, A History,* Oxford University Press, 2002*

Hosking, Geoffrey, *Russia and the Russians*, Penguin, 2012*

Kochan, Lionel, *The Making of Modern Russia,* Penguin 1962*

McCauley, Martin, *Stalin and Stalinism*, 3rd ed., Pearson/Longman, 2003*

Mosse, Werner E., *Alexander II and the Modernisation of Russia*, 2nd ed., I. B. Tauris, 1995

Nettl, John Peter, *The Soviet Achievement*, Thames and Hudson, 1967*

Nove, Alec *An Economic History of the USSR*, 3rd ed., Penguin,1990

Offord, Derek, *Nineteenth-century Russia: Opposition to Aristocracy,* Longman, 1999

Pares, Bernard, *History of Russia*, Methuen, Random House, 1975*

Read, Christopher, *From Tsar to Soviets*, UCL Press, 1996

Service, Robert, *The Russian Revolution 1900–1927,* Macmillan, 1991*

Saunders, David, *Russia in the Age of Reaction and Reform, 1801–1881*, Longman, 1992

Sixsmith, Martin, *Russia*, BBC books, 2011*

Smith, Stephen Anthony, *The Russian Revolution, a very short introduction*, Oxford, 2002

Ulam, Adam, B., *A History of Soviet Russia*, Holt Rinehart & Winston, 1976*

Volkogonov, Dmitri, *The Rise and Fall of the Soviet Empire*, HarperCollins, 1999*

Waldron, Peter, *The End of the Imperial Russia,* Macmillan, 1997*

Westwood, John, W., *Endurance and Endeavour*, 3rd ed., Oxford, 1987*

Wood, Alan, *The Romanov Empire 1613–1917*, Hodder Arnold, 2007

(* denotes book particularly recommended for exercises in interpretation)

Biographies and First-Hand Accounts

Deutscher, Isaac, *Stalin*, Penguin 1970

Lieven, Dominic, *Nicholas II Emperor of all the Russias,* Pimlico, 1994

Montefiore, Simon Sebag, *Stalin, The Court of the Red Tsar*, Phoenix, 2003

Serge, Victor, *Memoirs of a Revolutionary*, Writers and readers publishing cooperative, 1984

Service, Robert, *Lenin: A Biography,* Pan Books, 2002

Visual Sources and Websites

King, David, *Russian Revolutionary Posters*, Tate Publishing., 2012

King, David, *Red Star over Russia: a Visual History of the Soviet Union,* Tate Publishing, 2010

Kurth, Peter, *Tsar: The Lost World of Nicholas and Alexandra Back Bay*, 1998

Moynahan, Brian, *Russian Century: A Photographic History Weidenfeld*, 2000

https://www.marxists.org/archive/lenin/

http://hsc.csu.edu.au/modern_history/national_studies/russia/

http://www.choices.edu/resources/scholars_russian Rev.php

Index